TREATY OF CANANDAIGUA 1794

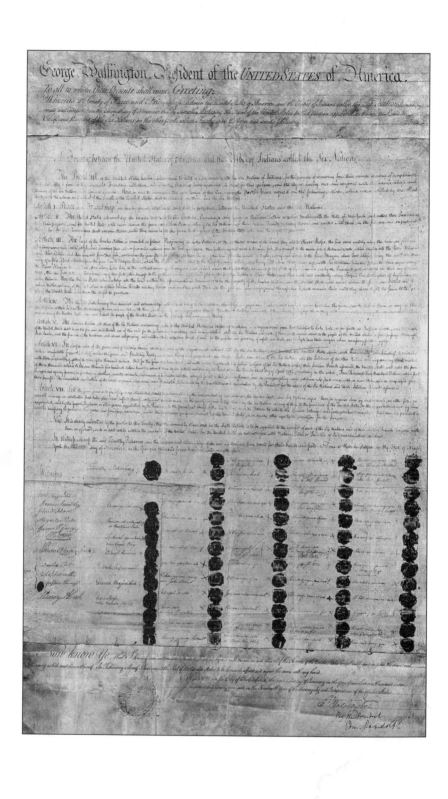

TREATY OF CANANDAIGUA 1794

200 Years of Treaty Relations between the Iroquois Confederacy and the United States

CHIEF IRVING POWLESS JR. ■ PAUL WILLIAMS
JOHN C. MOHAWK ■ CHIEF OREN LYONS
DANIEL K. RICHTER ■ ROBERT W. VENABLES
DOUG GEORGE-KANENTIIO ■ LAURENCE M. HAUPTMAN
JOY A. BILHARZ ■ RON LAFRANCE

EDITED BY
G. PETER JEMISON & ANNA M. SCHEIN

PREFACE BY **JOHN C. MOHAWK**
INTRODUCTION BY **G. PETER JEMISON**
EPILOGUE BY **DOUG GEORGE-KANENTIIO**

CLEAR LIGHT PUBLISHERS
SANTA FE, NEW MEXICO

*This book is dedicated to my father, Ansley C. Jemison, and
my mother, Margaret Jemison.* (Peter Jemison)

*In memory of our Elders who have gone before us,
in appreciation for those among us working for world peace,
and for all the children of the Seventh Generation,
especially for Teagan Ray.* (Anna Schein)

———————————————

Copyright © 2000 Peter Jemison & Anna M. Schein
Clear Light Publishers
823 Don Diego, Santa Fe, New Mexico 87501
Web: www.clearlightbooks.com

First Edition
10 9 8 7 6 5 4 3 2 1

Library of Congress Catalonging-in-Publication Data

Treaty of Canandaigua 1794 : 200 years of treaty relations between the
Iroquois Conferacy and the United States / edited by G. Peter Jemison &
Anna M. Schein.
    p. cm.
  Includes bibliographical references and index.
  ISBN 1-57416-052-4
    1. Iroquois Indians—Treaties. 2. Six Nations, Treaties, etc. United States,
1794 Nov. 11. 3. Iroquois Indians—Politics and government. 4. Indians of
North America—Government relations. I. Jemison, G. Peter. II. Schein, Anna M.

KF8228.176T742000
323.1'19755073'09—dc21   00-025416

Cover and frontise photograph of actual Canandaigua Treaty
Cover design by Marcia Keegan and Carol O'Shea
Interior design and typography by Carol O'Shea

Printed in Canada

Acknowledgments

Editing the manuscript has been challenging for all of us, as we have been attempting to respect the different styles of communication of the contributors while trying to achieve overall unity. Also, since the issues covered in these chapters are constantly evolving, we have worked to include pertinent new mateial even one week prior to publication.

We gratefully acknowledge the support of the many people who have helped to bring this book to publication. We would like to thank all of our contributors, not only for their chapters in this volume but also for the many contributions they each have made beyond that, especially Chief Jake Swamp, Chief Irving Powless Jr., Faithkeeper Oren Lyons, John Mohawk, and Robert Venables. We would also like to acknowledge J. Sheldon Fisher for his more than forty years of personal commitment to annually commemorate the Canandaigua Treaty in Canandaigua, New York, and for his encouragement of this project. We thank the following individuals and organizations for their support: Geraldine Green, Chief Vince Johnson, Martha LaFrance, George Heron, Sarah Schein, Melissa Taylor, Jane LeClair, Vernon (Barney) Jimerson and Carol Jimerson, Lillian Fisher, Douglas Fisher, Robert Gorall, Father Jack Lee, Lois Kuter, Leigh Jones, Sue Ellen Herne Dow, Max and Phyllis Lay, Joyce Breen, Arin Schein, Jeff Wegman, Martha Dixon, Ruth M. Jackson, Jim Lorenze and staff, Superior Photo, Inc.; Bernice Tennant and student staff, West Virginia University Mountainlair Academic Computing Lab; Frances O'Brien, Jing Qui, Todd Yeager, Judy McCracken, Christine Chang, David Foreman, Michael Ridderbusch, West Virginia University Libraries; Ed Varno and staff, Ontario County (N.Y.) Historical Society; Peggy Carroll and staff, Canandaigua *Daily Messenger;* Mary Jo Lanphear Barone, Ontario County (N.Y.) Records, Archives, and Information Management Services; Elisabeth P. Brown, Quaker Bibliographer, The Quaker Collection, Haverford College; Betty Jo Moore, Senior Archivist, Archives of Ontario; Jack T. Ericson, Daniel A. Reed Library, SUNY at Fredonia; Peter Drummey, Alyson Reichgott, Mary Fabiszewski, Jennifer Tolpa, Carrie Foley, and staff of the Massachusetts Historical Society; Kara Drake, Archivist, John Fitzgerald Kennedy Library; Linda A. Ries, Pennsylvania Historical and Museum Commission, staff of the Seneca Nation Library, Salamanca Public Library, Rochester Public Library, and New York State Library; and members of the 1794 Canandaigua Treaty Commemoration Committee. Special thanks go to the Eugene and Clare Thaw Charitable Trust for their support. Finally we would like to thank Harmon Houghton, Marcia Keegan, Carol O'Shea, and Sara Held with Clear Light Publishers for working with us to make this book a reality. Editing the manuscript has been challenging for all of us, as we have been attempting to respect the different styles of communication of the contributors while trying to achieve overall unity. Also, since the issues covered in these chapters are constantly evolving, we have worked to include pertinent new mateial even one week prior to publication.

Editors,

G. Peter Jemison
Anna M. Schein

Contents

Brother: We are of the same opinion with the People of the United States, you call yourselves free and independent, we as the Ancient inhabitants of this Country and sovereigns of the soil, say that we are equally as free as you, or any other nation, or nations under the sun . . .

Clear Sky, Onondaga Sachem
to General Israel Chapin
21st April 1794
Council at Buffaloe Creek

THE WHITE HOUSE

WASHINGTON

November 10, 1999

Warm greetings to everyone gathered in Canandaigua, New York, to celebrate the Treaty of 1794 between the Iroquois Nations and the United States.

This historic treaty, signed by President Washington, recognized the Six Nations and the United States as sovereign entities. Article 1 of this landmark document also established a foundation for peace and friendship between the people of the United States and the members of the Iroquois Nations. Now, more than two centuries later, we continue to build on this relationship, living side by side, learning from one another, appreciating one another's culture, and celebrating the gift of democracy that we all cherish.

In observing this special day, we honor the invaluable contributions of Native Americans throughout our history. Tribal America has brought to this country important values and ideas that have become ingrained in the American spirit: the knowledge that humans can thrive and prosper without destroying the natural environment; the understanding that people from very different backgrounds, cultures, religions, and traditions can come together to build a stronger future for their children; and the awareness that diversity can be a source of strength rather than division. As we continue to work toward these common goals and to strengthen our lasting friendship, I extend best wishes to all for a memorable event.

Clan Mothers

Alice Papineau (Onondaga),
Eel Clan Mother.
Photo © Helen M. Ellis.

Mary Lou Printup (Tuscarora) Turtle,
Clan Mother.
Photo © Helen M. Ellis.

Effie Jonathan (Tonawanda Seneca),
Wolf Clan Mother.
Photo © Helen M. Ellis.

Arlene Logan (Tonawanda Seneca),
Bear Clan Mother.
photo © Helen M. Ellis.

PREFACE

THE INDIAN LAND CLAIMS ARE A LEGACY
OF FRAUD, POLITICS, AND DISPOSSESSION

JOHN C. MOHAWK

The American Revolution ended with a victory for the Revolutionaries, which was something of a military miracle involving some innovative tactics and the assistance of French arms. The resulting Treaty of Paris failed to mention the rights or interests of those seen by both the United States and England as England's Indian allies. The ensuing treaty between the United States and the Haudenosaunee, or Six Nations, produced at Fort Stanwix, New York, left the Six Nations angry over land cessions the negotiators were not authorized to make. The Six Nations government on numerous occasions expressed a sentiment that they had lost lands through coercion or deceit. In the Mohawk Valley, some Indians who had fled during the confusion of war returned to find their homes and farms occupied by supporters of the Revolution, and they tried using the courts to regain their property. These two types of complaint—first, Indian warriors and governments complaining to officials, and second, individual Indians seeking return of assets through the courts and petitions to the legislature—were the earliest Indian land claims following the Revolution. The Indians, for their part, have never missed an opportunity to press their claims.

The new republic had won the war but was now immersed in a sea of problems that arose even before the hostilities had ceased. A very significant problem was that the English military continued to occupy a string of forts such as Fort Stanwix, Fort Oswego, Fort Niagara, and forts in present-day Ohio and Michigan, from which they encouraged resistance to encroachment into Indian country. The new United States was in many ways exhausted, its currency inflated, and its ability to enforce its laws challenged on every side internally. It did not want another war with England.

The United States government, the states, and private land companies viewed the western lands—a euphemism for Indian lands—as a source of dollars to repay their debts and to finance their needs. These three groups approached Indian nations with offers of money and other assets in exchange for land cessions. Some states, including New York

State, began selling parcels of land in areas long recognized as belonging to Indian nations even before negotiating a sale or other conveyance from them. During the years following the Revolution and while the U.S. government operated under the Articles of Confederation, it was not clear how such transactions would be handled, which ones would be legal and which not legal, or what could be done in the event of incidents of fraud or disagreement. Under the Articles the central government had little or no power to organize enforcement of its laws, and the states sometimes acted as though they had little or no obligation to act in the interest of the whole country, especially when that interest conflicted with their own.

The test of whether the central government would be able to survive and the union flourish came on two fronts: Indians and taxation. The taxation issue would be settled in a conflict known as the Whiskey Rebellion. The test provided by the Indian nations would prove to be much more complex.

The Indians had lived side by side with non-Indians in the Mohawk Valley for more than a generation. Problems had arisen because in incidents of conflict the courts were not available to the Indians. Indians were not permitted, for example, to bring suit or give testimony against an Englishman. The only workable peaceful solution was in the form of government-to-government agreements—treaties—and this reality greatly enhanced the influence of men such as Sir William Johnson, the British Indian agent who skillfully represented the interests of the Crown prior to the Revolution in negotiations with the Indians and settlers.

With the defeat of England, the Indians turned to negotiations with Albany and Washington in search of a way to expel squatters and other intruders without resorting to violence and ultimately to war. Some officials at Albany talked about expelling all Indians from New York, but this was not realistic because of the British forts which guarded British and Indian interests in central and western New York.

In 1768 the "Line of Property" had been established running south from a point about seven miles west of Rome, New York. No settlement could be made west of the line without a formal land cession by the Indian owners. By acts passed in 1783 and 1784 New York State created a commission to obtain cessions of land from the Indian nations. The Six Nations, as a Confederacy, responded to the first message from the commission, saying the Six Nations desired to make peace with the United States as a whole. Nevertheless, the state proceeded with plans to deal with each of the Six Nations separately. The so-called treaties that resulted have never been accepted as valid by the Indian nations.

In 1787 the American government passed the Northwest Ordinance, a historic step toward asserting central control over lands not yet part of existing states, to create rules in anticipation of the admission of new states, and to raise money to pay the national debt. The ordinance, however, had the effect of offering for settlement lands that had not been purchased or otherwise obtained from the Indians. When settlers moved to occupy these lands, Indians attacked and harassed them.

In 1789 the United States adopted a constitution which concentrated much more power in the hands of the federal government. U.S. forces, including local militias, moved to punish the Indians in the Ohio region for the raids which had caused property damage, injuries, and death on disputed lands. However, at this time President Washington and Congress resolved to conduct a fair treatment policy in regard to the Indians, and to retreat from bribery and coercion and move toward offering market value for the land. At this point it is possible to observe that the federal government was in favor of fair treatment of the Indians, and that the states were not in favor of fair treatment.

The history of the Indians' subsequent attempts to regain lands lost through fraud or coercion or other unfair means would confirm that while fair treatment occasionally was reborn as a federal policy, it was rarely invoked in Albany or other state capitals. This is essentially why Indian land claims have lingered for some two centuries.

American forces suffered two military defeats during this period, including a defeat of General Harmor's forces in 1790 and a disastrous loss of an army under General Arthur St. Clair in 1791. President Washington asked General "Mad" Anthony Wayne to create an army to defend U.S. interests in the Ohio region. Wayne was to march into the Miami River country to engage the Indians while avoiding military conflict with the British, who had built a fort there.

At this point, the states, including New York State, had interests that were distinct from those of the United States but also had the potential to interfere with federal policy. In 1790 George Washington invited a delegation of Six Nations' Chiefs to Philadelphia. They complained bitterly about fraudulent treatment of their people at the hands of the states, including, obviously, New York State. Washington promised to do what he could, and Congress subsequently passed what is now called the 1790 Trade and Intercourse Act, a promise that the federal government would guarantee that Indians would not be cheated by the states in dealings over land. By the summer of 1794, Wayne's army was marching toward the Indian towns in Ohio, and President Washington's envoy, Timothy Pickering, was assembling a treaty conference at Canandaigua, New York. Wayne's victory at Fallen Timbers, the first victory of the U.S. Army in the field, placed the federal government in a position of power in relation to the states.

The Canandaigua Treaty was one of the seminal documents in U.S. history because it confirmed the federal triumph over state assertions of rights to land transactions with Indians. Had state militias defeated the

Indians and had the states been able to assert control over the future of land dealings in the territories to the west, U.S. history might have been very different. This is especially clear when we think about what was coming in the future: the Louisiana Purchase, the Indian resistance organized by Tecumseh, the War of 1812 with England, the Mexican War, and the Civil War.

The 1794 treaty was also a defining document for the Native American Nations because it established a federal responsibility to guard the rights of the Indians against the ambitions and abuses of the states. It would not be lost on the Indians that this historically arises as a government-to-government arrangement, not one engineered by lawyers in courts.

Nevertheless, in the decades following this treaty, New York State aggressively followed a policy of dealing with the individual Nations of the Six Nations, and even with unauthorized individuals, obtaining land sales and cessions in defiance of the 1790 Trade and Intercourse Act. The only recourse against abuses open to the Indians was in the form of appeals for justice to the federal government, but the United States was on a path which was dominated by warfare with Indian nations across the continent.

In 1838, the U.S. Senate ratified a treaty that was quickly found to be fraudulent (the Buffalo Creek Treaty), and a long line of Indian law cases affirmed, first, that claims could not be brought against the United States without a special act of Congress. Second, the courts would not question the validity or fairness of a treaty that was legally signed and ratified by the United States. The courts were not open to Indian nations for claims against New York. As a result, there was no court open to the Six Nations for their most important claims. The Indians had no realistic recourse to assert their claims that their lands had been taken—most Americans two generations ago acknowledged that the Indians' lands were "stolen"—through political or judicial means.

The first case under the Trade and Intercourse Act was decided in 1920 and is known as *United States v. Boylan*. This case involved 32 acres of Oneida land, which was being seized for nonpayment of a loan and which the court held could not be seized because it was protected under federal law. This revelation led the New York Legislature to create the Everett Commission to study the question of Indian title to lands in New York. Assemblyman Edward Everett concluded that the Indians had been subjected to very serious abuses, but his final report was rejected by the legislature and Everett was treated as an outcast.

In 1946 Congress had passed the Indian Claims Commission Act which authorized certain Indian nations to bring claims against the United States. There was some dissatisfaction among the Native Americans, because the commission decided that claims could only be brought for money, and the amount of recovery was limited to the dollar value of the land at the time of taking. Because the law limited the lawsuits to actions against the federal government, it was not applicable to a whole category of cases in which the states or county or individual landowners would rightfully be the defendants, such as existed in New York State.

A major change occurred in 1974. Previously, in *Deere v. St. Lawrence River Power Co.*, another case brought under the 1790 Trade and Intercourse Act, it was ruled that such cases were barred, because they did not technically arise under federal laws. This ruling was overturned in 1974 by the Supreme Court in the first Oneida land claim to reach the Court, *Oneida Nation v. County of Oneida*. This decision, and the 1985 Supreme Court decision in the same case, made it possible at last for Indian nations to seek justice for their land claims in the United States legal system.

The Haudenosaunee Nations of New York, including the Onondaga, Cayuga, Seneca, Tuscarora, Mohawk, and Seneca, have never, until 1974, had a realistic opportunity to pursue claims for lands illegally taken, beginning two centuries ago and occurring well into this century. These modern land claims are merely the latest attempt by the Haudenosaunee Nations to secure the fair treatment that Washington had promised. History will judge this country as to whether or not it can finally fulfill this promise to be fair.

The current wealth that is enjoyed in New York and in the country as a whole was built on a foundation of illegally taken land and stolen natural resources. These land claims test whether this theft will be acknowledged and at least partially paid for. The Empire State was created when the state government violated federal law and illegally obtained 98 per cent of the native lands and forced 95 per cent of the Haudenosaunee people to flee from their aboriginal homeland.

The Nations of the Haudenosaunee have persevered through these many decades, sustained by the words of a Seneca prophet who, in the early nineteenth century, predicted that although times will be difficult, the Nations will survive. They have survived awaiting the fulfillment of a policy advocated by the United States' first president, George Washington. Fair treatment, the first order of the new country's business, has been a very difficult path to follow.

Marching with the George Washington Covenant Belt. Left to right: Chief Irving Powless Jr. (Onondaga), Chief Leo Henry (Tuscarora), Chief Jake Swamp (Mohawk), and Chief Emerson Webster (Tonowanda Seneca). Photo © Helen M. Ellis.

Introduction

G. Peter Jemison

History for many Americans is exclusively thought of as beginning with the arrival of Europeans on these shores. Many Iroquois people who today continue to inhabit portions of their aboriginal territory are not aware of their specific history. Instead, a general sense of loss of land and reduction of territory over centuries, leading to the present reservation era, substitutes for specifics.

Treaties, when and if they are known, remain vaguely understood by many Americans, often regarded as obsolete relics of a distant past. The most vociferous critics of treaties made with Native Americans wish to view them all as invalid because they were made a long time ago. Treaties with Native Americans belong in the past, best forgotten and certainly no longer legitimate after all these years.

This is a curious argument, and if we accept that logic, it can be as easily said that the United States Constitution is invalid because it was made so long ago. A friend reminded me that there are people who, in fact, do feel that way about the Constitution. What about the Declaration of Independence? That's a document with some age—let's put it to a vote, shall we? All those American citizens who would prefer to return to the status of a colony under England please stand up.

My point is that a *treaty,* according to *Article 4* of the United States Constitution, is the *supreme law of the land.* Treaties are solemn agreements between nations: they truly test the integrity of those who sign such agreements. Native Americans have not fared well when the United States government has been relied upon to uphold its word. A common expression holds that U.S. treaties are not worth the paper they are written on.

This book investigates the Canandaigua Treaty of 1794, one of the first treaties the United States entered into. The Canandaigua Treaty, also known as the Pickering Treaty, or the George Washington Covenant, is between the Haudenosaunee (Six Nations Iroquois Confederacy) and the United States of America. This treaty, which created a lasting peace and friendship between the Six Nations (Seneca, Cayuga, Onondaga, Oneida, Mohawk, and Tuscarora) and the United States, was signed November 11, 1794, and ratified January 21, 1795. Two copies of the treaty were drafted in Canandaigua, New York, on November 11, 1794. One copy is held in the collection of the Ontario County Historical Society in Canandaigua and the other is in the National Archives in Washington, D.C. The treaty bears the United States seal and George Washington's signature and is dated January 21, 1795.

Peace and friendship forever were the basis upon which the Haudenosaunee leadership signed the Canandaigua Treaty. This was totally consistent with the Great Law and the message of the Peacemaker, who united the Haudenosaunee. The United States government was equally desirous of establishing peace and exercising its authority as the sovereign government over the fifteen newly federalized states. The treaty recognizes the sovereignty of the Haudenosaunee *and* the United States and establishes in writing that the aboriginal lands belonging to the Haudenosaunee are theirs. There is recognition by the United States government that Haudenosaunee territories are an allodium (land that is the absolute property of the owner): this point is clear in Articles II, III and IV of the Canandaigua Treaty.

We Haudenosaunee remain indebted to the foresight of our Chiefs and Clan Mothers, who had the wisdom to negotiate an agreement that reaches into our lives today and that continues to have a life in the federal courts of the United States. Some of the terms of the Canandaigua Treaty are still being met. For example, treaty cloth still arrives by United Parcel Service to our territories during the fall of each year. This has been ongoing since 1794, although the cloth has gone from bolts of calico to unbleached cotton and now to inexpensive muslin. The allotment of cloth is tied to an amount of money established in 1794 and is distributed by our nations on a per capita basis.

Today the treaty is cited in all land claims cases affecting the Haudenosaunee. The recent claims of the Cayuga Nation and the Oneida Nation have been upheld all the way to the United States Supreme Court. Land claims have become a highly charged and emotional issue in New York State, particularly in counties affected by current claims. The Canandaigua Treaty remains, in the face of challenges, a valid legal document unaffected by its age.

However, as recently as December 1999, arguments were made that if a historical injustice occurred, it was long ago, "and those people are, after all, dead." Don't punish the innocent, the argument goes. Federal laws involving Indians, some individuals believe, have a time limit built in that extinguishes them automatically, particularly when that law legitimizes our aboriginal title to our land.

In fact, according to U.S. constitutional law, however, there are no statutes of limitations that apply to treaties. So convinced are we Haudenosaunee of our sovereignty that we issue our own passports to travel abroad, using them in countries that honor them. This writer has twice traveled to New Zealand to meet with Maori artists and others, each time with a Haudenosaunee passport. Our passports have made a great impression on the Maori people who are, of course, the aboriginal inhabitants of Aotearoa.

The historical record of speeches and correspondence between our Haudenosaunee Chiefs and George Washington prior to the Canandaigua Treaty give clear indication that the Chiefs fully understood the duplicity they were witnessing and well understood our relations with England and the Thirteen Fires (the thirteen original U.S. States). In fact, the Chiefs' remarks addressed to George Washington show remarkable insight and speak directly to promises made and violations of trust in the written word that had occurred. These carefully constructed remarks forced George Washington to examine the record and respond directly to the facts. The remarkable record of the dialogue that took place in 1790 addresses nearly everything that became the focus of Indian Commissioner Timothy Pickering's task as he negotiated the Canandaigua Treaty in 1794.

The Haudenosaunee had skillfully balanced their relationship with the English Crown and the emerging colonies for years, and they reminded George Washington that he himself had once been a loyal subject not so long before. It was King George III, who desired that the Haudenosaunee help him punish his willful children, who were now revolting against *their* father.

The Dutch, French, English, and the Thirteen Fires had required us to learn about *them* and their values. The Haudenosaunee had managed to become skillful trading partners and negotiators with all of these foreign interests. For the Haudenosaunee to engage in war with these interests was actually the exception; for the majority of time we dealt quite well with these competing forces. Diplomacy had allowed us to maintain a strained peace for several decades, alternating with open conflict. In time, we found it a necessity to protect ourselves from encroaching settlers who placed no value on our lives and who little heeded any written agreements.

In 1794 the British remained a concern for the newly established United States. Negotiations with the Haudenosaunee could not take place at Buffalo Creek (Buffalo, New York) because of the threat of an English army just across the Niagara River, eleven years after the end of the Revolutionary War and England's defeat. George Washington, or Hanadahguyus (Town Destroyer), was desperately interested in peace with the Haudenosaunee because he well knew that they, likewise, remained a formidable foe.

In the spring of 1794 efforts were ongoing to regroup and enlarge the American army, which had been twice defeated by a confederacy of western Indians. An excise tax on whiskey was levied on U.S. citizens to increase the existing army from 3,000 to 6,000 men. This unpopular tax was eventually passed, and the size of the army was doubled.

Against this backdrop of concerns, George Washington and Congress addressed the "Indian problem"—how to establish a lasting peace; then, how to address the problem of land taken illegally from the Haudenosaunee; and what safeguards could be created to consolidate power within the federal government. The Trade and Intercourse Act of 1790 established that independent land transactions must stop. Thereafter, Indian land could only be negotiated for legally when the federal government was a party to the action.

Today our leaders insist it is time to "polish the silver covenant chain of friendship," meaning that when we signed the Canandaigua Treaty, there was an acknowledgement that from time to time a rust would accumulate on the chain. When that happens, our people said, the Haudenosaunee and the United States must come together as two sovereigns and renew our commitment to peace and friendship.

However, first and foremost on our part, we Haudenosaunee must continue to be who we are. We were given distinct instructions by the Peacemaker, who united our people into a confederacy. Even before that, we were given a ceremonial way of life that we continue to carry out. We also have our own distinct languages that are spoken and taught within our territories.

When we meet, we will remind the president of the United States that we are still here, just as the United States of America is still here. Changes have occurred in America, and its citizens look quite different today than they did 205 years ago. What *is* important is that our two people are still at peace with one another. To insure that that will continue for another hundred years, Haudenosaunee Chiefs need to meet face to face with the president of the United States and remove the rust from the silver covenant chain of peace and friendship. There have been violations of the treaty, some grievous—as in the case of the Kinzua Dam, constructed south of the Allegany Reservation, which flooded 9,000 acres of Seneca land in 1965. This catastrophic event led to the annual observation of the anniversary of the Canandaigua Treaty in Canandaigua, New York, on the lawn of the Ontario County Courthouse, where the Treaty Rock rests.

In 1994 I cochaired the Canandaigua Treaty Commemoration Committee. I served as the master of ceremonies on November 11 and was the organizer of the symposium on November 12. In many ways it was gratifying to see those two events come together and to see the two parties to the Canandaigua Treaty represented, but something was missing. What was missing on that occasion was the president of the United States.

November 11, 1994, was sunny and warm. That day six thousand people met to commemorate the 200th anniversary of one of America's oldest agreements. U.S. and Haudenosaunee representatives came together on that day and spoke of the significance of the treaty. *The New York Times* reported the event, and National Public Radio covered the story, as did the *Economist* magazine. Hundreds of other stories appeared in other newspapers around the country. Most of the chapters included in this volume were papers delivered at the symposium, entitled "1794–1994: Polishing the Rust from the Chain," held on November 12, 1994, in Canandaigua.

The Haudenosaunee now call upon the President of the United States to join with us in a renewal of friendship at the beginning of this new millennium. Mr. President, let us polish the rust from the chain and commit ourselves once again to *peace* and *friendship*.

Doneh ho.

Pictured at the 200th Anniversary of the Canandaigua Treaty are Congresswoman Louise Slaughter, official U.S. Representative, and Tadodaho Chief Leon Shenandoa (Onondaga). Chief Oren Lyons is shown behind Congresswoman Slaughter. Photo © Helen M. Ellis.

Clayton Logan (Cattaraugus Seneca). Photo © Helen M. Ellis.

The Thanksgiving Address
DELIVERED BY
CLAYTON LOGAN

It's a blessing
to see all you people here today.
As we begin in our way of life,
we acknowledge
all our Creator's creations.

Beginning with the people
that have come here
and arrived in good health.
There may be small illnesses where we have come from.
We include them in our prayers,
that they'll return back to good health,
so that they can continue with us in our journey.

We give thanks,
and place our minds as one,
that we are here together today in good health.

And then we can begin with our Mother Earth.
We are instructed to refer to her as a relative.
She is our Mother.
We acknowledge her, all her responsibilities
that she continues to provide for us,
all life coming from her,
and that we continue to live on.

"The Thanksgiving Address" is part of the Haudenosaunee oral tradition. This English-language version, as spoken on the occasion of the 200th Anniversary of the Canandaigua Treaty Celebration on November 11, 1994, in Canandaigua, New York, by Clayton Logan, Seneca Nation, was transcribed and arranged by Anna M. Schein and is © 1997 Logan.

As our Creator had created,
He made everything in two.
Man and woman,
male, female, in all life,
so that we can continue in our reproduction.

We acknowledge our Mother Earth
and everything that she owns.
Beginning from underneath the surface of the water,
underneath the surface of the earth,
her veins of water that flow into streams, into big waters.

It's important to us
that we respect our Creator's creations,
that we acknowledge them
and give thanks.
It is a necessity for us to sustain in life.

And the various grass and leaves that He has planted
that can lift up our spirits as we observe.
And there are some that are rooted as plants and medicine.
And their only purpose is to interrupt small illnesses that we can live on.
We acknowledge them and give thanks
and place our minds as one.

Each item that we acknowledge,
we place our minds as one.
So by the time that we get through,
the path that we're going to cover,
our minds and spirits are strong,
so that we may accomplish
what we have come together for in good spirit.

There is one that we acknowledge
amongst the people in this particular area,
which is the wild strawberries.
It is so great that it gathers people.
And we conduct a ceremony in its honor.

And individually,
we acknowledge our Creator
and give thanks.

And the plant foods that He has provided us,
some can be referred to as the Sisters,
corn, beans, and squash,
referred to as the Three Sisters.
We acknowledge them and give thanks.

And beginning from the small brush,
and the trees, and the big timbers,
a place where we can turn to when the winds become cold,
and we can receive our warmth.
And the timbers that we can turn to
and construct our dwellings so that we can live in comfort.

And there is one particular timber that is among us
our people also acknowledge.
When the winds begin from cold
and turn to warm,
we receive sap from the maple tree.

And it's so great.
Again, it gathers people
and we acknowledge the tree with our prayers and ceremony.
We give them thanks
that they still continue to provide us with medicine.
And we can process the sap and make sugar.

We also acknowledge the wild game
that our Creator has placed here that run between us.
There are some that He has created,
they are in the waters.
And on the surface of the earth,
beginning from the small game into large game,
we acknowledge them.

And again, our Creator has created different.
There are some birds He has placed above our heads,
again, where we can turn to and take as part of our food.
And some of their items we use in our ceremony.
We are in relation.
We acknowledge them and give thanks.

What our Creator created, everything here on earth,
then He placed responsibilities above.
As far as the winds may originate,
we acknowledge them from all Four Directions,
that they still provide us with what is necessary
for us to live on.

And there are some
that He had placed the responsibilities on.
And we are instructed to refer to them as a relative.

We'll begin with the ones that travel from the West.
We refer to them as our Grandfathers, the Thunderers,
who resupply our water.
And where they strike, there is a purpose for them.
And we give them thanks that they still continue.

And then above our head,
we also acknowledge our Elder Brother, the Sun,
who provides us with daylight and warmth.
We tell our time as he travels.
Our people are not regulated by the clock.
Our time is as the sun travels.
We acknowledge him.

And there is a certain time
that our Mother Earth becomes shaded.
There is another relation above our heads.
We refer to her as our Grandmother.
She has various responsibilities
and she continues to provide us with assistance.

As she travels,
we count our time again.
We have our ceremonies according to the Moon.
She is in connection with our mothers
who bear our children.

She has a lot of strength,
enough to cause the differences in tides of water,
and also affects us
in our way of thinking.
We acknowledge her and give thanks.

And all the stars that surround her,
placed there for our guidance,
that some of us travel and reach nightfall,
we can continue our journey according to the stars.
And we can name them, we have names for them.

We also acknowledge the Spirit Beings
that protect us in our journey.
They are still conducting their responsibilities.
There are certain ones
that have been asked and invited
to arrive here today
and they have in good health.

These Four Beings,
their responsibility is to interrupt all the conflicts
that may be along our paths.
We have arrived here without accidents.
We acknowledge them and give thanks.

And there is one particular one
that was provided with information
to tell to his people, his relations.
We also include him
whenever we pass the path of our Creator's creation.
We refer to him as Sēdwāgo'wane Ganio dai'io.

And we arrive at the home of our Creator,
where He intended for Him to live,
and look over His children on a continuing basis.
And He intended for us to travel this path
so that we may return back to Him.

This is our way of life,
whenever we come together.
So at this time,
if you will follow me in my own language
what I have just covered in yours.

Chief Jake Swamp (Mohawk). Photo © Helen M. Ellis

The Edge of the Woods
DELIVERED BY
CHIEF JAKE SWAMP

Today
we have arrived at the appointed time
where we are supposed to be
here, in this place
where our ancestors had made solemn agreements.

And we rejoice in the fact
that our brothers from Washington
and the United States representatives
that have arrived here to be with us,
have arrived safely to be here today.

And now,
as to our custom in the olden times,
and as we do today also,
whenever we receive visitors that enter into our country,
then we say these words to them:

Perhaps, maybe,
when you came here,
you the people of the United States,
on your way here,
you traveled through many dangerous areas and places.

Those things that you went through,
maybe could have hurt you,
but we are thankful,
we, the People of the Haudenosaunee,
for you have arrived here safely to be with us today.

"The Edge of the Woods" is part of the Haudenosaunee oral tradition. This English version, as spoken on the occasion of the 200th Anniversary of the Canandaigua Treaty Celebration on November 11, 1994, by Chief Jake Swamp, Mohawk Nation, was transcribed and arranged by Anna M. Schein and is ©1996 Swamp.

In your travels maybe you have accumulated much dirt
from the roads that maybe were dusty.
And now we use a nice feather, a nice soft feather,
and from the top of your head to where your feet are resting,
we wipe away all the dust.

And sometimes when you went into
some bushes that contained thorns and briars,
then what we do now
is we take them away from your clothes,
so you can be comfortable while you are with us.

Now sometimes what happens to people,
when they arrive from different directions as we have today,
perhaps recently we have experienced a great loss in our family.
But because of the importance of our having a clarity in our mind,
we now say these words to you:

If you have tears in your eyes today because of a recent loss,
today we have brought a white cloth,
and we use this to wipe away your tears,
so that your future will become clearer
from this moment forward.

Perhaps maybe some dust has accumulated in your ears
because of the recent losses.
Then what we will do
is we will take a soft feather and wipe away the dust
so that your hearing will be restored.

And now we will give you a pure medicine water for you to drink
to wash away anything that might be obstructing your throat.
And so that your voice will be restored
and so may your words be good
when you start to speak to our peoples.

And so now we welcome you
into our territory of the Haudenosaunee People.
We hope that you have had a safe journey to be with us today.
And we give thanks to all the people
that have come forward to observe today's event.

Treaty Making

CHIEF IRVING POWLESS JR.

Sagooli. Niawenha skenon. I'm one of the leaders at Onondaga. In the language of the Onondagas it's Onondagega, which means "People of the Hills." We are one of the nations of the Haudenosaunee. Haudenosaunee means "People of the Longhouse." In the Longhouse are five nations of people. They are the Mohawks, Oneidas, Onondagas, Cayugas, and Senecas. The Longhouse represents the territory of the Haudenosaunee. In the rooms of this Longhouse are these nations. The Longhouse of the Haudenosaunee consists of what is now the state of New York. At one time in our history, the house of the Haudenosaunee covered the territory from what is now Canada to North Carolina and from the Atlantic Ocean to the Mississippi River.

Somewhere back in our history, we were wandering away from the mandates, the policies, and the Way of Life that the Creator had given us. He put us on Mother Earth to take care of his gifts to us. These gifts were the animals, the trees, the plants, and the waters; we were to make sure that the coming generations would be able to enjoy the same things that we enjoy today—today meaning whenever this was in our history but also meaning today, the present.

Many, many years ago, we had gone through a period of time when we wandered away from our mandates. We began to war against each other. This was contrary to how we were supposed to be conducting our lives. This was a dark period in our history for our people.

So a messenger was sent to us. This messenger came with a message of peace. We refer to this messenger as the Peacemaker. The Peacemaker told us that we have what we refer to as a Good Mind. With the Good Mind, we should be able to live together in peace and harmony with our brothers and sisters, our mothers and fathers, our relatives, our clans, our nations—all of the people who live on Mother Earth. This also includes our relatives in the forest, in the air, and in the waters here on Mother Earth. We can settle our disputes without violence.

The Peacemaker established among us a system of identification that consisted of nine clans. The clans that he established at this time were the Wolf, Turtle, Snipe, Beaver, Deer, Eel, Hawk, Bear, and Heron. Some of our clans, such as the Wolf Clan, are in all of the Five Nations, the

Mohawks, Oneidas, Onondagas, Cayugas, and the Senecas. He put leaders in charge of these clans. These leaders are Clan Mothers, Chiefs, and Faithkeepers. In our language the Chiefs are called Hoyana, meaning that they are of the Good Mind. He devised a system of putting leaders in place and taking them down. If they did not do their duties for the benefit of the people, then there was a process through which they would be removed as leaders of the community. This system is still in place and still carried out as formatted so many years ago.

It took a long time for this to become a reality. The Peacemaker started out on his mission and traveled to the various nations. He went among the Mohawks and told them that this is how we should be conducting ourselves as a people. The Mohawks agreed with this idea of peace. The Mohawk Nation became the Keeper of the Eastern Door of our Longhouse. Among the Mohawks he set nine leaders in place and he gave them three clans. These clans were the Wolf, Bear, and Turtle. Then he went among the Oneidas. The Peacemaker did the same thing at Oneida. He explained the way of peace, and the Oneida people accepted this message. He placed three clans and nine leaders. He came among the Onondagas. At Onondaga he wasn't able to work things out, and so he continued on to the Cayugas. At the Cayuga Nation, he installed ten leaders, then he went to the Senecas and installed eight leaders. The Seneca Nation is the Keeper of the Western Door. Then he came back to Onondaga to see what he could do with the Onondaga Nation.

Onondaga was a key nation for the formation of the Haudenosaunee because of one powerful, evil man. His name was Tadodaho. It was important that this man become a leader of the Haudenosaunee because of his powers. The Peacemaker and an assistant went before Tadodaho to convince him that he should be a part of the Haudenosaunee. The man helping the Peacemaker was named Hiawentha (sometimes known as Hiawatha). He was an Onondaga. Hiawentha agreed that this is the way that we should follow. Together Hiawentha and the Peacemaker convinced Tadodaho that he should become this special person among the Haudenosaunee, with special duties and special mandates for the Haudenosaunee. Tadodaho finally agreed to be a part of the Haudenosaunee. The Onondaga Nation was also given special duties. This nation would hold the wampum belts—the Wampum Keeper of the Haudenosaunee. The meetings of the Haudenosaunee would be held at Onondaga. Today that could be described as the capital of the Haudenosaunee. Our nations are known as Fires. The Onondaga Nation then became the Keeper of the Fire for the Haudenosaunee.

Now our house was complete. We had a Longhouse (territory) in which five nations of people lived. The nations live in the various rooms of this Longhouse that stretches across Mother Earth and covers much of the land. If anyone were to speak to the Haudenosaunee, they would have to come to Onondaga at the central Fire. In order to get to the central Fire a nation would have to come through one of our doors. If they came from the west they would have to get permission from the Keeper of the Western Door, the Seneca Nation. If they came from the East they would have to get permission from the Keeper of the Eastern Door, the Mohawk Nation. Then that nation would be able to meet the Haudenosaunee at their central Fire at Onondaga. This process and protocol was set up by the Peacemaker and is still followed today. This process, set in place so many years ago, gave us the protocol to meet the foreign nations that would come into our Longhouse. We have not changed this process. This is important for you to understand. Our western brothers did not have this process, so it was difficult for them to deal with the hordes of people that were coming into their territories and setting up residence in their rooms as they did among our people.

The process that was used by the Peacemaker to put leaders in place as he went among the nations was that he picked the most vicious, the worst people in the community. He asked for them specifically. He said, "Show me your worst." These men were brought before the Peacemaker. He said to them, "We are talking about a different concept, a different Way of Life for our people. A life of peace." He convinced these people that they should change their ways. They would be the leaders. The reason that he picked the worst people in the nation was to show us that people can be changed so that they are following the mandates of the Creator.

We bring this message to you from whenever it happened many years ago, that we have the minds to change our ways. We can become role models of the community, upstanding citizens, people that can control our own destiny and look to the future, so that we can take care of the people. When we look among us, we see these young people who seem to be unruly, who seem to be carefree, not caring. We know that one of these days these people will change, and they will be the role models and the leaders of tomorrow. You have the same young people in your communities. Watch them, for they might end up as circuit judges. They might end up as president of the United States. We don't know. But we know that this comes about, that people have the ability to take in this concept of peace, change their ways, and become upstanding citizens, not only in our communities but in yours as well.

Tadodaho has someone that sits alongside him to assist him. Sitting on the right-hand side of Tadodaho is Honoweaydee of the Wolf Clan. On the left-hand side of Tadodaho sits Dayhawtgawdoes of the Beaver Clan. And that's who I am. I am the leader of the Beaver Clan. That is the name that I use when I am out among the Haudenosaunee as one of the leaders. But when I was a little boy and I was introduced to the people of the Onondaga Nation, they hung a name around my neck that

I would use for the rest of my life. That name is Chawhdayguywhaw-dayh. Chawhdayguywhawdayh, meaning that wherever I go, everything will be equal. Chawhdayguywhawdayh is also one of the leader's name among the Mohawks.

When the Peacemaker put the Mohawk leaders in place, in order to show that we are of one family and to show that we are all related, he took Hiawentha, an Onondaga, and put him into the Mohawk Nation and made him the second leader of the Mohawk Nation. The reason that this was done was to show us that we are all in the same house. We are all from the same family, all living together. This means that we can put people in place as leaders that are from a different nation of the Haudenosaunee.

The third person that he put in place was Chawtdayguyleewadeh. Chawtdayguyleewadeh is of the Wolf Clan. Somewhere in our history the Onondagas took up that name and I now carry that name. It is the same name. It is just pronounced differently in Mohawk.

So my name, both of my names, are as old as the formation of the Haudenosaunee. And when I'm through using this name, after I have gone away, gone to another place, someone will step forward and take one of my names. Someone will be set in place as a leader of the Ononda-gas, of the Beaver Clan, and he will have the name of Dayhawtgawdoes. Some young baby of the Wolf Clan will then take my name, Chawh-dayguywhawdayh. These are names that have been passed on down throughout in our history. The names continue today, because the people still do their duties as put forth so many years ago. When I am through with these names, there will be two people who will have my names.

The process that was given to us was a way that we should work together. The Peacemaker gave us clans; each one is a member of a clan. My wife is Onondaga and belongs to the Eel Clan, so her children are Onondagas of the Eel Clan. They have a leader and a Clan Mother. When something comes up among the people, the Eel Clan will sit down and discuss this issue. The other clans have the same process. Then their spokesman will go before the Council and present what the Eel Clan's position is or what they think about an issue. This provides a way for all of the people to have a voice in the government.

This process was observed by the people who came to see how our government worked. The process was then introduced into your system, and so our clan meetings became town meetings in the villages of the colonists. Our process also ended up in your Bill of Rights. The freedom of speech, the right to meet, and the right of freedom of religion—all of these came from our way of being a free people.

We were also given a very precise process of protocol for us to meet foreign nations. A foreign nation at that time would mean the Hurons, Algonquins, Delawares, Chippewas, Blackfeet, Lakota, Seminoles, and whoever else wanted to meet with us. This process was also used when the Europeans came into our territory.

The Peacemaker and Hiawentha also installed us as spiritual leaders to take care of the ceremonies that the Creator had given to us—the way we give thanks for all of the gifts from the Creator. We have now traveled through our life and our history with these mandates. These ceremonies are still done today.

In 1492, a man came to our shores. We discovered him there in the seas. He was lost. His name was Christopher Columbus. Our relatives invited him ashore and gave him food. When he came ashore, he met our people. When he returned home he took some of these people back with him to Europe. He spread the word that there was this rich wholesome land across the waters. This land was rich in resources. He told them they should go to this land and claim it for the Queen.

Historically, if we look into our history books, we have a couple of dates: one, 1492, when Christopher Columbus arrived and another when the Pilgrims landed at Plymouth Rock. Those who landed at Plymouth Rock came from where? They came from England. So what did they name the place where they landed? New England, true. Then there were some people who came from York. They landed on an island. What did they call that island? New York; very intelligent people that were able to think up a name for this new place they were in. Today we still call these two places New England and New York.

Another group of people started up a river that went around this island. The gentleman that sailed up the river declared that he had discovered a river. No one knew it was there. He found this river. This man was Henry Hudson, so he named the river after himself. We now call it the Hudson River. The people who came up the river were the Dutch. They landed and settled in what is now the capital of the state of New York. The Dutch named their villages Albany, Troy, Rotterdam, and guess what? Right. A village named New Amsterdam.

We had been taught throughout our history that we should live together in peace and harmony, and that all people are equal. The people that we had been encountering were, as I said before, other Native Americans. We lived together, respecting each other's ways, each other's languages. The languages are different. But when we all became the Haudenosaunee, we didn't ask the Mohawks to change their language, and we never asked anyone else who joined us to change their language.

The English called us the Five Nations. The French called us the Iroquois. They were unable to say Haudenosaunee. That's not too hard to say. But Haudenosaunee is not in your history books. They talk about the Five Nations.

In the 1700s in North Carolina lived the Tuscaroras. They were driven out of their territory and came to live with us in 1724. Then we were referred to as the Six Nations. The French still called us Iroquois. Nobody called us Haudenosaunee. This is the name that we have always called ourselves. Haudenosaunee, Onondagega, and Ongwehoweh. Ongwehoweh, meaning the Real People, People of the Land. Not Indians, but Real People, Ongwehoweh. Each of the Indigenous people on Turtle Island that is now the United States refer to themselves as People of the Land, Real People. They have their own word to describe themselves, and so it is with us.

So, there we were, looking at what was coming into our territory: a group of people who were settling, building houses, chopping trees down, shooting the deer, shooting the muskrats, the rabbits, the pheasants, the partridges, and the turkeys. Wherever they went, they laid waste to the land. You were not a very conservative people then, and you still are not conservative today.

We knew that your ancestors would be coming to our territory, because we were told in the prophecies of our people that strangers would be coming into our territory. These prophecies said that the strangers would be destructive. What they didn't tell us was how destructive your people would be. In the short time that you've been here on Turtle Island, Mother Earth, you have destroyed much of the country. That destruction still continues today.

In the 1600s, when the Dutch had settled in what is now Albany and the surrounding area, we were looking at them as people who were coming into our territory with a different language, different concept, and different ideas. But we realized that they were a people, a people equal to us. Different language, different culture, different ideas, but a people. Runners came from the Mohawk territory. They came to Onondaga to ask Tadodaho to call a meeting of the leaders of the Haudenosaunee, because we had people coming into our territory. We must decide how we are going to live together with the people who had entered our house and were living in a couple of our empty rooms. They were uninvited and they were destructive.

Tadodaho sent runners out to the Five Nations, and he told them what the agenda would be. When the Five Nations met, we discussed the Mohawks' concerns about our brothers and sisters who were moving into our territory and how we were going to live together. Under the protocol set up by the Peacemaker, some delegates were chosen, and they went to Albany to meet with the leaders of the Dutch to discuss our concerns. After a time our leaders struck an agreement with the Dutch people, an agreement whereas they would live together in peace.

After they made their agreement, the Dutch said to our leaders, "We think that in the future when we meet, it would be our idea that you would refer to us as father and we will refer to you as son." Now we had a lot of men sitting there. How many men have been reprimanded by their fathers? Yeah. The father has authority, as you know. So we looked at what a family was like, and we realized that a father and son relationship would not be to our advantage. It would be better, because of our concepts, that we be equal. Brothers are equal in a family relationship.

Our leaders informed the Dutch people, "From this day forward, we will refer to each other as brothers." Greeting each other as "brother" is not a statement from the 1970s or 1980s but a statement from our people in 1613. The Dutch agreed that this would be how we would conduct ourselves and greet each other from that day forward as brothers. The Dutch said to us, "We have pencils and paper, and so we will record this event on a piece of paper."

We said, "That is fine for you." When the Haudenosaunee was formed, we were provided with a process to record events. This process is the use of wampum beads, which are made out of quahog shells. The quahog comes from the East Coast. Any of you who have attended clambakes know what a raw clam looks like. The shell of a quahog is white on the inside. In the center of the shell it is purple. So we were given a process at that time to make beads. We were to break the shell into fragments, make round beads out of the fragments, and drill holes through them. These beads were then white and purple.

We use these beads for identification, as carriers of messages, and as records of events. So when the Haudenosaunee was formed, wampum belts were made that told about this event and the history of our people, the Hiawatha Belt, the Tree of Peace Belt, the Fan Belt, and the Tadodaho Belt. We then informed the Dutch people that we would put our record of this event in a wampum belt.

"We think that in the future, there will come a time when you will not have your piece of paper, but we will still have our belt. Because we are meeting for the health and welfare of our people, we should make sure that this agreement lasts a long time, like forever."

"Forever" is described by our ancestors in this agreement in the following words: "As long as the grass is green, as long as the water flows downhill, and as long as the sun rises in the east and sets in the west." This is the first place that these words were spoken. Subsequently, you hear them in movies, you hear them in various places. The United States used these actual words in some of the treaties that were made in the 1800s. But they were first spoken here by the Haudenosaunee to show that we would make this treaty last forever. We did not think that your paper would survive the times.

Today the sun still sets in the west, just like it did in the 1600s. So that hasn't changed. The grass is still green. Next to my house there is a creek, and its water runs downhill. That agreement that we made back then is still in effect as far was we are concerned.

Unidentified Haudenosaunee man holding the Guswenta, or Two Row
Wampum Belt. © Rick Hill.

Now what did we agree upon at that time? The first agreement between the Haudenosaunee and the Europeans who were coming into our country was completed and recorded by the Haudenosaunee. It is called Guswenta, the Two Row Wampum Belt. I hold in my hand a record of that event. Where is your piece of paper? And what do you know of this treaty? What do you know of this agreement?

This is an agreement between our two peoples. This agreement is still in effect because the grass is still green. This was the grandfather of all treaties, this was the first one that we made. A very important concept was expressed at this time, that concept being that we were equal. At this time the Haudenosaunee were a very powerful, powerful people. We realized that you were a young people, that you were just learning, yet we realized that you were equal. This is a very important issue. You must understand the concept: we recognized you as people and that we were equal.

The Two Row Wampum belt is made of white and purple beads. The white beads denote truth. Our record says that one purple row of beads represents a sailboat. In the sailboat are the Europeans, their leaders, their government, and their religion. The other purple row of beads represents a canoe. In the canoe are the Native Americans, their leaders, their governments, and their Way of Life, or religion as you say it. We shall travel down the road of life, parallel to each other and never merging with each other.

In between the two rows of purple beads are three rows of white beads. The first row of white beads is "peace," the second row, "friendship," and the third row, "forever." As we travel down the road of life together in peace and harmony, not only with each other, but with the whole circle of life—the animals, the birds, the fish, the water, the plants, the grass, the trees, the stars, the moon, and the thunder—we shall live together in peace and harmony, respecting all of those elements. As we travel the road of life, because we have different ways and different concepts, we shall not pass laws governing the other. We shall not pass a law telling you what to do. You shall not pass a law telling me and my people what to do.

The Haudenosaunee have never violated this treaty. We have never passed a law telling you that you could not worship Sunday morning at nine o'clock in your church. We have never told you that you have to change your ways. We have never told you that our ways are better than yours. We have never passed a law telling you how to live. There are many things that you do that we do not understand. We do not understand why you throw water onto a baby's face. We know that you have many statues in your churches and that you have names for these statues. We do not know why you have chocolate rabbits bringing jelly beans on Easter Sunday. We have never passed a law telling you that you could not do this anymore.

You and your ancestors, on the other hand, have passed laws that continually try to change who I am, what I am, and how I shall conduct my spiritual, political, and everyday life. Because you don't understand the religions of the Native Americans, you have said, "They must be wrong; therefore, we must pass a law that prevents them from doing that."

You have passed a law that says that we are United States citizens. You have passed laws on jurisdiction. We did not agree to be citizens, and we did not agree that your governments could have jurisdiction over us. We do not accept these laws. We are not citizens of the United States, nor do you have the right to say that the state of New York has jurisdiction over us. The Department of Justice agrees with us. Recently the Justice Department submitted briefs in one of the cases that we were involved in, and these briefs stated that jurisdiction is not absolute, it is concurrent with the nations.

You have prohibited some of our religious practices. You prevent us from going to our sacred sites—a violation of our agreement. During the 1860s, you said, "Ghost dancing is no longer permissible." Many of the religions of our people went into hiding. They went underground because this agreement was being violated. We noticed that among your people there were many different kinds of religions, each one stating that this is the religion for everyone to follow. When your missionaries came to us, they said, "You should become a Christian and be like us."

We said, "We are not sure if we want to be like you. We have noticed that in your daily life, you argue about which church is better than the other. We would suggest at this time that you gather all of the leaders of your various churches, and let them decide which one is the best. After they have decided, then you can come to us and tell us which one is the best. Then we might think about joining that one. But in the meantime, I think that we shall continue to be as we have been instructed by the Creator as Ongwehowe, Onondagegah, and as Haudenosaunee."

Many of our people did change over to Christianity. However, there has been a core of people, not only among the Haudenosauneee but also among all of the Native Americans across what is now the United States, that have maintained their Way of Life. Many have done this secretly, because there were federal laws passed that said they weren't able to do these things any more.

We have never, never violated this first treaty. We stand before you today saying that we are equal, and we still recognize you as people. We ask the same courtesy and the same respect, that you honor us as people and allow us to continue to live as we have lived thousands of years before you came into our territory. From 1613, when the first treaty (Two Row Wampum Belt) was made, until after the Revolutionary War, the Haudenosaunee made somewhere between fifty and sixty treaties with the Dutch and the French and the British.

When the Haudenosaunee was formed, symbolically the Peacemaker lifted a tree out of the ground. Into the hole where the tree was, we put our weapons of war. Then he put the tree back into the ground, therefore planting the Tree of Peace. On top of the Tree of Peace sits an eagle that warns the Haudenosaunee of danger. Under the spreading branches of the Tree of Peace sit our people and their friends and allies in peace and in friendship.

So the Dutch, French, British, and many Native American nations have sat under our Tree of Peace, and they have agreed that we should live under this concept and this idea. As the various people mingled with us, they started to learn about a different Way of Life. They were under the rule of the king of England. Who ruled France, was that a king also? And the Dutch, was that also a king? The Europeans were people who were not able to sit down and discuss their destiny. They were told what they were supposed to do by those who ruled their country.

Our concept of government was very different. The people who came into our communities would say, "We have a suggestion for you. What do you think about this idea?"

The person who was being asked the question would say, "I don't know. I'll be back."

Your ancestors would then ask, "Where are you going?"

He'd say, "I'm going back to my Clan. I'm going back to my Nation and let the people decide about your idea." They would return to the Eel Clan, the Wolf Clan, the Beaver Clan, the Snipe Clan, or the Turtle Clan, and the Clan would meet and they would discuss what was being presented. Each of the people in the Clan had a voice on every issue. Each could stand up and say, "Well, I agree with them," or "I disagree." Maybe we would change their presentation.

But when they got through, they were of one mind. We have an expression among us. The expression is "Let us put our minds together as one." This is a concept that was not known among the Europeans. "Let us put our minds together as one and give thanks to the Creator for the gifts that he has given to us for our pleasure and benefit." We do this every time we meet. We put our minds together as one.

As individuals you have to have separate voices in order to put your minds together to become of one mind. You have to agree with your neighbor. You have to agree. You must compromise your differences until you become of one mind and you are agreeable to the situation. This is what we were taught. This is the way we lived. This is what we were telling the people who came into our territories. We were telling them that individual people have a voice. They can speak up. They have freedom to stand up and voice their opinions. They have the right to meet, so that they can voice their opinions in a group and become "of one mind." They have the freedom to choose how they are going to worship.

The people who were coming into our territory were looking at these concepts and saying, "How can we do that?" We suggested at the time that they join together as we had done. It would be advantageous for the Thirteen Fires up and down the East Coast to join together as one and become united so that they could speak as one, because unity is strength.

I would suggest to you that if you look into the archives of Europe in the 1600s, you would not find any record of those people sitting down at a meeting discussing their future. They were being told. They weren't given a choice. They weren't given a voice. But here in the territory of the Haudenosaunee this was happening. And not only here. It was also in the territory of what is New England. Because in New England today, they still have town meetings where the people go to meet and to voice their opinions about what is happening in their community. This concept and idea came from the Native Americans that your ancestors met.

George Washington, Thomas Jefferson, Benjamin Franklin, and others were coming into our territory asking us, "How does your government function?" We explained that to them, that we are free people. These events were happening in 1754, 1755, somewhere during this time period.

The people talked about this freedom for the next twenty years. Finally they said, "Well, let's revolt. We don't have to be under the direction of Great Britain. We can be free people like the Haudenosaunee. They've given us a concept, an idea of how a free government can work, where we can speak for and on behalf of the people. But before we do that, we know that the Haudenosaunee have made fifty to sixty treaties with the Dutch, the French, and the British. They're good friends with them."

Joseph Brant, a Mohawk, married Sir William Johnson's sister. Sir William Johnson was the ambassador to Great Britain. He lived up near Fonda, New York. Sir William Johnson's hall is where he lived and dealt with the Mohawks and other native nations. The hall is still there today. You can go visit it. Get off the thruway at Fonda and ask where the hall is. It's only a few miles away. In 1768, Sir William Johnson wanted to have a line of demarcation. From what is now Rome, New York, down to New Orleans, he drew a line. East of that line to the Atlantic Ocean would be for the new people to colonize, to build homes, and so forth. Everything west of that was Indian country. We agreed that this is how we would live together and we would share the gifts.

Because we had made all of these treaties, George Washington said, "In this upcoming Revolutionary War, it would be to our advantage to not have the Haudenosaunee fight with Great Britain. We know that they have a lot of friends there among the British."

They sent out the first federal agent, George Morgan, to the Haudenosaunee and its allies in 1775 to ask for a meeting. The purpose of this meeting was to insure that the Haudenosaunee be neutral during the upcoming Revolutionary War. You will not find the name George Morgan in your history books. He is just not there. Nor is the meeting between George Morgan and the Haudenosaunee. We agreed at this time that we would be neutral during this war. Our word is as good as it was in the 1600s, as it was in 1775.

But the colonists were not used to having people say, "This is how it's going to be" and only have to say it once. So in 1776, the request was repeated at Fort Pitt. George Morgan came again to the Haudenosaunee to make sure that we would be at peace, that we would not fight in the Revolutionary War. To commemorate this event, they made a belt using the same colors of white and purple. The belt has 2,500 beads. Through the center of the belt are thirteen diamonds, representing the Thirteen Fires. I don't know where this belt is. It is hidden in the archives of some museum, or some library, or maybe in the private collection of some individual. We do know that the belt exists. There was an allocation from the federal government for the funds to make this belt. This allocation is recorded in Washington, D.C. George Morgan carried this belt to the Haudenosaunee and asked us to be neutral during the fight between the colonists and Great Britain. The Haudenosaunee carried the belt to its allies and said, "We will be neutral in the upcoming war."

The war was fought. Some of our people, such as Joseph Brant, because they had made friends, fought with the British, not as members of the Haudenosaunee, but as individuals. Some of our people had made friends with the colonists, those revolting, and so they fought with the Revolutionaries. But politically, the Haudenosaunee were neutral during the Revolutionary War, contrary to what you read in your history books.

History books say there was a war. The books say the Haudenosaunee, or the Six Nations, fought with Great Britain and they lost; therefore, they were conquered. Well, who was at Valley Forge with George Washington? The Oneidas were there. They took seven hundred bushels of corn. Our people fought on both sides. Politically they were neutral. The record should show this in your history books. The history books should also state that we were not defeated by the United States in the Revolutionary War.

After the war, George Washington said, "We have to expand. We must expand to the west. But there is a group of people in our way called the Haudenosaunee, or the Six Nations. They must be annihilated. They must be destroyed. Terminate them. Extinguish them." Washington sent out Major General John Sullivan in 1779 to extinguish the Haudenosaunee.

If I requested that hunters go out and shoot all of the deer in the woods, what do you think would happen? The deer would run, because we're a noisy bunch of people. And when we got to the woods, there would be nobody there. The deer would run away. We might get one, but most likely we wouldn't get any. We'd return home. The next day, the deer would be running around in the woods again.

This happened when Sullivan came through our territory. He went to our villages but there was nobody there. Since he was there to destroy, that's what he did. He burned our villages. He burned our silos. He burned our cornfields. He burned our orchards. He destroyed our food storage bins. We had no food for the winter. When we returned to our villages, we saw that our villages and towns were destroyed. We then gave a name to George Washington. We hung a name on his neck. That name is Hanadahguyus, which means "Town Destroyer."

That is the custom of our people. We name our people and then we rename people with that same name. That way the name is passed down through our people and our history. There is the president of the United States who resides in Washington, D.C. His name is William Clinton. On April 29, 1994, we wrote him a letter, inviting him to Canandaigua on November 11, 1994, to assist and to celebrate the 200th anniversary of the Canandaigua Treaty. I'll let you guess what the first line of that letter said. Yeah, you're right. It said Hanadahguyus. Underneath that, it said "President William Clinton."

If you look at your past presidents and examine what they did during the time that they were in office, you will understand what I mean. Look at the era of Andrew Jackson, Harry Truman, Theodore Roosevelt, Franklin Delano Roosevelt, Jimmy Carter, and Ronald Reagan. How many towns did these presidents destroy? Each one of your presidents has been in a situation in which he made a decision that resulted in having a town destroyed. President Clinton looked overseas to the Persian Gulf and Saddam Hussein. So President Clinton destroyed some towns and villages in Iraq. The name is so appropriate. We still refer to the president of the United States as Hanadahguyus. Some of the troops were aboard an aircraft carrier. I'll give you one guess at the name of this ship. Yup. You're right again. The name of the ship was the *George Washington*. How ironic.

When our people came back into their villages, and they saw what had happened to them, they said, "We shall do the same thing." They went out on the frontier, the western frontier. Now the western frontier then was not where Cochise, Geronimo, and Sitting Bull were. That frontier came later. That was a hundred years later. The frontier that I'm talking about is the line that was drawn in 1768. That's the line. That's the frontier line. You won't read this in your history books either. Most of the information that I'm telling you about is not recorded in your history books. This is the oral history that my father and my elders told me. I didn't read about these events in the history books. Anyway, retaliation was the name of the game at this time. We went back and destroyed 1,500 miles of frontier land.

George Washington said, "I cannot afford to fight the Haudenosaunee and its allies." Remember that when we agreed to be neutral
there were 1,500 of us at Fort Pitt. These included leaders and some of
the warriors. There were more warriors who stayed home, who were
ready to fight for our protection. Each warrior that we had at that time
was equal to fifty soldiers in the Revolutionary War. So if we had a
hundred men, that total was equal to five thousand soldiers, a very formidable force. George Washington had just finished fighting the
Revolutionary War. He could not afford to fight with us. He did not
have enough money to pay the soldiers who fought for freedom in the
Revolutionary War, and therefore he did not have enough money to
finance another war against the Haudenosaunee and their allies.

George Washington said, "We must have a treaty. We must sit down
and agree to live in peace." He asked us to meet at Fort Stanwix, which
is now called Rome, New York. This was in 1784. There we made our
first treaty with the United States. This treaty was signed by the representatives of the United States and the representatives of the
Haudenosaunee. Article I stated, "Let there be peace and friendship
between us." At this treaty we drew some lines from Lake Ontario down
the Niagara River, around Lake Erie, down through Pennsylvania and
then south, down the Ohio River and then east, along the Susquehanna
back up around Rome, a huge circle. This was the land of the Haudenosaunee. All of the land outside of that huge circle could be used by
the Revolutionaries for settling their villages. It must be understood that
the line that we drew was not to keep our people in, but was to keep
your people out. But your ancestors didn't pay attention to the treaty
that we had just made. They continued to come into our territory. This
was a violation of the treaty.

We went back to George Washington and said, "Your people are violating this treaty."

We met again at Fort Harmar in 1789. There we struck another
treaty with the United States. Again, we said in Article I, "Let there be
peace and friendship between our peoples." We had a big problem—
people were still coming into our territory. There were land grabbers,
land speculators in the state of New York. George Washington passed a
law in 1790. It was called the Non-Intercourse Act. This act is still in
effect. The law states that there will be no legal transactions of Indian
land unless there is a federal agent present.

The thirteen colonies, when they joined together to form the United
States, gave up some of their power. Before the Revolutionary War, as an
entity, the state of New York was able to negotiate and make treaties
with the Native American people. But after the Revolutionary War, the
Articles of Confederation were set down. This did not work for them,
so the United States Constitution was written to replace the Articles of

Confederation. In order to have a central power, the Thirteen Fires would have to give up some of their powers to the central power. The central power, the United States, then took over these duties. One of the powers that the states had was to make treaties with foreign nations. States also had the powers to regulate trade and commerce with these nations, to declare war, and to set up an army. The state of New York now could not act on the same issues that it had acted upon before the war. Like the other colonies, New York had given up its rights. The United States now had what the courts of today refer to as "plenary power," meaning that it would now act for and on behalf of the states on these issues. These powers were then put into the Constitution of the United States.

People of the state of New York ignored the Treaty of Fort Stanwix, the Treaty of Fort Harmar, the Non-Intercourse Act of 1790, and the original agreement in 1613. They set out to take over the lands of the Haudenosaunee. They commissioned a group of people to extinguish Indian title to our lands. Their report to the state of New York is recorded in the *Proceedings of the Commissioner of Indian Affairs, Appointed by Law for the Extinguishment of Indian Titles in the State of New York* with an Introduction and Notes by Franklin B. Hough.[1] This two-volume record is known as the *Hough Report*. At the present time still, the state of New York has not been able to extinguish the title to our land. The land still belongs to the Haudenosaunee.

We looked at what was happening to us at that time and the protection that George Washington gave us. He put into law the Non-Intercourse Act and then he said to the Haudenosaunee, "Herein lies your protection." The settlers still came and they still violated the law. We went back to George Washington, Hanadahguyus, and said to him, "Your people are still violating the treaties."

George Washington sent out Timothy Pickering to meet with us. We gathered at Canandaigua, New York, in July of 1794. There for a six-month period we discussed the terms of an agreement between our peoples. Many issues were discussed during that six-month period, and these discussions were brought back to our separate nations. On November 11, 1794, we finally signed the treaty. This treaty was between the Haudenosaunee (the Six Nations) and the United States. Again, Article I states, "Let there be peace and friendship between our two peoples." This treaty was ratified by the United States Congress and was signed by George Washington, the president of the United States.

The treaty still exists and is used today by the Haudenosaunee and the United States. The Canandaigua Treaty, the Fort Stanwix Treaty, and the Fort Harmar Treaty have never been abrogated by the United States. The Canandaigua Treaty is also known as the Timothy Pickering Treaty and the George Washington Covenant Treaty. There is a wampum belt in the possession of the Onondaga Nation that is six feet in length. It has thirteen figures holding hands with two native figures. The two native figures are on both sides of a house that is in the center of the belt. This belt is known as the George Washington Treaty Belt and was made to commemorate the Treaty of Canandaigua in 1794.

Yearly, the federal government expends $4,500 for treaty cloth that is sent to members of the Haudenosaunee. Each of the Nations receives this cloth. That $4,500 used to buy a lot of things back in 1795. Because we didn't have any lawyers sitting with us at the signing of this agreement, we forgot to put in a cost-of-living clause. You can imagine what $4,500 would be like today if we calculated that at 10% compound interest over the years. The sum would be something that we could use for the benefit and welfare of our people. As it is now, since the Haudenosaunee has grown in numbers, the $4,500 buys a small amount of treaty cloth. This treaty cloth is sent to us, and we get about a quarter of a yard of material for each person. The material is muslin. The United States used to send us yards of cotton cloth. It is much too expensive today and it would not be very much cloth, so the United States sends us muslin instead.

When I was a child, the Longhouse used to be filled with calico prints, cotton prints, huge piles of cloth. Our people went into the Longhouse and took their share of treaty cloth. That treaty cloth still comes to us every year. The federal government in 1954 tried to buy out those treaty rights, those annuity rights. They sent a man to each of the Six Nations and asked if we would like to get a lump sum that would forever pay the annuities.

Each one of the Nations said, "No, we won't do that. As long as the cloth comes to us, that means that the treaty is still in effect. We cannot make a decision like that because we would be making a decision that affects our grandchildren. Some time in the future the children might ask us why we made that kind of decision."

A report made by the Senate and signed by Richard Nixon in 1954 explained this part of our history. In this report it says that the United States government has never laid claim to the land of the Six Nations. That means that land that you walk upon, the land that you enjoy today are the lands of the Haudenosaunee. We are here today telling you that you must honor these treaties. You are the other half of these treaties. Talk to any one of our people, not only the Haudenosaunee, but the other nations of native people. As I had mentioned before, there were about four hundred treaties that were made between the native people and the United States. These treaties were ratified by Congress.

Article VI of the Constitution says the treaties that are made, and are to be made, by the United States will be the *supreme law of the land*. The federal and state courts cannot change the agreements that were made. A court decision, *Jones vs. Meehan*, says that if there is a treaty dispute involving our people, because the Indian is unlettered, the courts are to interpret the treaties as the Indian understands them and not as they are written.

We, as a people, walk around with our mandates that we shall take care of Mother Earth, not only for our sons, but also for our coming generations. The land that we occupy at this time is very small compared to the land that we were in control of. We cannot fulfill our mandates as we did many years ago. We now remind you that you are the other half of that treaty. We ask that you, as people of the United States, remind your leaders that you have treaty obligations with the Native people. You, as a people, would like to have those treaties honored.

I would be very embarrassed if I were sitting at a table with a foreign country, requesting their country to have a treaty. And the foreign country asked me, "What is your treaty record?" I would have to say, as a citizen of the United States, "I have violated every treaty that I have made with Native Americans, but with you, I won't do that."

I would probably say, "Well, let's take another look at what we're going to do here." You, as the other half of the treaty, are supposed to be taking care of the environment. You are supposed to be respecting Mother Earth, the plant life, the trees, and the animals, because we're living together. What have you done that violates this concept, this idea? Think about this question and then answer it honestly.

I come from Onondaga. We are living on a small plot of land just eight miles south of Syracuse, New York, where there is a lake named Onondaga Lake. Onondaga Lake is known as the most polluted lake in the United States. It's 4 1/2 miles long and about a mile wide. Fish that used to be in that lake but are not there anymore include whitefish, sturgeon, and salmon. They ran from the creeks of Onondaga down into the Atlantic Ocean and back. The short period of time that the settlers have been in our territory began somewhere around 1780. One hundred years later, we had a polluted lake. Two hundred years later, we have the most polluted lake in the United States.

When I heard that, I said, "Wow! You know, that is really something terrible!" If we continue to pollute at this rate, how long will we last? I would like to give you students a math problem. Our people have been on this land for many thousands of years. The land was not polluted when the settlers came to our territory. In two hundred years, we *now* do not have the same gifts that existed when the settlers came to our territory. These gifts are extinct. They no longer exist. The problem is this: how long will we exist if we continue to pollute at this rate?

Natives—No Pollution > Settlers—Pollution = EXTINCTION
          5000 years   200 years

We must live by the laws of nature. These laws are very simple. I'll give you one for example: you must drink water to survive. How long will you last without water? Not very long. How many days? Not many. If you pollute the water so that you can't drink it, then you are looking at extinction. Only one percent of the water on earth is drinkable, yet you continue to pollute the water. This is a violation of this concept, this agreement that we shall live together in peace and harmony as brothers, not only with each other but also with the environment.

Just north of Onondaga Lake is another lake, Lake Ontario. That lake is huge—130 miles long, 10 miles wide, a few miles deep. I have a friend who lives up on South Sandy Creek, which flows into Lake Ontario. She had a dog. The dog was down by the banks, where it found the insides of a fish. Fishermen were down there and didn't want to take the fish home to make a trophy out of it. They decided to behead it and clean it. So the dog came down, and, seeing the remains of the fish, ate them. Three days later, the dog died of mercury poisoning. Lake Ontario is polluted. This huge body of water is polluted. This is another violation of the treaty. We are told not to eat the fish that come out of this lake. What a shame to have such a beautiful lake that once was so clean, and now it is so polluted that it is dangerous to our well-being to consume the fish!

We must continue to live together under this concept of peace and harmony, not only with each other but with our friends: the animals, the fish, and the birds. When you came into this country, there were many animals and birds. Some of these birds and animals do not exist anymore. They are extinct because you have destroyed them in the very short period of time that you have been with us here in what is now the United States. We, as Haudenosaunee people, ask that you respect us today the same way that we respected you when you first came here. We ask that you will recognize that we are equal, that we are human beings, and that we are your brothers and that we are a people. We ask you to remember that what you do to the web, you do to yourself. We continue to speak the words of our ancestors. We tell the people that this is what we're about. We have the mandate to preserve the gifts that we receive.

My knowledge about the woods and the animals was taught to me by my father. He said to me, "When you go into the woods, take only what you need, when you need it, and use what you take." When I went hunting, I shot only what I needed that day. When I went fishing, I only took one or two fish, depending on the size. I have taught my children the same ways that my father taught me, the same ways that his father taught him.

The history of our people has come to us by being passed on from generation to generation in our oral tradition. Today we still carry on the ways of our people.

We are a sovereign nation of people. We qualify to be a member of the United Nations. We have our own government. We have civil ceremonies such as marriage and funerals. We have our own language. We have a government that has the process and protocol to put our leaders in place or to remove them if they do not work out for the people. We have our own land base. This then means that we have the right to make treaties with foreign nations. We have made treaties throughout our history. We still have the right to make treaties with foreign nations. We travel around the world on our own passports. We have been in thirty-nine foreign countries with our passports. The treaties that we made were usually for the welfare, benefit, but most important, for the preservation of our heritage, culture, and the language of our people.

We are not citizens of the United States. We are citizens of the Onondaga Nation. We do not vote in your elections, nor are we a part of the Democratic or Republican parties. We do not accept federal funds from the United States. The funds and services that we do receive come to us as *treaty obligations.* As a sovereign nation, we do not accept the federal and state laws that violate the concepts and interpretations of our treaties, as we understand these treaties.

Our mandate of today is the same as it was yesterday. What we see today, we should preserve, so that our great-great-grandchildren will be able to enjoy the same things that we see today. If we have fresh water, then let there be fresh water three or four hundred years from now. If we have fresh air, then let there be fresh air. Let us live together in peace and harmony with each other, the forces of nature, and the environment, forever.

Dawnaytoh.

Based on an address by Chief Powless Jr., Onondaga Nation, at a symposium held at Finger Lakes Community College on October 26, 1994.

NOTES

1. This report was published from the original manuscipt in the Library of the Albany Insitute with imprint: Albany: Joel Munsell, 1861.

WORKS CITED

Proceedings of the Commissioners of Indian Affairs, Appointed by Law for the Extinguishment of Indian Titles in the State of New York. 2 vols. Introduction and Notes by Franklin B. Hough. Albany: Joel Munsell, 1861. Manuscript, Library of the Albany Institute.

Treaty Making: The Legal Record

PAUL WILLIAMS

If you had come this way four hundred years ago, you would have come singing, singing your song of peace down the path, along a forest path to the village. At the Woods' edge you would have stopped. You would have waited respectfully for the people to greet you. And at the Woods' edge they would have taken you by the hand and welcomed you, and cleared your eyes, and ears, and throat in the first part of the ceremony of condolence, so that you could enter into that circle of their people with a clear mind.

The clear mind, the Good Mind, is the beginning of peace. That is one of the most important lessons of the Kaianerekowa, the Great Law of Peace. A mind that is tired, that's worn down, troubled, affected by grief, distracted by enemies or by loss or uncertainty, a mind like that finds it difficult to reason. It's carried by emotion. It's quick to tire. It's quick to anger. When nations come together as friends, it is the duty of friends to ease each other's minds. In the law of the Haudenosaunee, this obligation to ease each other's minds is reciprocal. The condolence should take place in both directions; the support should take place in both directions.

In times of loss, the world is divided instantly and sharply between the grieving ones and the clear-minded ones, who must respect that grief but who must also raise up the minds of their friends. Eyes that can see clearly, ears that can hear well, a mouth that can speak without the throat clogging with tears or anger, and a heart and body that function without pain, these permit the Good Mind, and the clear mind, to make the right choices for the future. A good mind, working well, will always choose peace. It will always seek peace. It will find a way to join with other minds to create peace.

Four hundred years ago, as the Great White Roots of the Tree of Peace were spreading over this part of the world, that thinking, and the processes and ceremonies that flowed from it, were the strength of the people. If we look at what took place two hundred years after that at Canandaigua, we see that the way those Councils went, the things that took place, were not happening according to the processes, the structures, and legal guidelines of the United States. They were following the ways of the Haudenosaunee. The United States had learned from those ways, and borrowed those ways, and respected those ways, and, in Council, followed those ways.

In Council, there are no adversaries. There are friends bringing their minds together. Each side has full opportunity to present its thoughts without being interrupted, to take as much time as required to present its reply, to consider what it's going to say, and to use as much time as necessary to deliver its reply carefully. Each issue must be addressed in the order in which it was raised. Nothing can be ignored. Council ends at sundown because minds, tired minds, make mistakes in the dark.

The legal record of the United States, Canada, Great Britain, and France rarely mentions anymore that when nations bring their minds together, they also bring their most sacred thoughts and ways. There is no higher purpose than peace. What people do to bring their minds together also brings their spirits together to create this peace. Every Council of the Haudenosaunee begins internally and externally with the same words. Even before we put our minds together politically, we put our minds together as human beings with a place in this world, a humble place.

All of these principles still guide the laws and thoughts of the Haudenosaunee in Council today. And the Good-Minded ones, the ones that in English are called Chiefs, they carry certain responsibilities that guide and inform their thinking. In any Council, in any decision, the law requires that they ask themselves: what will this do to the seven generations yet to come? What will this do to the natural world? What will this do to peace? These are three lenses through which the lawmakers must see each question. They are lenses that I think every lawmaker in this world would do well to carry.

These same processes, thoughts, and circles of protection were present in 1794, over two hundred years ago. But the world had changed as much in the two centuries before as it has in the last two centuries.

When we think of the Treaty of Canandaigua, we think of its aftermath, about what has flowed from it. We rarely think about what flowed into it and before it. But the relations between the Indigenous nations of this land and the settler nations are like a river. Indeed, the Kaswentha, or Two Row Wampum, is symbolized by the river of life, dynamic, flowing. The two peoples travel down that river together. Its source is far upstream from 1794. Individual transactions, like the Treaty of Canandaigua, stand as rocks in the river, not as the river itself.

A treaty, the way I've been taught, isn't a written document. It's an agreement. It's a coming together of minds. The written document is merely evidence of that agreement. Usually, it's incomplete evidence. The Haudenosaunee keep a record of the treaties on wampum belts. But nobody says, "That is a treaty."

They say, "This helps us remember the treaty," because the treaty, the agreement, is kept in people's minds, the way it was made, in people's minds. And while it may be that details are kept better on paper, people who hold their treaties in their minds keep their treaties *in mind*, and are governed by them and live by them.

The power of the Iroquois Confederacy was never military invincibility. I think people who believe the myth of military power end up suffering by it as a result. Instead, the power of the Confederacy was the power of minds that could create a landscape of peace. It is true that the history, at least the first three centuries, of European presence in this land is one of intermittent warfare on all sides. It's true that the Confederacy played important and brave parts in that warfare. But if one reads the entire written record of the Councils, one sees that the Chiefs are constantly talking of peace—how to restore it, how to maintain it, how to create it. That to them is the power that mattered. That power is still present.

We tend not to see the world as it was in 1794. We tend to see the world today and impose our values and thoughts on the people who were there. There had been a tremendous amount of technological change during the eighteenth century, and that changed the society of the Haudenosaunee in profound ways. Men who could cut trees with steel axes and saws no longer had to take ten times as long to girdle them. Draft animals and steel plows meant that men could plow a field in half the time that it would take all the women in the village to do so. Single-family farms came along to replace palisaded villages. It was a time of religious and spiritual uncertainty and renewal. The people were reeling under waves of new diseases. They suffered the effects of the Mind Changer, alcohol. Those were difficult times. And the wars made them more difficult, more dangerous.

But it's a bad mistake to think of the world of the Haudenosaunee in 1794, or the world of the United States in 1794, as isolated or insular, primitive in technology or thought, or to think that any of the issues were simple or straightforward. In 1794, the world was a complicated place and the leaders were complicated people. They struggled with issues every bit as difficult as those we face today.

Let me give you some examples of the influences on the treaty that were taking place two hundred years ago. Back in the early 1790s, several New York State land transactions took place that remain controversial today. New York openly defied the federal government by engaging in these land treaties.

By late 1794, Supreme Court Chief Justice John Jay was in England negotiating a definitive treaty of friendship, commerce, and navigation that we now call the Jay Treaty. In the London negotiations, Britain had proposed an Indian buffer state in the Ohio Valley, south of Lake Erie. Britain's thinking was that if the United States ever invaded Canada, it would have to go through the Indian nations first. John Jay had been instructed to agree to this buffer zone if the British pushed hard enough. The British never pushed hard enough. They were much more concerned about the rise of Napoleon Bonaparte in France. Essentially, the British had made promises to the Indian nations, their allies, that they ended up not keeping. Everybody was looking east to the British-American negotiations, even as Canandaigua was being negotiated.

Everybody was also looking west to the Ohio country. It wasn't the wars between the British and the Americans that were exhausting the Indian nations. For the United States two hundred years ago, the Ohio country was very much like Vietnam twenty years ago. There were impossibly long supply lines. Many of the soldiers, the militia, had been called up and didn't really want to be there. The enemy was perhaps less technically well-armed than the American soldiers, but the enemy knew the territory. And the United States could never tell who was an enemy and who was not. In 1791, Arthur Sinclair lost one half of the standing U.S. army. That's three times as many men as Custer lost. Custer just had better public relations people.

We have to remember that in 1794, most of the population of the United States was hugging the East Coast. They were a maritime people. It was only after the 1780s that there was a real push westward, a stampede westward, perhaps. On the Indian side, the nations gathered together in the Ohio country and they put a wampum there, a moon of wampum, a big circle of wampum that stems from the Four Directions.

They said, "This is going to be the country of all the nations. It's going to be a house with four doors. Everyone who wants to can settle here." For the first time they weren't talking about each nation. They were talking about "people of our color." And they were saying, "This is where we make a stand."

During the negotiations at Canandaigua in 1794, everybody was looking westward. The reason that Thayendenegea, Joseph Brant, wasn't at Canandaigua was that he was meeting with the Sauks from the headwaters of the Mississippi to talk about the future with them.

In the middle of the negotiations, a runner came from Tuscarora, with news that Turkey Foot and the Miamis had been defeated in battle by General Anthony Wayne of the United States. That changed the tone of the negotiations. Just as everybody was looking east to what was happening in Europe, everybody was also looking west to what was happening in the Ohio country. This wasn't an isolated place. Nobody on either side was isolated.

After the American Revolutionary War, the Haudenosaunee found themselves badly battered. Internal scars were slow in healing. Getting caught between two warring brothers, as the Six Nations considered the British and the Americans, was even more painful than what had happened in the first half of the 1700s between the English and the French, because as a result of the U.S. Revolutionary War, land was lost. Even the western nations of the Confederacy now found themselves on the front lines.

The first treaty made between the United States and the Six Nations after the Revolutionary War was the Treaty of Fort Stanwix. It was a disaster. It was a disaster for the Confederacy because it involved the loss of huge amounts of land. Also, it was a disaster for the United States, because it lacked credibility. The United States commissioners had blatantly violated all the rules of treaty procedure. They had made their agreement with young, inexperienced, and unauthorized spokesmen. The Treaty of Fort Stanwix had all the ill feeling and humiliation of the Treaty of Versailles after World War I. It left the Confederacy smarting with shame and anger. Therefore it left the United States in danger rather than peace. After the Treaty of Fort Stanwix, a series of land frauds by New York State and by individual citizens of the United States occurred. Each of these increased the danger and the hard feelings. The Treaty of Canandaigua was made out of necessity on both sides.

In this uncertainty, there were men of vision. People like Thomas Jefferson and Benjamin Franklin, on the United States side, acknowledged their debt to the Confederacy and also the need to maintain peace. Timothy Pickering, the treaty commissioner, was an idealist. He wasn't like the men who had made the Fort Stanwix Treaty. He took the long view that peace with honor was necessary and possible.

He wrote to George Washington before the treaty and said, "Indians have been so often deceived by white people that *white man* is, among many of them, only another name for *liar*. Really, sir, I am unwilling to be subjected to this infamy. I confess I am not indifferent to a good name even among Indians."

On the side of the Confederacy as well, there were people who took the long view. For many years they had been seeking peace, stability, and certainty. In 1786, they wrote to the United States, and they said they were looking for a real treaty.

They said, "Let us pursue reasonable steps; let us meet half-way for our mutual convenience; we shall then bring into oblivion the misfortunes that have happened, and meet with each other on a footing of friendship."

The Chiefs of the Confederacy, in their quest for peace, were supported by thoughtful, energetic, literate men like the ones we know in English as Joseph Brant and Cornplanter. These Pine Tree Chiefs engaged in preliminary negotiations, setting up what happened in Canandaigua. This wasn't an instant treaty. It wasn't just people coming together in one place at one time. A lot of work went beforehand, just as any modern treaty requires a great deal of preparation.

We also shouldn't deceive ourselves that Canandaigua was the only option for the Confederacy. Eight years earlier the Senecas had met with British authorities and arranged with them that, if things went badly on the American side, land would be made available on the Canadian side. About a month before this treaty, Cornplanter had met with Governor John Graves Simcoe of Upper Canada. Simcoe reaffirmed that promise, the promise of land on the north shore of Lake Erie at Long Point. The Senecas were hoping to secure and recover their lands, but they were prepared to leave if the United States didn't make peace on the right terms.

If we look at the treaty itself, we see that for the Senecas, Canandaigua represented the recovery of much of their lost land. It delivered enough assurances for the future that they stayed on those homelands instead of moving west. For the rest of the Confederacy, it meant peace with the United States on terms that would also permit healing within the Confederacy. The Treaty of Canandaigua was a genuine effort by men of vision and integrity to create a peace that was not obvious and that would require real compromise on both sides. In its day, for its time, it worked.

But what's been the aftermath of the treaty? The land that was restored was taken again. And even more was lost afterward, taken in a chain of transactions that have bred misery for the Haudenosaunee and hard feelings and litigation on all sides. Those continue today. I'm not suggesting that things would have been any different on the Canadian side, where the same kinds of frauds and the same kinds of litigation are continuing today as well.

The political aspects of the Treaty of Canandaigua also lie in ashes. The state of New York constantly pierces the circle of protection of the Confederacy and its laws. There are constant confrontations over taxes, gambling, land, pollution, and many other issues. Internally, the Confederacy is beset by challenges from people whose values reflect the worst of those of the United States—the desire to prosper as individuals at the edges of the law, without regard for the rest of the people or for the future.

The United States government, which intervened in 1794 in the interests of peace, remains largely invisible in these crises today. Though the Confederacy continues to address the president of the United States in the way that was agreed in the treaty, to seek redress, to seek help, help hasn't been forthcoming. If what happened at Canandaigua two hundred years ago was an effort by people of intelligence and foresight to secure a lasting peace and coexistence, we really should be asking ourselves, "What would it take to do the same thing today?"

It would require the same intelligence and foresight, the same spirit of respect, the same desire for peace, and the same regard for future generations. It would take commitment and participation on the part of the United States, which has grown since then in both power and population. It would certainly require more than the symbolic delivery of a bolt of cloth. It would need the nations' leaders on both sides to be of the same Good Mind that brought their minds together at Canandaigua two hundred years ago.

If a treaty is a matter of spirit—and not just of laws and details and words—then what's most important about what happened at Canandaigua over two hundred years ago is the confirmation of a relationship—the open path between the Grand Council of the Haudenosaunee and the president of the United States. In 1794 this path had real meaning. It was kept free from brush. Today, it is overgrown with brambles and thorns.

In these times of deep trouble for the Confederacy, the president and the government of the United States have turned their backs. The chain of friendship remains tarnished. We've just been told that Congress can change treaties, unilaterally. What I've been taught, and law school didn't really change my mind that much, is that it takes two minds coming together to create a treaty. And it takes those same two minds to change it

We all need to think about the survival of the way of thinking that carries respect for our Mother the Earth and for future generations, for peace, and for other people—that thinking that continues to pervade the minds of the Haudenosaunee. In its survival—the lessons of the Good Mind from the few who continue to carry it—there is much to learn.

Most people in this country today, their parents, or their grandparents, came to this continent from another land. This tells us that something, to them, to those who left, was stronger than their attachment to their land. To people who can leave their own land, it becomes easy to leave another land afterward. It becomes part of their heritage. It becomes easy for them to accept the idea that land is a commodity that can be bought and sold, that land can be used and exhausted, and left for other lands, other greener pastures. It gives rise to the way of thinking that says treaties can be abrogated, and what comes instead is a right to compensation. But money is not land. Money doesn't replace land. There is no replacement for land. We now see that this way of thinking, that land and money are the same thing, is dangerous to all human life as well as all other life, because it ignores our responsibility to the land, and therefore to future generations of humans and all parts of the natural world.

Two hundred years ago, the recovery of part of their land left the Senecas convinced that they should stay and live on this land. We celebrate not that recovery, because it was short-lived, but the survival of the people who carry that view of the world, perhaps to teach others, perhaps only to pass it on to some of their children.

Perhaps too late.

At the treaty commemoration, though we don't see the Woods anymore, Chief Jake Swamp cleared everyone's eyes so they could see clearly; cleared their ears so they could hear clearly; cleared their throats so they could speak freely without tears or fears; cleared the passage to their hearts so each could feel truly and well; and cleared their minds so that all could understand and accept peace and the respect that maintains it. That respect is the spirit of Canandaigua. We honor its hopes and its promises for the future. What we cherish is the ember that remains of it.

Da ne toh.

This chapter is based on an address delivered at the "Symposium: Polishing the Rust from the Chain," held in Canandaigua, New York, on November 12, 1994, as part of the 200th Anniversary of the Canandaigua Treaty Celebration.

Timothy Pickering by Charles Willson Peale ca. 1792. Photo courtesy of the Independence National Historical Park Library, Philadelphia, Pennsylvania.

The Canandaigua Treaty in Historical Perspective

JOHN C. MOHAWK

The first half of the eighteenth century was a time of relative peace and prosperity in North America. By the fourth decade, however, a sense of impending doom began to appear among the Indians. This was caused by the continuing European encroachment into Indian country and a result of a century of dislocations of Indians, as Europeans pushed westward from the Atlantic coast.[1] European expansion was manifested in 1737, a year which also marked the beginning of a century of Indian revitalization movements. These produced both prophets and movements for Indian unity to face this threat. They also produced American Indian military leaders and armed resistance that would prove a real challenge to Euro-American westward expansion. Conscious efforts to produce a more satisfactory culture, these revitalization movements frequently involved prophets bearing messages from the great beyond that urged followers to participate in certain activities, including the revival of ancient spiritual practices, the refraining from destructive behaviors and dependencies introduced by Anglos, and unity, in the face of an enemy bent on destruction of the Indian nations. Such movements were often characterized by an early state of enhanced enthusiasm that tended to result in the group's inability to realistically assess the probability of success.

By 1740 some Iroquois bands had migrated to western Pennsylvania. The Americans called these people Mingoes, but they were refugees drawn from Delaware, Conestoga, Shawnee, Wyandot, and Seneca peoples.[2] They had drifted westward as refugees from white encroachment and fraudulent dealings.[3] Meanwhile, the Seven Years' War ended with an English victory and the expulsion of France from Canada and the Ohio region. As soon as the war was over, the English continued their encroachments into Indian country and adopted what was recognized by the Indians as a disrespectful demeanor at meetings and negotiations, and tensions grew. When Detroit fell to the British in November 1760, General Jeffrey Amherst pointedly discontinued the custom of giving gifts to the Indians, including arms and ammunition.

Three years following the war an Ottawa war chief named Pontiac organized a siege of the British at Detroit, which grew into a rebellion intended to drive the British from the Indian country. Pontiac's attempt to drive the British out was energized in part by several Nativist movements, among which was one authored by an individual known as the Delaware Prophet. The Delaware Prophet urged that the arrival of the white man and the Indians' adoption of the white man's ways had interfered with the Indians' spiritual life and destiny. If the Indians would revive ancient ceremonies, renounce the use of rum and firearms, and abandon other bad habits introduced by the whites, they could drive the invaders from their country.[4]

A party of men employed by the Susquehannah Company of Connecticut cut a road and took steps to occupy Delaware country at Wyoming, Pennsylvania, in pursuit of land claims based on colonial charters. This was part of a larger movement of penetration and occupation of Indian lands that in contemporary times might be seen as "ethnic cleansing." These men and their enterprise were opposed by the Six Nations and the Delaware, led by chief Teedyuscung, who was murdered—burned to death in his house while, it is rumored, under the influence of rum—probably by agents of the Connecticut interests, on April 19, 1763.[5] On April 27, Pontiac convened a Grand Council of the Potawatomie, Huron, and Ottawa and organized the attack on Detroit, sparking the war that became known as Pontiac's Rebellion. Pontiac altered the Prophet's message to fit the realities of his day and promoted the use of firearms and alliance with the French.[6]

Pontiac's Rebellion included an effort, unsuccessful at the time, to create a confederacy that would embrace the Ottawa and other Indian nations of the Great Lakes and Ohio country, including some Seneca of the Genesee Valley. During this war many British forts fell into Indian hands, including Fort Michilimackinac, Fort St. Joseph, Fort Ouiatenon, Fort Miamis, Fort Sandusky, Fort Le Boeuf, and Fort Venango. The Indians cut off the supply lines and attacked British posts from Niagara to Michilimackinac. Detroit survived a siege that lasted five months.

During a siege at Fort Pitt (present-day Pittsburgh) Sir Jeffrey Amherst, the British commander in North America, ordered smallpox-infested blankets distributed to the Delaware.[7] The Indians then suffered a significant defeat in the confrontation known as the Battle of Bushy Run, where English colonial soldiers under Colonel Henry Bouquet routed an Indian force, one of the first times this had happened in forest warfare.[8]

For centuries, European wars had been settled in great battles where decisive victories meant total conquest. Sometimes wars involved extensive sieges of powerful fortresses with the same effect. The Indian wars in the woodlands were not fought this way. Indians often refused to meet on a battlefield, preferring to whittle away at a pursuing enemy.

They built no forts, and they did not defend their towns as Europeans did, preferring to melt into the forest and to fight from there.

Pontiac's war ended in two stages. On October 7, 1763, the British issued the Proclamation of 1763, in which they promised to stop encroachments into Indian land,[9] but some Indians fought on for another year. Although armed conflict ended, the tensions that had provoked the war were far from resolved, and Pontiac was murdered in April 1769. From that time forward the Indians who had attacked the British continued efforts to unify under a Western Confederacy, which would include the Shawnee, Delaware, Wyandot, Potowatomie, Chippewa, Cherokee, and other western Indian nations.[10]

The Proclamation of 1763 was not universally or adequately honored by the colonists. In 1773 the governor of Virginia, Lord Dunmore, moved to claim land on both sides of the Ohio River, in violation of the Proclamation and in defiance of the Indians. When surveyors appeared west of the Ohio, a Shawnee warrior who went to them unarmed to warn them to go back was murdered. The Shawnee then attacked the surveyors, killing several and sending a message that all who crossed the Ohio would be killed. Further attempts at negotiations were marked by murders of Indians by frontiersmen, which were followed by retaliations and killings of frontiersmen by Indians. In June 1774 Lord Dunmore declared war against the Indians (this is called Lord Dunmore's War) and raised a militia. Dunmore's forces under Andrew Lewis engaged in a fierce battle with the Indians at Pleasant Point, Ohio, on October 10, during which some 222 militiamen and half as many Indians were killed or seriously wounded.[11] It is said that Tecumseh's father, Pucksinwa, was killed at this battle.[12]

Daniel Boone became famous with the successful defense of the siege of Booneville, Kentucky, just before the American Revolution on April 6, 1774.[13] Neither side was enthusiastic about continuing the war and a truce was signed on October 26, 1774.

Although raids and retaliations continued in the Kentucky and Ohio country in 1775, squatters continued to arrive. Kentucky was claimed by Virginia, and the following year George Rogers Clark arrived in Williamsburg, colonial Virginia's capital, seeking help in the border wars. In July 1776, at about the same time that the American colonists gathered in Philadelphia to sign the Declaration of Independence, the Shawnee held a grand Council with Cherokees, Delawares, Ottawas, Wyandots, and others at Muscle Shoals on the Tennessee River. At this meeting Cornstalk, the most prominent chief of the Shawnee, abandoned neutrality and announced for the British cause.

Early the following year Shawnee war chief Black Fish led attacks against the settlements in the Kentucky region. Virginia designated Kentucky a county of that commonwealth, and Clark planned to assemble a force to attack the Shawnee. Shawnees, Mingoes, Wyandots, and Cherokees raided the area around Wheeling during the summer of 1777. The Americans planned to retaliate with an expedition against a British supply depot near Cleveland. Hearing this, Cornstalk approached Fort Randolph at the confluence of the Ohio and Kanawha Rivers under a flag of truce to try to convince the Americans to abandon the expedition. He was seized by the fort commander who ignored the truce flag, and Cornstalk and his son Silverheels were held hostage to ensure against attacks by the Shawnee until November 10, when a group of white hunters murdered Cornstalk, Silverheels, and another warrior. This incited the Shawnee to more raids under Black Fish, Black Hoof, and Blue Jacket. In February 1778, Blue Jacket captured Daniel Boone.

In September Black Fish and more than four hundred warriors laid siege to Boonesboro and in May to Fort Randolph. That same month Clark marched on Kaskaskia and Cahokia and captured both without a fight. Clark continued to Vincennes, where the British surrendered after a brief fight. At this point, the British forts in the Old Northwest were in American hands, and the Shawnee and their allies were divided about how to defend their country. In July 1779 Colonel John Bowman of the Continental army attacked the Shawnee town of Chillicothe, and during this encounter Chief Black Fish was mortally wounded. This motivated an October Grand Council of Miamis, Wyandots, Tuscaroras, Shawnees, Ojibwas and others to meet with the Tory frontiersman Simon Girty to plan retaliatory attacks on the Kentucky settlements. The following spring an Indian-British force attacked and captured Ruddell's Station, killing its defenders.

In 1779 General John Sullivan led a coordinated expedition against the Six Nations, which penetrated the Genesee Valley towns of the Seneca. Cornfields were destroyed, houses burned, and, in the fashion of Indian warfare, the Indians retreated, many to Fort Niagara. The following year British General Sir John Johnson led an expedition of Tories and Indians into the Mohawk Valley, where they attacked Caughnawaga and overran Canajoharie. Joseph Brant led an expedition down the Ohio River, where he encountered and thoroughly defeated a force of Pennsylvania militia under Archibald Lochry. Brant and the Tories then invaded Tryon County in New York. Brant and Seneca War Chief Cornplanter joined forces and pushed through the Schoharie and Mohawk river valleys, destroying everything they encountered. By 1781 the American-allied Oneida had been driven to refuge in Schenectady. Only two thousand settlers remained in the New York counties in and around the Mohawk Valley when Colonel Marius Willet assumed command of the American forces. Willet led his forces against Captain Walter Butler and a force of Tories, British regulars, and Indians near Corey's Town and later at Canada Creek. Butler was killed in the second skirmish, and most of his forces retreated into the wilderness. Willet's success halted raids in western New York for the time.[14]

In early 1782 a band of Moravian Indians were forced by famine to move back to their mission towns on the Tuscarawas River in western Pennsylvania at Gnaddenhutten. These Moravian Delawares were considered peaceful Indians and not involved in the war. In spite of that, an American force under Colonel David Williamson captured them and announced they would be put to death for the depredations committed by the pagan Delaware. Ninety men, women, and children were executed by mallet blows to the back of the head.[15]

This act of mass murder was denounced by prominent American politicians and predictably incited more Indian raids in retaliation. In May Colonel William Crawford was sent to destroy the Indian towns at Sandusky in the Ohio country. On June 4 Crawford's force encountered Indian forces near Sandusky, and during his retreat, forty to fifty of his men were killed, and Crawford was captured and tortured to death. This set off a new round of raids. In August a force, including Simon Girty and three hundred Indians and rangers, surrounded a stronghold called Bryant's (or Bryan's) Station, 5 miles north of Lexington. Girty's forces retreated and were pursued by 180 Kentucky militiamen, including Daniel Boone. At Blue Licks the perusing Americans were ambushed and more than half were killed, the worst defeat of the Kentucky militia thus far.

American General William Irvine assembled a force of 1,200 Continentals and militia for an assault on Sandusky, and George Rogers Clark invaded the Ohio country at the head of more than 1,000 Kentucky militia. He burned Shawnee towns and destroyed cornfields, but the expedition managed to inflict minimal losses on the enemy: ten Indians were killed and ten were captured. Meanwhile, British General Cornwallis was surrounded by a French fleet and a French and Continental army and forced to surrender following a siege at Yorktown. In November, the preliminary articles of peace between the United States and Great Britain were signed in Paris, and in that treaty Britain ceded whatever rights in sovereignty Britain claimed in the Old Northwest to the new United States.

The treaty that ended the war failed to mention the British government's Indian allies. The Indian Committee of the Continental Congress submitted a report to Congress in the fall of 1783 urging that the terms of peace include a demand that the Indians surrender part of their country without compensation to the United States.[16] The New York Assembly produced a proposal to expel all the Mohawks, Onondagas, Cayugas, and Senecas—the nations whose warriors fought mostly for the British cause—from New York State.[17] Even the Tuscarora and Oneida peoples who had supported the American cause in arms were to be exiled to "vacant" Seneca lands in Western New York.

United States officials met with representatives of the Six Nations at Fort Stanwix and concluded the war with a treaty. At these negotiations the American representatives were very aggressive and insulting, even demanding hostages from the Indians. They insisted on land cessions, which the delegates had not been empowered to grant, and urged that the Indians were a conquered people and had thus forfeited their right to their lands.[18] The Indian representatives, including very few sachem chiefs, were "warriors" who made land cessions they were not authorized by their nations to make, including lands along Lake Erie, in Pennsylvania, and Ohio.[19] The treaty was not ratified by the Six Nations, and its terms were soon rejected publicly by its spokespeople.[20] Cornplanter, the spokesman for the warriors, separately negotiated with Pennsylvania a land cession which left him with land south of the New York border and a pension.[21]

The humiliation suffered by the Iroquois warriors at Fort Stanwix was not lost on the western Indians. The New York Iroquois were exposed to the expansionist ambitions of the new United States, but the Indians in the Ohio region were determined that they would not suffer the same fate as their Iroquois brethren. The United States pressed its conquest theory at the Treaty of Fort McIntosh with the Delaware and Wyandot in January 1785 and at the Treaty at the Mouth of the Great Miami with the Shawnee in February 1786.[22]

The first meeting of the new Western Confederacy took place in Detroit in the autumn of 1785.[23] The United States ignored this new confederacy and now claimed to own the whole Ohio country. The Western Confederacy responded in the fall of 1786 with a four-point position. They denied the legitimacy of the conquest theory and repudiated the three treaties of Fort Stanwix, Fort McIntosh, and Fort Finney (1786).

Tensions mounted and war appeared more certain. In October 1786, a raid against the Shawnee resulted in eleven Indian casualties. During this raid Hugh McGary, a Kentucky militiaman, murdered Delaware Chief Moluntha. In March of the following year McGary was court-martialed and found guilty. His sentence was light: a one-year suspension of rank. This raid had the unintended result of uniting the Shawnee in Ohio and western Pennsylvania.

The United States, meanwhile, found itself on the edge of bankruptcy. The states were not paying into the treasury and a national tax was a failure. Partly in response to this crisis, on July 13, 1787, Congress passed the Northwest Ordinance. It then sold parcels of land for cash. Some of these investors were gentlemen of influence, poised to use public office to enhance their personal fortunes in the lucrative business of land speculation. The United States' claim to these lands continued to be based on the theory that the Indians who occupied these lands had been conquered along with the British during the American Revolution—a theory the Indians hotly contested—and the results of three treaties which the Indians had renounced as illegal.

This was to be the first large real estate deal by the United States. Governor Arthur St. Clair received an appropriation of $14,000, with orders to implement Congressional policy, meaning he was to obtain Indian land. Before he could arrange a treaty negotiation with any Indians, however, hordes of white squatters descended on the Ohio country with the covert approval of the United States government:

> Along the Ohio, the end of the Revolution simply commenced a new phase of the struggle between American and Indian villages for control of the Ohio country. Fed by the flood of settlers coming down the Ohio—more than twelve thousand landed in Limestone from 1786 to 1788 alone—Americans pushed across the river in violation of both law and treaty . . . 'The Indians seem determined to defend themselves,' wrote the governor general of Canada, "and make the Americans feel the difference of a war carried on in their own manner."[24]

History had proven that once these settlements were established, they were impossible to uproot. The Indians of the Ohio region were forced to fight or surrender.

Joseph Brant emerged as a leader of moderates in the Western Confederacy, as undeclared low-intensity warfare proceeded between the whites and Indians in Kentucky and along the Ohio River. Brant had negotiated a hard-won compromise by which the Western Confederacy expressed willingness to cede significant lands west of the Ohio in exchange for peace. Arthur St. Clair negotiated with the Indians for the settlers, but he proved to be an inept diplomat. He blamed the Western Confederacy for a raid conducted by Ojibwa of the far west—Indians who were not part of and not related to the Western Confederacy—and refused to meet Joseph Brant's proposals half way. This had the effect of damaging Brant's credibility and strengthening the Shawnee factions which favored war.

St. Clair was successful in organizing a conference at Fort Harmar with the Senecas and Wyandots in 1789, and the resulting treaty continued the spirit of St. Clair's insistence on Indian capitulation to the United States. This treaty was not attended by important Indian chiefs and was described as a farce by one of St. Clair's own men. Following the Fort Harmar treaty, the Shawnee stepped up attacks in Kentucky. In September a delegation from the Western Confederacy journeyed to Buffalo Creek to meet with the Six Nations in the hope they might secure approval for their part of the war in the Ohio region. They were met by Joseph Brant, who represented the nations of the Six Nations except the Seneca. Brant expressed the sentiment that they need not wait for advice from the Six Nations Confederacy and that, if possible, they should negotiate some kind of agreement with the Americans. The Seneca speakers expressed similar ideas.[25]

The American settlers on the frontier were becoming desperate because, in addition to the violence of an ongoing Indian conflict, they had no access to markets. The British continued to block access to the water routes of the Great Lakes and the St. Lawrence with their occupation of forts from Michilimackinac to Niagara. The Spanish were imposing an impossibly high tax on river cargo on the Mississippi. The only route to markets for the people in Kentucky and Ohio was by road over the Appalachians, a course which was both expensive and exhausting.[26] Most generally believed the British were the source of the materials of war which supplied the Indians with the capacity to keep the frontier in a state of constant alert and potential danger[27] (although, at the same time, in poverty). There was talk in the frontier towns of sedition. They might declare themselves an independent country and make war or a peace treaty with Spain, or they might rejoin Great Britain. Such thoughts threatened to tear the fledgling United States apart.

Major John Doughty was dispatched to meet with the southern Indians, but his party of fifteen was attacked on the Tennessee and only five survived. Governor St. Clair sent a representative to meet with the Miami, but he was in their town for three days when, in a gesture of disdain, the Miami burned a white prisoner. The only solution, in the eyes of many, was a military strike against the Indians.[28]

In 1790 Cornplanter and several Seneca chiefs gained a meeting with President Washington, at which they complained of the terms of the Fort Stanwix treaty and of unfair land deals at the hands of the state of New York.[29] This may have been a factor in shaping Washington's policy toward Indian land cessions to adopting treaty making and a principle of fair and honest treatment of the Indians, because he did cause several small tracts of land to be returned to the Seneca. The spirit of this exchange was implemented when Congress passed the Non-Intercourse Act of July 23, 1790, which guaranteed federal protection against unfair land transactions at the hands of the states. It said:

> that no sale of lands made by an Indian or any nation or tribe of Indians within the United States, shall be valid to any person or persons, or to any state, whether having the right of preemption to such land or not, unless the same shall be made and duly executed at some public treaty, held under the authority of the United States.[30]

At the Treaty of Fort Harmar, the Americans had paid what amount-ed to a reasonably fair price for land, and sentiment was growing for following a course of treating the Indians with justice and humanity. As Kelsay would note, "It was the one course the Americans had not yet tried, and no doubt a certain amount of frustration over the results of their previous conduct prodded them on."[31]

In addition, a popular theory among some Americans was that as white settlement approached the Indian country, the game population would plummet, making the area less attractive to the Indians. This ecological impact of white settlement, it was thought, would be a factor that would cause the Indians to want to sell the land. Purchasing land was less expensive than mounting military expeditions. This was another reason why, at Washington's urging, Congress had passed the 1790 Non-Intercourse Act creating a federal promise to protect the Indians from unfair dealings at the hands of the states. Isabel Thomp-son Kelsay's summary is concise:

> The United States had now put the finishing touches on its com-plete about-face. Gone was the uncompromising stand that the Indians had lost their lands in the war. Kindness, conciliation, generosity, humanity: these would be the watchwords, hence-forth, of the new American Indian policy.[32]

Meanwhile, white settlements had encroached north of the Ohio River at Marietta, Fort Washington (Cincinnati), and Steubenville.[33] The undeclared warfare with the Indians was proving costly. An esti-mated fifteen hundred men, women, and children and been captured, killed, or injured in the Ohio country between 1783 and 1790. At least two thousand horses had been captured by Indians, and property losses were estimated at around $50,000.[34]

In June 1790, General Harmar was authorized to mount an expedi-tion against the Indians to destroy the Indian towns, especially those of the Miami.[35] Harmar's army of some 320 troops and 1,133 local militia was mostly untrained and unprepared for a wilderness campaign. The nearly-destitute United States could not afford a war with Great Britain or with a wide coalition of Indian nations, and Philadelphia dispatched messages to neutral Indians that the expedition was strictly limited as a exercise in chastising some Miami and Shawnee Indians who had been involved in raiding white settlements. Diplomatically and militarily, pacification and conquest of the Ohio region was to be a complex affair.

There were skirmishes near present-day Fort Wayne, Indiana, which produced heavy casualties among Harmar's forces and relatively light casualties among the Indians. An engagement near a destroyed Miami village produced the most important battle of the campaign.[36] More than

150 Americans were killed and, although Harmar was able to engineer an orderly retreat to Fort Washington, his expedition was considered a significant defeat for the Americans. Harmar's report reached George Washington in December. He reported he had burned the Miami towns and declared the expedition a success, but the disproportionate losses were noted, and it was soon dubbed "Harmar's Defeat." Harmar resigned his command.

In the spring of 1791 the U.S. secretary of war dispatched Colonel Thomas Proctor to meet and negotiate a peace with the Indians. His effort was successfully frustrated by the British, who wanted to be part of any settlement involving lands they felt they had a chance to regain. That summer Colonel Timothy Pickering was sent to the country of the Six Nations, and in June and July he held meetings with all but Mohawk representatives at Newtown on the Chemung River,[37] site of an important battle between Revolutionary forces and British and Six Nations fighters. Over a thousand Six Nations delegates attended these meetings, and Pickering was able to extract a promise of continued neutrality. Pickering was also exposed to numerous complaints by the Six Nations people that they had been abused at the hands of the Americans and the states, and that these abuses included murders for which no one was punished and land deals which were not proper.

During the summer of 1791 the Mohawk war chief Joseph Brant met with the Western Confederacy in an effort to help move matters toward a negotiated peace. While he was there, American forces moved toward the Indian country, and Brant was recruited by the Western Confederacy to lead a delegation to meet with Britain's Lord Dorchester, to plead for military aid and for a fort to protect the Indians on the Maumee. He reported to Lord Dorchester that the Indians were willing to agree to a boundary at the line of the Muskingum,[38] but Dorchester departed for England with no promise of military help from the British to their Indian allies. Brant, severely disappointed, returned to his home on the Grand River, while the Indians who had delegated him as their representative waited hopefully for his return to their towns on the Maumee, with British military aid in tow.

Arthur St. Clair, the territorial governor who had failed at peace negotiations with the Indians, was selected to succeed Harmar. By September he was collecting militia and planning a massive campaign against the Miami towns. Within a short time his army of more than two thousand had dwindled to some seventeen hundred.[39] St. Clair's army encountered bad weather and food shortages, and the general became so ill he was transported by litter.[40] When the delegates who had accompanied Brant to Quebec reported there would be no British aid, the Indians were bitterly disappointed but nevertheless gathered their forces and moved eastward to meet St. Clair's army. Their leader was the well-respected Little Turtle, and their warriors had come from many different Indian nations, including some from the Seneca and Cayuga.

On November 4, 1791, St. Clair and his army, now reduced to about fourteen hundred because some were deployed protecting supplies, were camped at one of the tributaries of the Wabash River. Little Turtle launched a surprise attack shortly before dawn. The militia panicked and in the confusion the American army was surrounded. St. Clair, realizing the whole of his army could be lost, ordered a retreat. The Miami pursued them for about 4 miles but allowed 580 survivors to escape.[41]

More than nine hundred men were killed. Among the officers, thirty-nine were dead and twenty-one wounded. Cannon were lost, and many of the men threw away their arms even after the pursuit had ended. It was the worst defeat of Europeans at the hands of Indians since the British rout on the road to Fort Duquesne at the beginning of the Seven Years' War. One of those captured and killed was Richard Butler, superintendent of Indian affairs for the northern district. A short time later Joseph Brant received a package from the Shawnee containing Butler's scalp and a message which expressed bitter resentment at what they considered his desertion of their cause.[42] When news of the defeat reached Philadelphia, some of George Washington's critics wanted to know how Americans had acquired the right to invade Indian land, especially in light of the cost of the invasion in lives. St. Clair, who had been raised to the highest rank in the American military, resigned.

"Mad" Anthony Wayne was a popular hero during the Revolution because he had captured the British fort at Stony Point in 1779. Wayne's civilian life had fallen upon difficult times. He had suffered the bankruptcy of his Georgia farm and had been elected to Congress, but the election and his residency were challenged and his seat was subsequently declared vacant. Wayne did not believe in peace with the Indians and set about the task of building a credible U.S. army during 1792 and 1793.

In 1792 George Washington turned to the Six Nations for help persuading the Western Confederacy to sell some lands and to make peace. Early that year letters were sent to Iroquois chiefs and leaders, including Joseph Brant, inviting them to Philadelphia. Cornplanter and forty-eight Seneca chiefs arrived at Philadelphia, where they received goods worth $1,500, some domestic animals, and a promise that a like amount would be paid annually.[43] The Americans asked that the Seneca intervene in negotiations on their behalf, and Cornplanter and some of his associates agreed to attend a meeting of the Western Confederacy in the fall and to urge a peaceful settlement. Joseph Brant was also coaxed to Philadelphia, where he met President George Washington and was given a letter by Secretary of War Henry Knox in which the United States offered peace and promised to take no lands which were not freely sold by the Indians under conditions of just compensation.[44] Washington then stated that for this to be meaningful, a treaty must be entered into, and Brant was asked to assist in arranging such a treaty. Brant, who had reason to worry about his reputation among the Indians of the Western Confederacy and the British governors of Canada, declined the offer and returned instead to his home on the Grand River.

War Chief Cornplanter, at considerable risk to himself and his fellow travelers, led a delegation to a meeting on the Glaize (now Auglaize) River at Defiance, Ohio. Red Jacket, the most persuasive orator in the Six Nations, made a credible effort to argue in favor of peace and a settlement with the Americans. At one point, his speech lasted five hours, but it was to no avail. The victorious Shawnee treated Cornplanter and his delegation with contempt and chided them for their subservience to the American cause.[45] Their arguments had great strength because of the lengthy history of mistreatment at the hands of the Americans and because, on several occasions, the Six Nations had ceded lands in Kentucky without the permission of the Indians using those lands. The general sense of the Western Confederacy was that the Americans intended to take their country from them despite their words, and there was an underlying belief that, in the end, the British would be there for them. The meeting lasted from September 30 to October 9, and by its end discussions produced feelings which were much improved over the previous hostility. By the time Brant arrived at the meeting place most of the delegates had departed. Cornplanter and the others were not successful in their mission but were greeted with great warmth in Philadelphia upon their return.

The British governor of Upper Canada, Lieutenant Governor John Graves Simcoe, was concerned the Americans would become powerful enough to invade Canada. He hoped to build a buffer zone between Canada and the United States consisting of an Indian country conforming roughly to the Fort Stanwix line of 1768. The only way such a line could be achieved would be if the British were part of a treaty between the United States and the Indians.[46] The British, working behind the scenes, orchestrated the meeting on the Glaize River to include a demand that the Americans accept the boundary to the Indian country as the Ohio River, along with a demand that the British mediate the dispute between the Indians and the United States.[47] Although the Western Confederacy demand that Indian country begin at the Ohio River was not conciliatory, the United States appeared to genuinely desire peace and evinced a willingness to make concessions.[48] The United States, however, was unwilling to accept British mediation in a dispute with Indians over land inside the boundaries of the United States.

During the spring of 1793 war broke out between Britain and France, and although France had been a critical ally which provided much-needed naval support crucial to Cornwallis' surrender at Yorktown at the end of the Revolution, the United States declared its neutrality. From this point on, continuing through the Napoleonic wars until the battle at Waterloo, war with France would occupy Britain's attention. Canadian officials could well suspect that American sympathies rested with their old ally France.

A peace Council was opened at Sandusky, Ohio, on July 31, 1793. Colonel Timothy Pickering was among the American delegates, and hopes were high among the Americans that a peaceful settlement could be reached. Before anything productive could be accomplished, however, a number of the leaders of the Western Confederacy signed an ultimatum demanding that the American settlers fall back beyond the Ohio River, stating that unless the Ohio was the recognized boundary, there would be no reason to conduct a peace negotiation. The American delegation was authorized to make significant concessions, but this demand went well beyond that authorization. Many of the Indians present, including some from the Iroquois Confederacy, felt the Western Confederacy missed an excellent opportunity to preserve much of their country and that a British agent had been instrumental in their decision.[49] When the conference broke up with no agreement and no progress made toward peace, there were serious signs the Western Confederacy was weakened by internal division, because many of its members had little interest in a war and others felt the negotiators had missed an opportunity for peace and an honorable settlement.

Leaders of the Western Confederacy, notably including the Delaware chief Buckongehala, continued to meet with American representatives through the summer. The Americans offered considerable concessions, including an admission that the United States had not acquired Indian lands by conquest. They offered to recognize as Indian country all the land west of the Ohio, except those areas already occupied by American settlers, and they offered to pay handsomely for any land the Indians would sell.[50] Buckongehala and his delegation rejected any settlement short of removal of all whites beyond the Ohio River. In the discussion that followed, the various nations of the Western Confederacy were strongly divided. Two victories over the Americans in the field, several decades of revitalization movements which produced prophets who predicted Indian victory under positive spiritual conditions, and the intrigue of British agents and provocateurs combined to energize the factions which favored war.

Lord Dorchester, governor of Lower Canada, met with a delegation of Canadian Indians who were carrying inquiries about British support for the Western Confederacy. Dorchester made a speech in which he stated that there was little chance that Britain could intervene and produce a peaceful settlement, that war was very likely, and that if the Indians should win, the dispute would be settled in their favor. Word of this speech leaked out and caused considerable alarm, because it was interpreted as tantamount to a declaration of war.

To underscore British resolve to remain in the area, Simcoe led troops to the Maumee, where they built a fort as part of the defense of Detroit. The Indians had been requesting that the British build such a fort and assumed it was for their protection. In words and deeds the British seemed to be poised to protect and support their Indian allies.

These intrigues and failed negotiations provided General Wayne time to train and equip a credible fighting force, giving birth to the United States Army. Wayne marched to the southwest branch of the Maumee River and established Fort Greenville, where he passed the winter. In the spring of 1794 Pennsylvania proposed to occupy Presque Isle (at present-day Erie) on Lake Erie. An American settlement at that place would cut communications between the Seneca and the Western Confederacy. Cornplanter, who had signed treaties at Fort Harmar and Fort Stanwix ceding this area and whose reputation among his own people had suffered because of land sales, now claimed that those land cessions were illegal and that the land in the so-called Erie Triangle belonged to the Seneca. In June and again in July Indian councils were convened at Buffalo Creek to discuss the proposed settlement at Presque Isle. During the course of these discussions threats were directed against the Americans. In response to these threats and the very strong likelihood that an attempt to build a post at Presque Isle would lead to war, President Washington prevailed on Pennsylvania's Governor Thomas Mifflin to abandon the plan for the settlement.

Beginning in June more than two thousand warriors gathered on the Maumee and Auglaize Rivers to await the American army. Meanwhile John Jay arrived in England to begin negotiations toward a new treaty addressing matters left unsettled by the treaty of 1783.[51] England wanted peace because its fortunes on the continent were not going well, and the United States wanted a treaty because it could ill afford another war with Britain. The situation that emerged was that while peace negotiations were taking place thousands of miles away, an American army was marching into country peopled by British military garrisons and Indians determined to give battle.

The next serious military event occurred on June 29, 1794,[52] when Little Turtle's forces attacked an outpost at Fort Recovery, site of St. Clair's defeat. The main force of the Western Confederacy—estimated at between fifteen hundred and two thousand warriors—was allegedly led by British officers and accompanied by Tories. The attack was repulsed and the Indians and their allies retired with losses rumored at around seventy warriors. Following this battle and consistent with Indian custom, some of the warriors abandoned the campaign to return home. Little Turtle began advocating peace, but the Miami and their allies were in no mood for negotiations. As a result, Little Turtle lost considerable standing among his people as a chief, and he also lost control of the warrior army which had defeated St. Clair. He was replaced by Turkey Foot, a warrior considered by many to be less able than Little Turtle. In late July the United States had authorized the negotiation of a federal treaty with the Six Nations at Canandaigua on September 15.[53]

Wayne advanced cautiously to the Glaize River, where he built Fort Defiance. He moved through Indian country, where he pointedly declined to burn villages abandoned in his path. He was careful to avoid ambush while sending messages to the Indians seeking a truce and negotiation for peace. Some of Turkey Foot's forces, as was custom in Indian campaigns, had left camp to seek provisions, and it is not known how many Indians were in the vicinity as Wayne advanced. On August 20 Wayne advanced toward Fort Miamis, the British fort the Indians had been led to believe was built for their protection. Not far from the fort a tornado had left a mass of decaying tree trunks in the forest—this engagement is called the Battle of Fallen Timbers—and as Wayne's forces moved into this area, the Indians began firing from the grass and trees. About sixty Tories from Detroit joined them in a battle that lasted about an hour. The Indians and Tories were routed, and Turkey Foot fell on the battlefield. Some Indians fled to the British fort, where they found the doors barred. It is said some were killed at the walls of the fort.[54] Wayne did not attack the British at Fort Miamis or Detroit but instead returned upriver, now destroying Indian villages as he went. The Indians were militarily defeated, the Western Confederacy effectively scattered, and peace between Britain and the United States, for the time, preserved, but it would be several weeks before official word of the outcome of the battle would reach western New York.

The invitation to a treaty conference at Canandaigua reached the Allegheny Seneca on August 23, before the arrival of reports about Wayne's victory. The Seneca were adamant that they would take up the hatchet to prevent white settlement at Presque Isle and wanted no part of negotiations unless these were accompanied with an agreement that some lands already lost must be restored. Over the next few weeks Cornplanter and other Seneca rebuffed the invitation to Canandaigua, stating they had not requested a treaty meeting and that they didn't want the presents which accompanied Pickering's invitation. Cornplanter and some of the warriors continued to favor war, but at this moment the Seneca women began to intervene with an insistence that custom provided them with a veto power over war. Iroquois custom did indeed provide such power to the Iroquois matrons. Cornplanter would shortly argue that the women should not have this power, that a decision to go to war should belong to the warriors.

About one hundred Seneca warriors took part in the Battle of Fallen Timbers.[55] Cornplanter and others were at Council when the first account of Wayne's victory and the locked British fort reached them. At Buffalo Creek the news was greeted by a stunned silence. Many, including Cornplanter, had strongly believed the Western Confederacy would crush Wayne's newly formed army. Timothy Pickering had appeared at Canandaigua and had sent invitations to the Seneca to come to a treaty negotiation there, but the British were urging the meeting be held at Buffalo Creek. Many of the Seneca chiefs blamed Cornplanter for their troubles, and the following day an elder rose in Council and suggested that the best they could do would be to go to Canandaigua and make the best agreement they could make. No one dissented, and most of the assembly soon set out for Canandaigua.

The Seneca and Onondaga contingents arrived and ceremoniously entered Canandaigua on October 14.[56] Altogether about sixteen hundred members of the Six Nations attended,[57] a number which represented a significant majority of the population. Some Seneca towns sent almost the entire population. A delegation of Quakers was present as observers, and their written accounts of the proceedings are an important part of the record. The opening ceremonies of this negotiation adhered to Indian customs that required expressions of condolences for people who had passed away since the parties last met. Following these formalities, Colonel Pickering announced himself the commissioner representing the United States and offered to hear their grievances. He introduced the Quakers, who attended as witnesses to the proceedings, and an Onondaga chief, Clear Sky, acknowledged the words spoken and adjourned the meeting for the day. An evangelist, Jemima Wilkinson, asked to be heard and spent the time until dark praying and preaching at the center of the assembly. It was an embarrassing display to the participants but a historically significant event in the country that was to become New York's Burned Over District, the birthplace of numerous sects and religions. Pickering proceeded to convene private meetings with selected individual Indians.

Red Jacket served as speaker on behalf of the sachems, and this was to be as much his treaty as Pickering's. The first order of business involved Indian complaints about land cessions at three earlier treaties— Fort Stanwix, Fort Harmer, and Fort McIntosh. There was a discussion about what lands the Six Nations claimed as their own. Pickering replied with seven points which recounted recent attempts to settle these claims, some of which had been frustrated by British agents.[58] He went on to assure the Indians that the 1790 Non-Intercourse Act was insurance against land frauds perpetrated by the states, and he suggested the land along Lake Erie south of Buffalo, ceded in the 1784 treaty, might be returned to Seneca hands.

When the British Indian interpreter Johnson arrived, Pickering denounced him as a British spy and accused the British of frustrating recent years' attempts at peace between the Indians and the Americans. Pickering complained the British had failed to relinquish forts inside United States territory in accordance with the treaty that ended the American Revolution. He had orders from President Washington, he said, to refuse to allow any British agent to attend the negotiations, and he put it to the Six Nations that they, as a free and independent people, should decide whether to send Johnson away or to cover the Council fire and go home themselves. Cornplanter took responsibility for inviting Johnson, but in this contest of wills Pickering was triumphant, and Johnson left the meeting and returned to Canada. Johnson had served another purpose because he had carried Joseph Brant's affirmation of the defeat of the Western Indians at Fallen Timbers, and he returned with letters to Brant from people assembled at Canandaigua.

Pickering continued the strategy of holding private meetings with selected Senecas, most notably the war chief Cornplanter. This caused considerable distress among the sachem chiefs, who felt Cornplanter had usurped the role of a sachem, and Little Billy admonished him directly for this behavior.[59] Pickering returned to discussing the terms of the treaty in public Council. During the course of subsequent discussions, Cornplanter's role at the treaty at Fort Stanwix become more publicly known. It was discovered that he had received $800 from Pennsylvania and had in turn been granted 1,500 acres for a farm, information that cast Cornplanter in a negative light among the Seneca.

In the eyes of the Indians, the burning issues were predictable: murders of Indians by whites, the unfairness of the land cessions at Fort Stanwix in 1784, and the dispute over the land at Presque Isle. The Seneca insisted that the warrior chiefs who had negotiated the peace at Fort Stanwix had failed to submit the treaty to the Council for ratification.

Pickering proposed the Seneca relinquish a strip of land 4 miles wide along the south of the Niagara River from Cayuga Creek to Buffalo Creek. Red Jacket replied that this was not acceptable because it would constitute a threat to their fisheries and their settlement at Buffalo Creek, and Pickering dropped the issue and settled for a road, to be owned by the Seneca, from Fort Schlosser to Buffalo.[60] The negotiations continued until there was a general consensus that both sides had achieved all they could. On November 9, however, Cornplanter complained of past dealings with the United States and offered that the sachems alone, and not the warriors, would sign the treaty. Pickering was unwilling to do this. He felt that if the warriors did not sign, divisions would rise among the Indians which would undo the treaty.[61] The treaty was signed on November 11, 1794, and went into effect under United States law on January 21, 1795.

The primary objective of the United States was to settle the question of the claims of the Six Nations to lands in Ohio and the Erie Triangle and to embark on a policy of sincere negotiations and fair payment in land transactions. The day following the treaty Pickering wrote to Secretary of War Henry Knox:

> You will see the great object is obtained; an express renunciation, which takes in all of the lands in Pennsylvania, including the Triangle which comprehends Presqu'Isle; and a pointed declaration that they will never disturb the people of the U. states in the free use and enjoyment of them, or any other lands not contained within the present described boundaries of the lands of the Six Nations.[62]

In return, Pickering relinquished lands earlier ceded along Lake Erie upon which the Six Nations had built settlements, and he abandoned for the time ambitions of securing the 4-mile-wide strip along the Niagara River. He secured, however, a right of passage along the river from Fort Schlosser to Buffalo Creek.

The text of the treaty speaks to the issues that occupied the people who negotiated it. Article 1 establishes peace and friendship between the Six Nations and the United States. Article 2 guarantees to the Oneida, Onondaga, and Cayuga Nations the lands they possessed on the day of the treaty, including words which guarantee the United States will not claim these lands or disturb them "nor their Indian friends residing thereon and united with them, in the free use and enjoyment thereof . . ." Article 3 describes the boundaries of the Seneca lands, a description of which carefully omits and therefore disallows Six Nations claims to lands in the Ohio region. This article also includes recognition as Seneca land some land along the Niagara River "ceded" to Sir William Johnson in 1764, acknowledging as Seneca land

> from the mouth of O-yong-wong-yeh Creek to the river Niagara, above Fort Schlosser, being the eastern boundary of a strip of land, extending from the same line to Niagara river, which the Seneca Nation ceded to the King of Great-Britain, at a treaty held about thirty years ago, with Sir William Johnson.) Now, the United States acknowledge all the land within the aforementioned boundaries, to be the property of the Seneca Nation.[63]

In Article 4, the Six Nations promise never to claim lands outside these boundaries. In their minds, most importantly, in the light of the history of the previous decade, were the lands in Pennsylvania and Ohio. Article 5 provides the United States the right to use a road along the Niagara River and to use the waterways, a right which was strongly desired by farmers and others in the Ohio-Kentucky region who needed an economical way to transport their goods to the markets.

In Article 6, the United States promises to pay goods valued at $10,000 and an annuity of $4,500, a considerable sum in 1794 and evidence of the United States' commitment to a policy of "fair dealings" with the Indians. In Article 7 the United States agrees that when a crime—murder, assault, robbery—is committed by either side, that no act of revenge shall take place. Rather, the representative of the victim will enter a complaint. The Six Nations will enter a complaint to the president or his appointed superintendent. If an Indian commits such a crime, the president will submit a complaint to the "principal chiefs" of the Six Nations and "such prudent measures shall then be pursued as shall be necessary to preserve our peace . . . until the legislature . . . of the United States shall make other equitable provision for the purpose."

The Canandaigua Treaty was important because it provided the United States with security at a time when continued warfare with Britain and the Indians of the Great Lakes was not only possible but, as history would prove, inevitable. The treaty represents a historical moment when "fair treatment" of the Indians was not only the Indian policy of the moment followed by the United States but was arguably the best policy for the survival of the country.

There are promises in this treaty which the people of the Six Nations believe the United States has not kept. The promise that the United States will never disturb the Six Nations in their enjoyment of their lands, for example, is interpreted to mean that the United States had no right to condemn Seneca land to build the Kinzua Reservoir in the 1960s or other construction projects which disturbed the Mohawk, Tuscarora, and Onondaga peoples. The Termination Era of the 1950s and its threat to assimilate the Iroquois into American society would contradict any reasonable interpretation of the promise not to claim the land or disturb the Indians in its use. The intent of the treaty in the eyes of the Iroquois and the United States at the time it was written was to underscore the United States' acknowledgement that the lands of the Six Nations belong to the Six Nations, not to the United States. Many Iroquois believe, with some justification, that such a principle would preclude the United States, or New York State, from collecting taxes or enforcing a variety of laws and regulations on lands they have acknowledged through an international treaty as having status as a sovereign domain.

Finally, many Iroquois believe that Article VII constitutes a promise of recognition of parallel legal jurisdictions far greater than they have enjoyed since 1794. The section states that in the event of a crime, the two parties will pursue prudent measures involving the president or the superintendent until some other "equitable" provision shall be made. Some United States spokespersons claim that federal laws that transferred criminal and civil jurisdiction to New York State fulfilled the requirement for equitable or equal provision that both parties would be involved in resolving the problem. Many Iroquois, most notably the traditional chiefs, have long complained that there was nothing equitable in either the spirit or practice of the American legal system as it relates to this article.

The Treaty with the Six Nations of 1794 remains a seminal document in Iroquois–United States relations. It is also an important part of the history of both peoples, because it marked a new and inevitable kind of relationship with the emerging United States and is evidence of one United States road in American Indian policy. In light of the history of other roads taken, some of which are among the most tragic and dishonorable in American history, the Canandaigua Treaty stands as a symbol of what might have been almost as much as it is a symbol of what came to be.

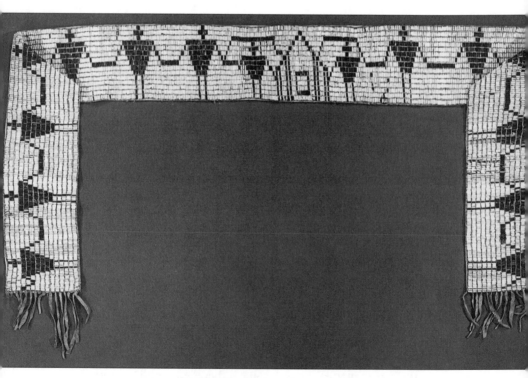

George Washington Covenant Belt.
Photo courtesy of Chief Irving Powless, Jr., Onondaga Nation

NOTES

1. Gregory Evans Dowd, *A Spirited Resistance: The North American Indian Struggle for Unity 1745–1815* (Baltimore: Johns Hopkins University Press, 1991), 27.

2. Frederick E. Hoxie, ed., *Encyclopedia of North American Indians: Native American History, Culture, and Life from Paleo-Indians to the Present* (New York: Houghton Mifflin, 1996), 380. The Wyandot Nation were descendants of the Huron Confederacy, which was dispersed in the mid-seventeenth century. These refugees had moved to the Ohio country. They were later resettled in Wyandot County, Oklahoma. *See* Olive Patricia Dickason, "Huron/Wyandot," in Hoxie, ed., *Encyclopedia of North American Indians*, 263–65. The Mingo would eventually become known as the Sandusky Seneca and, later, the Cayuga-Seneca of Oklahoma. *See also* Wallace, 166; NYHS, O'Rielly Collection, vol. 8, 45, and vol. 9, 34; W. Stone, 1838, vol. 2, 295, 313, 405; and App. xxi–xxvi. PA, 2nd series, vol. 4, 557. In the 1790s, most of the pro-British Delaware, now known as Muncees, moved to an area near the Thames River in Ontario. Jay Miller, "Delaware," in Hoxie, Ed., 157–59.

3. *See* generally Paul A. W. Wallace, *Indians in Pennsylvania* (Harrisburg: Pennsylvania Historical Commission), 1961.

4. Charles E. Hunter, "The Delaware Nativist Revival of the Mid-Eighteenth Century," in Bruce A. Glasrud and Alan M. Smith, ed., *Race Relations in British North America, 1607–1763* (Chicago: Nelson-Hall, 1982), 263–75.

5. Anthony F. C. Wallace, *King of the Delewares Teedyuscung, 1700–1763* (Syracuse: Syracuse University Press, 1949, 1990), 258.

6. Alan Axelrod, *Chronicle of the Indian Wars: From Colonial Times to Wounded Knee* (New York: Konecky & Konecky, 1993), 96.

7. Axelrod, 97.

8. *See* Bouquet's report to Amherst. Sylvester K. Stevens and Konald H. Kent, ed., *Wilderness Chronicles of Northwestern Pennsylvania* (Harrisburg: Pennsylvania Historical Commission, 1941), 265.

9. Axelrod, 98.

10. Anthony F. C. Wallace, *The Death and Rebirth of the Seneca* (New York: Alfred A. Knopf, 1970), 154.

11. Axelrod, 100.

12. John Tebbel and Keith Jennison, *The American Indian Wars* (New York: Bonanza Books, 1960), 147.

13. Axelrod, 114. He was captured and adopted by the Shawnees. He later claimed he did not collaborate with the Indians, and after the war he was court-martialed as a traitor, but the trial found Boone had acted as a hero and his strategy had probably saved the Kentucky settlements.

14. Axelrod, 120.

15. Dowd, 86, 88.

16. William N. Fenton, *The Great Law and the Longhouse: A Political History of the Iroquois Confederacy* (Norman: University of Oklahoma Press 1998), 604.

17. Fenton, 605.

18. Fenton, 617–19.

19. Fenton, 620. "Of the listed signatures, two from each of the Six Nations save a lone Cayuga, none bears the title of a league founder."

20. A. F. C. Wallace, *Death and Rebirth of the Seneca*, 152. Repudiation of the treaty is found in State Historical Society of Wisconsin, Draper Collection, 11 F7, and Governor Blacksnake's account at SHSW DC, 16 F.

21. Fenton, 820. Red Jacket would later use this information to destroy Cornplanter's reputation.

22. Wiley Sword, *President Washington's Indian War: The Struggle for the Old Northwest, 1790–5* (Norman: University of Oklahoma Press, 1985), 41.

23. A. F. C. Wallace, *Death and Rebirth of the Seneca*, 155.

24. John Mack Faragher, *Daniel Boone: The Life and Legend of an American Pioneer* (New York: Henry Holt and Co., 1992) 249–50.

25. Isabel Thompson Kelsay, *Joseph Brant 1743–1807: Man of Two Worlds* (Syracuse: Syracuse University Press, 1984), 434.

26. Kelsay, 434.

27. The belief that Great Britain was poised to aid the Indians in a war with the Americans was, at this moment, erroneous. See Kelsay, 440–41.

28. Kelsay, 435.

29. John C. Mohawk, "Cornplanter," in Hoxie, ed., 136.

30. Felix S. Cohen, *Handbook of Federal Indian Law,* Washington: U.S. Government Printing Office 1942, 69.

31. Kelsay, 443.

32. Kelsay, 443.

33. Sword, 5.

34. John Tebbel and Keith Jennison, *The American Indian Wars* (New York: Bonanza Books, 1960), 131.

35. Kelsay, 436.

36. Tebbel and Jennison, 134.

37. Kelsay, 453.

38. Kelsay, 451.

39. Kelsay, 455.

40. Kelsay, 453.

41. Tebbel and Jennison, 137.

42. Kelsay, 457.

43. Kelsay, 464.

44. Kelsay, 471.

45. Hoxie, 136.

46. Kelsay, 486.

47. Kelsay, 487.

48. Kelsay, 488.

49. *See* Kelsay for an account of the role of British officer Alexander McKee. Kelsay, 498–99, 502.

50. Kelsay, 500.

51. Kelsay, 510.

52. Fenton's account states June 30. Fenton, 656.

53. Fenton, 652.

54. McKee, the British officer who had done so much to encourage the Indians to forgo negotiations until British participation could be secured, later thought around four hundred Indians were engaged in the battle. Kelsay, 511.

55. Fenton, 658, Knopf 1960, 357.

56. Fenton, 669.

57. Fenton, 687.

58. Fenton, 676.

59. Fenton, 683.

60. Fenton, 695.

61. Fenton, 699.

62. Fenton, 705.

63. Treaty With the Six Nations, 1794, Article III.

Jay Claus (Tuscarora), Runner for the Six Nations, and Tadodaho Chief Leon Shenandoah at the parade for the 200th Anniversay Commemoration. Photo © Helen M. Ellis, 1994.

Chief Oren Lyons (Onondaga). Photo © Helen M. Ellis.

The Canandaigua Treaty:
A View from the Six Nations

CHIEF OREN LYONS (JOAGQUISHO)

Nyáwéhá skán. Today is history. It pleases me a great deal to see that our Chiefs are still around. By this fact we proclaim that we are not just a part of a past age or history; the history is now. Some time in the future, when our grandchildren and our great-grandchildren look at pictures of the 200th Anniversary Commemoration of the Canandaigua Treaty, they'll see who was there, just as we have this great interest to see who had been there at that time in 1794. They will see the continuity of our independence.

The Canandaigua Treaty was also called the Pickering Treaty and the George Washington Covenant. The treaty was signed at a period of time when the United States was on the threshold, on the cusp, of becoming a great nation, and when the future of Indian nations was being threatened, on the cusp of being destroyed and extinct.

The history of North America began a long time ago. It began long before the white man ever got here. For us it began thousands upon thousands of years ago, longer than our white brothers care to acknowledge or admit. During those times Indigenous people resided here and prospered. They understood life and the laws of nature and they lived, by and large, in peace.

As you know, human beings, being the way we are, will always have problems and trouble. Thus it becomes incumbent upon each society to develop a process by which you control these problems, and have a forum and a process that can accommodate the differences and the problems within a community of people. The Indigenous peoples worked very hard at that. Separate and apart from the development of Europe, we developed our own standards, principles, values, and civilizations.

By the time that Christopher Columbus came here our nations were ancient. Christopher Columbus has been called the discoverer of America. How can that be? We disagree vigorously, because here in what is now called America, here in this great Turtle Island, were many nations, great civilized nations, and millions of peoples. There was history, great history, as well as economic, scientific, and social development. We had good health here. We did not have the diseases that were ravaging Europe at the landfall of Christopher Columbus, but we soon would. He brought us suffering and death.

The health of the European population was poor. They were starving. They were being swept by plagues, one after the other. People were dying in the streets. Europe was a terrible place to live. There was no future for the human beings, for the common people; they were in bondage. There was no freedom in Europe for the common people. There was a great hierarchy of power, with rule by kings and queens, and there was starvation because of overtaxed populations and no lands for the common people.

Christopher Columbus landed on our shores bringing with him a philosophy of Christian dominion over heathens and pagans. This Christian doctrine declared all the peoples of the Western Hemisphere to be heathens, pagans, and infidels. With this simple declaration our lands became open for conquest. The European nations sat down and concocted a law called the "Law of Nations," or the "Law of Discovery." This declaration said simply that if there are no Christians on any of the lands that you discover, and if you are the first Christian nation to make this land claim, then this land will be declared vacant: *terra nullus*, "empty lands." And you can acquire the land into the realm of Christianity. That was how they came here. There was no hope for us with this kind of a philosophy.

In 1823, Supreme Court Justice John Marshall sealed our fate in U.S. courts with his now famous (infamous?) *Johnson v. McIntosh*, 21 U.S. 543, (1823) decision regarding Cherokee land. He based his decision on the Christian "Doctrine of Discovery," although he did not use the word "Christian." He did use the word "heathen," which is of Christian origin. He referred the basis of his decision back to the 1493 Declaration of the Cabots of England that announced in their charter by King Henry VII of England: "To seek out, discover, and find whatsoever islands, countries, regions or provinces of the heathens and infidels...To subdue, occupy and possess..." There was at that time a prevailing attitude that all Christians were in a state of war with all heathens and infidels. (That's us). Today, I suppose that, as long as we remain loyal and true to our original and traditional way of life and continue to carry on our ceremonies, we will still be regarded as enemies according to this Christian doctrine.

One hundred and thirty-two years later this same doctrine was applied to a contemporary Indian nation by the Supreme Court of the United States, in the case of *Tee-Hit-Ton v. United States*, 348 U.S. 272, 185 (1955). At that time the Tee-Hit-Ton Nation was told that their land claim was denied because: "Indian occupation of land without government recognition of ownership creates no rights against taking or extinction by the United States protected by the Fifth Amendment or any other principle of law...." The justices referred to the 1823 *Johnson v. McIntosh* case as the basis of their decision. We believe this Christian doctrine to be racist and abhorrent in these supposedly enlightened times.

But wait, it doesn't stop there. In 1991 the Supreme Court of British Columbia, in the case of *Delgamuukw et al. v. The Queen in Right of British Columbia et al.*, or the Gitksan Case, 79 D.L.R. 4th 185 (1991), argued that "'Indian title' is not an ownership right; it is only a right to use the land, and this mere right to use land can be taken away at any time 'at the will of the sovereign'" (*R. v. St. Catherine's Milling & Lumber Co.* (1885) (79 D.L.R. 4th, 415). It appears that the Christian doctrine continues to prevail in contemporary North American courts.

These cases are important because they chart the development and continuance of "legal fiction" that forms an insulation of American courts against Indian land claims. Steven T. Newcomb pursues this discussion in depth in his treatise "The Evidence of Christian Nationalism in Federal Indian Law: The Doctrine of Discovery, *Johnson v. McIntosh*, and Plenary Power." Newcomb cites a statement by Vine Deloria Jr., to "uncover the historical mythologies" that have dominated federal Indian law since the time of the Johnson Decision; that the "mythical doctrine [that] determined history which is now entrenched in federal Indian law will be replaced with a more accurate history only with exceptional difficulty and hardship."

To say that we are at a disadvantage is a monumental understatement that makes it all the more imperative to protect the treaties between our nations and to keep the delineation of our separate sovereignties clear and distinct. That is why we Haudenosaunee issue our own passports. The passport is a reaffirmation of our Nation, our independence, and the future of our people.

During the commemoration of the treaty, as our two nations came together in a ceremonial reenactment of the historic 1794 meeting, the United States was represented by a Native American now in the employment and political position of undersecretary of the interior of the United States. All the rest of the U.S. delegation were non-Indians. The contrast of our two delegations was striking as we, the Haudenosaunee, walked in our full ceremonial dress, carrying our flag with eagle feathers. As the military of the United States approached from the opposite direction I thought of the Two Row Wampum.

This wampum instructed us to be joined by the Chain of Friendship, "we in our canoe, and our white brother in his boat." We were instructed to go down the river of life in peace and friendship. It cautioned us to stay in our canoe and our brothers in their boat and not to interfere with one another. I wondered what our Native American sister was thinking as she approached our Haudenosaunee delegation, we in our canoe, so to speak, and she, clearly in our white brothers' boat. It was a symbol of our times and very graphic. I wondered how many of our people were somewhere between our two nations, in a state of limbo and perhaps even confusion. It was clear to me that we must strive hard to maintain our identity and control of our lands. If we are not ever vigilant we may *all* wind up on the other side as American citizens. Then who would be here to hold up the treaties? Clearly, as a voting American citizen you can't have a treaty with yourself.

So then the grand plan of the Americans would be complete. We would all be tax-paying American citizens and all titles to our lands would be extinguished by our own hands. Our peoples paid a terrible price to keep our sovereignty and lands as the original peoples of Turtle Island, and we must have the same passion to see our Nations continue for the next seven generations.

The 1794 treaty was a treaty of accommodation, one of military and political necessity. Both parties could put men in the field. Both parties could do battle. Everything was at stake. As a consequence, the father of this country, George Washington, signed an agreement with the Haudenosaunee to forever, in perpetuity, keep peace and friendship among us. So there it is. The result is we are here today as a Nation.

Our leaders were present at the 200th Anniversary Treaty Commemoration, but the President of the United States was not. This makes us wonder. How important is this treaty to the United States? Since treaties are considered the supreme law of the land, why must we struggle to get treaty obligations recognized?

Nineteenth-century history was a terrible history for American Indians. Lands and lives were taken. In 1887, the Dawes Act was enacted. That act separated Indians from their lands and was a great vehicle to clear title to Indian lands. It's been our observation and our understanding that from the beginning that the primary purpose of the United States has been to clear title to Indian land. There's never been, in our observation, any lessening of that pressure. The 1978 American Indian Education Act reads very clearly that the purpose of the act is to assimilate the American Indians into the mainstream of American life.

We've always taken the position that you must maintain your separateness and your own identity to protect treaties and land. From the beginning, with our discussion with the Dutch in 1613, we established a treaty called the Two Row Wampum, the Guswenta. We said at that time, "You will know us by the way we dress." We take that literally. So today, you'll know us by the way we dress, and that is to clarify our identity.

Indian nations, and leaders of Indian nations, have the obligation to protect the welfare of their people, and they have the obligation to protect the people's lands and territories. Fundamental to that is the understanding that there are three primary boundaries you must protect. The first boundary is geographic. You must delineate the boundaries, mark them, and keep them alive, so other people know what your boundaries are. Your next boundary is political. You must delineate your political boundary, so that you do not become infused and confused with the United States governing system. The political boundary is extremely important to keep, because that means the way you operate as a nation. The third boundary is economic. This is the boundary that gets most obfuscated and is the most difficult to keep clear, because of monies that come to our nations for health, education, welfare, and economic support of our governments.

Our problems begin with the process that Congress goes through to ratify treaties. Changes made by one party mean the treaty has to be renegotiated. However, treaties made with American Indians were changed by Congress but were not renegotiated. There were unilateral changes that Indian nations were never informed about.

Red Cloud, a Lakota leader, went to Washington to find out why provisions in the Fort Laramie Treaty of 1868 were not being implemented. He was told that the treaty had been changed by Congress. He thundered, "I have been deceived!" Not only were the Congressmen cowardly in their actions, they left the only American Indian in government, Ely Parker (the head of the Bureau of Indian Affairs, a Seneca and former general under Ulysses Grant), the unsavory job of giving the bad news to Red Cloud.

On a related subject, I will continue with a little history of the Haudenosaunee, in particular, the Seneca near Buffalo. In 1912 or 1913, a couple of Seneca men were spearing fish in one of the creeks in Buffalo. They were picked up by a New York State conservation officer and were charged with fishing without a license.

Their response was, "We think we can hunt and fish anywhere in New York without a license." So they went to the United States Attorney General, who defended them, and indeed, they found in court that according to treaty rights, they could hunt and fish in all ceded lands. This did not sit well with New York State, who assumed they had jurisdiction over Indian nations in the state.

Next, in 1917, an Oneida person sold a piece of land to a farmer and immediately was told by other people, "You can't do that. That's Nation land. Lands cannot be sold or transferred without the consent of the Oneida Nation." They also went to court. And lo and behold, it was true. This disturbed the state of New York because they thought that they had a jurisdictional hold on our territories, our welfare, and our lives, but they found it was not true. It was pointed out in court that Haudenosaunee Nations had superior relations with the federal government because of our treaties.

As a result, New York organized the Everett Commission in 1918. Edward Everett was commissioned to look into the "problems" with the Indians of New York State. And what were these problems? Well, we were outside the jurisdiction of the state. Who has jurisdiction on your land is key to whether you are sovereign or not. Our people know that. Our leaders know that. The commission found that, yes, our Nations are not only sovereign but still owners of all those lands taken back to the 1784 Fort Stanwix Treaty. Well, there was a great effort on our part to file a land suit at that time. But due to disunity, it didn't come about. In 1923, the commission's findings were denounced by the state, and only Everett signed the report. To this date, the full report has not been made available to the Haudenosaunee.

On June 2, 1924, Congress passed legislation that "granted citizenship to Indians and for other purposes." All of a sudden, the United States said it's about time all these Indians should be citizens. And so the Citizenship Act came about. Curious, wasn't it, that this happened shortly after the finding of the Everett report.

Well, the Haudenosaunee, being ever vigilant, sent a letter (maybe one of the few in the whole country) to the United States government saying, "Thank you, but no thanks. We never were, we are not now, nor do we ever intend to be citizens of the United States." This was the gist of the letter from the Chiefs.

Knowing that we had a treaty, we understood that when you have an agreement between nations and you obfuscate your national identity, there's going to come a point in time when you're not going to be sure what side of the line you *are* on. If you were an American citizen, it just seemed elementary to us that you could not have a treaty with yourself. So it was extremely important to keep the definition between our nations, because the treaties really are our last bastion to protect our lands. They are the last. We have to maintain them not only for us but also for all the Indian nations across this country. There are many, many treaties that have gone by, some good, some bad, and some that have taken advantage of our peoples. Nevertheless, definition remains extremely important to us.

In 1934 Senator Wheeler and Senator Howard introduced legislation called the "Wheeler-Howard Act." This act, under the title of the Indian Reorganization Act (IRA), repealed the devastating Dawes Act of 1887. The new act was brought about by the efforts of John Collier, commissioner of Indian Affairs under President Franklin Roosevelt. Collier studied British colonialism and followed their example of "indirect rule" in establishing the IRA. The legislators said that they wanted to reorganize Indian governments, so we'd be in tune with the twentieth century. But this was a reorganization of power, and what they were doing was removing the Chiefs. They rescinded the Dawes Act by establishing the IRA, but they tagged onto it, "Reorganize your government."

And that's where the elected systems came from. The Haudenosaunee voted down the Indian Reorganization Act. The United States was not able to force us to reorganize our government. Nor were they able to bring that power against the Navajos and the Seminoles. There were others. But most people were kind of swept away by that 1934 Reorganization Act called the IRA. I hear a lot of grieving and crying today about the government that now rules on these territories. Indians are fighting Indians, and that's very hard when you fight your own government. But there it is, control by "indirect rule."

And so in 1994, when we came to commemorate the Canandaigua Treaty, the Haudenosaunee came with a history of having fought off a great deal of these events that have happened to a lot of other Indian people. And how have we done that? Well, only in my short memory and experience do I know. It's the adherence to the principles of the sovereignty of the people, to the spiritual unity, and to the spiritual strength of the Great Law, the basis of Western democracy.

The Concurrent Resolution 76, which went through the U. S. Senate in 1987, recognizes and acknowledges the contribution of the Iroquois Confederacy of Nations in the development of the United States Constitution and reaffirms continuing the government-to-government relationship between Indian tribes and the United States established in the Constitution. The Senate of the United States saw fit to do this, and there was a Concurrent Resolution in the House.

This is very contemporary. It's recognition of the work of our grandsires, those men and women, those elders who looked after the welfare of the people. And as I heard it said, they were concerned not for the welfare of a few individuals but for the welfare of the whole. That's the strength of the Confederacy.

Our leadership today, in contemporary times, is pretty much the same as it was. We still receive no salary. We are not paid that I know of. There is no budget for the Chiefs that sit at Onondaga, Tuscarora, Tonawanda, Akwesasne, and Oshweken. Since we don't get paid; it's true service. And the Clan Mothers and the Clans that put us there are pretty tough. What they say is, "If you can't do the job, get out of the way and we'll put somebody in there who can."

It's that kind of service that is very hard to find in the continental United States today, I would think. When you look at the budgets of BIA Indian nations (IRA), the first item is for government. And how high are the salaries of the people there? Enormous. This money includes education for their children and retirement for themselves. For the Chiefs of the Haudenosaunee, there is none. Free government for free people.

I find it a great honor to sit with these men, because they are so selfless and because they have such passion for our welfare. They have such great love for the future and the children. It's astounding to me how our government continues to stand. I've been around the world and I've met and talked to a lot of people in a lot of governments. I've not seen a government like this. The only time that I come near it is when I'm with other Indian nations, the traditional people. I see how they continue to think of their future children, and that is the same with us.

So I think that when we talk, we have to keep those things and histories in mind. The passion that makes a nation, the *political will* to be who you are—that's the definition of a nation. If your people want it, the young people want it, and the nation wants it, then you will have it. You put leaders there who will hold that line. And you demand accountability from your leaders because that's their job.

In our process we have Clan Mothers who have power of recall. They can take their representatives out, but this has to be proper and according to law. The process is there, and they don't have to wait for a four-year term. Individuals can take themselves out by their own conduct. It's no fun being a Chief, let me tell you, but there is satisfaction when something goes right for the people. There's great satisfaction. I think that's all that the Councils demand of themselves.

The great turnout at the commemoration was also very satisfying. It was great to see that the two nations came together, clearly defined, and shook hands again. I was very, very pleased to hear the words of the U.S. federal government, the state government, and the leaders. They showed that, although things may be tarnished, the chain can be polished and should be polished.

Today's times are very perilous for all. It's not only Indian children who are endangered. It's not only white people's children who are endangered. It's not only black people's children who are endangered, or any of our brothers around the world's children; it's *all* of *our* children who are endangered. We have to set our houses straight. We have to take care of these land claims. We have to take care of these treaty obligations. We have to recognize and respect one another's positions. And then we have to, as the treaty says, be friends, and allies, and brothers, shoulder to shoulder. And, to take on those terrible obligations of survival that we face today, we must support one another.

That's how it's going to be. We're going to have to be united to survive on this great Turtle Island. I'm not just talking about Indians. I'm talking about everybody; we must be united on principles. We must remember the spiritual law that governs everything, and continue thinking, really, truly, about the seventh generation coming. We must continue to have great compassion and love for the unborn in future generations.

Dahnato (now I am finished).

Joagquisho (Oren Lyons) is Faithkeeper, Turtle Clan, Onondaga Nation. This chapter is based on an address delivered on the occasion of the 200th Anniversary of the Canandaigua Treaty at the symposium "Polishing the Rust From the Chain," held in Canandaigua, New York, November 12, 1994.

WORKS CITED

Newcomb, Steven T. "The Evidence of Christian Nationalism in Federal Indian Law: The Doctrine of Discovery, *Johnson v. McIntosh*, and Plenary Power." *New York University Review of Law and Social Change* 20, 2: 303–41.

Phillip, Kenneth R. *John Collier's Crusade for Indian Reform, 1920–1984*. Tuscon: University of Arizona Press, 1977.

Onondaga longhouse at the Onondaga Nation. Photo © Helen M. Ellis.

The States, the United States & the Canandaigua Treaty

Daniel K. Richter

A few months before the Canandaigua Treaty was negotiated, Pennsylvanian John Adlum traveled from Pittsburgh to Fort Franklin, intending to survey a million-acre tract of Allegheny land to which his employer, James Wilson, had recently acquired title. Escorted by the Seneca leader Half-Town, Adlum's flotilla of canoes received a strained ceremonial reception at Cornplanter's village; welcoming shots fired by young Seneca riflemen whizzed suspiciously close to the surveyor's head. Shortly thereafter, in a crowded Council house where Adlum was seeking permission to conduct his work, he attempted to read elaborately beribboned messages he carried from Secretary of War Henry Knox and Pennsylvania Governor Thomas Mifflin. His interpreter had barely finished the first paragraph of Knox's letter when "the young Indians" sitting in the rafters "saluted" Adlum with "a univer[sal] roar, *vulgarly called farting.*" The women seated below soon joined in with cries of "*shame, scandalous;*" whether they were speaking to the young men or commenting on the proceedings as a whole is not clear. Whatever the case, Cornplanter "reprimanded" the rude music-makers, who then, Adlum said, "descended from their roosts, and sneaked off." Next morning, in a more decorous meeting, Adlum received begrudging permission to plat approximately half the territory he intended, but not before Cornplanter informed him "that all persons who encroached on their lands were their enemies."[1]

This little story does more than indicate how tense relations between Anglo-Americans and Senecas were in 1794. It contains several themes that are crucial for understanding the complicated political environment in which the Canandaigua Treaty took place. First is the emphasis on surveying land—and lots of it. At the risk of stressing the obvious, it is worth remembering that land was at the heart of the issues involved with the Canandaigua Treaty. Second is the fact that Adlum was a Pennsylvanian, representing Pennsylvania interests, and not a representative of the U.S. government (although he carried a letter from the secretary of war) or of the state of New York, so frequently mentioned in con-

nection with the Canandaigua Treaty. Multiple state and federal jurisdictions were competing for rights to the lands in question. Third,
Adlum was not even an official representative of Pennsylvania (though
he also carried a letter from the commonwealth's governor). He spoke,
instead, for the private interests of a particular group of land speculators. The competing aims of such groups also powerfully shaped the
environment in which the Canandaigua Treaty took place. And, fourth,
Adlum was negotiating, not with the Haudenosaunee or even the Seneca
Nation, but with a particular Seneca village and its Council. Such divide-
and-rule tactics are another important part of the picture. In these
contexts, perhaps the best way to understand the Canandaigua Treaty of
1794 is to see it as an effort by its parties to undo some of the damage
done in a series of earlier treaties among various Native leaders, the
United States, New York, and Pennsylvania—damage epitomized by the
competing forces at work during Adlum's visit to Seneca country a few
months earlier.

*   *   *

The most significant of the prior treaties that Canandaigua redressed took
place (note that I do not say "was negotiated") at Fort Stanwix in 1784.
There the Senecas present signed a document that surrendered nearly all
their lands now within the boundaries of Pennsylvania and most of those
now within the state of New York. In 1794, the new treaty returned a substantial portion of the New York territory to the Senecas.

The timing of these two treaties is crucial. Fort Stanwix occurred
after the end of the U.S. War for Independence but before the imple-
mentation of the U.S. Federal Constitution in 1789, which provided the
greatly enhanced centralized powers that made the Canandaigua Treaty
of 1794 possible. In 1784, then, not only had Euro-Americans and
Native Americans, enemies in the recent war for independence, been
attempting to come to terms with each other; they had been doing so in
an environment in which neither the respective authorities of the parties
involved nor the map of the vast region of which ownership was in contention was clear to any of the participants.

The Articles of Confederation provided for a notoriously weak
central government for the United States—although on paper, at least,
the Continental Congress's powers were not quite as limited as we sometimes might think. The Articles gave the Continental Congress the "sole
and exclusive right and power of . . . regulating the trade and managing
all affairs with the Indians not members of any of the states." That grant
of powers would seem to be clear except for two flies in the ointment.
No one, Euro-American or Native, agreed on which Indians were or

were not "members of any of the states" or what exactly that phrase meant. Moreover, under the Articles, the Continental government had no means of enforcing its will on states that disagreed with its decisions on this or any other question.[2]

To understand more fully why it was such a difficult matter for Euro-Americans to determine which Indians should be considered "members of any of the states," we need to return to the situation immediately following the end of the War for Independence. A map of the region, on which none of the modern lines had yet been clearly drawn, showed only two fixed reference points. The first, to which all Euro-American officials and many Native American parties agreed, was the "Line of Property," drawn before the War for Independence in the Fort Stanwix Treaty of 1768. This Line of Property stretched in a southwestwardly direction, roughly from modern Binghamton, New York, to Pittsburgh and the Ohio River. East of it, Anglo-Americans and Indians at least begrudgingly agreed that the soil belonged to the United States. West of the boundary, however, even Anglo-Americans admitted that no treaties had ever clearly transferred ownership from Native to Euro-American hands.[3]

The second reference point was drawn by the Treaty of Paris of 1783, which ended the war between Great Britain and the United States, recognized the new nation's independence, and essentially created the modern borders between Canada and the United States in the Great Lakes area. For some of the more fanciful elements within the governments of the United States and the states, the Treaty of Paris was enough to make the land west of the 1768 line theirs by what they referred to as a "right of conquest." Most cooler heads, however, following long-standing Anglo-American legal tradition, still distinguished between a "right of preemption" (which—to the extent it legitimately existed—the Treaty of Paris *did* unquestionably transfer from Great Britain to the United States) and an actual land-cession treaty, to which Indian leaders had to be signatories.

Of course, no one could pretend that any Native people had had anything to do with negotiating, much less signing, the Treaty of Paris. So, from the perspective of state and United States officials, before any of the lands west of the 1768 line could be offered for sale to Anglo-Americans, some sort of paper trail had to be created through the mechanism of land-cession treaties with the Indian owners of the soil. The problems centered on just who was to negotiate treaties with whom.[4]

The U.S. War for Independence had at least temporarily emptied much of the territory of its human inhabitants. Some of the conflict's most brutal fighting had destroyed the many ethnically mixed Native villages of the upper Susquehanna watershed and the Wyoming Valley and killed or dispersed their populations. Farther west and north, in what is today much of western New York and extreme northwestern Pennsylvania, the Sullivan, Clinton, and Brodhead campaigns of 1779 had burned most of the Seneca, Cayuga, and Onondaga villages and sent the vast majority of their inhabitants into nearly two years of exile at the British post of Niagara. Beginning in 1781, many Senecas returned to their homelands to build new homes on the Cattaraugus and Buffalo Creeks. Others resettled villages in the Genesee region and in the Allegheny River area. Well into the 1780s, these places remained communities in the making, or re-making. Their populations were very much in flux, as families moved back and forth among the four major areas of Seneca resettlement.[5]

Meantime, Anglo-American squatters were pouring into large parts of the region west of the 1768 boundary line, particularly in the area near Pittsburgh and along the Ohio River. These people were under the effective control of no Euro-American government. In fact, it was uncertain which government that might be, because state boundaries had not yet been drawn. New York and Pennsylvania authorities agreed on only the vague outlines of the border between their two states; surveys would not be completed until well into 1787.

That was the simplest of many jurisdictional disputes among states competing for the right to make the Indian treaties that would give them property rights on paper. Under its colonial charter, for instance, Massachusetts claimed much of what is now western New York; that matter would not be resolved until December 1785, when the two states agreed that Massachusetts should own the soil, but New York would exercise governmental jurisdiction over the area. To the south and west, a jumble of competing claims among New York, Pennsylvania, Connecticut, and Virginia had only recently and very roughly been worked out. The Northwest Territory, created in 1785, would not have an organized government until 1787; its boundaries with Pennsylvania and Virginia would not be surveyed until 1786. Meanwhile, competing claims between Pennsylvania and Virginia for the lands surrounding Pittsburgh dragged on for years and were still, to some extent, live issues as late as 1794. Similarly but more violently, rival claimants from Connecticut and Pennsylvania were actually killing each other in the "Pennamite Wars" over possession of the Wyoming Valley in what is now the Keystone State.

So, in the 1780s, it was not at all clear among Anglo-Americans who was supposed to be in charge over the land west of the 1768 line. Enormous power struggles were going on, not only between Indians and Anglo-Americans, but also among various state governments seeking the right to claim the Senecas as "members" of their states. At the same time, the Confederation government was seeking to assert its general authority. As historian Dorothy Jones has pointed out, of some twenty-one major treaties held in eastern North America between 1783 and 1786, the Confederation negotiated only six; the majority were made by states, and several by private interests. "No where along the seaboard or in the backcountry on either side of the Ohio River was there a clear-cut center of authority, white or red," Jones concludes. "There was no power great enough or with enough prestige to impose a system of stable relationships or to persuade groups into voluntary associations that could be counted on from one day to the next."[6]

Amidst this confusion, the issue of who was able to claim jurisdiction over Indians lands took on added urgency for financial reasons. State and Confederation governments alike planned to use western lands to redeem their debts—particularly those to soldiers paid in paper money and promises during the war. Illustrative is Pennsylvania's financial situation and its plans for Indian lands to which it did not have clear title. Strapped for cash, in 1780 the Pennsylvania legislature had voted to fulfill many monetary obligations to its troops with promises of land. A "donation" of acreage would serve in lieu of an enlistment bounty, and "depreciation certificates" redeemable at the state land office were to compensate officers and men for the lost purchasing power of their paper-money pay. By war's end, the depreciation certificates comprised an enormous portion of the state's debt. Entries in the Supreme Executive Council minutes between 1783 and 1785 approve interest payments alone of over $116,000. As late as 1790, the outstanding principal was calculated at nearly $1.5 million, roughly three-quarters of the remaining obligations incurred by the state on its own, rather than the Continental government's, behalf.[7]

For Pennsylvania, the beauty of the depreciation certificate plan was that redemption of this substantial liability would cost this commonwealth and its taxpayers next to nothing, provided sufficient "free" real estate were available. As one historian puts it, for Pennsylvanians, "land" promised to be "the path to solvency."[8] Depreciation certificates could be used to purchase any unpatented acreage, and a significant portion of them paid for newly platted city lots in Philadelphia. Clearly, however, given the size of the financial obligation the certificates represented and the overwhelmingly agricultural nature of the late eighteenth-century Pennsylvania economy, much larger and more rural tracts seemed necessary. Accordingly, in March 1783 the Pennsylvania legislature declared most of the southern half of the territory west of the Allegheny River to be "Depreciation Lands" set aside for redemption of the certificates and instructed surveying parties to lay out lots for sale. Meanwhile, plans were being drafted to set aside the northern half of the region as "Donation Lands" for war veterans. As mutiny by unpaid Pennsylvania soldiers rocked the capital in June of that year, and as squatters pouring across the Allegheny and Ohio threatened to overrun the region before land could be distributed to law-abiding citizens who would help to cancel the commonwealth's liabilities, the rapid and cheap acquisition of legal title to Indian lands assumed vital importance. With this much at stake, it is clear how important it was to determine just where the boundary lines between states lay, which Indian owners of the land were "members" of what state, if any, and which government would be able to get treaties signed. This government would profit enormously.[9]

Complicating things even more was the fact that large portions of the whole area west of the Line of Property remained active war zones. West of Pittsburgh, the Shawnees, Delawares, and others (who had never recognized the validity of the first Treaty of Fort Stanwix in 1768 or the Iroquois pretensions to negotiate it in their names) continued their war against the Anglo-American squatters pouring into the Ohio Valley. These Native groups in turn were part of a broader Western Indian Confederacy, in which the Mohawk Joseph Brant and other Iroquois, who were in the process of establishing new homes on the Grand River in Ontario, were important figures. Despite the peace of Paris, this Western Confederacy sought, and sometimes received, the support of British officials at Detroit, Niagara, and elsewhere in the region. British Niagara remained the main center of European power and trade in the contested area of what became western New York.[10]

*   *   *

By 1794 much, though not all, had been clarified. Boundary lines had been drawn, the federal Constitution was in effect, and the Trade and Intercourse Act of 1790 had forcefully asserted federal supremacy over the states in relations with Indian nations. But power relationships remained unstable. In the resolution of those relationships, the Treaty of Canandaigua combined with two other crucial events of that year to establish firm federal supremacy over the states. These other two events were the Whiskey Rebellion, with its massive western Pennsylvania challenge to the authority of the central government and Anthony Wayne's campaign against the Western Indian Confederacy, which would culminate in the Battle of Fallen Timbers.

In each of these three events, the federal government was exerting its power not just over particular issues but over the Anglo-American population of the vast region west of the mountains. First, the resolution of the Whiskey Rebellion established not only federal supremacy on the issue of taxation but also the federal government's ability to enforce its taxes and laws on the Anglo population of the trans-Appalachian region.[11] Similarly, the Fallen Timbers campaign and the subsequent Greenville Treaty not only defeated the Western Confederacy but, perhaps more importantly in the long run for both Anglo-Americans and Indians, it established a federal monopoly of military force. This marked a change in a region where freelance raiders and state-organized militias had previously done most of the fighting.[12]

Finally, the Canandaigua Treaty asserted the supremacy of the federal government in the area of Indian-Anglo treaty-making, marking a turning point in the complex and conflicting rivalries of private, state, and federal authorities illustrated by John Adlum's visit to Cornplanter's town a few months earlier. Had the Washington administration failed to establish a monopoly of force in any of these three events, the future development of the entire region, the United States, and the Native peoples of the continent might have turned out quite differently. The Canandaigua Treaty was deeply embedded in the creation of a broader system of political power that, for better or worse, has shaped the lives of both Native and Euro-Americans ever since.

NOTES

1. Merle H. Deardorff and Donald H. Kent, "John Adlum on the Allegheny: Memoirs for the Year 1794," *Pennsylvania Magazine of History and Biography*, 84, no. 3 (July 1960), 287–324, quotations from 304. Portions of this chapter were published previously in somewhat different form in Daniel K. Richter, "Onas, The Long Knife: Pennsylvanians and Indians, 1783–1794," in Ronald Hoffman and Peter Albert, eds., *Native Americans and the Early Republic* (Charlottesville: University Press of Virginia, 1999), 125–61.

2. Jack Campisi, "From Stanwix to Canandaigua: National Policy, States' Rights and Indian Land," in Christopher Vecsey and William A. Starna, eds., *Iroquois Land Claims* (Syracuse: Syracuse University Press, 1988), 49–65.

3. Dorothy V. Jones, *License for Empire: Colonialism by Treaty in Early America* (Chicago: University of Chicago Press, 1982), 36–119.

4. Francis Jennings, "The Indians' Revolution," in Alfred F. Young, ed., *The American Revolution: Explorations in the History of American Radicalism* (DeKalb: Northern Illinois University Press, 1976), 341–44.

5. Peter C. Mancall, "The Revolutionary War and the Indians of the Upper Susquehanna Valley," *American Indian Culture and Research Journal*, 12, no. 1 (1988), 39–57; Colin G. Calloway, *The American Revolution in Indian Country: Crisis and Diversity in Native American Communities* (Cambridge: Cambridge University Press, 1995), 129–57.

6. For brief overviews of Pennsylvania's boundary disputes see Solon J. Buck and Elizabeth Hawthorn Buck, *The Planting of Civilization in Western Pennsylvania* (Pittsburgh: University of Pittsburgh Press, 1939), 156–74; and Peter S. Onuf, *The Origins of the Federal Republic: Jurisdictional Controversies in the United States, 1775–1787* (Philadelphia: University of Pennsylvania Press, 1983), 49–73.

7. Statistics calculated from various entries in *Minutes of the Supreme Executive Council of Pennsylvania, from Its Organization to the Termination of the Revolution* (Harrisburg, Penn.: T. Fenn, 1853), vols. 13–14, 16. JoAnna McDonald assisted in compiling these figures.

8. Norman Wilkinson, "Land Policy and Speculation in Pennsylvania, 1779–1800: A Test of the New Democracy" (Ph.D. diss., University of Pennsylvania, 1958), 19.

9. Richter, "Onas, The Long Knife," 133–35.

10. Wiley Sword, *President Washington's Indian War: The Struggle for the Old Northwest, 1790–1795* (Norman: University of Oklahoma Press, 1985); Colin G. Calloway, *Crown and Calumet: British-Indian Relations, 1783–1815* (Norman: University of Oklahoma Press, 1987).

11. Thomas P. Slaughter, *The Whiskey Rebellion: Frontier Epilogue to the American* (New York: Oxford University Press, 1986).

12. Gregory H. Nobles, *American Frontiers: Cultural Encounters and Continental Conquest* (New York: Hill and Wang, 1997), 91–115; Andrew R. L. Cayton, "'Noble Actors' upon 'the Theatre of Honour': Power and Civility in the Treaty of Greenville," in *Contact Points: American Frontiers from the Mohawk Valley to the Mississippi, 1750–1830*, ed. Cayton Teute and Fredrika J. Teute (Chapel Hill: University of North Carolina Press, 1998), 252–67.

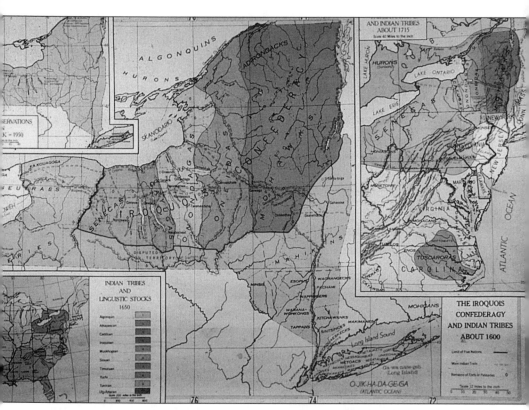

A map of original Haudenosaunee territories about 1600 and an inset illustrating the increase of Seneca territory about 1715. Originally edited by Arthur C. Parker, published by Denoyer Geppert Co., Chicago, 1967.

Some Observations on the Treaty of Canandaigua

ROBERT W. VENABLES

In 1755, Edmond Atkin, a South Carolinian merchant and colonial official, wrote a report to London's Board of Trade describing colonial Indian affairs. Atkin noted that

> no people in the World understand and pursue their true National Interest, better than the Indians.... In their publick Treaties no People on earth are more open, explicit, and Direct. Nor are they excelled by any in the observance of them. Witness in particular the Treaties of the five Nations with the Government of New York; in which there hath been no Breach yet on their Part, since 1609 at first under the Dutch, and since 1664 under the English.[1]

That Atkin, a Southerner, chose the Haudenosaunee as his example of fidelity to treaties is an indication of the high regard many colonists had for Haudenosaunee diplomacy. And while the Haudenosaunee continue to abide by their treaties with the United States, the fact is that the United States has continued its English colonial heritage by continually breaking its treaty obligations to the Haudenosaunee, right down to the present day.

In 1910, a remarkable book was published as one of a series of volumes called "The Harvard Classics." Entitled *American Historical Documents*, this book was edited by one of the foremost educators of the day, Charles W. Eliot. Until the previous year, 1909, Dr. Eliot had served as one of the greatest presidents Harvard University had ever had. For his book *American Historical Documents,* Eliot chose just forty-seven documents to illustrate what he called "a selection of the most important documents which record in contemporary terms the great events in the history of the country."[2] One of those forty-seven documents was the "Treaty with the Six Nations." Dr. Eliot placed the Treaty of Canandaigua alongside the Declaration of Independence, the United States Constitution, and the Gettysburg Address. Yet, eighty-four years later, in 1994, the Treaty of Canandaigua is not widely known.

It is time to reassert—to all peoples—the significance of the Treaty of Canandaigua and its recognition of Haudenosaunee sovereignty.

How important is the treaty? Even the Haudenosaunee's political opponents have conceded the point. In 1892, the United States government published a special report entitled *The Six Nations*. The authors of that official United States report concluded that no unilateral action could be taken by either the New York state or the federal government with regard to the Haudenosaunee, and these authors reluctantly admitted Haudenosaunee sovereignty. One of the authors, Thomas Donaldson, noted:

> The conclusion is irresistible that the Six Nations are nations by treaty and law, and have long since been recognized as such by the United States and the state of New York, and an enlightened public will surely hesitate before proceeding to divest these people of long-established rights without their consent—rights recognized and confirmed in some cases by the immortal [George] Washington and by more than a hundred years of precedents and legislation.[3]

Among the "rights recognized and confirmed" by George Washington are those in the 1794 Treaty of Canandaigua, negotiated during his second administration as president of the United States.

In the 1892 report, Thomas Donaldson also noted:

> If the Iroquois, native or foreign (i.e., Canadian) born, want to become citizens of the United States they must renounce allegiance to their own people.... The several reservations belong to them, and neither the state of New York nor the United States can break them [the reservations] up without the Indians' consent, or through conditions analogous to those of war. They have always been recognized as nations.[4]

Towards the end of this 1892 U.S. government report, the other major author, General Henry B. Carrington, noted:

> The alleged absurdity of the Six Nations of New York being a "nation within a nation" does not change the fact or nullify the sequence of actual history.[5]

Remarkably, Carrington calls upon the United States to accept the Haudenosaunee claim to "independence," and goes on to suggest that international law take precedence over *both* United States and Haudenosaunee law:

Accepting all that the most technical advocate of the Indians' claim to prolonged independence can advance, a higher and equally consistent principle of international law supplies the wholesome remedy.

As contiguous nations must have political intercourse, and upon a basis of mutual benefit, so there must be, on the part of each, some representative authority to adjust conflicting issues between them.[6]

Thus Carrington was calling for two permanent liaison authorities, one authorized by and representing the Haudenosaunee, and the other authorized by and representing the United States. This proposal extends Article 7 of the Treaty of Canandaigua, which calls for communication between representatives when there is an immediate crisis.

In 1910, Charles Eliot chose to include the Treaty of Canandaigua in his volume of historic documents, because he felt that the treaty with the Six Nations "fixed the limits of the territory to be left in the possession of these tribes." In turn, we can also examine what "limits" and obligations exist on the part of the United States as set forth in the Treaty of Canandaigua. We can ask why the United States citizenry remains largely ignorant of the limitations and obligations that set them apart from the sovereign Haudenosaunee, the People of the Longhouse.

Eliot also noted another reason to include the Treaty of Canandaigua in his volume of significant historical documents: the treaty was a part of the evidence of how the United States acquired, in Dr. Eliot's words, "each successive increase of territory."[7] In this context, Eliot also included the Louisiana Purchase, the Treaty of Ghent in 1815, the Monroe Doctrine, the 1848 treaty with Mexico which transferred so much of Mexico to the United States, the purchase of Alaska from Russia, and the annexation of Hawaii.[8]

The fact that the America of Dr. Eliot's day gloried in the United States' aggressive expansion provides a clue as to why today's generation virtually ignores the treaty. While there are many reasons why the Treaty of Canandaigua does not seem to be high on the political agenda of non-Indian governments today, one reason is national embarrassment. While the America of Dr. Eliot's day may have been proud of the United States' violent expansion across the North American continent, the American citizens of the present day would rather forget the details of exactly how a nation managed to expand over 3,000 miles in just one century, from 1789 to 1890.

Perhaps it is time for some reality therapy. Yes, Virginia, there is a "Town Destroyer" ("Hanadahguyus") named George Washington,[9] whose orders to General John Sullivan during the American Revolution enabled Sullivan to burn Haudenosaunee towns in 1779. Sullivan did so with a thoroughness not seen again until William Tecumseh Sherman marched from Atlanta to the sea.[10]

Overall, the Treaty of Canandaigua is a treaty between two sovereigns—the Six Nations on the one hand, and the United States on the other. In addition to setting limits for each sovereign, the treaty defines reciprocal obligations.

In defining these limits and obligations, there are some problems of terminology. In this context, the Supreme Court decision *Worcester v. Georgia* (1832) specifically noted that in cases of conflicting interpretation, the U.S. courts must use the interpretation presented by a First Nation, an American Indian nation—provided that the Indian nation can *prove* that its interpretation has a historical basis. And that of course is the trick, because most of the treaty records acceptable in court just happen to be documents written by Anglo-Americans.[11]

With this Supreme Court case in mind, it is interesting to examine Article 2 of the Treaty of Canandaigua, which defines lands reserved "to" the Haudenosaunee by the state of New York. Non-Indians, especially United States government lawyers, often contend that this implies that the United States is granting lands "to" the Haudenosaunee, which in turn implies that the United States is the sovereign. This non-Indian interpretation is contradicted in the very next two articles, because both Articles 3 and 4 state that the United States will never "claim" the Haudenosaunee lands set forth in the treaty. If the United States was sovereign, it clearly *would* claim these lands. Instead, Articles 2 and 3 define a more limited right, a right known as the "right of pre-emption." Pre-emption means the right of purchase is exclusively established for one particular European or Euro-American nation. Thus Articles 2 and 3 use the same wording and define pre-emption as follows: Haudenosaunee lands "shall remain theirs, until they choose to sell the same to the people of the United States, who have the right to purchase."

"Pre-emption" referred only to land, and did not alter Indian political systems on that land. Pre-emption was originally a European concept that competing European powers used to settle which European power would have the right to negotiate with a specific Indian nation in order to purchase or otherwise obtain some or all of the lands of that Indian nation. Pre-emption was not an assertion of sovereignty over Indian nations, their societies, or their political systems.

In addition, pre-emption does not mean that the United States can force a sale of lands. In fact, pre-emption regarding lands only means that if and when an Indian nation decides to sell lands, the Indian nation—by agreeing to pre-emption—must approach the United States first—the United States has to be the first nation to which the Indians offer to sell their land.

The right to pre-emption on land does not give the United States other jurisdictional powers, for the simple reason that the land retains its status as Indian territory until the Indians agree to sell it, and only then do those lands pass into the jurisdiction of the United States.

Pre-emption affects Haudneosaunee sovereignty only in the sense that it "pre-empts" another non-Indian power, such as British Canada, from entering into land negotiations with the Haudenosaunee. Pre-emption is a mutual agreement regarding a single, specific *future* action—the Indian nation has a legal, contractual obligation to sell to only one other nation, such as the United States.

The right of pre-emption also depends on its recognition by other European or Euro-American powers. British Canada, for example, maintained that it had pre-emption rights in Canada even as the United States claimed pre-emption rights south of the Great Lakes. By respecting each other's rights of pre-emption, both Euro-American nations avoided conflict. This reciprocal recognition between the United States and British Canada of its own particular rights of pre-emption is dealt with in the last sentence of the treaty: "The United States do not interfere with nations, tribes or families, of Indians elsewhere resident." This was an assertion both the United States and the Haudenosaunee recognized in the treaty. The immediate reason for the inclusion of the right of pre-emption was to restrict annuities only to those members of the Six Nations who resided south of the Great Lakes, thereby excluding those of the Six Nations who lived in Canada. But the fact that the treaty ends with the overall statement of pre-emption indicates that the United States was clearly declaring that in matters of land it would not deal with any Haudenosaunee who lived in Canada. By extension, the treaty implies that no state within the United States has the right to deal with any Haudenosaunee living in Canada with regard to land. The full text of the last paragraph of the Treaty of Canandaigua thus reads:

> NOTE. It is clearly understood by the parties to this treaty, that the annuity, stipulated in the sixth article, is to be applied to the benefit of such of the Six Nations, and of their Indian friends united with them, as aforesaid, as do or shall reside within the boundaries of the United States: for the United States do not interfere with nations, tribes, or families of Indians, elsewhere resident.

Pre-emption meant Haudenosaunee lands are not on an "open market." If Great Britain in Canada had had an equal right or access to the purchase of Haudenosaunee lands, for example, the United States feared that Britain could buy up lands on the western frontier of the United States and prevent the United States from expanding.

If the United States had sovereignty over the Haudenosaunee, or if it had plenary rights under the 1787 United States Constitution, it would have been totally unnecessary to state the right of pre-emption. Thus the larger context of Article 3 is:

> the United States will never . . . disturb the Seneka nation, nor any of the Six Nations, or of their Indian friends residing thereon and united with them, in the free use and enjoyment thereof: but it [that is, the lands] shall remain theirs, until they choose to sell the same to the people of the United States, who have the right of purchase.[12]

Pre-emption as it was understood at the time of the Treaty of Canandaigua is reviewed in an 1815 Senate speech by Rufus King during the Senate's discussion of the Treaty of Ghent, the peace that would end the War of 1812 with Great Britain. King stated that the right of pre-emption, and not sovereignty, was the claim the United States could make against Indian nations. King noted that the United States

> hold[s] that Discovery gives them the exclusive right [pre-emption] to extinguish the Indian title of occupancy by purchase or conquest—possessing such a degree of Sovereignty, as the rights of the natives will allow them to exercise, the U.S. have an absolute right to the soil, subject to the Indian right of occupancy, and also the absolute right to extinguish that right. This division includes a complete title to the soil either in the U.S. or the Indians. The sovereignty of the U.S. is therefore limited not absolute.[13]

This last sentence deserves emphasis: "The sovereignty of the U.S. is therefore limited not absolute."

In 1831, a decade and a half after the Treaty of Ghent, statesman Henry Clay (one of the U.S. negotiators at the Treaty of Ghent) described what he was absolutely certain of with regard to Indian rights under the Treaty of Ghent. He noted that Indian nations had the right "quietly to possess and enjoy its lands, subject to no other limitation than that, when sold, they can only be sold to the U. States."[14] The full text of Clay's statement indicates the context of the above quote:

> I had supposed that the principles which had uniformly governed our relations with the Cherokee and other Indian nations had been too long and too firmly established to be disturbed at this day. They were proclaimed in the negotiation with Great Britain at Ghent, by the American commissioners who concluded the

treaty of peace; and having been one of those commissioners, I feel with more sensibility than most of my fellow citizens, any violation of those principles; for if we stated them incorrectly, we deceived Great Britain; and if our government acts in opposition to them, we deceive the world.

According to those principles, the Cherokee nation [and by Clay's definition, all other Indian nations] has the right to establish its own form of government, and to alter and amend it from time to time, according to its own sense of its own wants; to live under its own laws; to be exempt from the operation of the laws of the United States; and quietly to possess and enjoy its lands, subject to no other limitation than that, when sold, they can only be sold to the U. States.[15]

Clearly, the fact that the United States claimed only the right of pre-emption is a major proof in the non-Indian records that Haudenosaunee oral tradition is correct: the Haudenosaunee are a free and independent nation.

The issue of sovereignty is indeed complicated with semantic arguments. Since that is the case, how would the Haudenosaunee have perceived treaty provisions when they were translated into their own languages? How did the Haudenosaunee perceive phrases such as "the lands reserved to," "to be their property," and "the United States will never claim the same [lands], nor disturb them [the Six Nations]?"

Such questions cannot be answered with total certainty. But there is a provocative clue. One of the signers of the Treaty of Canandaigua was Handsome Lake. Beginning in 1799, Handsome Lake was inspired by messages provided to him by spiritual messengers from the Creator. Until his death in 1815, Handsome Lake shared these messages with the Haudenosaunee through teachings known as the "Gaiwiio." One of these teachings reviewed a vision Handsome Lake had seen of George Washington in the afterlife, living in a special place provided by the Creator, because Washington had been responsible for the United States' acceptance of the terms of the Treaty of Canandaigua, terms which included Haudenosaunee freedom and independence. The teachings of Handsome Lake assisted the Haudenosaunee as they created a spiritually motivated and spiritually guided renaissance and reformation, and these teachings—based on spiritual messages and therefore of unquestioned credibility—clearly indicate that the Haudenosaunee perceived themselves, in the years immediately following the Treaty of Canandaigua, as a free and independent people.[16]

If United States citizens, and their elected officials, ever begin to appreciate the position of sovereignty taken by the Haudenosaunee in the Treaty of Canandaigua, it may depend upon first casting aside a powerful stereotype imbedded in the American culture: the stereotypical Western Indian, especially the Plains Indian, as the Indian "standard," the Indian "Everyman." Native American cultures are all different, and each First Nation's internal political systems are all different. Just as important, however, not all treaties are the same. That is, the terms of treaties vary from decade to decade, and vary according to which First Nation the United States is negotiating with. Generally, as United States history progressed through the decades of the nineteenth century, the more power the United States amassed, and the more the United States was able to impose its own agenda. In this context, the Treaty of Canandaigua is clearly a treaty between sovereigns. For example, an important phrase in the Treaty of Canandaigua is the recognition by the United States in Articles 3 and 4 that the United States will never "disturb...any of the Six Nations, or their Indian friends residing thereon and united with them, in the free use and enjoyment" of Haudenosaunee lands. This is a recognition of the sovereign right of the Haudenosaunee to determine who could live within their borders. After all, a long-established tradition among the Haudenosaunee was the adoption of other Indians into their midst. This United States recognition in 1794 is in stark contrast to the provisions the United States imposed upon the Crow Nation, a western Indian *ally* of the United States, in 1868:

> set apart for the absolute and undisturbed use and occupation of the Indians herein named, and for such other friendly tribes or individual Indians as from time to time they may be willing, with the consent of the United States, to admit amongst them.[17]

It is significant that the United States imposed this provision requiring "the consent of the United States" on one of their Indian allies, because similar restrictive provisions which required the consent of the United States were imposed upon First Nations which had resisted United States expansion, such as the Lakotas and Navajos in treaties that same year, 1868.[18] Yet three-quarters of a century earlier, at Canandaigua, no such restrictions applied. In fact, the Haudenosaunee were recognized by the United States as having the complete freedom to determine who lived within their territories.

To indicate further that there is no such legal entity as a generic Indian treaty, and to emphasise that the Treaty of Canandaigua has terms that are different from other treaties, it can be noted that the various 1868 treaties with the Crows, the Lakotas, the Navajos, and other First Nations also imposed a provision that the United States could unilaterally alter the internal property rights of these Indians, forcing them from communal land base onto individually owned plots of land.

No such provision exists in the Treaty of Canandaigua. In fact, in Articles 3 and 4, the Treaty of Canandaigua specifically notes that the United States will *not* disturb the Haudenosaunee in "the free use and enjoyment" of their lands.

In this context, another term used in the Treaty of Canandaigua in both Articles 2 and 3 seems to be especially significant: the United States recognizes Haudenosaunee lands "to be their property." At the time, in 1794, these lands were controlled communally, and both Articles 2 and 3 define a recognition by the United States that the Haudenosaunee have the sovereign right to continue their communal use of land.

One of the most significant aspects of the Treaty of Canandaigua is the recognition by the United States that the Haudenosaunee are indeed a Confederacy of Six Nations.[19] This acknowledgement by the United States of Confederacy sovereignty, rather than a recognition of separate sovereignties for *each* of the Six Nations, is vital to an understanding of the renaissance of the Confederacy following the devastations of the Sullivan campaign during the American Revolution.

An issue raised in the records of the negotiations which led to the Treaty of Canandaigua is the Haudenosaunee right to hunt in *all* of their territories, including those now within United States jurisdiction. William Savery, a Quaker observer at the 1794 Treaty of Canandaigua, noted how these rights had been acknowledged both in the 1794 treaty negotiations and in previous treaties.

> The commissioner [United States negotiator Colonel Timothy Pickering] observed . . . that the Indians shall have the right of hunting on . . . those [lands] ceded at the treaty of Fort Stanwix [in 1784]; and on all other lands ceded by them since the peace [of 1783].[20]

The right of the Haudenosaunee to travel and hunt even across ceded lands seems to have been assumed. Although Colonel Pickering voluntarily reiterated this right when he orally reviewed the treaty in the presence of the Haudenosaunee, the final text of the Treaty of Canandaigua does not include this provision. Of course, the omission from the final text may have been intentional on the part of the United States negotiators. None of the participants representing the Confederacy could read English well enough to critique its legal contents, and one of the negotiators, "Farmer's Brother," noted his unease at the end of the negotiations: "as we cannot read, we are liable to be deceived."[21] The importance to the Haudenosaunee of their hunting rights cannot be overemphasized, given the spiritual and political worldview of the Haudenosaunee.

Haudenosaunee Concepts of the Land at the Time of the Treaty of Canandaigua

Haudenosaunee concepts of land were defined by the original founders of the Confederacy, and this worldview of the land evidently also existed prior to the founding of the Confederacy. In this Haudenosaunee tradition, two types of land coexist harmoniously within the Haudenosaunee economy and polity: (1) the Clearings, and (2) the Woods.[22]

THE CLEARINGS

The Clearings were and are lands belonging to one of the member Nations of the Confederacy (that is, the nations of the Mohawks, the Oneidas, the Onondagas, the Cayugas, the Senecas, and—after 1722— the Tuscaroras). The Clearings include the occupied towns and the communal agricultural fields currently in use and primarily controlled by the women. Descent and communal property were matrilineal. The women had the major responsibility for each town's communal field agriculture (especially the cultivation of corn, beans, and squash) and for the gathering of non-domesticated berries and other plants.

THE WOODS

The Woods are defined as the areas beyond the villages and agricultural fields. These Woods even include the sites of former towns and abandoned fields that were being encouraged to rejuvenate their strengths by lying fallow. The Woods were primarily controlled by the Haudenosaunee men. In this sphere beyond the towns, Haudenosaunee men hunted, fished, traded, and made their living.

While the Clearings were and are national lands, belonging to only one of the Nations (such as the Oneidas) within the Confederacy, the Woods (also known as "the Forest") have a dual identity. The Woods are Confederacy lands, belonging to all the member Nations of the Confederacy, but they are simultaneously recognized as being divided into what were originally the specific responsibilities and domains of the five founding Confederacy Nations: Mohawks, Oneidas, Onondagas, Cayugas, and Senecas. These national "boundaries"—more accurately, national spheres of responsibility and influence—had existed prior to the formation of the Confederacy. No hierarchy is implied, and thus the Woods are the equal responsibility of the Confederacy as a whole and, in their different local contexts, the responsibility of one of the five founding Nations. Because there is no ultimate sovereign power, these simultaneous and equal responsibilities have no real parallel in Western law, including Western property law. These simultaneous and equal responsibilities are also what make the Confederacy a unique and delicate balance of equal responsibilities among its confederate parts. The concept of the Woods exemplifies a broader fact with regard to Haudenosaunee politics: the Confederacy is not centralized, and has no centralized supreme power with subordinate political entities such as the "federal-state" structure of the United States.

The separation of territories into the Clearings and the Woods evidently existed in some form prior to the founding of the Confederacy. The specific details of the concepts could have been different—for example, before the Confederacy was founded, it is not known whether or not the women controlled the Clearings. In any case, the origin of the concepts is extremely logical. In a world where one could monitor one's territory only by sight, approaching humans fell into two categories: those who came in peace, and those who were enemies. Because it was unlikely that enemies would announce themselves, a formal announcement of a person's approach indicated peaceful intentions. To convey that one was a friend, a person emerged from the Woods and stopped at the edge of the Woods, which was of course also the edge of the Clearing. There it was the custom to light a fire or shout loudly. The people of the Clearing would be alerted by the smoke or shouts. At this point, a messenger might be sent out to ascertain the identity of the visitor and to escort the visitor into the Clearing and into the town. The people of the Five Nations were already familiar with this ritual before the Confederacy was established. This was such an important concept that during certain significant occasions, there was (and is) a ceremony known as "The Edge of the Woods."

Tradition records that leaders such as the Onondaga named Hayonhwatha (popularly known as Hiawatha) followed this ritual during the long process that led to the founding of the Confederacy. For example, when Hayonhwatha and some warriors approached a Mohawk town, they stopped before emerging from the edge of the Woods. As described by the Seneca scholar Arthur C. Parker,

> this was the custom, to make a smoke so that the town might know that visitors were approaching and send word that they might enter without danger to their lives. The Mohawks knew the meaning of the signal so they sent messengers and invited the party into the village.[23]

Arthur C. Parker also described the custom of pausing at the edge of the Woods before emerging into the Clearing, as the custom existed prior to the founding of the Confederacy.

> In those days [before the founding of the Confederacy] it was necessary to build a fire on the outskirts of a village about to be

entered. If necessary to kill an animal for food, its pelt must be hung on a tree in plain sight because it is the property of the nation in whose territory it is killed.[24]

When trade began with the musket-bearing Europeans, musket shots fired into the air became a new way to signal one's emergence from the Woods into the Clearing. For example, in 1634, a group of Mohawks were escorting three Dutch traders westward out of Mohawk lands and into the lands of the Oneidas. The Mohawk escorts stopped just a short distance from the first Oneida town—the first Oneida Clearing. One of the Dutchmen, Harmen Meyndertsz van den Bogaert, wrote:

> The Indians asked us to shoot. We fired our weapons, which we reloaded, and then we went to the castle [a Mohawk town surrounded by a wooden palisade].[25]

THE WOODS, HUNTING RIGHTS, AND THE TREATY OF CANANDAIGUA

The most prominent founder of the Iroquois Confederacy, the Peacemaker Dekanawideh (also spelled Deganawidah), made the Confederacy's control of all the Woods one of the foundations of the league, defining the right of the entire Confederacy to hunt anywhere within "the Woods."

> Then [the Peacemaker] Dekanahwideh continued and said: "We have still one matter left to be considered and that is with reference to the hunting grounds of our people from which they derive their living."
>
> They, the lords [sachems in Council, representing all five of the founding Nations of the Confederacy], said with reference to this matter: "We shall now do this: We shall only have one dish (or bowl) in which will be placed one beaver tail and we shall all have co-equal right to it, and there shall be no knife in it, for if there be a knife in it, there would be danger that it might cut some one and blood would thereby be shed." (This one dish or bowl [notes Seneca editor Arthur C. Parker] signifies that they will make their hunting grounds one common trace and all have a co-equal right to hunt within it. The knife being prohibited from being placed into the dish or bowl signifies that all danger would be removed from shedding blood by the people of these different Nations of the confederacy caused by differences of the right of the hunting grounds.)
>
> Then Dekanahwideh continued and said: "We have now accomplished and completed forming the great Confederacy of the Five Nations together with adopting rules and regulations in connection therewith."[26]

DIFFERENT TREES IN A DIFFERENT FOREST: THE CLEARINGS, THE WOODS, AND THE HAUDENOSAUNEE PERCEPTION OF THE TREATY OF CANANDAIGUA

Physical space is just one dimension of the Haudenosaunee environment. The philosophical premises of the Haudenosaunee are very different from "Western" beliefs. Therefore, the different questions and solutions posed by Haudenosaunee philosophy are more than just choices of different paths through the same forest. The entire reality for traditional Haudenosaunee is different: the Haudenosaunee see different trees in a different forest. For example, they see the trees as having spiritual components equal to human spirituality, and in fact they believe that each and every mortal being, human and non-human, has a spiritual essence ("soul") of equal spiritual value.

The Haudenosaunee view of the land has always been based on the premise that both humans and non-humans are consciously interactive. The environment is interdependent spiritually as well as biologically. From this strong sense of interdependence comes a stress on "communal" ethics. The entire world is alive with the spiritual energies of all these beings—deer, eagles, trout, and all others. Each species has its own function, assigned by the Creator, and each species has a sense of its own community. Each species has religious instructions that have been provided by the Creator and which each species is obliged to carry out. All beings are equally conscious of the other beings. There are no unconscious objects, no inferior beings. There are simply beings with different functions. In this sense, all beings, with their equal souls, are your relations, your relatives. Communal human ethics are thus a logical extension of how the Haudenosaunee perceive a communal, interdependent world. Since the Creator filled the world with symbiotic, equal souls who nevertheless carry out specific functions, the most logical premise upon which to base an organized human community was also communal.

Haudenosaunee women and men did not (and do not) define themselves as only members of a single communal group. Each person was/is a member of a Nation; each is a member of the Confederacy as a whole; and each is a member of a specific Clan. Because the same Clans existed throughout the Confederacy, people of one nation literally had relatives in other nations across the Confederacy. The people in the towns were also divided in half (each half is called a moiety by anthropologists). This added still another dimension to personal identity.

Membership in a Clan was matrilineal—that is, determined by the Clan of one's mother. The matrilineal Clans determined who occupied the communal, multi-family longhouses. Husbands had to be from a different Clan. Among other things, this meant that husbands moved in with their wives, and it also meant that the status of all children was matrilineal. The women made up, and continue to make up, Clan Councils. These women's Councils resolve who the "Clan Mother"—the Clan's leader—would be. Each Clan Mother, after consulting the women of her Clan, would designate a Chief from among the men, and the man's name would be submitted to a Council of male Chiefs for approval, and eventually submitted for approval to the Confederacy's grand Council. These all-male Councils are monitored closely by the women. Chiefs serve as long as they have the support of their particular Clans. Any inept Chief of a Clan may be removed by the Clan Mother after consultation with the women of her Clan. Such a removal must then be sanctioned by the entire Confederacy's Grand Council, and if approved, the Chiefs of the Onondaga Nation have the responsibility of finalizing the end of the deposed Chief's tenure.[27]

THE CLEARINGS, THE WOODS, AND THE PERPETUATION OF HAUDENOSAUNEE SOVEREIGNTY

The Haudenosaunee would have never given up the males' rights to hunt, travel, or trade, for to do so would have deprived half of the population—the male half—of their livelihood, their right to earn a living, beyond the female-oriented towns. Had the Haudenosaunee given up these rights, the entire balance of male and female roles, reinforced as they were by spiritual as well as temporal rationales, would have been shattered. Haudenosaunee religion, society, and political structures were and are focused upon the continuing need to maintain "balance:" a balance of Clearing and Woods, a balance of male and female, and a balance of virtually all opposites. (This effort at maintaining a balance continued even when the reservation land bases were reduced, as responsibilities for men and women were redistributed so that balance could be maintained. The most apparent indication of this rebalancing to accommodate a diminished land base was that the responsibility for farming was given, at the direction of the Creator, to men. The women maintained their political and spiritual roles, and the Haudenosaunee remained matrilineal.)

Although males control the Woods, women also had the right to travel, hunt, fish, and trade throughout all the territory of the Confederacy—just as men, of course, had the right to live and work in the towns and assist the women in the fields. However, for purposes of obtaining the foods necessary to sustain day-to-day living, each town depended primarily upon local sources. Thus each Haudenosaunee town had specific hunting and fishing territories which were used by village hunters to provide deer meat, other animal meats, and fish to eat as a balance to the maize and other agricultural foods produced by these towns. How Haudenosaunee women, as well as men, could travel and trade throughout the entire territory of the Confederacy was clearly recorded in December 1634 by Dutch colonist Harmen Meyndertsz van den Bogaert. While in a Mohawk village, he noted the arrival of three women, perhaps Oneidas, carrying dried salmon, which they then sold in at least two Mohawk villages:

> Three women came here from the Sinnekens [a general Dutch term often referring to any Iroquois living west of the Mohawks, as well as to the "Senecas" proper] with some dried and fresh salmon.... They also brought much green tobacco to sell, and had been six days underway. They could not sell all their salmon here, but went with it to the first castle [that is, a Mohawk village further east].[28]

Haudenosaunee traditional religion reflects these perceptual boundaries. Haudenosaunee traditional religion incorporates and recognizes the equal (not hierarchical) spirituality of an environment far larger than a human community or an agricultural area. This religion, in fact, integrates the specific environment in which the Haudenosaunee hunt and fish. Prayers include giving thanks to the animals and fish themselves as well as giving thanks to the Creator of those beings.[29]

ADOPTION OF OTHER NATIONS AND THE TREATY OF CANANDAIGUA

The Treaty of Canandaigua recognizes the right of the Haudenosaunee to continue to carry out their responsibilities towards groups of people adopted into the Confederacy, those the treaty defines as "their Indian friends residing thereon and united with them."[30] An understanding of these adoptions is important in understanding what the rights of the adopted "Indian friends" were, and just as importantly, what limitations the Haudenosaunee had placed on these Indian friends. These Indian friends are not adopted individuals, because adopted individuals became citizens of one of the Confederacy's Nations. These Indian friends are whole groups of people whom the Haudenosaunee allowed to retain their distinct national characteristics.

The Haudenosaunee welcomed other Indian peoples as refugees, because adoption helped to counter colonial pressure along the eastern and southern frontiers of the Haudenosaunee by bolstering their population. This tradition also helped the Haudenosaunee offset the continual depopulation brought on by war and by white diseases such as smallpox. Thus adoption was one of major survival strategies of the Haudenosaunee.

The Haudenosaunee concepts of the Clearings and the Woods have a direct role in defining the status of people who are adopted by the Haudenosaunee. As noted above, the Haudenosaunee practiced two basic forms of adoption. One was when an individual was adopted into a Clan and a Nation, becoming, for example, a member of the Wolf

Clan in the Mohawk Nation. While the adopted individual was permitted to recall their past national heritage with pride, the individual became a full citizen of a Clan and Nation, and was expected to act accordingly. Essentially, the adoption of individuals meant that an individual was absorbed into a Haudenosaunee town—a "Clearing." The second form of adoption was of an entire group into "the Woods"—Woods that were within the sphere of a particular Nation and simultaneously within the Confederacy. In these cases, the groups of refugees did not become citizens of one of the Confederacy's founding Nations, but instead essentially retained their own national rights, rights such as language and religion. However, the adopted group, while controlling its own internal affairs according to its own systems and language, were represented within the Confederacy by the Nation whose Woods or sphere of influence they lived within. The adopted group also forfeited control over external diplomacy, which the Confederacy managed for them. For example, by 1722, Tuscarora refugees from North Carolina had been adopted as a people, not as individuals, and they took up residence within that part of the Woods that was within the sphere of influence of the Oneida Nation. Therefore, the Oneidas represented them in Council.[31]

On the eve of the American Revolution, during 1773 and 1774, a clear example of the adoption of an entire group occurred. At that time, a refugee people known as the Brothertons were brought into the Confederacy as a whole people, not as individuals. This event also demonstrates the Haudenosaunee concept that any lands not occupied by a town were Woods and therefore were under the authority of the entire Confederacy, not simply of one of the Nations. More than a decade of negotiation with East Coast Algonquins from New York, Connecticut, and Massachusetts preceded a more intense discussion by the Grand Council in 1773 and 1774. Then, in January and February 1774, the Haudenosaunee Grand Council gave permission to one of their member Nations, the Oneidas, to grant land to refugee New England and Long Island Indians. Haudenosaunee spokesmen carrying appropriate wampum belts of authority first delivered the terms from the Grand Council—which included, of course, Mohawk representatives—to both the Algonquin refugees and English officials awaiting them at Johnstown, New York. Then the English drew up a written agreement based on the Grand Council's intent.

In this agreement, the Grand Council and the Oneidas specifically excluded these refugee New England Algonquin Indians, soon to be known as the Brothertons, from participating in the beaver trade with the following restrictive clause:

> The said Oneidas do grant to the said New England Indians, and their Posterity without power of Alienation, the aforedescribed

Tract…Also full liberty of Hunting all Sorts of Game throughout the whole Oneida Country, Beaver Hunting only excepted.[32]

Thus it is clear that the Oneidas did not believe they could, as a Nation, take action to invite foreigners into their territory without the permission of the Grand Council. What is all the more significant is that some of the lands onto which the Oneidas were proposing to admit foreigners were lands which were "old towns"—abandoned over the years because of epidemic disease and war.[33] These abandoned town sites—which had once been Clearings—had reverted to Woods both in their physical appearance *and* in their relationship to the Confederacy. Thus even lands once occupied by towns were *not* under the authority of an individual Nation, but of the entire Confederacy through the Grand Council.

Colonial history certainly illustrates the complex issues involving adoption into the Iroquois Confederacy and the definition of "friends" in the Treaty of Canandaigua. But the Brothertons' 1774 example also helps define how, in the present day, the Confederacy's debate over treaty rights with both the state of New York and the United States federal government is complicated by the fact that the national lands of each member Nation of the Confederacy are the dual responsibility of both the Confederacy and of each particular Nation. It is a complication the United States and the state of New York choose to ignore. And as individual entrepreneurs among the Haudenosaunee have created businesses and other economic endeavors on Confederacy lands, it is a complication also conveniently ignored by some of those individuals who claim to be Haudenosaunee.

The colonial era also demonstrated that the Haudenosaunee understood and initiated restrictive clauses in treaties. Any restrictive clauses in negotiations and treaties would not have gone unnoticed. Haudenosaunee perceptions of the Treaty of Canandaigua and of related treaty rights, such as those defined by Britain and the United States in the Jay Treaty of 1794 and the Treaty of Ghent of 1815, were shaped by a Haudenosaunee worldview that had already been honed by experience.[34]

Furthermore, this long-established Haudenosaunee worldview of treaties included the concept that treaties were reaffirmations of precedent, a continuum of custom. They opened treaty negotiations with tradition and expected the Europeans to open negotiations with a reference to Indian tradition. This is why, throughout the centuries, so many Haudenosaunee diplomats took the time in treaty Councils to recite the past history of their current relations with the Europeans. These Haudenosaunee diplomats were reiterating what they believe is still in effect. They were emphasizing, and they continue today to emphasize, what has not changed.[35]

In contrast, Europeans perceived treaties as marked changes or progressions in their dealings with various Indian groups: that progression usually meant that the Europeans could expand either their trade or their settlements.

THE HAUDENOSAUNEE CONCEPT OF SOVEREIGNTY AND THE TREATY OF CANANDAIGUA

Haudenosaunee sovereignty was defined succinctly just before the outbreak of the American Revolution. General Thomas Gage, the commander in chief of all British forces in North America, was also in charge of Indian affairs. On October 7, 1772, Gage wrote to Indian superintendent Sir William Johnson:

> As for the Six Nations having acknowledged themselves Subjects of the English, that I conclude must be a very gross Mistake and am well satisfied were they [the Haudenosaunee] told so, they would not be well pleased. I know I would not venture to treat them as Subjects, unless there was a Resolution to make War upon them, which is not very likely to happen, but I believe they would on such an attempt, very soon resolve to cut our Throats.[36]

General Gage's clear separation of the non-Indian colonists on the one hand and the sovereign Haudenosaunee on the other is the "world" that the United States inherited in 1783 at the end of the American Revolution in the Treaty of Paris. Whatever states may claim about state constitutions defining the states' rights prior to the end of the American Revolution, the fact is that the Treaty of Paris was between Great Britain and the United States as a single nation that consisted of a united confederacy of states. Whenever claims of states' rights with regard to Indian lands are raised, it is important to note that Great Britain did not make thirteen separate treaties with each of the thirteen states, and it was also the responsibility of the Congress of the United States to ratify the treaty. Furthermore, no state boundaries were defined in the 1783 Treaty of Paris; only national boundaries were defined.

Of equal importance, the treaty only referred to the transfer of claims to lands and boundaries, not to a transfer of direct jurisdiction over Indian nations. Thus Article 1 of the Treaty of Paris states clearly that Great Britain "relinquishes all claims to the Government, proprietary and territorial rights of the same [that is, the United States], and every part thereof [that is, every part or state within the United States]."[37] That there are only two parties to the treaty is also clear in Article 2 ("the said United States" with no mention of individual states); Article 3 ("the people of the United States"); Article 4 ("either side" implying only two parties); Article 5 (regarding the treaty's terms concerning property confiscated from Loyalists, "the Congress" has the initiative to deal in turn with the states); and Article 6 ("America"). Article 1 does not transfer jurisdiction, only "claims." This transfer of claims is essentially a transfer from Great Britain to the United States of the right of pre-emption. Not the same as jurisdiction, pre-emption was a concept defined by the European powers when they colonized North America to clarify which European nation would have the right to negotiate over specific areas with the Indian nations whose political systems preceded European contact. That every Indian nation was absent from the Paris negotiations was a travesty, but in retrospect is also a further indication that what was transferred was pre-emption, not jurisdiction.

If the United States actually had sovereignty over the Haudenosauee, no treaties would have been necessary after the 1783 Treaty of Paris. The Haudenosaunee treaties that followed the American Revolution refer to cessions of land but not to the cessation of Haudenosaunee government or society and the absorption within the United States of Haudenoaunee people. No Haudenosaunee governments were dissolved. The 1794 Treaty of Canandaigua defines a clear separation of the United States on the one hand and the Haudenosaunee on the other.

THE TERMS OF THE TREATY OF CANANDAIGUA REAFFIRMED IN THE 1815 TREATY OF GHENT

The terms of the Treaty of Canandaigua were not regarded as temporary, and were among those Indian rights recognized by both Great Britain and the United States in the Treaty of Ghent, which ended the War of 1812. In Article 9, both nations guaranteed to Indian nations "all the Possessions, Rights, and Privileges, which they may have enjoyed, or been entitled to in 1811."[38]

Under the 1815 Treaty of Ghent, the United States gained no new rights with regard to the Haudenosaunee or other Indian nations. Under the treaty's call for a return to the antebellum Indian rights, the United States still only had the right of pre-emption, which it had already possessed prior to the War of 1812. This right of pre-emption, however, was never to be imposed unilaterally. The right of pre-emption had to be exercised through the mutual agreement by treaty between U.S. government on the one hand and each particular Indian nation on the other. Even the notorious 1830 Indian Removal Act stated that Indians could not be removed from their lands if they did not make a treaty with the United States agreeing to exchange their lands east of the Mississippi for lands west of the Mississippi.[39]

Attempting to define what the status of the Indian nations were within the Constitution (which defines Indians who still live within their nations as "not taxed"), the Supreme Court of John Marshall invented the term "domestic dependent nation" in 1831 *(Cherokee Nation v. Georgia)*.[40] In the next year, 1832, the Marshall Court outlined these nations' rights in *Worcester v. Georgia* that

> [A] weaker power does not surrender its independence—its right to self-government, by associating with a stronger, and taking its protection. A weak state, in order to provide for its safety, may place itself under the protection of one more powerful, without stripping itself of the right of government, and ceasing to be a state. Examples of this kind are not wanting in Europea. "Tributary and feudatory states," says Vattel [prominent Swiss legal authority Emmerich de Vattel (1714–1767)] "do not thereby cease to be sovereign and independent states, so long as self government and sovereign and independent authority are left in the administration of the state."[41]

After the American Revolution, one of the most important opinions with regard to American Indian sovereignty and United States Indian policies was voiced by Rufus King, the United States Senator representing New York State. He defined his learned opinions in 1815 during the Senate's consideration of the Treaty of Ghent. King had been born and raised in Massachusetts. During the American Revolution, King had been in combat as an officer in the Patriot army. King was a Harvard-educated lawyer who, in the decades following the Revolution, was continually in a position to understand the legal reality of United States Indian policy and its ramifications. In 1786, Rufus King had been one of the Massachusetts negotiators who settled the conflicting land claims of Massachusetts and New York to Haudenosaunee lands. In 1787, at the age of thirty-two, he represented Massachusetts at the Philadelphia Convention, where he was regarded as one of the convention's most outstanding orators. (King's notes in the Philadelphia Convention describing the formation of the new U.S. Constitution are today a widely respected scholarly resource.) King moved to New York and was elected by the legislature to be one of the first two U.S. Senators representing New York (his Senate colleague was another figure long familiar with Haudenosaunee issues, Philip Schuyler). King served in the Senate during all the negotiations with the Haudenosaunee that led to the Treaty of Canandaigua in 1794. Then, beginning in 1796, he served as the United States ambassador to Great Britain under Presidents George Washington, John Adams, and Thomas Jefferson.[42]

In his 1815 Senate speech, King reviewed Indian policy within the context of the Senate's debate over the Treaty of Ghent. King, a conservative Federalist, surveyed the history of United States–American Indian relations. (The internal structure and ideas of John Marshall's

1832 Supreme Court decision *Worcester v. Georgia* indicate that Marshall may have had a copy of King's speech when he researched and wrote his decision. In any case, Marshall agreed with much of what Rufus King had already outlined in 1815.) As noted earlier in this chapter, King concluded that "the sovereignty of the United States is therefore limited not absolute."[43]

In a recital of European diplomatic relations with the Indians, Rufus King declared that Europeans, including Great Britain and the United States, did not have absolute sovereignty over Indian people because of the existence of "the rights of the primitive Inhabitants" which "were not overlooked, tho' they were somewhat impaired." King even maintained that the United States only had "such a degree of Sovereignty, as the rights of the natives will allow them [the United States] to exercise." As a senator and lawyer, he maintained that various European nations' claims to land on the basis of "discovery" were intended to exclude other European nations and were not claims "against the native inhabitants."

Admitting all of this, Senator King also took the position that Britain should not have inserted the Indian rights into the Treaty of Ghent. King regarded the provision as foreign interference—which, since King was a Revolutionary and Founding Father, is not a surprising position for him to have taken.

Nevertheless, while Rufus King disputes the right of Britain to interfere in what he maintains as the internal matters of the United States, King twice reaffirmed Indian rights to cross borders freely. His first reference is declared as the right of all Indians. But later in his speech he specifically referred to the Haudenosaunee and to the 1713 Treaty of Utrecht.

Rufus King had served in Great Britain as the United States ambassador under Washington, Adams, and Jefferson, and so he was entirely familiar with Britain's viewpoint. In his Senate speech King told his colleagues that in 1713 Britain claimed the exclusive right of purchase, but no dominion over the Haudenosaunee people or Haudenosaunee government. In this speech, he also defined the historic—and limited—meaning of "dominion" as it applied to relations with Indians. In this context, he concluded that in the United States there is "a complete title to the soil either in the U.S. or the Indians. The sovereignty of the U.S. is therefore limited not absolute."

As a dedicated Federalist, Rufus King was a pragmatic fiscal conservative who took an interest in human rights issues, because he believed that ethics were logical and that violations of the human rights of Indians and blacks would weaken the social and political fabric of the United States. This point is significant, because King's conclusions regarding the United States' relationships with Indian nations were based on strong pragmatic political principles. King had no patience for ideological extremes of any shade and followed the Enlightenment's guide of reason.[44] Thus Rufus King's statements on the political status of Native Americans are not those of a romantic, but of a calm objective observer who most often either sat in the Senate or was representing his country's policies to Great Britain.

One point the British had raised was that "the Indians must in some sort be considered as an independent people."[45] King's response was that the Indians' status was unique, because the Indians about which the British were concerned all lived within the internationally recognized boundaries of the United States. Determined to blunt British interference in U.S.-Indian relations, King reviewed the history of these relations. His major theme was that the Indians were independent nations in laws, government, and custom who had nevertheless signed treaties which gave one European power or another, and then the United States, the exclusive right to purchase the title of the Indians' lands. Granting specific Anglo nations the exclusive right of purchase was a limitation on Indian sovereignty, but this was the only limit he regarded as significant.

At a time when the United States was busy settling all the lands to the Mississippi as well as those purchased from France in the Louisiana Purchase west of the Mississippi, Rufus King stated that

> Indians [east of the Mississippi] *are not citizens of the U.S., but perpetual inhabitants living in Tribes[,] independent of each other*, and possessing by occupancy title to the soil where they inhabit. Those natives west of the Mississippi [who were not yet within the boundaries of any new state, as the Louisiana Purchase was still in territorial status] are now, as they probably were at the discovery by Columbus, independent Tribes.[46]

Rufus King declared that the European right of "discovery gave no dominion over the Indians, except in cases of conquest" and that titles to American soil were defined among various European countries to minimize conflict among the Europeans. The right of discovery was therefore intended and exerted by the various European governments "not against the native inhabitants, but against each other."[47]

Interestingly, this description is virtually the same as that given by Lord Dorchester, governor of Canada, in 1791 to the Six Nations and other Great Lakes Indians. This similarity indicates that this concept was widely understood. At Quebec, on August 15, 1791, Dorchester strongly affirmed that

> the King's rights with respect to your territory were against the Nations of Europe . . . the King never had any rights against you but to such parts of the Country as had been fairly ceded by yourselves with your own free consent by Public convention and sale.[48]

In his 1815 Senate speech, Rufus King stated that the Indians were *"the rightful occupants of the soil, with a just claim to retain and use the same, according to their own discretion."*[49] Thus the Indians could retain and use their lands at their own discretion, and not the discretion of the Anglos. But even though Indians were "independent nations," their "right to the soil, as independent nations, was diminished by the denial to the natives the power to dispose of the soil at will to whomsoever they pleased."[50]

That Senator King did not lightly regard the interdependency of the United States and Indian nations is illustrated by his opinion regarding a crucial subtlety in treaty negotiations, which is applicable to an examination of British policy as well. The question was: when Indian lands were set aside as "reservations," did the Indians reserve this part of their original homelands unto themselves, or did the United States claim all of their lands *and return to the Indians*—reserve for the Indians—the reservation lands?

King maintained that the Indians reserved the lands to themselves. Otherwise, if the Indians got *back* their reservations from the United States, any total transfer ended the U. S. government's pre-emptive right of purchase—a principle which is a cornerstone of the 1815 Senate speech quoted above. King explained his firm view on this in a letter from Washington, D.C., February 12, 1818, to his son, Edward King. Rufus King, then serving in the Senate, wrote the letter to explain why the Senate had rejected a treaty drawn up by General McArthur and General Lewis Cass with the Great Lakes Indians, forcing a reconvening of the negotiators and the Indians and a postponement of the sale of acquired lands to white settlers. King defended Indian rights because they were intertwined with the rights of the national federal government against the governments of the states and, more importantly, those individual citizens who wished to make purchases of Indian land directly from the Indians:

> the late commissioners [McArthur and Cass] departed from all former examples. They required the Indians to cede their whole territory to the U.S., and then by an article for that purpose, the U.S. are made to *retrocede* or grant in fee simple a portion of these lands to the Indians; the effect of such measure is to deprive the U.S. of their pre-emptive Right to obtain a future grant of these lands, so conveyed to the Indians. Other parts of the Treaty, which confirmed to the individuals of the Indian Tribes such grants in severalty as the chiefs of the Tribes might make to them, with authority or power to such individual Indians to sell their shares, or several grants to any person, Indian or white man, is reprehensible; is inserting our Laws relative to property so as to affect the Indians and their regulations. Our policy has been to leave the Indians to manage these lands as they pleased; to assign portions of it to portions, or individuals, of their Tribes, and not

to meddle with these dispositions and regulations. Under the proposed Treaty, Ohio would have been embarrassed with ejectments, trespasses, covenants, and all sorts of real Contracts, between Indians & whites, and confusion, as well as fraud, would have been the consequence, had the Senate confirmed the Treaty. It is as true in managing Indian affairs, as in attending to those of the Church, that we shd. be careful "stare (supra) vias antiquas" [consider above all the old ways].[51]

King then gave another example, noting how some Cherokee mixed bloods, having heard of the McArthur-Cass treaty provisions, had asked to have a recent Cherokee treaty retroactively include similar provisions:

Before this Treaty had reached the Senate, a Deputation of Cherokee Indians, whose tribe have lately made a cession of Lands to the U.S., having heard of this Treaty, applied to have the Treaty made with their Tribe, reformed and settled on the Plan of Genl. McArthur's and Cass' Treaty.

The halfbreeds among the Tribes would all prefer the new project, as it wd. enable them to make money out of it; and the novelty of the U.S. granting *in fee*, instead of the Indian Tribes reserving their unceded lands, wd. have put an end to the preemptive Rights of the U.S., and not only been the means of preventing their acquiring future and profitable cessions; but would have opened a scene of fraud, speculation and Indian controversy of the most immoral and dangerous character.[52]

HAUDENOSAUNEE EXPECTATIONS AT THE TREATY OF CANANDAIGUA

Regarding sovereignty, what did the Haudenosaunee expect as a result of the 1794 Treaty of Canandaigua? Speculation is exactly that, especially from this Anglo-American author. In all probability, because the Haudenosaunee viewed treaties as a part of a diplomatic continuum, the Treaty of Canandaigua would have been an extension of the premise of the "Guswenta," or "Two Row Wampum Belt." Symbolically, the primary elements of the Guswenta are two parallel rows made of purple wampum, separated by three rows of white wampum.

This belt refers to a diplomatic concept of Haudenosaunee-European/Euroamerican relationships that had been ongoing since the seventeenth century. The Guswenta represents the two separate but parallel rivers (or paths) along which each society, Haudenosaunee and European, have each promised the other to perpetually follow. The Two Row Wampum vividly asserts the Haudenosaunee commitment to independence. At the same time, it also affirms an intention, evident since the seventeenth century, to communicate with, rather than confront, non-Indian governments. These are parallel and thus continually distinct developments. The symbolism of separate rivers or paths is not intended to be adversarial. So long as there are no attempts to force the ways of one people upon the other, neither path becomes blurred and useless, and each path remains viable.

The three rows of white beads which intervene between the parallel paths simultaneously represent both the physical space that will forever remain between peoples and the method by which these separate people should communicate, mutual communication based on truth, justice, and spiritual thinking. The concepts of the Guswenta are in turn a part of the Haudenosaunee worldview. The goals of the Guswenta are certainly reflected in Articles 2, 3, and 4, in which the United States promises not to "disturb" the Haudenosaunee, and in Article 7, which provides for a resolution of conflicts that is to be followed by both the United States and the Haudenosaunee: "The United States and Six Nations agree, that...complaint shall be made by the party injured to the other." Another detail of the Guswenta and the Haudenosaunee worldview it represents may also apply to the Treaty of Canandaigua: one end of the wampum belt remains unfinished, to symbolize the fact that the belt must be continually renewed by both peoples, a concept promised in Article 1 ("Peace and friendship are hereby firmly established, and shall be perpetual between the United States and the Six Nations") and, in Article 7, in the procedure for resolving conflicts.

There are also other possibilities that may suggest what Haudenosaunee perceptions were at the time the Treaty of Canandaigua was made in 1794. One is the importance of the continuation of hunting and fishing guaranteed by U.S. negotiator Timothy Pickering during his discussions with the Haudenosaunee. This concept seems paramount, and is perhaps related to the Haudenosaunee concept of the Woods as common to all. During the 1780s and 1790s, even the manipulative officials representing the state of New York had guaranteed that the Haudenosaunee would be able to maintain continuous hunting and fishing rights throughout *all* of what is now New York State.

At the Eastern Door of the geopolitical Longhouse, the Mohawks had lived and cooperated with Dutch, English, German, and other European colonists for three-quarters of a century. Occasional disputes aside, this diverse population had used the same Mohawk River and the same streams, and they had all hunted in the same forest. To a lesser extent, the Oneidas, the Onondagas, the Cayugas, the Senecas, and the Tuscaroras had also lived interdependently with non-Indians, especially through the Covenant Chain of trade. Perhaps the Haudenosaunee also saw that the new United States was simply another layer of political complexity that would be added to the already complex duality of the Woods. Perhaps the Haudenosaunee envisioned a future with the United States and its member states simply as the most recent addition to this Haudenosaunee concept of the Woods— Woods which had always been simultaneously both the lands of a particular Nation within the Confederacy and simultaneously the domain of the entire Confederacy.

There was perhaps an expectation on the part of the Haudenosaunee in 1794 that the Treaty of Canandaigua would reestablish the Covenant Chain of peace and mutually beneficial economic relations. After all, the Covenant Chain had more than a century of history before the American Revolution had disrupted it, and that disruption had lasted less than a decade, from 1775 to 1784. The Confederacy itself had frequently faced disruptive internal challenges and had survived. There was no reason to suspect that the English-speaking people of the United States would, in the long run, be any less or more difficult to live among than the Dutch, English, and other European colonists who had preceded these Americans of 1794.

Whatever these possibilities may or may not have been, no speculation is necessary to discern one aspect of Haudenosaunee confidence with regard to their future. Between 1800 and 1815, the Creator assured the Haudenosaunee, through spiritual messages imparted to a teacher named Handsome Lake, that they would survive as a people. Those messages, the "Gaiwiio," have sustained the Haudenosaunee down to the present day. The Haudenosaunee remain confident that eventually the non-Indian world will fall into step with the Creator's intentions.

Conclusion

Today, the Haudenosaunee continue to maintain their rights under the Treaty of Canandaigua. And what expectations of the Treaty of Canandaigua can be held by non-Indians? At the start of the twenty-first century, the reality of global politics is that we are all interdependent peoples. The successful maintenance of that interdependence will depend upon all of our abilities, throughout the globe, to work with each other as sovereign peoples. But what if the citizens of the United States cannot persuade their government to uphold the principles of the Treaty of Canandaigua? What if the United States fails to take actions which recognize the sovereignty of the Haudenosaunee, our immediate neighbors? The answers to such questions may reveal how successfully the United States is likely to understand other cultures and nations in the global economy of the twenty-first century. The answers may also reveal who will dare to believe our word, and trust us.

Chief Jake Swamp (Mohawk) addresses *The Edge of the Woods* at the 200th Anniversary of the Canandaigua Treaty. Louise M. Slaughter, official United States Representative, is at his left. Also pictured are J. Sheldon Fisher, Chief Leo Henry (Tuscarora), Jonathan Hopkins (Tlingit), and Chief Emerson Webster (Seneca). Photo © Anna M. Schein.

Appendix A: The Proclamation of October 4, 1774

PROCLAMATION
Contemporary Copy
[At Guy Park, on northern bank of the Mohawk River, New York, October 4, 1774]

By Guy Johnson Esqr. sole Agent & Superintendent of Indian affairs for the Northern Department of North America &c&c—

Whereas the Indians of Mohegan, Naraganset, Montock, Pequods of Groton & of Stonington, Nahanticks, & Farmington inhabiting with the New England Governments did last year represent that they were much straightened & reduced to such small Pittances of land that they cou'd no longer remain There, & did thro the Channell of Sir William Johnson Bart. [Baronet] late superintendent apply to the Six Nations for some land to live upon, which was at length agreed to in my presence at the last Treaty, and a Tract allotted to them by the Oneidas, And Whereas some of them have since in Company with the Oneida Chiefs viewed the said Lands, & determined on its Boundaries as follows, desiring [that] a Certificate of the same, and that it might be entered in the Records of Indian Affairs, vizt. Beginning at the West end of Scaniadaris or the Long Lake which is the head of one of the branches of Orisca Creek, & from thence about twelve Miles Northerly so far as that an Easterly Course from a certain Point on the first mentioned Course shall intersect the Road or Path leading from old Oneida to the German flats where the said Path crosses the Scanandowa Creek running into the Oneida Lake—then the same Course continued to the Line settled as the Limits between the Province of New York & the Indians at the Treaty of Fort Stanwix in 1768, Thence Southerly along the said Line about 13 miles, or so far as that a Westerly Line from thence keeping one mile South of the most Southerly [Bounds] Bend of Oriscany Creek shall reach the Place of beginning so as to comprehend the Lake first mentioned—I do therefore in compliance with the Joint Request of the said Oneidas and New England Indians declare that the said Oneidas do grant to the said New England Indians, and their Posterity without power of Alienation, the aforedescribed Tract with its Appurtenances in the amplest manner, Also full liberty of Hunting all Sorts of Game throughout the whole Oneida Country, Beaver Hunting only excepted, with this particular or Reservation that Same shall not be possessed by any persons, deemed of the said Tribes, who are descended from, or have intermixed with Negroes, or Mulattoes.—

Given under my hand & Seal at Arms at Guy Park
    October the 4th. 1774 —

INDORSED:
Certificate of the Oneidas Grant of a Tract of Land to the
New England Inds.
Guy Park 4th. Octr. 1774.

(Guy Johnson, October 4, 1774, "Proclamation," in James Sullivan, et al., eds., in Vol. XIII, *The Papers of Sir William Johnson,* [Albany, New York: University of the State of New York, 1921–65], 683–84.)

Appendix B: The 1815 U.S. Senate
Speech of Rufus King

BACKGROUND OF THE SPEECH

Two years after Rufus King was defeated by James Monroe in the presidential election of 1816, King's character and viewpoints were summarized in the July 4, 1818, issue of the *National Register*:

> Mr. R King is a senator from the State of New York, and was once, you will recollect, minister resident at the Court of St. James. He is now about 60 years of age, above the middle size, and somewhat inclined to corpulency. His countenance, when serious and thoughtful, possesses a great deal of austerity and rigor, but at other moments it is marked with placidity and benevolence. Among his friends he is facetious and easy; but when with strangers, reserved and distant....
>
> As a legislator he is perhaps inferior to no man in his country. The faculty of close and accurate observation, by which he is distinguished, has enabled him to remark and treasure up every fact of political importance that has occurred since the organization of the American government, and the citizen, as well as the stranger, is often surprised at the minuteness of his historical details, the facility with which they are recalled, and the correctness and accuracy with which they are applied. With the various subjects immediately connected with politics he has made himself well acquainted, and such is the strength of his memory and the extent of his information, that the accuracy of his statements is never disputed....
>
> His object is more to convince and persuade by the force of reason than to play upon the mind by the fantastic embroidery and gaudy festoonings of fancy. His style of eloquence is plain, but bold and manly; replete with arguments and full of intelligence.... Facts form the basis of his reasoning. Without these his analysis is defective and his combinations and deductions often incorrect. His logic is not artificial, but natural, he abandons the formal divisions, non-essentials, moods and figures of logic to weaker minds, and adheres to the substantials of natural reason.

(Charles R. King, ed., *The Life and Correspondence of Rufus King*, Vol. 6 [New York: G. P. Putnam's Sons, 1894–1900], 183–185.

THE TEXT OF THE SPEECH

The text of Rufus King's entire speech is as follows:

The required arrangement [in the Treaty of Ghent] upon the subject of Indian pacification and Indian Boundary suggests an enquiry of what has been the practice in like cases between other nations. When the territorial limits are settled, as those of the U.S. and G.B. are, it is believed that in no instance of a like foreign interference in behalf of persons, in the situation of Indians, has occurred. No principle seems better understood, or more universally admitted than that the Dominion or Sovereignty of every nation is exclusive and co-extensive with its Territory. All within such limits whether men or things being subject to such Dominion.

Thus the Indian Tribes within the U.S. by different Compacts or Conventions have all admitted themselves to be under the Dominion of the United States. It is true that they are included within, not subject to their [the United States'] ordinary Jurisdiction, having their own laws, customs and government, which are acknowledged and allowed by the U.S. It is also true, that, according to these privileges, they may pass out of the U.S. into the territories of the neighbouring powers, and may allow other Indians of remote tribes to come into their cantons and hold intercourse with them. But their subordination is such that they may not enter into Conventions with the sovereign of a neighbouring territory; and it is an infringement of the Sovereignty of the U.S. for another sovereign to form Compacts or Conventions with them.

No such interference is known to have occurred. When France possessed Canada, and England the U.S., they made war and peace without stipulation concerning the Indians—except that in the Treaty of Utrecht [1713], provision is made by the XV Article thereof, that the Indians might pass and repass from the territory of one to that of the other—France engaging not to molest the 5 cantons of Indians [the Haudenosaunee], *subject to the Dominion of G.B.,* nor other nations of America who are friends to the same.

It may be true that the treatment of the Indians by the U.S. is inequitable and injurious as well to them, as to the character of the U.S.; but does this give a right to G.B. or any other foreign nation to interfere? Will not the sovereignty of the U.S. preclude such interference? They are responsible to the tribune of public opinion, and their reputation will be affected by this as by any other act of Injustice; but they are the sole keepers of their own reputation and rights, and from the very nature of sovereignty are not accountable to others.

The Spaniards wasted the population of their American Territories. The English have overrun and destroyed as well the governments as the inhabitants of the E. Indies. The Caribbee Islands, in modern times, have been some of them depopulated and the spared remnant of the Caribs, but a few years since, were removed entirely from the Islands on which they were born.

The Settlement of the Colonies, now the U.S., was by gradual encroachment upon the Indians, who by war and other causes arising from the society of the whites, have been, from numerous and populous tribes inhabiting the whole maritime frontier of the U.S., driven back during the colonial Govt. of G.B., in like manner as they have since been obliged still further to retire by the U.S. Much of hardship, of injustice, and not unfrequently of cruelty has been in this way inflicted upon persons in the circumstances of the Indians actually within the U.S.

But no foreign nation has ever claimed to interfere in favor of the Indians of So. America, or of those of the E. Indies, or of the inhabitants of the W. India Islands, or of the American Indians, while the territory of the U.S. belonged to G.B. or that of Canada to France. Why should G.B. now insert herself into affairs, for the good or ill direction whereof, she is in no manner responsible, and over which we have the exclusive power of decision? With what right could she make an alliance with Indians, who were under the dominion of the U.S.—or how does she derive a right to enter into stipulations with the U.S. respecting them? The Indians and the U.S. may, as they before have done, settle their own concerns; and it imports the safety of the U.S. to exclude the interference of G.B.—Indians *are not citizens of the U.S., but perpetual inhabitants living in Tribes independent of each other,* and possessing by occupancy title to the soil where they inhabit. Those natives west of the Mississippi are now, as they probably were at the discovery by Columbus, independent Tribes.

Discovery gave no dominion over the Indians, except in cases of conquest; for the sake of peace among the discoverers, it was established as a principle of Law between themselves, not against the native inhabitants, but against each other—a title capable of being consummated by possession. This title gave to the respective discoverers, the exclusive right to acquire the soil occupied by the natives and of establishing settlements upon it.

As between the discoverers and the natives, the relations between them remained to be regulated by themselves. The history of the Eng. discoverers, demonstrates that in regulating the relations between them and the native Tribes, the rights of the primitive Inhabitants were not overlooked, tho' they were somewhat impaired; *they were* considered to be *the rightful occupants of the soil, with a just claim to retain and use the same,* according to their own discretion. But their right to the soil, as independent nations, was diminished by the denial to the natives the power to dispose of the soil at will to whomsoever they pleased; it being assumed that in virtue of the Discovery, the discoverers acquired a title to the soil, subject to the Indian right of occupancy.

This principle seems to have been recognized throughout America from the earliest Discovery. Eng. derives her title by discover from the Cabots, who [beginning in 1497] discovered the continent of N.A., as far South as Virginia.

[Describing the Louisiana Purchase:] The country west of the Mississippi ceded by G.B. to France; of France south of the actual boundary of Canada ceded by Fr. to G.B.—after a cession by France to Spain and a retrocession by Spain to France of the territory west of the Mississippi; the latter power ceded the same to the U.S., who hold that country in full right, subject only to the Indian right of occupancy, the exclusive power to extinguish which is vested in the U.S.

They [the United States] hold that Discovery gives them the exclusive right to extinguish the Indian title of occupancy [on both the sides of the Mississippi,] by purchase or conquest—possessing such a degree of Sovereignty, as the rights of the natives will allow them to exercise, the U.S. have an absolute right to the soil, subject to the Indian right of occupancy, and also the absolute right to extinguish that right. This division includes a complete title to the soil either in the U.S. or the Indians. The sovereignty of the U.S. is therefore limited not absolute.

The claims of the U.S. have been established as far west as the Mississippi by the sword—beyond we have had no war few treaties. The limits of Conquest are prescribed by the conqueror; but humanity and justice call upon us to prescribe limits to conquest.

(Charles R. King, ed., *The Life and Correspondence of Rufus King*, Vol. 5 [New York: G .P .Putnam's Sons, 1894–1900], 550–553.)

Robert W. Venables, Ph.D., American Indian Program and Department of Rural Sociology, Cornell University, paper presented at Canandaigua, November 11 & 12, 1994.

NOTES

1. Edmond Atkin, *The Appalanchian Frontier: The Edmond Atkin Report and Plan of 1755*, ed. Wilbur R. Jacobs (Lincoln: University of Nebraska Press, 1967), 38.

2. Charles W. Eliot, ed., *American Historical Documents, 1000–1904*, in the series *The Harvard Classics* (New York: P. F. Collier & Son Corporation, 1910), 3.

3. Thomas Donaldson [Henry B. Carrington, and Timothy W. Jackson], United States Department of Commerce, Bureau of the Census. *Extra Census Bulletin. Indians. The Six Nations of New York* (1982; reprint with new introduction by Robert W. Venables, Ithaca, New York: Cornell University Press, 1995), 4.

4. Ibid., 3.

5. Ibid., 79.

6. Ibid.

7. Ibid., 3 and 229.

8. Eliot did not include the 1794 Jay Treaty. Eliot, *American Historical Documents*, 3.

9. Wilbur R. Jacobs, *Wilderness Politics and Indian Gifts: The Northern Colonial Frontier, 1748–1763* (1950; republication, Lincoln: University of Nebraska Press, 1966), 135, fn 121. Jacobs notes that the name was originally given to Washington's grandfather.

10. The analogy is not at all inappropriate. At the centennial "celebration" of the Sullivan campaign in 1869, one of the keynote speakers in Elmira, New York, was none other than General William Tecumseh Sherman, whose two speeches on that occasion reveal how he believed both the Sullivan campaign and the Civil War "purified the atmosphere...wherever men raise up their hands to oppose this great advancing tide of civilization, they must be swept aside, peaceably if possible, forcibly if we must."— General William Tecumseh Sherman, first speech at Elmira, August 29, 1879, in Frederick Cook, ed., *Journals of the Military Expedition of Major General John Sullivan Against the Six Nations of Indians in 1779 with Records of Centennial Celebrations* (Auburn, New York: Knapp, Peck & Thomson, 1887), 440.

11. Specifically, *Worcester v. Georgia* states: "The language used in treaties with the Indians should never be construed to their prejudice. If words be made use of which are susceptible of a more extended meaning than their plain import, as connected with the tenor of the treaty, they should be considered as used only in the latter sense. . . . How the words of the treaty were understood by this unlettered [i.e., pre-literate, not illiterate] people, rather than their critical meaning, should form the rule of construction." (*Worcester v. the State of Georgia* [315 U.S. 515, 1832], in Wilcomb E. Washburn, ed., *The American Indian and the United States: A Documentary History*, vol. 4 [Westport, Connecticut: Greenwood Press, 1973], 2637).

12. Charles J. Kappler, ed., *Indian Treaties* (1904; reprint, New York: Interland Publishing, 1972), 35.

13. Rufus King, 1815 speech before the U.S. Senate regarding the ratification of the Treaty of Ghent, in Rufus King, *The Life and Correspondence of Rufus King*, ed. Charles R. King, vol. 5 (New York: G. P. Putnam's Sons, 1894–1900), 553. King also sweepingly asserts that "the claims of the U.S. have been established as far west as the Mississippi by the sword." But the treaties with the Haudenosaunee after 1784 indicate that the Haudenosaunee were not a conquered people. Indeed, until the enforcement in 1796 of the 1794 Jay Treaty, Great Britain maintained Fort Niagara and Fort Oswego as forts and trading posts on Haudenosaunee lands. Samuel Flagg Bemis, *Jay's Treaty: A Study in Commerce and Diplomacy* (revised edition; New Haven: Yale University Press, 1962), 3–4.

14. Henry Clay, letter to John Gunter, June 6, 1831, *The Papers of Henry Clay*, ed. Robert Seager II, vol. 8 (Lexington: University of Kentucky Press, 1984), 358.

15. Ibid.

16. This perspective is detailed in Robert W. Venables, "Iroquois Environments and 'We the People of the United States,'" in *American Indian Environments,* eds. Christopher Vecsey and Robert W. Venables (Syracuse, New York: Syracuse University Press, 1980) 81–127, specifically at 108–9.

17. Treaty with the Crows at Fort Laramie, Dakota Territory, May 7, 1868, in Charles J. Kappler, ed., *Indian Affairs: Laws and Treaties,* vol. 2, *Treaties* (1904; reprint, New York: Interland Publishing, 1972), 1008.

18. Treaty with the Sioux...and Araphaho, April 29, 1868; Treaty with the Navaho, June 1, 1868; and Treaty with the Eastern Band Shoshoni and Bannock, July 3, 1868, in Ibid., 998, 1016, and 1021.

19. The fact that the Mohawk Nation is not mentioned specifically is neatly covered in Articles II, III, and IV by the phrases "the Six Nations," which clearly implies Mohawks, and the term "their Indian friends residing thereon and united with them."

20. William Savery, *A Journal of the Life, Travels, and Religious Labors of William Savery,* ed. Jonathan Evans (Philadelphia: published for the Friends' Bookstore, 1873), 124.

21. Ibid., 151.

22. An excellent summary of this balance between the Clearings and the Woods is related by Hazel W. Hertzberg, in a chapter she entitles "Patterns of Space: Forest and Clearing" in her *The Great Tree and the Longhouse: The Culture of the Iroquois* (New York: Macmillan, 1966), 23–34. Cf. William N. Fenton, "Northern Iroquoian Culture Patterns," in Bruce G. Trigger, ed., *Northeast: Volume 15 of the Handbook of North American Indians* (Washington, D.C.: Smithsonian Institution, 1978), 296–321; Matthew Dennis, *Cultivating a Landscape of Peace: Iroquois-European Encounters in Seventeenth Century America.* (Ithaca, New York: Cornell University Press, 1993), 105–11; and Elizabeth Tooker, "Women in Iroquois Society," in Michael K. Foster, Jack Campisi, and Marianne Mithun, eds., *Extending the Rafters: Interdisciplinary Approaches to Iroquoian Studies* (Albany, New York: State University of New York Press, 1984), 109–23.

23. Arthur C. Parker, in *The Constitution of the Five Nations* (Albany, New York: New York State Museum, 1916), 22.

24. Ibid., 22, fn 1.

25. Harmen Meyndertsz van den Bogaert, *A Journey into Mohawk and Oneida Country, 1634–1635,* trans. and ed. Charles T. Gehring and William A. Starna, with wordlist and linguistic notes by Gunther Michelson (Syracuse, New York: Syracuse University Press, 1988), 12.

26. This English translation is by Seth Newhouse, an Onondaga at the Six Nations Reserve in Ontario, Canada. The version quoted here was edited by the Seneca scholar Arthur C. Parker, in *The Constitution of the Five Nations* (Albany, New York: New York State Museum, 1916), 103. William N. Fenton [Willam N. Fenton, ed., *Parker on the Iroquois* (Syracuse, New York: Syracuse University Press, 1968), 38–47] notes that Newhouse had completed a draft in English as early as 1880. Fenton also notes that another version was later drawn up by a committee of Chiefs at Six Nations who rejected the Newhouse version. (*Cf.* Sally M. Weaver, "Seth Newhouse and the Grand River Confederacy at Mid-Nineteenth Century," in Michael K. Foster, Jack Campisi, and Marianne Mithun, eds., *Extending the Rafters: Interdisciplinary Approaches to Iroquoian Studies* (Albany, New York: State University of New York Press, 1984), 165–82). While Fenton discusses the differences and issues involving these two versions, both versions present similar concepts of the communal, Confederacy-wide hunting domain. The similar wording used by the committee of Chiefs is found in Duncan Campbell Scott, ed., "Traditional History of the Confederacy of the Six Nations, Prepared by a Committee of the Chiefs [at the Six Nations Reserve, Ontario, Canada]," in Royal Society of Canada, *Proceedings and Transactions of the Royal Society of Canada,* third series, vol.

5 (Ottawa: The Royal Society of Canada, 1912). Scott read the Chiefs' version at the Royal Society annual meeting in 1911. At page 228 of the *Proceedings,* the chiefs' version explanation appears:

> We shall only have one dish (or bowl) in which will be placed one beaver's tail and we shall all have a co-equal right to it, and there shall be no knife in it, for if there be a knife in it there will be danger that it might cut some one and blood would thereby be shed. (This one dish or bowl signifies that they will place their hunting grounds in one common and all have a co-equal right to hunt within its precin[c]ts; and the knife being prohibited from being placed into the dish or bowl signifies that all danger would be removed from shedding of blood by the people of these different Nations of the Confederacy caused by differences of the right of the hunting grounds, etc.)

The metaphor of sharing/eating the beaver's tail as a definition of territory was also used by Indians who were not members of the Iroquois Confederacy. The Jesuit Joseph Aubry, a Jesuit missionary among the Western Abenakis on the St. François River which drains into the St. Lawrence, described how the Abenakis used the term in 1723: "to eat the beaver's tail there,"—that means, "to pursue our Hunting, and make our abode there." Joseph Aubry to the Marquis de Vaudreuil, October 3, 1723, in Reuben Gold Thwaites, ed., *The Jesuit Relations and Allied Documents,* vol. 67 (Cleveland, Ohio: Burrows Brothers, 1896–1901), 128, 129.

27. William N. Fenton, "Northern Iroquoian Culture Patterns," in *Northeast: Volume 15 of the Handbook of North American Indians,* ed. Bruce G. Trigger, (Washington, D.C.: Smithsonian Institution, 1978), 296–97, 306–7, 309–12.

28. Harmen Meyndertsz van den Bogaert, *A Journey into Mohawk and Oneida Country, 1634–1635,* trans. and ed. Charles T. Gehring and William A. Starna, with wordlist and linguistic notes by Gunther Michelson (Syracuse, New York: Syracuse University Press, 1988), 6.

29. Jake Thomas, "Words That Come Before All Else," trans. Ronald LaFrance, in "Indian Roots of American Democracy," *Northeast Indian Quarterly* (Ithaca, New York: Cornell University American Indian Program, 1988), 2–3; and Jake Swamp, "Thanksgiving Address," in Jose Barreiro and Carol Cornelius, eds., "Knowledge of the Elders: The Iroquois Condolence Cane Tradition," *Northeast Indian Quarterly* (Ithaca, New York: Cornell University American Indian Program, 1991), 16–18.

30. Treaty of Canandaigua, Kappler, *Indian Treaties,* 35.

31. Matthew Dennis, *Cultivating a Landscape of Peace: Iroquois-European Encounters in Seventeenth Century America* (Ithaca, New York: Cornell University Press, 1993), 105–11; and Elizabeth Tooker, "Women in Iroquois Society" in Michael K. Foster, Jack Campisi, and Marianne Mithun, eds., *Extending the Rafters: Interdisciplinary Approaches to Iroquoian Studies* (Albany, New York: State University of New York Press, 1984), 119.

32. Guy Johnson, October 4, 1774, "Proclamation," in James Sullivan, et al., eds., *The Papers of Sir William Johnson,* vol. 13 (Albany, New York: University of the State of New York, 1921–1965), 683–84.

33. Samson Occom, "The Diary of Samson Occom," reprinted in Gaynell Stone, ed., *The History & Archaeology of the Montauk.,* 2d ed. (Stony Brook, New York: Suffolk County Archaeological Association, 1993), 250.

34. William N. Fenton, "Structure, Continuity, and Change in the Process of Iroquois Treaty Making"; Mary A. Druke, "Iroquois Treaties: Common Forms, Varying Interpretations"; Michael K. Foster, "Another Look at the Function of Wampum in Iroquois-White Councils"; and "Glossary of Figures of Speech in Iroquois Political Rhetoric," in Francis Jennings, ed., *The History and Culture of Iroquois Diplomacy* (Syracuse: Syracuse University Press, 1985), 3–36, 85–124.

35. Michael K. Foster, "Another Look at the Function of Wampum in Iroquois-White Councils," and "Glossary of Figures of Speech in Iroquois Political Rhetoric," in

Francis Jennings, ed., *The History and Culture of Iroquois Diplomacy* (Syracuse: Syracuse University Press, 1985), 99–124.

36. General Thomas Gage, letter to Sir William Johnson, 7 October 1772, in James Sullivan et al., eds., *The Papers of Sir William Johnson*, vol. 12 (Albany, New York: University of the State of New York, 1921–1965), 995.

37. "Treaty of Peace," September 3, 1783, in Henry Steele Commager, ed., *Documents of American History*, 9th ed. (Englewood Cliffs, New Jersey: Prentice-Hall, 1973), 117–18.

38. Treaty of Ghent, December 24, 1814, with ratifications February 17, 1815, in F. I. Israel, ed., *Major Peace Treaties of Modern History, 1648–1967*, vol. 2 (New York: Chelsea House Publications, 1967), 357.

39. "An Act to Provide for an Exchange of Land with the Indians Residing in any of the States or Territories, and for Their Removal West of the River Mississippi, May 28, 1830," in Wilcomb E. Washburn, ed., *The American Indian and the United States: A Documentary History*, vol. 3 (1973; reprint Westport, Connecticut: Greenwood Press, 1979), 2169.

40. *The Cherokee Nation v. the State of Georgia* (30 U.S. 1, 1831), in Wilcomb E. Washburn, ed., *The American Indian and the United States: A Documentary*, vol. 4 (1973; reprint Westport, Connecticut: Greenwood Press, 1979), 2556.

41. In Wilcomb E. Washburn, ed., *The American Indian and the United States: A Documentary*, vol. 4 (1973; reprint Westport, Connecticut: Greenwood Press, 1979), 2622.

42. The standard work on Rufus King is Robert Ernst, *Rufus King: American Federalist* (Chapel Hill: University of North Carolina Press, 1968).

43. Rufus King, speech in the United States Senate, 1815, in Charles R. King, ed., *The Life and Correspondence of Rufus King*, vol. 5 (New York: G. P. Putnam's Sons, 1894–1900), 553. The complete text of this speech, with this writer's commentary, is in an appendix to this report.

44. Robert Ernst, *Rufus King: American Federalist* (Chapel Hill, North Carolina: University of North Carolina Press, 1968), 53–54, 86, 93, 100–101, 217, 222, 291, 308, 361, 369–381, 405–412.

45. Rufus King, Speech in the United States Senate, 1815, in Charles R. King, ed., *The Life and Correspondence of Rufus King*, vol. 5 (New York: G. P. Putnam's Sons, 1894–1900), 549.

46. Ibid., 552.

47. Ibid.

48. Lord Dorchester at Quebec, August 15, 1791, Speech to the Confederated Indian Nations, Archives of Ontario, F47, A-1, letterbook 17.

49. Rufus King, Speech in the United States Senate, 1815, in Charles R. King, ed., *The Life and Correspondence of Rufus King*, vol. 5 (New York: G. P. Putnam's Sons, 1894–1900), 552–53.

50. Ibid., 553.

51. Rufus King, letter to Edward King, February 12, 1818, in Charles R. King, ed., *The Life and Correspondence of Rufus King*, vol. 6 (New York: G. P. Putnam's Sons, 1894–1900), 114–16.

52. Ibid., 115–16.

The Mohawk Nation & the 1794 Treaty of Canandaigua

Doug George-Kanentiio

Is there any more politically divided area on earth than the Mohawk community of Akwesasne? Located astride the St. Lawrence River where it absorbs the Adirondack-born Racquette and St. Regis Rivers, the region is marked by once-fertile soils, dozens of islands, and one of the largest freshwater marshes in North America. From its grounds archaeologists have extracted flint arrowheads, uncovered fire pits, and identified village sites that indicate continuous human occupation in the region dating back many thousands of years. This is hardly surprising to Akwesasne's contemporary residents, for they recall stories passed down through the generations of a time when the waters were full of fish and the forests were home to a wealth of animals ranging from meandering black bears to the majestic *wapiti* (elk).

The name Akwesasne refers to the drumming sound made by the male partridge as it marked territory or sought a mate beneath the branches of the skyscraping eastern white pines, trees which grew in abundance along the river banks to a height of over 200 feet. Besides expansive stands of pines, spruces, and cedars, there were also groves of sugar maples, oaks, beeches, hickory trees, ashes, and elms.

Added to the natural resources was the area's strategic position along the most important trade and travel route in the northeast. People transporting goods, such as furs from the continental interior or manufactured products from the east, used the St. Lawrence River as the principal highway of commerce. Military expeditions also used Akwesasne's waterways, as did Jesuit missionaries and intrepid explorers.

According to oral tradition, the Akwesasne region was once extensively populated by the ancestors of the Mohawk people. Village sites have been identified not only within the current boundaries of the reservation but also on islands to its immediate west and along rivers some distance into the foothills of the nearby Adirondack Mountains. More villages existed to the north of the St. Lawrence in what is now the province of Ontario.

After the initial contact with Europeans in the mid-sixteenth century, the overall Mohawk population experienced a significant decline, which was aggravated by decades of warfare with Indigenous nations to the north, east, west, and south. Compelled to retreat from their northern borders for tactical reasons, the original Mohawks of the Akwesasne area left to join their relatives in the Mohawk Valley some 175 miles to the south. There was, however, never any doubt as to their jurisdiction over the territory.

Across the river from Montreal the community of Kahnawake was founded around the year 1668 by a small band of Catholicized Oneidas; about two years later they were joined by some Mohawks. The community of Kanesatake (Oka) was established west of Montreal on the banks of the Ottawa River in 1721.

As the years passed Kahnawake expanded, with additional Mohawks making their way to the settlement. Within a generation it had become the largest of all Mohawk communities, as it began to play a vital role in the lucrative fur trade, which had come to dominate the economic lives of Native people throughout the northeast. With a growing population the residents of Kahnawake expanded their food-gathering activities to the north and south. Hunting parties entered the Adirondack and Laurentian Mountains in search of game, which supplemented the fields of corns, beans, and squash planted by the women next to the town.

In time, the Mohawks realized it would be impossible to provide an adequate diet for everyone, hence the decision to search for a new settlement site. Akwesasne, with all of its natural resources, seemed a natural choice. By the 1740s a number of Mohawk families already in the area were joined by their Kahnawake relatives, which in turn led to the founding of the Catholic mission in 1755, when the first Catholic priests visited the community. The priests named the mission after St. Francis Regis, a Jesuit priest from Lyon, France, who had expressed an interest in preaching his faith to the Iroquois but had died before coming to America.

While the heart of the Nation remained in the valley, other Mohawks decided they would prefer to distance themselves from the steady encroachment upon Native lands in that area. In addition, the Catholic missionaries had made considerable progress converting many Mohawks to the Christian faith, resulting in a decision by many individuals and families to relocate along the St. Lawrence. The Mohawks were once again establishing a firm, permanent presence along the Nation's northern boundary, and there was much interaction between the widely scattered Mohawk communities.

In the following years the settlements grew to include a sizable number of men capable of bearing arms. They first saw action during the so-called French and Indian War. The Mohawks were present when the English, with active Iroquois support, wrestled forts Niagara and Duquesne from the French before moving against Quebec and Montreal. There were instances during this conflict when Mohawks allied with the French encountered their cousins on the side of the English, a situation which usually compelled both sides to retreat.

With the French surrender of Canada, a primary threat to the westward expansion of the English colonies was removed. Left without adequate resources to prevent the intrusion of colonists onto territory in Kentucky, Ohio, Tennessee, Pennsylvania, and New York, the Native nations could not hope to stem the flow of land-hungry immigrants. Mohawks began to abandon their homes in the valley for the St. Lawrence, despite the assurances of English authorities, such as Sir William Johnson, that their government would take decisive steps to protect Iroquois territory. In response to Iroquois demands, the English government issued the Royal Proclamation of 1763 prohibiting settlement by Europeans west of the Allegheny Mountains. This was followed by the 1768 Treaty of Fort Stanwix between the Haudenosaunee Confederacy and Britain, which also affirmed Iroquois lands.

Conflict between a distant government in London and its independent-minded colonies was inevitable, given the need by the Crown for money to pay for its many wars, the lack of colonial representation in Parliament, and the attempt to frustrate the lucrative speculation in Native lands. The Iroquois saw the rebellion as less an assertion of natural rights than an effort to forge a nation whose wealth would be derived from Indigenous resources, primarily land. Despite this, they tried to sustain a policy of strict neutrality, even when they were confronted with demands by their Native allies in the midwest to enforce the Fort Stanwix Treaty and make use of their standing with the English government to remove the settlers.

By this time, the valley Mohawks found it impossible to respond collectively to a land incursion situation characterized by violence and corruption. The Mohawks were reduced to a few hundred individuals in the valley, surrounded by the farms and villages of German and English émigrés. The leadership of the Mohawk Nation realized it would be impossible to have these people evicted, so accommodations were made, including the selling of additional land.

The St. Lawrence Mohawks were not inclined to follow the suggestions of their distant valley relatives. Each community in the northern area formed its own governing entity, modeled after the traditional system of Clan Mothers and life Chiefs but holding authority only in its immediate area. There was a loose alliance of Catholic communities called the "Seven Nations of Canada" which met from time to time to debate issues of common concern. This group consisted of the Mohawks of Kahnawake, the Mohawks of Kanesatake, the Hurons of Lorette, the Abenakis of Odanak, the Nippissings of Oka, and the Oneida-Onondagas of Oswegatchie (near Ogdensburg, New York). The Akwesasne Mohawks were said to be "under the wing" of Kahnawake and did not assume a formal position with the Seven Nations until the Oswegatchie community was forced from its land by New York State in 1806. They subsequently removed to Akwesasne, where their descendants live today.

Despite the distances and differences, all Mohawks did acknowledge the Haudenosaunee Confederacy as the primary representative agency for the Iroquois. Delegates from the St. Lawrence Iroquois were often in attendance when the Grand Council was called into session at Onondaga or when the Haudenosaunee met with representatives from other nations.

During the American Revolution the Mohawks of the valley tried valiantly to secure neutrality, although their northern relatives were actively supporting the English. In August of 1775 the valley Mohawks secured a treaty with the colonies, which was meant to honor their status as nonbelligerents, only to have that agreement compromised when New York sent a military unit in 1776 to arrest Sir John Johnson, the British Indian agent, then residing in the home of his father. Alarmed by this breach, a group of Mohawks escorted Johnson from the valley and through the Adirondacks before finally reaching Akwesasne. After the war, Johnson joined other non-Native refugees in eastern Ontario. Called the "United Empire Loyalists," they populated the region north of Akwesasne and founded the town of Johnstown, later renamed Cornwall.

Little Abraham was the representative of the valley Mohawks most inclined towards peace. As the hostilities intensified, Abraham found himself at great odds with military commanders such as Joseph Brant, a Mohawk from the Canajoharie district, former secretary to Sir William Johnson and a noted exponent of the British Crown.

Although not one of the Confederate Nations ever made a formal declaration of war against the United States, Iroquois by the hundreds elected to pick up arms, mostly against the land-rapacious Americans. Of all regions affected by the Revolution no region suffered as greatly as New York State. In spite of its neutrality, the valley region in particular witnessed repeated invasions, guerrilla attacks, ambushes, crop burnings, and atrocities as the displaced loyalists and their Iroquois allies attacked the rebels.

In time, the few remaining Mohawks in the valley had little choice but to leave the region. Little Abraham died as a result of a prolonged imprisonment in Fort Niagara, ordered at the insistence of Joseph Brant, then a captain in the British army. The starving remnants clustered around Niagara, on Carleton Island at the eastern end of Lake Ontario or across the river from Kahnawake. Their homes were looted by their former neighbors, then confiscated by New York before being given to American refugees.

There was no doubt that the Iroquois were effective fighters in the war. Their skills as guides and woodsmen were highly prized by both English and American military leaders. The Iroquois played decisive roles in the battles of Oriskany and Saratoga, with some, particularly the Oneidas, enlisting outright in the U.S. Army. However, the majority of the Iroquois fighters fought against the rebels in defense of their homelands.

The Iroquois were to pay a high price for their efforts. At the conclusion of the war, which caught the Confederacy by surprise, the English government ceded their territory to the Americans. The Mohawks were left without any land base in the valley, while the lands of the other Nations were thrown to revenge-minded Americans.

The infant U.S. government did have a serious problem with the Native Nations in the Midwest that tempered its attachment to Iroquois territory. A much-reduced American army was not in a position to wage a prolonged war with a grand alliance of Native nations, so efforts were made to secure the neutrality of the Haudenosaunee Confederacy. Laws such as the 1790 Federal Non-Intercourse Act prohibiting individual states from engaging in land cession "treaties" with Indian nations were passed as a concession to the Confederacy. In 1794 the United States authorized a delegation to meet with the Grand Council at Canandaigua in part to address the concerns of the Iroquois while keeping the Confederacy from being tempted to join their western allies.

The Mohawks were represented at Canandaigua by Henry Young Brant. By that time, the Mohawk valley refugees had settled on lands given to them by the British Crown, north of Lake Ontario at a place called Deseronto as well as along the Grand River near the Niagara peninsula.

The split was caused in part by some of the Mohawks' unwillingness to live alongside Joseph Brant. At Akwesasne, Kahnawake, and Kanesatake, Brant was also a figure of considerable controversy. His rare trips to the St. Lawrence area commanded sufficient hostility as to require the captain to have an armed escort.

With the lack of a Mohawk Nation Council in the valley, its status and interests were held in trust by the Confederacy. Almost a century would pass before the Grand Council at Onondaga returned the Council fire to the Mohawks by acknowledging Akwesasne as the capital for the People of the Flint.

At the large Iroquois settlement along the Grand River the community continued to be governed by a traditional administration which was seen as an extension of the Confederacy rooted at Onondaga. Leadership was determined by Clan Mothers, sanctioned by the Clans and ratified by the national Council. All formal leaders held ancestral titles in accordance with Iroquois law.

While the negotiations leading to the signing of the Canandaigua Treaty were being held, Mohawks were present, although the actual treaty did not specifically cite them. The repeated references to the "Six Nations" clearly was designed to include all the Nations of the entire Confederacy, who were assured they would retain active possession of their lands along with exclusive jurisdiction over their citizens. The treaty also established a rule of law regarding the surrender of aboriginal lands to the United States. Individual states were denied the authority to usurp Native territory without federal participation and congressional sanction.

Since Canandaigua, the Mohawks have argued that they may claim its protection because it was an integral part of the Confederacy, even though its Council fire had been held by the Grand Council. Such a status is normal within the customs of the Haudenosaunee, which currently retains the national wampum, or "charter," of the Oneidas. The Treaty of Canandaigua has been cited in many instances, such as appeals by the Mohawks to the U.S. president in 1986 and 1989 to remove illegal gaming devices transported from Nevada to Akwesasne. The Mohawk Nation has also made reference to Canandaigua in its land claims against New York State.

Shortly after the enactment of the Treaty of Canandaigua, several groups convened to create the "Seven Nations Treaty" of 1796. As a result of this treaty, a small reservation was set aside for the "Indians at St. Regis" with annual annuities paid to those Mohawks who reside on the "U.S." side of the border. By virtue of this document, the "Seven Nations" had surrendered their territorial claims in northern New York.

The Mohawk Nation at Akwesasne maintains that this so-called Seven Nations Treaty does not apply to their Nation for several compelling reasons. First, the Nation is not mentioned nor alluded to in the document nor cited in the negotiations leading up to its signing. In addition, the Nation Council has determined that two of the signatories to that agreement were not Mohawk, one being an Anglo Revolutionary War veteran and one a citizen of the United States. In fact, the Mohawk Nation at Akwesasne was not, in 1796, a formal member of the so-called Seven Nations.

Also, when Joseph Brant signed the alleged "Mohawk Nation" treaty in 1797, he had long been a controversial figure in Iroquois life. Never selected as a traditional leader, his lack of status as a legitimate representative of a then-scattered Mohawk Nation did not prevent him from selling great stretches of Native territory along the Grand River (for his personal enrichment) as an "agent" for the Iroquois there. His assumptions of control extended to the ancient lands of the Mohawks, when he seemingly convinced New York State and U.S. officials that he had the power to enter into a treaty to extinguish Mohawk title to millions of acres.

Finally, the Mohawk Nation Council has challenged Brant's treaty as a cession in blatant violation of the Treaty of Canandaigua, since the Grand Council of the Confederacy retained the sovereign status of the Mohawks in trust and no Confederate delegate was present at the signing of the Brant treaty. The Mohawks on their own did not have the authority to enter into such a treaty.

Subsequent attachments of Native land included in the original reservation by New York in clear violation of federal law form the current basis for the Mohawk land claims in that region. Despite its lack of formal recognition in Albany or Washington, the Mohawk Nation Council continues its involvement in the affairs of the Haudenosaunee Confederacy as it presses for the full adherence to the Canandaigua Treaty. At forums before the United Nations or in the halls of Congress, the Mohawk Nation has joined its Iroquois brethren in insisting that the Treaty of Canandaigua was not only a United States acknowledgment of the Confederacy's status as an independent people but also a recognition of the Confederacy's right to the unimpeded "free use and enjoyment thereof" of its aboriginal lands.

Chief Lewis Farmer (Onondaga).
Photo © Helen M. Ellis

Who Owns Grand Island (Erie County, New York)?

Laurence M. Hauptman

In recent years, eastern Indian land claims based upon violations of the Federal Trade and Intercourse Acts have received much attention in historical and legal literature. The Seneca Indians, both the Seneca Nation of Indians and the Tonawanda Band of Senecas, have sizeable land claims to large chunks of western New York State. One such claim is to Grand Island, New York. Grand Island, which contains 17,385 acres of land and over 17,000 permanent non-Indian residents, is the main access route between two of New York State's major cities: Buffalo and Niagara Falls. The New York State Thruway Authority maintains the major road and bridges that connect the two cities. The island contains well-appointed suburban-style homes, a regional amusement park, two golf courses, access to two state parks, a sandy beach, hotels, and other tourist facilities. The author concludes that the Senecas still have title to Grand Island as suggested by New York's interest in buying the island in 1802–1815, the lack of the presence of a federal commissioner at the signing of the treaty of 1815 conveying the island to New York, Governor George Clinton's claim that New York had no jurisdiction in 1819, the failure of the United States Senate to ratify the 1815 accord, and the fact that the United States-Canadian boundary was not formally set at the time of the treaty.

Introduction

In recent years Iroquois Indian land claims have received much attention in the historical literature.[1] Most of the focus, however, has been on the Oneida, and, to a lesser extent, the Cayuga efforts at redress. Yet, the Seneca Indians—both the Tonawanda Band of Senecas and the Seneca Nation of Indians—also have sizeable land claims to large chunks of western New York State, claims largely ignored by state officials as well as by contemporary historians. The present article will

focus on one of these Seneca claims, namely their assertion of ownership of the islands in the Niagara River, most notably Grand Island, in
Erie County, New York.

Grand Island has been associated with Seneca Indian history since the
seventeenth century. Although centered from Canandaigua Lake westward to the Genesee Country prior to Euroamerican contact, the Senecas
expanded their influence and territory well westward and southward in
the middle decades of the seventeenth century. Between the late 1630s
and the mid-1670s, they were able to expand their territory perhaps as
much as threefold, defeating and absorbing other Iroquoian peoples. In
1638, they defeated the Wenros, who controlled the territory directly
west of the Genesee River to the Niagara River; in 1651, they defeated
the Neutrals, who occupied Grand Island and other islands in the
Niagara River; and, in 1657, they defeated the Eries, who occupied lands
south of the present city of Buffalo and lands along Lake Erie.[2] In defeating these and other Indian communities, they absorbed these diverse
peoples through an elaborate adoption process into a Seneca reality.

By the end of the seventeenth century, right through the French and
Indian War (Seven Years War), the Niagara River region was occupied
by Senecas, mostly in temporary fishing and hunting camps. Although
the Seneca resisted and opposed the growing European presence at
nearby Fort Niagara at Youngstown, New York, they increasingly
became dependent on this trade. According to ethnohistorian Donald H.
Kent, the Senecas filled the vacuum caused by the defeat of the three pre-
vious-mentioned Indian groups, located a temporary village at the
mouth of the Niagara River, negotiated with both the French and
English in this vicinity, worked in the employ of the French, from the
building of Fort Niagara in 1720 to the end of the French presence in
1759, and frequently traversed this region, crossing the Niagara River
onto the Ontario peninsula in their hunting pursuits.[3] According to one
local history, the Tonawanda Senecas continued to seek food sources
and hunt on Grand Island well into the nineteenth century.[4] Thus, it is
little wonder that the Indian Claims Commission in its Finding of Fact
in 1968 clearly indicated that the Niagara Frontier and the Niagara
River islands were Seneca Country, and that, from 1701 onward, both
the French and English dealt with the Seneca "as the owners and con-
trollers of the area."[5]

Today, Grand Island, which contains 17,385 acres and over 17,000
permanent non-Indian residents, is the main access route between two of
New York State's major cities: Buffalo and Niagara Falls. The New York
State Thruway Authority maintains the major road and bridges that
connect the two cities. The island contains well-appointed suburban-style
homes, a regional amusement park, two golf courses, access to two state
parks, a sandy beach, hotels, and other tourist facilities. Hence, the

Seneca land claim to Grand Island has far-reaching political and eco-
nomic implications. It should be noted and emphasized that, unlike
Connecticut, Maine, Massachusetts, Rhode Island, and South Carolina,
New York State has never settled an outstanding Indian land claim.

The Devil's Hole Massacre

In 1763, a group of Seneca including Guyasuta, an uncle of Handsome
Lake, the Seneca prophet, proposed driving the English out of the Iroquois
Country. These western Seneca centered at Chenussio (Geneseo), not the
Seneca nation as a whole, soon became part of the famous Indian uprising
known in history as "Pontiac's War" or "Pontiac's Conspiracy." Indeed, as
anthropologist Anthony F. C. Wallace has written, this contingent of
Seneca "struck perhaps the severest blows of the war, destroying the forts
at Venango, Le Boeuf, and Presqu'Isle and at Devil's Hole almost annihi-
lating two British detachments on the newly cut road along the cliff above
the whirlpool at Niagara Falls."[6] The Seneca war party of 500 warriors
ambushed a convoy of twenty-five horse and ox-drawn wagons containing
thirty-one British soldiers. When the company was soon reinforced by two
other companies composed of eighty more men, these new forces were
overwhelmed by the Seneca warriors. In all, seventy-two British soldiers
"lay dead on the trail, scalped and stripped of their clothing."[7]

After the collapse of Pontiac's War, the British authorities demanded
reparations for this "massacre." After summoning Senecas to Johnstown
in August, 1764, Sir William Johnson, the British Superintendent of
Indian Affairs exacted a price from the "Chenussio [Geneseo] Indians."
The cession of August 1764 came after a formal treaty of April 1764
that Johnson negotiated with the entire Seneca Nation after the French
and Indian and Pontiac's Wars:

> Preliminary Articles of Peace, Friendship and Alliance, entered
> into, between the English, and the Deputies sent from the whole
> Seneca Nation, by Sir William Johnson Bart His Majty's sole
> agent and superintendant of Indian Affairs for the Northern parts
> of North America, and Colonel of the Six United Nations their
> Allies and dependants ettc.[8]

In both the April and August agreements of 1764, Johnson specifically
served as the Crown's Agent, not as an individual land speculator. In the
accord of August 6, 1764, made by Johnson, article 5 specified the
islands in the Niagara River.[9]

This August 1764 "treaty" was a cession to the King of England by
a portion, not all, of the Senecas. When Sir William Johnson died in
1774, his will never mentioned Grand Island or other Niagara River

islands, proof that Johnson had subsequently transferred these lands to the Crown and that Great Britain's monarch had title to these lands, although Seneca occupancy of Grand Island continued.[10] As crown lands, not individual loyalist property, they were not subject to simple state legislative acts of confiscation which occurred in New York State during the American Revolution. Later, in 1790, the Cornplanter recalled the events surrounding the Seneca cession of 1764, when he was in council with President Washington in Philadelphia. Referring to Fort Niagara, Cornplanter maintained: "Sir William Johnson came and took that fort from the French; he became our Father and promised to take care of us and did so until you [Americans] were too strong for his King. To him we gave four miles round Niagara as a place of trade."[11]

THE EARLY IROQUOIS TREATY PERIOD, GRAND ISLAND, 1783–1794

In March 1783, the United States and Great Britain signed the Treaty of Paris ending the American Revolution. Although ambiguous, article II of the treaty appears to confirm United States jurisdiction of Grand Island:

> And that all Disputes which might arise in future on the Subject of the Boundaries of the said United States, may be prevented, it is hereby agreed and declared, that the following are & shall be their Boundaries, viz. . . . Thence along the middle of said River into Lake Ontario; through the Middle of said Lake until it strikes the Communication by Water between that Lake and Lake Erie; *thence along the middle of said Communication into Lake Erie, until it arrives at the Water Communication* between that Lake and Lake Huron.[12]

In the immediate aftermath of the American Revolution, the cession of 1764 involving Grand Island was alluded to by Joseph Brant, the Mohawk war chief with little authority at that time to speak for all of the Six Nations, including the Senecas on the American side of the British Canadian-United States border. In the state negotiations at Fort Stanwix on September 10, 1784, Governor George Clinton asked representatives of the Six Nations for lands "in the Vicinity of Niagara and Oswego" to establish and settle boundary lines.[13] Brant replied specifically making reference to the Niagara River cession to the Crown in 1764:

> Brothers! You have particularly expressed your Wish to have Lands at Niagara and Oswego, for the Accommodation of your ancient Settlement at those Places. We have formerly ceded some Lands to the Government of the late Colony of New York *for the Use of the King. This already belongs to You by the Treaty with Great Britain.*[14]

Yet, article III of the federal treaty of Fort Stanwix that followed on October 22, 1784 never mentioned the Niagara River islands, while defining the boundary between the United States and the Six Nations.[15] In the federal Iroquois treaty at Fort Harmar in 1789, there is also no specific reference or clear indication about the cession of 1764 or ownership of the islands in the Niagara River.[16] On December 16, 1786, New York State and Massachusetts, at a meeting at Hartford, Connecticut, settled their existing dispute over western lands, but once again did not mention the islands in the Niagara River.[17]

The famous Pickering Treaty (Treaty of Canandaigua) of November 11, 1794, with the Six Nations does make reference to the islands in the Niagara River.[18] Article III of the treaty specifies that the land of the "Seneka Nation" is bounded as follows:

> Beginning on Lake Ontario at the northwest corner of the land they sold to Oliver Phelps, the line runs westerly along the lake as far as Oyongwongyeh Creek at Johnson's landing place, about four miles eastward from the Fort of Niagara; thence southerly up that creek to its main fork then straight to the main fork of Stedman's Creek which empties into the Niagara River above Fort Schlosser and then onward from that fork continuing the same straight course to that river. *This line from the mouth of Oyongwongyeh Creek to the River Niagara above Fort Schlosser being the eastern boundary of a strip of land extending from the same line to Niagara River which the Seneca Nation ceded to the King of Great Britain at a treaty held about thirty years ago with Sir William Johnson,* then the line runs along the River Niagara to Lake Erie; then along Lake Erie to the northeast corner of a triangular piece of land which the United States conveyed to the State of Pennsylvania as by the President's patent dated the third day of March 1792, then due south to the northern boundary of that state; then due east to the southwest corner of the land sold by the Seneca Nation to Oliver Phelps and then north and northerly along the Phelps line to the place of beginning on Lake Ontario. Now the United States acknowledge all the land within the aforementioned boundaries to be the property of the Seneca Nation and the United States will never claim the same nor disturb the Seneca Nation nor any of the Six Nations or of their Indian friends residing thereon and united with them in the free use and enjoyment thereof but it shall remain theirs until they choose to sell the same to the people of the United States who have the right to purchase.[19]

In the most recent analysis of the Pickering Treaty, ethnohistorians Jack Campisi and William A. Starna throw light on this remarkable accord with the Six Nations, most directly the Senecas. They insisted that: (1) it secured for the United States whatever title the Six Nations had to the Ohio Valley; (2) it returned to the Senecas the land they had lost at Fort Stanwix in 1784; and (3) it secured by treaty, which seemed a stronger assurance than legislation to the Six Nations, their reservations in New York, laid out in state agreements. In many ways it resolved longstanding issues that had never been resolved between the Iroquois, most notably the Seneca, and the federal government at the end of the American Revolution. The treaty was an "unconditional affirmation by the United States of the Six Nations' reserved lands." With a recent end to a bloody war with the Indians of the Ohio Valley and a continuing and menacing British presence as close as Fort Niagara, Pickering's treaty was much more than other Indian-White accords, as ethnohistorians Starna and Campisi have brought out, "without a doubt, a treaty between sovereigns." In agreeing to their permanent cession of the Erie Triangle, and the Ohio Country claims, the Senecas were getting something much more valuable to them, namely federal confirmation of their primary lands in 1794 and federal protection from the lust of land companies and the speculators' state legislative allies. This treaty, then as now, "remains the primary basis for Iroquois assertions of sovereignty." Then as now its "clear and unequivocal language, and its explicit guarantees, however, have afforded little protection or comfort" to the Senecas and other Iroquois.[20]

In three specific pieces of correspondence, Pickering stated his awareness of the 1764 cession and believed the United States now (1794) had sovereignty over the islands.[21] This interpretation of the Pickering Treaty was also confirmed in the Indian Claims Commission's Opinion in 1968 which found that the Six Nations recognized American "interest in the southern strip and in the islands" of the Niagara by this 1794 accord, and that: "Any subsequent disposition of the lands by the Seneca would be under the protection of the Trade and Intercourse Act."[22] The former attorney for both the Seneca Nation and Tonawanda Seneca, George P. Decker, insisted that the Pickering Treaty operated to release the Niagara shore above Stedman's Creek, thereby receding Grand Island to the Senecas. Pickering's treaty, a unique accord, made promises of protection to the Senecas, "subject only to the new privileges expressly stipulated in favor of the United States by article 5 for land and water passageways and harbor accommodations."[23]

NEW YORK STATE'S EARLY EFFORTS AT SECURING TITLE TO
GRAND ISLAND, 1794–1812

New York State's continuous efforts to buy Grand Island and the other islands in the Niagara River from the Senecas—a further indication that the state did not have title to them—intensified in the years approaching the War of 1812. New York's questionable title was revealed in other ways. Despite an offer by land speculator John Livingston to buy these islands on February 4, 1793, no state action in this regard was taken.[24] The federal Treaty of Big Tree of 1797 and the federal treaties of 1802 did not deal with Grand Island or the other islands in the Niagara River.[25] In one of the 1802 treaties, the lands north of Buffalo Creek Reservation—the so-called "New York Reservation" lands—were ceded by the Senecas, but the treaty did *not* involve the Niagara River islands. By 1805, this shoreline cession was being laid out in lots; however, Grand Island was not.[26]

On March 19, 1802, the New York State Legislature authorized state officials to trade with the Senecas for a one-mile-wide strip along the Niagara River from Stedman's Farm northward including Black Rock, but did *not* specify acquisition of the Niagara River islands.[27] Despite this limited authorization, New York State officials and representatives of the Holland Land Company pushed for a larger Seneca land cession of the islands throughout the spring and early summer of 1802. Nevertheless, the Senecas, after the debacle at the Treaty of Big Tree in 1797 when they were dispossessed of much of their lands in western New York, refused to part with the islands, although they did finally agree to make a cession of the "New York Reservation," namely the shoreline. Red Jacket, the Seneca leader, addressing John Tayler, the commissioner on the part of the United States and later governor of New York State, and Governor George Clinton, specifically insisted:

> *We propose to sell you the whole tract, with the reservation however of all of the islands* [in the Niagara River]; the line to the edge of the water, but the use of the river to be free to you—We wish to reserve also the privilege of using the beach to encamp on, and wood to make fires, together with the uninterrupted use of the river for the purpose of fishing; And likewise the privilege of passing the bridge and the turnpike, when made, free from Toll, and of keeping a ferry service across the river—For the whole tract we ask $7500. We think this reasonable, and that in a few years it will refund you much more than this sum.[28]

The next day, New York State concluded a land transaction with the Senecas. The August 20, 1802, agreement had a federal commissioner (John Tayler) present as well as the governor of New York State (George

Clinton) and Seneca leaders (Red Jacket, Farmer's Brother, Young King, Pollard, and others) in attendance. This accord stated that the Indians "do sell, cede, release and quit-claim to the people of the State of New York, all that trust of land one mile wide on the Niagara River, extending from Buffalo to Stedman's Farm including Black Rock, *and bounded Westward by the shore or waters of said river.*"[29] Nowhere in the accord are the islands in the Niagara River specifically ceded. Importantly, the Senecas reserved the right to camp, fish, collect driftwood, and pass freely on bridges, on ferry, or by established boat service. Under this accord Jasper Parrish and Horatio Jones both received one mile square land cessions for their service. The legal giant Chancellor James Kent notarized the accord of August 20, 1802. The United States Senate approved this state agreement on December 30, 1802.[30]

Governor Daniel D. Tompkins of New York State clearly indicated his anxiety about the Niagara River islands and ill-defined nature of the United States-British Canada boundary under the 1783 Treaty of Paris in a letter to the U.S. Secretary of State on December 10, 1810.[31] On the same day, Governor Tompkins wrote a second letter to Congressman Peter B. Porter, chairman of the House Foreign Relations Committee, further reflecting his concern about the ambiguity of the Treaty of Paris of 1783. Tompkins, seeing war clouds on the horizon with Great Britain, reflected on the strategic and economic importance of these Great Lakes islands to both New York State and to the United States as a whole, and urged its final resolution by Congress.[32]

On March 8, 1811, the New York State Legislature specifically authorized the governor to purchase the islands in the Niagara River from the Senecas.[33] Governor Tompkins wrote Jasper Parrish, the sub-agent for the Seneca Indians, on April 11, 1811, attempting to facilitate negotiations with them for the purchase of the Niagara River.[34]

With a war with British Canada on the horizon, Tompkins' position on the Niagara River islands hardened by 1812. On February 12 he reported to the New York State Assembly Committee on Indian Affairs about a meeting he had had with a delegation of Seneca chiefs. Tompkins told the Assembly that in his estimation the Seneca cession to Sir William Johnson in 1764 and the 1794 Pickering Treaty with the Six Nations denied the Seneca claim to the islands and that the Niagara River islands belonged to New York, but that he was willing to pay the Senecas for the islands. He insisted that New York State had no legal obligation to pay the Senecas, but that state officials would do so in order to ensure friendship and amity with the Indians.[35] Yet, in the same report, Tompkins readily admitted: "The timber on Grand Isle, in Niagara River, *belonging to the Senecas* is some of the best in the vicinity."[36] The governor then revealed the increasing pressures on the Senecas caused by trespassers, namely timber strippers, on the island.[37]

Tompkins' hardened view stands in sharp contrast with Seneca words and actions related to Grand Island. On September 16, 1810, the Seneca Chief, Little Billy, addressed a Six Nations Council at Buffalo Creek, telling the Indians that Governor Tompkins had inquired about a Seneca land sale of Grand Island to Sir John Johnson. Little Billy claimed that he had held three meetings and interviewed the oldest chiefs about this matter. He insisted that there was "no recollection of any grant to Sir John [Johnson]. We view the islands as our own, and shall claim them." Little Billy recalled that Joseph Brant at Onondaga "produced a paper— 16 years since." Once again the oldest chiefs were consulted, but "[n]o one could tell anything about it." They then sent the paper back to Sir John Johnson.[38] Little Billy, addressing Erastus Granger, the federal Indian agent, further insisted: "We own all the islands. Do not wish at present to sell them, but remain as they are." Cornplanter reiterated Little Billy's sentiments to Granger: "He hopes the white people will not trespass on the islands and wishes me to prevent [them]."[39]

Seneca determination to hold this territory was manifest in other ways, especially when they rallied after a British-allied force of Mohawks from Canada threatened an invasion of Grand Island in July 1812. These Senecas soon after joined the American side in the War of 1812. Anthropologist Arthur C. Parker, himself of Seneca ancestry, claimed that Senecas of Neutral Indian Nation ancestry at that time had urged Iroquois alliance with the Americans since it meant not only war against the British and their allied Indians, but also "it meant the defence of the graves of their [Neutral] forefathers" on Grand Island.[40]

PETER BUELL PORTER

In order to fully understand the background to this Grand Island claim, how the Senecas were finally and illegally separated from their lands, and the complex forces at work that undermined the Indians' estate, it is necessary to introduce Peter Buell Porter, the most influential white man in western New York dealing with the Iroquois in the first three decades of the nineteenth century. He was also one of the great proponents of transportation, namely road and canal building, as well as national defense. On the surface, he presented himself as a friend of the Indians and served as the commander of Indian troops in wartime; however, in reality, he was one of the major state officials dispossessing the Senecas and, with it, one of the greatest promoters of the rise of western New York.[41]

Born in Salisbury, Connecticut, on August 14, 1773, Peter Buell Porter was the son of Colonel Joshua Porter, a leading land speculator of southern New England. His older brother Augustus was an associate of Oliver Phelps in his land jobbing activities and later served as a surveyor and agent for the Holland Land Company from the late 1790s onward. After Porter's graduation from Yale University in 1791, he attended law school at Litchfield, Connecticut. Subsequently, he moved to Canandaigua, New York, where he practiced law in this frontier community and entered local politics. Between 1797 and 1805, he held the position of clerk and, for one term, state assemblyman from Ontario County, which at the time included most of western New York. Although beginning his career as a Democratic Republican allied to Aaron Burr's Tammany Hall machine, Porter was the crass political opportunist, shifting affiliations frequently—from Burrite faction of the Democratic Republicans, to Clay "War Hawk," to Van Buren Bucktail, back to Democratic Republican during John Quincy Adams' administration, and then back to Clay and the Whigs.

In 1810, Porter moved to Black Rock, then a village at the mouth of the eastern branch of the Niagara River three miles north of the village of Buffalo. In the same year, he was appointed by Governor Daniel D. Tompkins as one of the seven original members of the New York State Board of Canal Commissioners. Because of the strategic location of the harbor at Black Rock, partly in Lake Erie and partly in the Niagara River, Porter lobbied for the village's becoming the end terminus for the planned Erie Canal. His arguments were aided by his gift for oratory and boundless confidence and his clear leadership skills. At Black Rock, Porter established his firm—Porter, Barton and Company—which soon held a monopoly in the transportation business in the portage area below Niagara Falls and Fort Schlosser above the falls. His firm also became the dominant force in the salt trade from central New York to Lake Ontario and throughout western New York. His salt depot at Black Rock was vast, and his firm handled from 15,000 to 18,000 barrels of salt until the British destroyed the operation during the War of 1812.[42] Even before the Erie Canal, the salt, that largely came from the environs of the present city of Syracuse, was carried by bateau along the Seneca, Oswego, and Oneida Rivers to Three-River Point, near Cicero, and then to Oswego. At Oswego, it was transshipped to larger lake craft to make the 160-mile water passage to Niagara. Since Porter and Barton had a monopoly at the Niagara portage between the lakes, the company made a fortune before the War of 1812 since two-thirds of the salt exported from Oswego in 1810 made its way to consumers in the Ohio River Valley.

Black Rock, the company's headquarters, was only a short distance from Lewiston, New York, the end terminus of the famous Ridge Road, the natural transportation link to the Genesee River Valley. With other salt supplies found around the Montezuma Marsh and near the Cayuga Reservation in the eastern Genesee region, the Ridge Road became antiquated with mule-team traffic, and other roads and turnpikes needed to be developed. The Porter brothers first pushed the development of a toll road between Utica and Canandaigua and sought state subsidies for the project. Subsequently, the Porters fervently promoted the development of a canal linking eastern and western New York. Hence it was no accident that in 1810 Porter was appointed as one of the original members of the New York State Board of Canal Commissioners.[43]

Porter's activities were also in land speculation. Because of his brother Augustus' early ties to the Holland Land Company, which at times hired him to undertake their surveys, Peter B. Porter had advanced knowledge and got in at the ground level on land purchases as well as in the company's plans for road development. When the Holland Land Company sold its preemptive right to Seneca lands to David A. Ogden in 1810, Porter soon became an associate of the new firm, the Ogden Land Company, and remained tied to its operations for the next fifteen years.

Prior to the War of 1812, Black Rock had largely outdistanced its rival Buffalo. Unlike Buffalo, the harbor at Black Rock was not impeded by sandbars, and dredging was not required to improve its existing natural advantages. Consequently, the village had grown as the principal harbor at the eastern end of Lake Erie. By 1811, the New York State Assembly had designated Black Rock as the port of entry for the eastern end of Lake Erie during the navigation season. Yet, its future was never completely secure in part because of the ever existing presence of British forces close by, by an ill-defined international boundary, and by existing Seneca claims to the islands in the Niagara River, most notably Grand Island, the massive land mass that divided the Niagara River into eastern and western branches and served as a buffer with British Canada. In the end, it was none of these factors—all overcome by Porter's ability—that led to Black Rock's demise, but rather the frontier boom town's physical limitations: seven-knot currents in the Niagara River, crippling winter ice jams which choked up the neck of the river, and dangers caused by frequent fog. By April 1853, the village, the former rival of Buffalo, was annexed by the city of Buffalo and disappeared as a separate entity. Thus, while Porter was able to deal with both the British and the Iroquois successfully from 1814 onward, he could never deal with the "lake effect," namely the vicissitudes of western New York's climate and weather conditions.[44]

From 1809 to 1813, Porter served in Congress. There he promoted the interests of transportation, unsuccessfully advocating federal moneys for roads, canals, and other internal improvements. It was during his two-term congressional career that he became a leader of the "War Hawks," which condemned British policies, especially their Orders in Council, which had pushed the United States to employ the embargo, nonintercourse, and nonimportation acts to ensure Britain's sovereignty and its rights to freedom of the seas; their impressment of American seamen into the British navy; and their actions stirring up the Indians on the Great Lakes-Ohio Valley frontier. On November 29, 1811, Porter's House Committee on Foreign Relations, less than three weeks after the Battle of Tippecanoe, reported that the time had come when the United States "must now tamely and quietly submit, or we must resist by those means which God has placed within our reach."[45] Hence, the leading political voice of western New York's interests, an area that bordered British Canada, was now calling for armed action. Besides, twisting the British lion's tail was always a successful political tactic that won votes for aspiring American politicians in non-Federalist districts. For New York State to arise as a major force in the new nation, its borders had to be secured. Porter's goal of making Black Rock and the Niagara region a major center of commerce could be achieved only by bringing permanent peace one way or another to the New York frontier.

Porter, who did not seek reelection to Congress in 1812, entered military service where he distinguished himself and furthered his political career. He became quartermaster general of New York while serving in the militia. In 1813, he was commissioned a brigadier general and authorized by General John Armstrong, the U.S. Secretary of War, to raise a brigade of volunteers and merge them with a corps of Iroquois Indians. Armstrong's response was conditioned by the fact that New York was one of the most exposed fronts of the war and the state's officials were in panic, faced with far superior British forces along a vast Canadian frontier boundary, inadequate roads to transport troops, and British control of the Great Lakes.[46]

After the British, with upwards of four hundred men, crossed the Niagara River and sacked and burned Black Rock in July 1813, then proceeded south to Buffalo, Porter regrouped the American forces, including one hundred Indian troops, and helped drive the British back across the Niagara River. Porter, going against orders, then began a series of unauthorized incursions into Canada that quickly won him fame in local political circles as the hero of the Niagara frontier. In July 1814, General Jacob Brown and his U.S. force of 3550 regular militia men, volunteers, and allied Indian warriors from New York, New Jersey, Pennsylvania, as well as New England, crossed the Niagara River and began a major assault on British Canada. On July 5, Brown's forces, in which Porter's contingent excelled, won a brilliant victory at the Battle of Chippawa against a British contingent that included Senecas and other Iroquois from the Six Nations Reserve along the Grand River. At the battlefield, Porter's corps of Indians suffered one of the heavier casualty rates: nine killed, four severely injured, four wounded, and ten missing in action. Two days after the Battle of Chippawa, Porter led a force that helped recapture Fort George. In September 1814, Porter's men helped raise the siege of Fort Erie, later resulting in his promotion to major general and a special citation by Congress.[47]

After the conclusion of the War of 1812, much of General Porter's attention was focused on rebuilding the devastated Niagara frontier, promoting the development of the Erie Canal, and fixing the international boundary between the United States and British Canada. As the great statesman-hero of the Niagara frontier with close ties to national leaders such as Henry Clay, Porter continued to dabble in politics, being reelected to Congress in 1814 and running unsuccessfully against De Witt Clinton for the governorship of New York State in 1817. A second defeat occurred in the same year when Buffalo was chosen as the western terminus of the Erie Canal instead of Porter's Black Rock, a decision that was not finalized until a meeting at the Eagle Tavern in Buffalo in 1822. Thus, for a five-year period, Porter pressed on with his campaign to make Black Rock the seat of commerce of western New York.

THE SENECA–NEW YORK STATE "TREATY" OF 1815

After the conclusion of the war and two months before the New York State-Seneca "treaty" in 1815 involving Grand Island, Governor Tompkins wrote Jasper Parrish about the details for negotiating an accord with the Indians. Tompkins once again insisted:

Although it is questionable whether these Indians have any title to the lands [islands in the Niagara River], yet I am willing (with a view to avoid any collisions, and to perpetuate the good understanding which at present exists between them & the government) to pay Twelve thousand dollars for the relinquishment of their right to all the Islands—This sum is however to cover all the incidental expenses attending the purchase.[48]

On September 12, 1815, New York, with Congressman Porter serving as a "state commissioner," made an accord with the Seneca Nation relative to the islands in the Niagara River. The Senecas, fearing the loss of their remaining ten reservations, reluctantly agreed to the cession made to their former military commander, General Porter. In return for $1000 payment and an annuity of $500 paid to the "Chiefs, Sachems and Warriors of the Seneca Nation of Indians," the Senecas, in this September 12, 1815, "treaty," "hereby sell, grant, convey and confirm to the people of the State of New York, all the islands in Niagara river between Lake Erie and Lake Ontario & within the jurisdiction of the United States. . . ." The Senecas also reserved "equal right and privileges with the citizens of the United States in hunting fishing and fowling in & upon the water on the Niagara river" as well as the right to camp on the islands.[49]

Besides General Porter, the New York delegation "purchasing" the islands included Governor Tompkins and state commissioners Henry

Crocheron, Samuel Younge, Rodger Skinner, Esec Cowan, Robert Tillotson, and Louis Livingston. Witnesses included Jasper Parrish, Horatio Jones, J.C. Brown, and L. Harrison. Among the Seneca signatories were Red Jacket, Little Billy, Colonel Pollard, Young King, Little Beard, and Captain Shongo.[50] With growing talk about concentrating Indian populations to the Allegany Reservation or removing the Iroquois altogether from the state, the Seneca strategy appeared to be agreeing to piecemeal cessions of lands in order to delay and prevent these two disasters from happening. With the hovering shadow of the planned Erie Canal, which they knew would bring rapid changes and white population growth, the Indians had little choice but to cede over the islands, lands that were less central to their cultural existence when compared to Buffalo Creek or their other reservation communities.

At this September 12, 1815, accord, no federal commissioner was present at the negotiations and treaty council. Even the federal agent, Erastus Granger, was not present. There are no federal instructions about this land deal. Two of the witnesses to this deal were sub-agent Jasper Parrish and interpreter Horatio Jones, who benefited significantly by Seneca land deals. Both Parrish and Jones, white men, had been captured as youths by the Senecas and had learned the Iroquoian languages and mores. They served as intermediaries between the white and Iroquois worlds from the late 1780s to the late 1820s. Jones received Seneca lands at the Little Beard's Reservation cession under one of the federal treaties with the Seneca in 1802, while Parrish was "allowed" to purchase the 131-acre Squaw Island, one of the islands in the Niagara River at the foot of the Black Rock rapids, after the "treaty" of 1815 by a special act of the New York State Legislature in 1816.[51] General Peter B. Porter, along with his brother Augustus, soon secured Goat Island as well as other river properties. The motivating factors for this New York land deal were: (1) to secure a safe western border with British Canada after the War of 1812; (2) to further the development of Black Rock, Porter's residence, as an important site for the proposed Erie Canal; and (3) to further individuals', land companies', and New York State's land interests.[52]

With the "extinguishment" of Seneca title in the illegal agreement of 1815, Porter now turned to a second piece of the puzzle, namely securing final British recognition of United States ownership of the islands in the Niagara River adjacent to Black Rock and the Niagara peninsula. The Treaty of Ghent, which ended the War of 1812 between the United States and Great Britain and was signed on December 24, 1814, had provided a mechanism for settling the controversy over ownership of the Niagara River islands.[53] The treaty was ratified by the U.S. Senate on February 17, 1815, and proclaimed by the President the next day. Article VI dealt with determining the meaning of the following language set forth in the Treaty of Paris of 1783: "along the middle of the said River into Lake Ontario, through the middle of said Lake until it strikes the communication by water between that Lake and Lake Erie thence along the middle of said communication into Lake Erie through the middle of said Lake until it arrives at the water communication into Lake Huron."[54] The treaty provided for the appointment of two commissioners, one from the United States and one from Great Britain, to meet first in Albany, and later elsewhere, to determine ownership, among other things, of "the several Islands lying within the said Rivers, Lakes & water communications" to be "in conformity with the true intent of the said Treaty of one thousand seven hundred eighty three."[55] What ultimately resulted was the creation of the "Joint Mixed Boundary Commission" which formally reported in 1822 on article VI of the treaty, but which continued in operation until December 24, 1827, determining a multitude of boundary issues stretching across the immense United States-British Canadian boundary.[56]

THE ANGLO-AMERICAN JOINT MIXED BOUNDARY COMMISSION, 1816–1822

On January 16, 1816, Porter, then serving as New York State's Secretary of State, received his official federal appointment to head the American delegation to the Joint Mixed Boundary Commission. Porter's appointment was a controversial one, leading to delays in his Senate confirmation, because some members of Congress questioned Porter's nomination due to the general's entrepreneurial activities and land speculation. Finally, on November 18, 1816, Porter was sworn in as boundary commissioner. Yet, throughout Porter's tenure as commissioner, charges of conflicts of interest were leveled at him, especially concerning his business ties to David A. Ogden, the founder of the Ogden Land Company.[57]

Besides Porter, the United States contingent on this Joint Mixed Boundary Commission included: Donald Fraser, the secretary; Samuel Hawkins, frequently at odds with Porter, and Major Joseph Delafield, who served as agents; Richard Delafield as draftsman; David P. Adams as astronomical surveyor; and William A. Bird, Porter's nephew and resident of Black Rock, and James Ferguson, as assistant surveyors. The British contingent was first headed by John Oglevie, who died in 1819, and later by Anthony Barclay. John Hale served as agent, David Thompson as surveyor, and Dr. John Bixby and Alexander Stevenson as assistant surveyors.[58] Joseph Delafield's memoir is the more complete and revealing account of Mohawk and Seneca discontent and their fears of losing their lands. The Senecas at Buffalo Creek in 1819 told the commission that the United States was supposed to protect them under the 1794 Pickering Treaty. Delafield was also rather frank about David A. Ogden's involvement in facilitating the workings of the Commission.[59]

From their initial meeting at Albany, New York, this Joint Mixed Boundary Commission set forth certain guidelines regarding their individual and collective responsibilities and procedures about settling controversies. Both groups of surveyors were to proceed on their own. The entire border region was to be twice surveyed trigonometrically. Both governments' commissioners had to agree after the calculations made by each group of surveyors were compared. Maps were to be prepared in the winter months, and four sets of maps were drawn for each section, one set for each government and one for each commissioner. From the outset, the commissioners agreed that no island would be divided in ownership even though by their rules the true boundary line would be the mid-distance from main shore to main shore. If the more sizeable part of an island lay in the United States' half of a body of water, the United States would receive the island; if it lay mostly on the Canadian side of the waterway, it went to British Canada.[60] Another way the commission ascertained ownership of the islands "was to determine the deepest channel or navigable channel as the case might be."[61]

The commissioners and their staffs dealt with issues related to the eastern regions, the St. Lawrence River and Lake Ontario, including making a decision negatively affecting Indians, the assignment of Mohawk-claimed territory (Barnhart and other islands in the St. Lawrence River). By June 1819, the Commission set their sights on the islands in the Niagara River. The Commission held meetings on Iris Island (Goat Island) on June 4 and on Navy Island on June 14, 1819. Soon after these meetings, Grand Island was "awarded" to the United States along with all the other islands in the Niagara River except Navy Island.[62]

Although astronomy and mathematics have been cited as the reasons for determining ownership of the islands, except for Navy Island, other forces were also at work. The presence of Porter, the leading entrepreneur of the Niagara frontier and first citizen of Black Rock as U.S. commissioner, obviously did not hurt American chances to secure these islands. Moreover, compromise, not confrontation, was the British goal in the aftermath of war. British policies in the post-War of 1812 were clearly designed to build amity and commerce with the United States, culminating in the Rush-Bagot Treaty of 1817 and British encouragement of John Quincy Adams' Monroe Doctrine of 1823. On June 18, 1822, the Joint Mixed Boundary Commission's report under article VI of the Treaty of Ghent was finalized and signed at Utica, New York. On July 24, 1822, Joseph Delafield formally presented this report to Secretary of State John Quincy Adams.[63]

Despite the conclusion of his service on the Joint Mixed Boundary Commission, Porter's personal and political fortunes did not wane. He remained, along with his brother Augustus, one of the richest men in the state, becoming involved in Niagara Falls water power development, while maintaining major land and shipping interests. He later served as Secretary of War, once again having a major impact on decisions affecting the Iroquois and other Indians, this time the extensive Seneca estate in the Genesee Valley. Although not a Jacksonian Democrat, he continued to push for frontier settlement and Indian removal beyond the Mississippi as well as the extension of state laws and jurisdiction over the Indians.[64]

The long career of the "Bashaw of the Border" who died in 1844 was largely marked by his strong advocacy of the interests of western New York. His involvement in state and federal politics was also marked by an era of Iroquois decline. Porter's life clearly shows the connections among transportation, land interests, national defense, and the unmaking of the Iroquois world in the early republic.

NEW YORK STATE "SECURES OWNERSHIP" OF GRAND ISLAND, 1819–1824

New York State began efforts to assert its jurisdiction over Grand Island long before the Joint Mixed Boundary Commission made its final report on article VI of the Treaty of Ghent. Governor De Witt Clinton wrote the New York State Senate on March 11, 1819, that a number of families had settled on Grand Island since 1815 who "disclaim the authority of the state" and who may inflict "great injury on the public property" as well as "become a serious annoyance to that part of the country." In his message, Clinton claimed that this situation on the island had worsened "since the extinguishment of the Indian title [by the state]" but admitted that the situation was largely the result *"because the jurisdiction over the islands in that river has not been settled under the treaty of Ghent."*[65] In response, on August 13, 1819, the New York State Legislature enacted "An Act Authorizing the Removal of Certain Intruders from Grand Island in the Niagara River."[66] On December 9, 1819, a state force of fifty-three men began carrying out the forced ejectment from the island of the "squatters." Seventy houses were burned and 150 men, women, and children were removed from the island in the five-day "mopping-up" operation that cost the state $568.99.[67]

Despite this state action, even the New York State Surveyor-General, Simeon De Witt, whose office carried out cartographic surveys and administered state lands from the time of his appointment in 1784 to the 1830s, and who was one of the major state officials dealing with the Iroquois in the period, wrote to Henry Livingston on April 15, 1820: "Nothing will probably be done with Grand Island in the Niagara River *till the boundary line between us and the British is settled which may not be done in some years from this."*[68]

In 1824, the state authorized a survey of Grand Island into farm lots. The next year, this survey was completed, and immediately these lots were put up for sale at the state's land office in Albany. New York State sold these lots for $76,230. The largest purchaser of these lots was Mordecai Noah, a leading American Jew, former consul general of the United States in Tunis, and editor of the *National Advocate*. Noah believed that the nearby Seneca and Tuscarora Indians were the lost tribes of Israel and that creating a "great" city of "Ararat" on Grand Island would lead to the redemption of the Jewish people and a Zion where his oppressed brethren could worship freely and live in peace. Despite the dream, Noah's experiment was to fail miserably.[69]

Conclusion

Several questions throw doubt on New York State's claim to Grand Island: (1) Why was New York State so interested in buying Grand Island from 1802 to 1815 if, as it claims, it already had title? (2) How could New York purchase or "confirm" its existing title to Grand Island in 1815 if the "treaty" with the Senecas had no federal commissioner present and was not ratified by the U.S. Senate? (3) Where was the federal trust responsibility carried out by President Madison and the War Department in 1815? (4) How could New York State claim or even "confirm" its existing title to Grand Island in 1815 when the island was still in dispute between the United States and British Canada until 1822? (5) How could the New York State Legislature pass a law extending its jurisdiction to the island if, at the same time, the governor of New York, the eminent De Witt Clinton, claimed in 1819 that the state had no jurisdiction? (6) How could the governor of New York claim title to Grand Island in 1819, yet suggest that the United States did not have jurisdiction at the time?

Although the history of Grand Island is, as we have seen, a convoluted one, the Senecas appear to still own it as well as other islands in the Niagara River. Without question, the strongest support for the Seneca position is found in the Indian Claims Commission Findings of Fact decided December 30, 1968:

> The Commission finds that the Seneca were granted, by the Treaty of 1794, a compensable interest in the southern strip and islands (but not the riverbed) described in the conveyance to New York of 1802 and 1815. The Trade and Intercourse Act of 1790 imposed an obligation on the United States to insure that the Seneca received a proper consideration for these cessions; any failure to meet this standard would amount to less than fair and honorable dealings under the Indian Claims Commission Act.[70]

Professor of History, State University of New York, New Paltz, Laurence M. Hauptman has authored twelve books on American Indians. He has served as an historical consultant to the Mashantucket Pequot, Oneida, and Seneca Indian Nations.

NOTES

1. *See, e.g.*, IROQUOIS LAND CLAIMS (Christopher Vecsey & William A. Starna eds., 1988).

2. *See generally* Robert W. Bingham, *The History of Grand Island, in* 36 NIAGARA FRONTIER MISCELLANY 59-78 (Robert W. Bingham ed., 1947); DANIEL K. RICHTER, THE ORDEAL OF THE LONGHOUSE 63, map (1992).

3. *See* Donald H. Kent, *Historical Report on the Niagara River and the Niagara River Strip to 1759, in* IROQUOIS INDIANS II: INDIAN CLAIMS COMMISSION 194-95 (1974).

4. *See* I HISTORY OF THE CITY OF BUFFALO AND ERIE COUNTY 429 (H. Perry Smith ed., 1884).

5. 20 IN D. CL. COMM. 177 at 194. Findings of Fact decided Dec. 30, 1968, *in* IROQUOIS INDIANS II: INDIAN CLAIMS COMMISSION 388 (1974).

6. ANTHONY F. C. WALLACE, THE DEATH AND REBIRTH OF THE SENECA 115-16 (1969).

7. *Id.*

8. 7 JOHN ROMEYN BRODHEAD, DOCUMENTS RELATIVE TO THE COLONIAL HISTORY OF THE STATE OF NEW YORK 621-23 (E. B. O'Callaghan et al. eds. 1856).

9. *See id.* at 652-53.

10. *See* Will of Sir William Johnson *in* 4 RECORD OF WILLS PROVED AT ALBANY, 1799-1829, at 35-48 (on file in the New York State Archives, Albany).

11. Cornplanter et al., Address Before the Great Councillor of the Thirteen Fires (Dec. 1790), *in American State Papers*, II INDIAN AFFAIRS 18-20 (Walter Lowrie & Matthew St. Claire eds., 1982).

12. Treaty of Paris, Sept. 3, 1783, U.S.-Gr. Brit., art. II, 8 Stat. 80-83 (emphasis added).

13. *See* I PROCEEDINGS OF THE COMMISSIONERS OF INDIAN AFFAIRS APPOINTED BY LAW FOR THE EXTINGUISHMENT OF INDIAN TITLES IN THE STATE OF NEW YORK 57 (Franklin B. Hough ed., 1861).

14. *Id.* at 61 (emphasis added).

15. *See* Oct. 22, 1784, art. III, 7 Stat. 15.

16. *See* Jan. 9, 1789, N.Y.-Mass., 7 Stat. 33.

17. *See* Assembly Doc. No. 51 (N.Y. 1889), known as JAMES W. WHIPPLE, THE WHIPPLE REPORT 107-08 (1889).

18. Nov. 11, 1794, 7 Stat. 44.

19. *Id.* at art. III (emphasis added).

20. *See generally* Jack Campisi & William A. Starna, *On the Road to Canandaigua: The Treaty of 1794*, 19 AM. INDIAN Q. 467 (1995).

21. *See* Letter from Timothy Pickering to Henry Knox (Nov. 12, 1794) regarding negotiations with the Six Nations (on file with the Massachusetts Historical Society); Letter from Timothy Pickering to Henry Knox (Dec. 26, 1794) (on file with the Massachusetts Historical Society); WILLIAM L. STONE, THE LIFE AND TIMES OF SA-GO-YE-WAT-HA, OR RED JACKET 475-77 (1866).

22. 20 IND. CL. COMM. 177, at 181. Opinion of the Commission, Dec. 30, 1968, *in* IROQUOIS INDIANS II: INDIAN CLAIMS COMMISSION 375 (1974).

23. *Diversion of Water from the Niagara River, Trace of Title of Seneca Indians: Hearings on* H.R. 2498, 11756, 16542, 16547, 16587 *Before the House Comm. on Foreign Affairs*, 63d Cong. 26-27 (1914) (statement of George P. Decker).

24. *See* CALENDAR OF N.Y. COLONIAL MANUSCRIPTS INDORSED LAND PAPERS 908 (E. B. O'Callaghan comp., 1987).

25. *See* Sept. 15, 1797, 7 Stat. 601; June 30, 1802, 17 Stat. 72; June 30, 1802, 7 Stat. 72; WHIPPLE, *supra* note 17, at 214-15.

26. *See* WHIPPLE, *supra* note 17, at 214-15. The treaty was approved by the Senate on December 31, 1802. I JOURNAL OF THE EXECUTIVE PROCEEDINGS OF THE SENATE 427-28 (1828). Map of Niagara Frontier showing shoreline subdivision lots, but Grand Island not subdivided (1805) (on file with the Buffalo and Erie County Historical Society).

27. *See* Act of Mar. 19, 1802. ch. XLVII, 1802 N.Y. Laws 73-75.

28. Red Jacket, Address to Governor of New York (Aug. 19, 1802) (on file with the New York State Archives) (emphasis added).

29. *See* WHIPPLE, *supra* note 17, at 214-25.

30. For the U.S. Senate's approval, see I JOURNAL OF THE EXECUTIVE PROCEEDINGS OF THE SENATE 427-28 (1828).

31. *See* 2 DANIEL D. TOMPKINS, PUBLIC PAPERS OF DANIEL D. TOMPKINS 303-09 (1902).

32. *See id.* at 339-40.

33. *See* Act of Mar. 8, 1811, ch. XXXVII, 1811 N.Y. Laws 50-51.

34. *See* TOMPKINS, *supra* note 31, at 480-81.

35. *See id.* at 483.

36. *Id.* (emphasis added).

37. *See id.*

38. *See* Erastus Granger, *Notes on Little Billy's Speech of September 16, 1810, in* RED AND WHITE ON THE NEW YORK FRONTIER 40 (Charles M. Snyder ed., 1978).

39. *Id.*

40. Arthur C. Parker, The Senecas in the War of 1812, Address Before the N.Y. State Historical Ass'n, *in* 15 PROCEEDINGS OF THE N.Y. STATE HISTORICAL ASS'N 83 (1916).

41. For an account of Porter's career, see generally Joseph A. Grande, The Political Career of Peter Buell Porter 1797-1829 (1971) (unpublished Ph.D. dissertation, Notre Dame University) (on file with University of Michigan); and I. Frank Mogavero, Peter Buell Porter: Citizen and Statesman (1950) (unpublished Ph.D. dissertation, University of Ottawa (Ontario) (on file with University of Ottawa). For information about the Porter family, especially Peter Buell Porter's brother Augustus, see BUFFALO HIST. SOC., VII PUBLICATIONS 229-322 (1904).

42. *See* WILLIAM W. CAMPBELL, THE LIFE AND WRITINGS OF DE WITT CLINTON 28 (1849).

43. *See* Marvin Rapp, The Port of Buffalo 1825-1880, at 13-14 (1947) (unpublished Ph.D. dissertation, Duke University) (on file with University of Michigan); CAMPBELL, *supra* note 42, at 122-23; Grande, *supra* note 41, at 7-8.

44. *See* Rapp, *supra* note 43, at 13-14.

45. ROBERT H. BROWN, THE REPUBLIC IN PERIL: 1812, at 55 (1964).

46. *See* Grande, *supra* note 41, at 62-69.

47. For an account of the Battle of Chippawa, see OFFICIAL LETTERS OF THE MILITARY AND NAVAL OFFICERS OF THE UNITED STATES DURING THE WAR WITH GREAT BRITAIN 368-73 (John Brannan comp., 1823).

48. Letter from Daniel D. Tompkins to Jasper Parrish (July 10, 1815) (on file with the Seneca Nation of Indians, Department of Justice).

49. WHIPPLE, *supra* note 17, at 211-13.

50. *See id.*

51. Both Jones and Parrish were involved in swindles of Seneca lands through 1826. For Jones's "reward in the 1797 to 1802 doings," see June 30, 1802, 7 Stat. 72. For Parrish's "payment" (Squaw Island) for the 1815 state "treaty," see Act of Apr. 5, 1816, ch. LXII, 1816 N.Y. Laws 65-66. *See also* Letter from Daniel D. Tompkins to N.Y. State Senate (Feb. 21, 1816) *in* DOCUMENTARY HISTORY OF THE IROQUOIS INDIANS (Francis Jennings et al. eds.).

52. For histories of the land companies which pressured the Senecas during this period, see PAUL DEMUND EVANS, THE HOLLAND LAND COMPANY (1924); A. M. SAKOLSKI, THE GREAT AMERICAN LAND BUBBLE (1932); WILLIAM CHAZANOF, JOSEPH ELLICOTT AND THE HOLLAND LAND COMPANY (1970); TURNER'S PIONEER HISTORY OF THE HOLLAND PURCHASE OF WESTERN NEW YORK (1850); WILLIAM WYCKOFF, THE DEVELOPER'S FRONTIER: THE MAKING OF THE WESTERN NEW YORK LANDSCAPE (1988).

Sovereignty & Treaty Rights— We Remember

G. PETER JEMISON

Nyaweh Skannoh gah gwe goh![1] We, the Haudenosaunee, have made many treaties, not only with the United States; we have also made them with other countries. Perhaps the first one that we made was with the Dutch. We used a wampum belt, that is, a Two Row Wampum Belt with two parallel lines on a field of white. We used wampum belts to help us commemorate our treaties. As you may know, wampum is made of shells, a combination of quahog and periwinkle, cut and made into tubular beads then strung into a belt. The purpose of the belt, to use an anthropological term, is as a mnemonic device for remembering important ideas, so that when the reader of the belt holds it in his hands, the idea literally comes from the belt.[2]

The two parallel lines signify this to us: on the one hand, we are traveling in our canoe, down the river of life, and traveling in a parallel line in their boat are those Europeans or Euro-Americans who are here on our land, Turtle Island. We are traveling along, and we have an agreement with one another. I am not going to get out of my canoe and get into your boat and try to steer it. And I am going to ask you not to get out of your boat and get into my canoe and try to steer it for me. We are going to allow one another to exist. We are going to accept the notion that we each are sovereign, that we have our own form of government and that you have yours. We have our own way of life, and you have yours, and we are not trying to convince you to be us. We are trying to convince you that, because of our long history here, we have a knowledge of this place where we live. Even now, we use this Two Row Wampum Belt as the basis for all treaties, as we have since that time.

The treaty I wish to discuss is the one that we commemorated on November 11, 1994. On that day we reached the 200th anniversary of a treaty that has been called the Pickering Treaty, and is also known as the Canandaigua Treaty.[3] We have, I believe, the oldest treaties in the United States.

We gathered on that eleventh day of November 1994 to polish the silver covenant chain of peace and friendship between our people and the

United States. While the chain has been strained, it has not been broken. We met to brighten the chain and renew the relationship between the Six Nations (the Haudenosaunee) and the people of the United States. Some six thousand people came to Canandaigua, New York, to commemorate that treaty. Indian and non-Indian people came together. It was one of the largest gatherings of Iroquois people I have seen in my lifetime.

Leading up to the commemoration, the *New York Times* ran an article on it,[4] the *Economist* magazine ran an article on it,[5] and National Public Radio aired a program on it.[6] Within a 300-mile radius, we had coverage of the commemoration of this treaty in all of the major papers.[7] I mention this because one of our efforts is to bring this treaty to a level of recognition by not only the federal but also the international community. We recognize that we have to take this treaty to an international forum if we are going to have these treaties actually recognized as the legal and binding documents that they are.

We invited President Clinton to come. The man George Washington sent to negotiate the original treaty was Timothy Pickering, his direct ambassador. He was Indian Commissioner (1790–1795), a special position that Washington had created. Since the treaty was made with George Washington, we invited Bill Clinton. President Clinton did not come. The highest level government representative attending was a United States House of Representatives member, Louise Slaughter. The assistant secretary for the Department of the Interior, Ada Deer, was also present. We had messages delivered by aides of Senator Alfonse D'Amato and Congressman Bill Paxon.

I want to give you a little of the background of this treaty, because most people are totally ignorant about it. Most people do not know what it means today. Incidentally, I know I am speaking the truth when I talk about this, because each time that I invited a federal representative to come to this commemoration, I had to explain the significance of the treaty. I cannot tell you how many times I faxed federal officials copies of the treaty—and how many times I faxed to the offices of House and Senate members copies of this treaty, which they had never seen.

In June, the chairman of the Canandaigua Treaty Committee, Vernon Jimerson, and I flew to Washington, D.C., and spent two entire days walking the halls of Congress to meet people. We were aided by Representative Louise Slaughter. She took us by the hand through the House and she took us to their dining room. During lunch we met all these representatives and explained that were going to commemorate this 200-year-old treaty in November. I told them, "We are here to personally invite you, and we are going to follow up by sending you a letter, letting you know that we mean it. We want you to come."

I cannot begin to tell you how many people did not know. They had never heard of this treaty. So think about that, those of you who vote.

When you elect these people, think about the kinds of people you are electing. Recognize that the people who make all of the decision for them are the aides that work for them. The aides are actually the people with whom we spent most of our time talking after we went through this process.

November 11, 1994, marked two hundred years of peace and friendship between the Six Nations of the Iroquois Confederacy and the United States government. It was a fitting time to celebrate the Treaty of Canandaigua.

The historic Canandaigua Treaty of 1794 was negotiated by the Six Nations that make up the Iroquois Confederacy: the Seneca, Cayuga, Onondaga, Oneida, Mohawk, and Tuscarora. These aboriginal occupants of lands surrounded by New York State collectively call themselves the Haudenosaunee. Some of the negotiators at the treaty Council were Farmer's Brother, Red Jacket, Little Billy, and Cornplanter, all Seneca. Fish Carrier, Cayuga, and Clear Sky represented the Onondaga.

To represent the United States, George Washington sent his commissioner, Colonel Timothy Pickering, accompanied by General Israel Chapin. For this reason, the treaty is also known as the Pickering Treaty. Quaker representatives, led by William Savery of Philadelphia, also attended the treaty Council. Trusted as mediators, they had been invited by the Seneca to look out for the Haudenosaunee interests, because in 1794 we had very few people who read English. The Quakers were peaceful people and they read English, so they were asked to come to ensure that what the United States representatives were saying in negotiations was in fact the same language that they wrote in the treaty.

Why the Need for a Treaty?

During the Revolutionary War, from 1775–1783, the Haudenosaunee initially had taken a position of neutrality; however, loyalty to the British Crown eventually induced some Mohawk and some Seneca to side against the thirteen colonies. Meanwhile, some Tuscarora and Oneida sided with the American colonies. After the war, the British pulled back to Canada, and the Haudenosaunee found its land opened to settlement by the American colonists. The result was frequent skirmishing with settlers along the Pennsylvania borders. In 1779, on orders of George Washington, Major General John Sullivan led an army into the Finger Lakes region of New York State. Though few lives were lost on either side, the campaign destroyed upwards of fifty Haudenosaunee towns, along with valuable croplands.[8]

There was a similar tension between the American settlers and the confederacy of Indian nations in the Ohio region of the northwest territories. These Indian nations included the Hurons, the Ottawas, the Miamis, the Shawnees, the Ojibwa, the Cherokees, the Delawares, the Potowatami, and the Wabash.[9] In 1791, the Northwest Confederacy won a stinging victory when it defeated the U.S. Army, commanded by Arthur Sinclair.[10]

Failure to include the interests of the Six Nations in the 1783 Treaty of Paris, which ended the Revolutionary War between the British and the United States, had resulted in the 1784 Treaty of Fort Stanwix.[11] In this treaty, warriors Joseph Brant of the Mohawk and Cornplanter of the Seneca conceded land in western New York State and in the Ohio Valley, land which the Six Nations were now trying to win back. Also, tension was growing with white settlers immigrating into the Finger Lakes regions of New York State.

George Washington recognized the urgency of a treaty between the Haudenosaunee and the United States. He concluded that if the Six Nations warriors joined the Northwest Confederacy, their combined strength could prove insurmountable for the now fifteen states. He persuaded Congress to raise taxes to double the size of the regular army to almost 6,000 men. It was a very unpopular decision. Taxation without representation was, of course, partly the reason for the Revolutionary War. Now the American army was at about 3,000, and there was an excise tax on whiskey, which many, many people wanted removed. However, with the notion that they had to double the army, they also would have to increase the whiskey tax. So there was a big debate taking place in the Congress in Philadelphia.[12] Eventually, Washington and Secretary of War Henry Knox won over opponents, and the army of the United States was increased to 6,000 men.

The Chosen Spot

General Israel Chapin called for a treaty Council to be held in Canandaigua, New York, during the fall of 1794. From their respective territories, the Haudenosaunee set out on foot for the "Chosen Spot," the heart of the Seneca Nation, in what is today known as Canandaigua, New York, on the north end of Canandaigua Lake.[13] William Savery, the Quaker representative, records that the Oneida were already in camp when the Quakers arrived on September 25.[14] Next to arrive were the Cayuga, Onondaga, and the Tuscarora. The 800 strong Senecas arrived last on October 14, and as Savery reported, in their ceremonial entrance they made a truly terrific and warlike appearance. All told, 1,600 Haudenosaunee assembled for the treaty.[15]

The pro-British Mohawks, who sent a single representative, stayed in Canada. Our people made temporary bark shelters in Canandaigua and sent out our hunters. Our hunters were taking as many as one hundred deer a day and bringing them back into camp to feed the people there. We were fishing and hunting waterfowl available at that time of the year—the ducks, geese, and other migratory birds that were on the lake.[16] Preliminary treaty negotiations centered around the restoration of the Iroquois land ceded in the Fort Stanwix Treaty.[17] As Pickering was taking the matter under consideration something unexpected happened.

The Western Indians Defeated

On October 27, a Tuscarora runner burst into camp with news that American General "Mad" Anthony Wayne had defeated the western Indians under the leadership of Little Turtle, with great loss of life on both sides.[18] News of the battle made it clear to the Six Nations that a peace agreement with the Fifteen Fires was in their best interest. They decided to continue negotiations with Colonel Pickering in good faith and to reach the best possible terms.[19]

Rust in the Chain

Red Jacket addressed the Council. "Brother, we the Sachems of the Six Nations will now tell our minds. The business of this treaty is to brighten the Chain of Friendship between us and the Fifteen Fires. We told you the other day it was but a small piece that was the occasion of the remaining rust in the Chain of Friendship."[20]

The so-called rust in the chain referred to two points of contention for the Haudenosaunee. One was the building of a four-mile-wide portage road that would run basically along the Niagara River from Fort Schlosser to Buffalo Creek; the other was the desire to run a four-mile-wide road between Cayuga Creek and Buffalo Creek. Literally, the settlers would cut down all the trees for four miles to make a wagon road to transport their goods. When you reach the Niagara River you cannot travel between Lake Ontario and Lake Erie on the Niagara River because of Niagara Falls, so you get out and you portage. The United States wanted to increase the size of that road. Our people objected to that notion.[21]

The two sides reached a negotiated settlement by which the Six Nations agreed to allow the wagon road between Lakes Erie and Ontario. Colonel Pickering agreed to relinquish the U.S. request for a similar road between Cayuga Creek and Buffalo Creek. Pickering concluded, "I confess, brothers, I expected that you would have agreed to my proposal, the Cayuga Creek and the Buffalo Creek road, but as this is not the case, I will give it up, only reserving the road from Fort Schlosser to Buffalo. There has been a mutual condescension which is the best way of settling business."[22] After carefully reviewing the articles of the Pickering Treaty, the Six Nations and the United States signed a document on November 11, 1794, creating the lasting peace and friendship between our two peoples.

The Treaty's Significance Today

Land issues dominated the 1794 Canandaigua treaty, and two hundred years later they remain equally critical to the Six Nations and our sixty thousand members of the Iroquois people who live both in the United States and in Canada. The treaty restored to the Six Nations land in western New York State that had been ceded by the Fort Stanwix Treaty. The Haudenosaunee also won recognition of their aboriginal land right and their sovereignty to govern and set laws as individual nations.23 In return, the Haudenosaunee recognized and continue to recognize the sovereignty of the United States government. That was the outcome of the treaty.

Although the treaty has been violated a number of times, it has never been broken. The Congress of the United States would have to abrogate that treaty in order for it to be broken, or we Six Nations would have to discontinue observance of that treaty in order to break it. One example of the violation of the treaty by the United States government occurred in 1964 with the construction of the Kinzua Dam on the Allegheny River. The dam flooded 9,000 acres of Seneca land on the Allegany Indian Reservation in western New York. This required our people to be relocated.[24] It required moving our cemeteries from that location to another location. It required us to extinguish the fire of our traditional Longhouse, to move it to another Longhouse, to build another fire there, and to hold the ceremony that is involved in the moving of a fire.

Following that, we were relocated on the Allegany Reservation in suburban-type communities at Steamburg and at Jimersontown, away from the rich valley where we always had lived. We saw the land inundated with water. Our elders wept openly, and, as a result of that, we lost many of them in the succeeding years. In 1964, the United States created the St. Lawrence Seaway, which destroyed great areas of the Mohawk Nation and caused untold destruction of traditional fishing grounds.

That would not be the worst of it. Reynolds and General Motors would build plants in that area and pollute the entire St. Lawrence River which, as you may know, flows from the south to the north. The result was that PCB levels in the water grew to some of the highest in the world—and they still are at this moment.[25] For example, through studies of snapping turtles, they found these incredibly elevated PCB levels, because snapping turtles remain embedded in the earth for long periods of time.

In 1967, the Niagara River project flooded the Tuscarora land, another violation of the Canandaigua Treaty of 1794. However, the Haudenosaunee continue to receive annually treaty cloth.[26] Today we may be the only Nations that still receive treaty cloth from the United

States. They give us a muslin cloth that now amounts to a yard and a quarter per person. We also receive a per capita payment going back to that Treaty of 1794. The United States annually provides some $4,500 for the distribution of cloth, which we have received continuously for two hundred years. The cloth began as a calico, and then it went to a cotton, and today it's a nearly worthless muslin. But I do not care if it gets to be the size of a postage stamp. It's the principle of the fact that the United States is still having to distribute that treaty cloth because of its obligations it made two hundred years ago.

I want to go further and point out that this treaty is still in place. To do that, I need to refer to an article that is in the treaty. Article 7 says:

> Lest the firm peace and friendship now established should be interrupted by the misconduct of individuals, the United States and the Six Nations agree that for injuries done by individuals on either side, no private revenge or retaliation shall take place, but instead, thereof, complaint shall be made by the party injured to the other, by the Six Nations or any of them to the President of the United States. Or the Superintendent by him appointed, and by the Superintendent or other persons appointed by the President, to the Principle Chiefs of the Six Nations or of the Nation to which the offender belongs, such prudent measures should then be pursued as shall be necessary to preserve our peace and friendship unbroken until the legislature or great Council of the United States shall make other equitable provisions for the purpose.[27]

I want to make it very clear that the treaty spells out which branch of the United States that we address when there is a violation of our treaty. It is not the Congress, it is *the President of the United States*, the executive branch, that we address.

> Onondaga Nation Chiefs mailed a letter to President George Bush in the spring of 1991, telling of a chemical dump discovered on the reservation. They said the toxic waste likely came from citizens of the United States, invoking Article 7 of the Treaty of Canandaigua. They asked him to see about cleaning up the mess. A year later the Federal Environmental Protection Agency removed 1,300 drums of solvents and billed a Delaware Chemical Company believed responsible.[28]

Every Iroquois nation took notice. By invoking Article 7, the Onondaga Chiefs forced the Environmental Protection Agency to act on a violation where there was evidence of chemical dumping on their territory. This is one more example of the Treaty's present importance.

At one particular time, I believe it was in March of 1990, a heli-copter flying over a Mohawk territory was shot at, allegedly by individuals who were living inside that territory.[29] The United States, seeking to resolve the issue, turned to the Mohawk Nation, and even-tually turned to the Haudenosaunee Grand Council for resolution. The United States resolved this issue by invoking Article 7 of the Canan-daigua Treaty. As recently as 1990, Article 7 was invoked again. The treaty was ratified by George Washington on January 21, 1795, and is still in place today.

Not too very long ago, J. Sheldon Fisher, his wife Lillian, and his son Doug went to Washington, D.C. They went to the National Archives and asked, "Can we see that original treaty?" It took a long time; they went through a bureaucratic maze. They had to sign their names about twelve times, at different points, as they penetrated the National Archives. My friend remarked, "It's like getting into Fort Knox." The guard said, "Oh no, it's worse than that." Eventually they were brought to a drawer by the guard; as he opened the combination lock and that drawer, they all had to sign their names one more time. He noted the exact time that that drawer opened, and then out came one of the copies of the original treaty. Sure enough, there it was, that treaty that was written in 1794 at Canandaigua. They had sewn a piece of paper to the top and they had sewn a piece of paper to the bottom. On the top it said what this treaty was about and on the bottom was sewn a piece with George Washing-ton's signature. Sure enough, there was the date, January 21, 1795, accompanying his signature and ratifying that treaty.

After a great deal of effort, the Fishers got the National Archives to photograph that copy of the treaty for us. At Canandaigua, on Novem-ber 11, 1994, we already had a life-sized photographic copy of that treaty, in addition to the other copy in the Ontario County Historical Society in Canandaigua. We compared the two of them, and yes, the language is the same. As William Savery said, two documents were made that day, November 11, 1794. We have the proof; we have both of them. So, no one can say they cannot find a copy of the treaty. And they cannot say they do not know what it says, because we have a copy of the one the United States preserves. We know where it is and we know what it says.

A conflict arose recently within the Seneca Nation of Indians between the elected President of the Nation, Dennis J. Bowen Sr., members of the Tribal Council, three program directors, and Ross John Sr. In a case filed in the New York Supreme Court, the defendant-inter-venors charged that President Bowen had overstepped his constitutional authority when he removed and appointed councilors and department heads of a Nation enterprise and some programs, following his election in November 1994. The defendants sought declaratory and injunctive relief against Bowen, and on that same day, Justice Vincent E. Doyle issued an *ex parte* order enjoining Bowen from:

a. removing or attempting to remove any of the plaintiffs from their seats on the Council of the Seneca Nation of Indians;
b. appointing or attempting to appoint anyone to replace any of the plaintiffs on the Council of the Seneca Nation of Indians;
c. removing or attempting to remove department heads, the Human Resource Director and the Seneca Gaming Enterprises CEO from their employment with the Seneca Nation of Indians;
d. removing or attempting to remove any other employees of the Nation who, pursuant to the Government Law or Human Resources Policies and Procedures Manual, can only be removed by the Council or department heads or commissioners; and
e. otherwise acting or continuing to act in a manner that impedes the meetings of the Council of the Seneca Nation of Indians.[30]

Justice Doyle failed to recognize the Seneca Nation of Indians Peacemakers Court and its authority in the nation's judicial matters. The judicial power of the nation is vested in two Peacemakers Courts, two Surrogate Courts, and the Court of Appeals. The Seneca Constitution provides that

the judicial power shall extend to all cases arising under [the] Constitution, the customs or laws of the nation, and to any case in which the Nation, a member of the Nation or any person or corporate entity residing on, or doing business on any of the Reservation shall be a party.[31]

President Bowen maintained that he could not accept the jurisdiction of the New York State Court because it was in direct violation of a Peacemakers Court decision, and he is, by Seneca Nation Constitution, obligated to uphold Seneca Nation law. President Bowen further maintained that the state court lacks jurisdiction over such matters, and that because of the Canandaigua Treaty of November 11, 1794, the Seneca Nation retains the right of self-government and exclusive jurisdiction over its internal matters. Mr. Bowen and his lawyers were successful in moving the case to federal court, and on February 27, 1995, federal District Judge Richard Arcara issued a preliminary injunction.[32]

Judge Arcara prohibited New York State courts from exercising jurisdiction in the case of *John v. Bowen,* and cited previous case law, including the United States Supreme Court decision *Oneida Indian Nation v. County of Oneida.*[33] Arcara stated:

> As these decisions show, under the Treaty of 1794 [Canandaigua Treaty], the Nation holds the right of self-government and retains exclusive jurisdiction over its internal affairs. This authority includes the power to interpret the Constitution and laws of the Nation in such matters, to determine the composition of the Council, and to resolve employment disputes involving employ-ees of the Nation's government. The State Court action at issue clearly implicates the internal affairs of the Nation. Indeed, it would be difficult to imagine a more intrusive intervention into the internal affairs of the Nation than that which results from the Orders issued by the State Court.[34]

The Peacemakers Court of the Seneca Nation found that Dennis Bowen Sr., then president of the Seneca Nation of Indians, acted legally within "unwritten customary and traditional rules or laws" in removing from office councilors who were appointed by the outgoing "lame duck" president, Barry Snyder. Further Councilors appointed "for the day" to conduct tribal business are not duly elected but rather serve *pro tempore* appointments. President Bowen was found to have the author-ity to align his administrative staff, Nation-appointed officials, salaried or otherwise, and employees pursuant to the reorganization activities of a new administration. These staff realignments are allowed the Peace-makers Court of the Seneca Nation of Indians, ruled on August 14, 1995, Honorable Joyce Gates, Acting Senior Peacemaker, and Ronald Patterson, Peacemaker, presiding.

The United States District Court Western District of New York in the *Bowen vs. Doyle* case entered a judgement filed on October 28, 1997. The document number 84 was signed by Rodney C. Early, Clerk, U.S. District Court, Western District of New York. The decision by the Court ordered and adjudged that the Court grants plaintiffs and plaintiffs intervenors' motion for summary judgment and denies the State and the State Defendants motion for summary judgment for the reasons stated in the Court's February 27, 1995, Decision and Order:

> Judgment is entered in favor of plaintiff and the plaintiff-intervenors
>
> 1. declaring that the State Defendants and the New York State Courts lack jurisdiction to adjudicate a civil controversy between Seneca Nation Members that solely concerns issues of tribal self-governanace as recognized and protected by the Treaty of November 11, 1794, 7 Stat. 44, and the Supremacy Clause of the

United States Constitution, and which is subject to adjudication in the courts of the Seneca Nation; and

2. permanently enjoining the State Defendants from asserting jurisdiction over the parties, the subject matter of the dispute, and the internal affairs of the Seneca Nation in the case captioned Ross L. John, Sr., et al. Dennis J. Bowen, Index No. 1994–12582.[36]

The shame is that three men had to die in the conflict that arose over these matters and that the aftermath has left families and former friends deeply divided.

This recent case is cited to illustrate the living nature of the Canandaigua Treaty and the importance of keeping it alive because clearly it legally defines our *sovereignty*.

Sovereignty has become a front page story in the *New York Times* on Sunday March 8, 1998, in an article entitled "New Prosperity Brings Conflict to Indian Country," when the writer Timothy Egan examined the implications of sovereignty. Storage of nuclear waste, gambling casinos, cigarette sales, and gasoline sales are economic initiatives that have sent state and congressional representatives into a rage trying to prevent or capitalize on American Indian economic initiatives. The headline on the second page of the article read, "A growing Prosperity Brings New Conflicts to Indian Country." The author picked one of the most extreme instances of sovereign authority when he detailed the Goshute Indians' plan, to "lease part of their reservation as the temporary storage ground for high-level civilian nuclear waste," to bring a "multimillion-dollar infusion" to their desert community in Utah.

In the view of John Echo Hawk, executive director of the Native American Rights Fund, a non-profit legal defense fund, "Tribal rights are finally being enforced because more and more tribes have the resources to have their own lawyers." Kevin Gover, a Pawnee, and the Assistant Secretary of the Interior Department, said in the article, "Sovereignty sounds like something from the King of England, but what it really boils down to is the right to make your own laws and be ruled by them." All over Indian country and not just in the west, this concept is being tested on a daily basis. It's not a new idea. The Haudenosaunee have for a thousand years lived by this principle, but now that money has entered the picture, a sharper focus has been drawn to the issue by non-Indian governmental officials and private businessmen competing with the nations.

NOTES

1. "I give thanks that all of you are well!"

2. The wampum was critical to the Iroquois diplomats in establishing channels of communications. For a discussion of the significance of the wampum belt *see* Robert A. Williams Jr., "Linking Arms Together: Multicultural Constitutionalism," in *A North American Indigenous Vision of Law and Peace*, 32 CAL. L. REV. 981 (1994) 1017–18.

3. Treaty of Canandaigua, November 11, 1794, U.S.–Six Nations (American Indians), Art. 7. Stat. 44. For an in-depth analysis of the 1794 Treaty of Canandaigua *see Cayuga Indian Nation v. Cuomo*, 758 F. Supp. 107 (N.Y. 1991).

4. Francis X. Clines, "On Sunday; Peace Prevails in an Offering of Simple Cloth," *New York Times*, 25 September 1994, sec. A, p. 39.

5. "Indian Affairs," *Economist*, 12 November 1994, 35.

6. "200th Anniversary of U.S.–Iroquois Treaty Commemorated." in "Morning Edition," National Public Radio broadcast, 12 November 1994.

7. "Bruno Supports Majority Leader," *Albany Times Union*, 12 November 1994, sec. B, p. 2; Francis X. Clines, "A Treaty of Strong Moral Fiber; Government Upholds 200-Year-Old Peace With Iroquois," *Houston Chronicle*, 26 September 1994, sec. A., p. 7; Agnes Palazzetti, "U.S.-Iroquois Treaty Marked by Ceremony, 4,000 Observe 200th Anniversary," *Buffalo News*, 12 November 1994, sec. Local, p. 1.

8. *See* William E. Coffer, *Phoenix: the Decline and Rebirth of the Indian People* (1979)52; Francis Jennings, *The Founders of America* (1993), 301–02; Wiley Sword, *President Washington's Indian War: the Struggle for the Old Northwest, 1790–1795* (1985) 134; Pat Dowell, "Touching on Wines & Waterfalls, Paperweights & Piglets," *Washington Post*, 30 July 1989, sec. E., p. 1.

9. Lewis H. Morgan, *League of the Iroquois* (1962), 9.

10. Clines, "On Sunday," sec. A., p. 39; "200th Anniversary of U.S.-Iroquois Treaty Commemorated," NPR, 12 November 1994.

11. Treaty of Fort Stanwix, October 22, 1784, U.A.–Six Nations (American Indians), Art. 7 Stat. 15.

12. *See* David P. Currie, *The Constitution in Congress: Substantive Issues in the First Congress, 1789–1791*, 61 U. CHI. L. REV. 775, 779 (1994).

13. William Savery, *A Journal of the Life, Travels, and Religious Labors of William Savery* (Philadelphia 1873), 90.

14. Ibid., 93.

15. Ibid., 103.

16. Ibid., 100.

17. *See* Treaty of Canandaigua, Nov. 11, 1794, U.S.-Six Nations (American Indians) Art. 7 Stat. 44 (modifying land boundaries established in the Fort Stanwix Treaty).

18. Harry E. Wildes, *Anthony Wayne: Trouble Shooter of the American Revolution* (1970), 422, 426.

19. Savery, *A Journal*, 118–19.

20. Ibid., 137.

21. Ibid., 138–39.

22. Ibid., 145–47.

23. Treaty of Canandaigua, Arts. 2–4.

24. Act of August 31, 1964, Pub. L. No. 88–553, 7, 1964 U.S.C.C.A.N. (78 Stat.) 738.

25. Anne McIlroy, "River in Crisis: St Lawrence Clean-Up Action Plan Drifting," *Ottowa Citizen*, 15 January 1995, sec. A. p. 5.

26. Treaty cloth represents honor of the agreement. The United States still delivers $4,500 worth of coarse white muslin to reservations every year. Robert L. Smith, "Celebrating Sovereignty: Members of the Six Nations Gather in Canandaigua Friday to Keep

Alive a Treaty Signed in the Era of George Washington that Endures in the Age of George Bush and Bill Clinton," *Syracuse Post-Standard,* (Syracuse, N.Y.), 10 November 1994, sec. B, p. 1.

27. Treaty of Canandaigua, Art. 7.

28. Smith, "Celebrating Sovereignty," sec. B., p. 1.

29. The Mohawk Nation denied that they were responsible for shots that injured a civilian doctor fired at a military helicopter on an emergency medical flight on 30 March 1990. As a result, both state police and the Mohawk Indians set up roadblocks. "N.Y. Standoff Continues," *Washington Post,* 1 April 1990. (PAGE NUMBER?) The standoff lasted eleven days when both sides agreed to an investigation of the helicopter incident. However, the FBI issued about fifteen arrest warrants charging Mohawks with impeding the investigation. Laurie Goodstein, "Sparks in the 'Land of the Flint,' Shooting Incident Spotlights Secrecy in Mohawk Splinter Group," *Washington Post,* 21 April 1990. (PAGE NUMBER?)

30. *John v. Bowen,* 12582 N.Y. Sup. Ct.

31. Seneca Constitution (1848).

32. *Bowen v. Doyle,* No. 95-CV-00438, W.D.N.Y. (1995).

33. *Oneida Indian Nation v. County of Oneida,* 414 U.S. 661, 671–72 (1974). (The treaty of 1794 reflects the United States' acknowledgment that certain territory is the property of the Seneca Nation, and that it shall remain theirs unless and until they choose otherwise; this treaty determines the nature of these rights and is the supreme law of the land.)

34. *Bowen v. Doyle,* No. 95-CV-00438, at 34, W.D.N.Y. (February 27, 1995) .

Lu Ann Jamieson (Tonawanda Seneca).
Photo © Helen M. Ellis.

"Broken Promises Come High"

JOY A. BILHARZ

The decades following World War II held both peril and promise for Indian peoples in the United States. Twenty-two of the twenty-five thousand Indian men in the armed forces (90 percent of whom enlisted) served on the front lines; nearly three hundred Indian women joined the nurses' corps, military auxiliaries, or the Red Cross; and fifty thousand men and women worked in war industries (Fixico 1986, 4–7). Their heroism and willingness to serve indicated to many that Indians should be assimilated into mainstream America; moreover, they assumed that Indians shared this goal. Termination of treaty relations was perceived as an end to government paternalism that would allow Indian peoples to take their rightful place within the American system.

The Bureau of Indian Affairs initiated a Voluntary Relocation Program in 1952 with the goal of relieving the crowding on some reservations by encouraging Indians to move to cities, where they were promised improved housing and job opportunities (Madigan 1956). Concomitantly, the Indian land base was reduced. In 1954, 3½ percent of all acreage held by Indian individuals was removed from trust or restricted status and passed into the hands of non-Indians (Washburn 1971, 147). The assumptions that an expanding economy would welcome Indian job seekers and that Indians wanted to leave reservations were unquestioned by government planners. But despite their record of valor in the recent war, anti-Indian prejudice sometimes ran high in urban areas, and finding decent jobs and housing was often difficult despite a booming economy.

Industrial expansion and suburban growth required increased power, and large-scale hydroelectric projects were the primary source. Traditionally, many tribes lived in river valleys; therefore, the construction of dams for electricity or flood control tended to have a more severe impact on Indian groups whose traditional homelands and/or reservations were flooded by the new reservoirs. The Pick-Sloan Plan, which began in 1944, led to the construction of four dams on the Missouri River and "caused more damage to Indian land than any other public works project in America" (Lawson 1982, xxi). Although it was aware of the impact the plan would have on Indian lands and that enactment of the plan would violate existing treaties, the Bureau of Indian Affairs raised no objections to it during congressional debate. Several groups, including the American Bar Association and the Daughters of the American Revolution, supported the Standing Rock Sioux who sent a delegation to Washington to protest their treatment by the corps. As a result of the problems created by the plan, Congress enacted legislation in September 1959 that made the army chief of engineers and the secretary of the interior responsible for negotiating settlements between Indians and the government. The plan also required payment for Indian relocations as well as lands in order to allow the re-establishment of community life (Lawson 1982, 65). For the most part, this came too late for the victims of the Pick-Sloan Plan.

Ironically, however, the Cold War between the United States and the Soviet Union provided moral advantages to Indian groups who were willing to challenge termination and the condemnation of their lands for hydroelectric projects. Despite the creation of the United Nations as a means of maintaining peace, the former World War II allies divided into two camps whose relations became increasingly hostile. With the spread of nuclear weapons and the ensuing arms race, Americans increasingly saw Communism as the personification of evil and the Soviet Union and China as its instruments. The spread of Communism through Eastern Europe created what Churchill referred to as an Iron Curtain, dividing (in the inflammatory language of the day) the forces of democracy in the west from godless Communism in the east.

The greatest tension was focused on the city of Berlin, divided among Soviet, French, British, and U.S. areas of occupation, but located within the Soviet-controlled German Democratic Republic. In 1948–49 when the Russians attempted to cut off NATO access to West Berlin by means of a blockade, the West responded with the Berlin airlift, flying in tons of supplies. Backed by the Marshall Plan, the economies of Western Europe began to recover from wartime losses; however, the Soviet Union, which had suffered the heaviest casualties, did not experience the same recovery, and this extended to those countries under Soviet domination. In the divided city of Berlin, people in the eastern sector increasingly fled to the western sector in search of jobs and freedom. Unable to staunch the flow of people, the East Germans and their Russian allies constructed the Berlin Wall in 1959, physically dividing the city with a concrete and barbed wire barrier manned by the military. Individuals who attempted to climb over or tunnel under were shot. The Russians were portrayed by the American media as people who consistently violated the most basic of human rights and whose word could not be trusted.

Hard line foreign policy was complemented by a hard line domestic policy in the United States. Senator Joseph McCarthy and the House Un-American Activities Committee sought to uncover and destroy anyone perceived as ever having had Communist sympathies, conveniently for-getting that the Communists had been U.S. allies in World War II. Thousands of lives and careers were ruined before the scourge of McCarthyism ran its course.

The construction of Kinzua Dam on the upper Allegheny River can best be understood within these national and international contexts.[1] Although the 179-foot-high dam was in Pennsylvania, its reservoir flooded all but 69 acres of the Cornplanter Grant in Pennsylvania and one-third of the 30,000-acre Allegany Reservation of the Seneca Nation of Indians in New York. These lands were guaranteed to the Senecas under the terms of the Canandaigua Treaty. They could be sold only by the consent of the Senecas, which meant, under the Seneca Constitution, the consent of three-quarters of the mothers of the Nation.

Since 1908 Pittsburgh industrialists had championed a series of dams on the Allegheny River as a means of encouraging growth and provid-ing flood control. Seneca opposition to dam construction that would imperil the Allegany Reservation and the Cornplanter Grant in Pennsyl-vania was voiced as early as 1927 (Hauptman 1986, 90), and the help of anthropologists was sought in 1935 (Cornplanter Tribe 1935, 66). During the administrations of Franklin Roosevelt, the Senecas had pow-erful allies in Aubrey Lawrence and C. C. Daniels in the Public Lands Division of the Department of Justice and Harold Ickes, secretary of the interior. Assistant Secretary of the Interior Oscar Chapman rejected plans for a dam in 1940, citing the treaty relationship between the Senecas and the federal government. Although under the Canandaigua Treaty Seneca land could be alienated with the approval of the Senecas, Chapman felt that even if the Seneca Nation agreed, Congress would need to pass a separate bill in recognition of the treaty relationship (Hauptman 1986, 93).

The inauguration of Dwight Eisenhower as president in 1953 sig-naled a reversal in the perspectives of both departments. Eisenhower's election was prompted more by his military record as commander of Allied Forces in Europe in World War II than by his political positions, and once in office he turned to military friends for advice. Two key pres-idential advisors had close ties to Pittsburgh. Major General John Bragdon, named to the post of special assistant for public works plan-ning on the White House staff, was a Pittsburgh native and former deputy chief of the Army Corps of Engineers. General Lucius Clay had served in the Pittsburgh district of the corps in the 1930s and been an early proponent of a dam. In advising the president, Bragdon came to rely almost exclusively on the opinions of the corps rather than seeking outside advice, with the result that the relationship between his office and the corps became, in the words of Laurence Hauptman (1986, 109) "near incestuous."

Flood control was also an important issue, especially after a record-setting flood in Pittsburgh in 1936 (Brant 1970, 43). Although industrialists had long desired a dam to maintain water levels and reduce the pollution which was rusting their boilers (Hauptman 1986, 92), public support could be more easily gathered for a project that protected people rather than raised profits. This safety concern became the primary justification for the construction of a dam. It is likely that fear the Cold War might turn hot also played a role in the army's push for a dam. This factor had been noted during World War II by Charles Congdon, a New York attorney, who stated, "I hear they are going to tie the Kinzua Dam to the Defense Program as a power necessity and build it right away, so that if someone drops a firecracker down the chute at Niagara they can make juice at Kinzua" (Deardorff Papers, Box 2). If there was concern about the vulnerability of hydroelectric power generation at Niagara Falls in 1941, the advent of intercontinental ballistic missiles, atomic warheads, and the Cold War in the 1950s served only to increase it.

The Cornplanter Grant had been given to Cornplanter, a Seneca war chief, in 1791 by the Supreme Executive Council of Pennsylvania in recognition of his aid in deterring tribes in the Ohio Valley from taking the warpath against the new United States. Subsequent court decisions determined that the land would be tax free as long as it was held by Cornplanter and his descendants. Unlike the Seneca Nation, where enrollment is based on matrilineal descent, the heirs of Cornplanter are reckoned bilaterally. Jack Ericson (2000), genealogist of the Cornplanter Descendants' Association, states that although most descendants today have some Seneca blood, not all are enrolled Senecas, and there are some enrolled Cayugas and Onondagas. The grant did not have federal recognition as a reservation, and its inhabitants had no organization other than kinship until they formed the Cornplanter Landowners' Corporation to fight the dam. Although the Cornplanter heirs coordinated some of their efforts with those of the Seneca Nation, the Seneca Nation was the primary focus of the effort to stop the construction of a dam that would flood its land. Later, failing in that effort, the Seneca Nation worked to gain the best possible settlement for its people. The Cornplanters' Descendants were left to deal with the corps as individual landowners.

The government of the Seneca Nation of Indians (SNI) is unusual in that it has jurisdiction over three reservations, Allegany, Cattaraugus, and Oil Spring,[2] in western New York. An executive branch, consisting of president, clerk, and treasurer, is elected on a biennial basis, as are half of the members of the Council. By tradition the president and treasurer are from different reservations, with each serving as the "head" of his or her reservation, and these change at each election. Therefore, although a team can hold the offices of treasurer and president through a series of elections, the individuals involved will switch offices every two years. Until the 1960s, the primary function of the SNI government was to sign oil, gas, gravel, and mineral leases and, as a result, it met only twice each year. Election was based on personality and family rather than on issues and ability. There was no government office and no permanent (or temporary!) employees.

By the mid-1950s it was clear to at least some Senecas that their lands would not be protected by the federal government on the basis of the Canandaigua Treaty. The government of the Seneca Nation of Indians (SNI) was clearly no match in organization or personnel for the federal bureaucracy, especially the extremely powerful Corps of Engineers.

What the Senecas did have to counter the federal threat was a relationship with the Philadelphia Yearly Meeting of Friends (Quakers) going back nearly two centuries. Unlike the nominal support given to the Sioux by the Daughters of the American Revolution and the American Bar Association, the Quakers mounted an offensive alongside the Senecas that was long-term, highly visible on a national level, and utilized powerful images which brought to the fore the moral significance of breaking a treaty in order to take Seneca land. Although this chapter focuses on the public relations campaign and use of the Canandaigua Treaty, it is important to note that the Quakers sent Walter Taylor and his family to the Allegany Reservation, where they stayed for several years. The presence of the Taylors was an important symbol to the Senecas that the Quakers, unlike the federal government, were standing by the commitments they had made to protect Seneca interests. Taylor served as editor of the *Kinzua Planning Newsletter*, worked on issues of housing and resettlement, and served as an informal advisor to the Cornplanters. Thirty years later, and though residents of British Columbia, the Taylors still frequently return to Allegany, where they are well loved and honored for their contributions to the dam fight.

The Quaker-Indian association has had a long history in the northeast, and relations between the two were generally good. George Fox, the founder of the Society of Friends, believed that the Indians would confirm his doctrine of "inner light" through discovery of their past or present illumination by Christ, which he believed would be found preserved in their traditional lore (James 1963, 91–93). The first formal organization to aid Indians was set up in 1756 by a member of the Philadelphia Yearly Meeting. Although the organization failed to gain official recognition by the Society, its membership formed the core of the Philadelphia Yearly Meeting Indian Affairs Committee set up in 1795 and made permanent the following year (Deardorff and Snyderman 1956, 585–586).

Nearly two hundred years later, this committee would be in charge of mobilizing the Quaker effort to aid the Seneca Nation. From the beginning of their involvement, the Quakers believed that land issues lay at the heart of Indian-Anglo hostilities, and unless the Indians felt secure in their land base peace would be ephemeral. Therefore, they adopted a pattern of attendance at treaties to ensure that the Indians were dealt with fairly. Within Pennsylvania, lieutenant governors could not treat with Indians unless Quakers were present to oversee the proceedings (James 1963, 179).

The relationship between the Quakers and the Senecas began in 1790 when Cornplanter, Big Tree, and Halftown traveled to Philadelphia to complain to President Washington about white inroads on Seneca lands. Washington guaranteed the Senecas' boundaries and control of their lands. Cornplanter requested that Washington recommend men who might serve as teachers at his settlement along the Allegheny River, and the president suggested the Quakers. Cornplanter's request appears in the minutes of the Philadelphia Yearly Meeting of 21 April 1791.

Encroachment on Seneca lands did not cease, and in an effort to keep Seneca warriors from joining the Ohio tribes on the warpath, Washington sent Timothy Pickering to meet with the Six Nations at Canandaigua. The Senecas requested the presence of the Quakers, so four Friends, three of whom kept diaries of the trip, departed Philadelphia for the eight-day journey to New York (Journal of James Emlen, pertaining to the treaty at Canandaigua, David Bacon's journal of the treaty at Canandaigua, in Jennings et al. 1984; Savery 1844). Bacon reports in his journal that although four Iroquois met secretly with the Quakers and asked for their advice on particular issues, the Quakers told them, "You have been informed we can take no part in war, which is one great reason why we cannot be active in civil Government and therefore are not capable of judging of all your grievances, especially as the transactions at Indian Treaties of late years have not fully come to our knowledge" (Jennings et al. 1984). The following day Farmer's Brother, after thanking the Friends for their willingness to attend the Canandaigua deliberations at the Indians' request, asked them to review the articles of the treaty that had just been signed and assure the Indians that they had not been deceived by themselves signing the treaty. William Savery reported (1844, 155) that the Friends could not agree to sign because the articles of the treaty confirmed rights to land taken by conquest and without just and adequate compensation. Neither Bacon nor Emlen mention the Indians' request.

Article 3 of the treaty states:

Now, the United States acknowledge all the land within the aforementioned boundaries, to be the property of the Seneka nation; and the United States will never claim the same, nor disturb the Seneka Nation, nor any of the Six Nations, or of their

Indian friends residing thereon and united with them, in the free use and enjoyment thereof; but it shall remain theirs, until they choose to sell the same to the people of the United States, who have the right to purchase.

The public campaign to halt construction of a dam that would flood Seneca land can best be traced through a survey of the *New York Times* from 1956 through 1967. While there was obviously more in-depth coverage in local newspapers, the *Times* best reflects the information available to the informed general public, whose support the Senecas were seeking. From the beginning, the primary focus was on the Canandaigua Treaty. Of the forty-eight articles, editorials, columns, and letters to the editor that appeared from 1956 through 1961, twenty-six made direct reference to the breaking of the treaty. The treaty received less attention in subsequent years (only twelve references in seventy-six items) due primarily to the fact that the dam had become a reality and the focus shifted to obtaining an adequate settlement for those whose homes and land were taken for the reservoir.

In appealing to the American public, the Senecas and their Quaker allies used a series of strategic political activities, media events, and manipulation of prevailing stereotypes to mobilize support. From the beginning it was apparent to them that public pressure on the president and members of Congress was the best way to prevent the taking of Indian land. There have been few successful attempts to stop involuntary relocations, in part because those targeted for removal are usually of low social and economic status with few, if any, political allies (Scudder and Colson 1982, 268). Only one American Indian group, the Fort McDowell Yavapai, was able to stop a dam that would have inundated its land, and this occurred in 1977, long after the Kinzua experience.

As previously noted, Quaker aid to the Allegany Senecas was of a practical as well as symbolic nature. It was a Quaker who suggested to Seneca president Cornelius Seneca that Arthur D. Morgan, former head of the Tennessee Valley Authority and longtime opponent of the Corps of Engineers, be recruited to spearhead an effort to demonstrate the engineering difficulties of the proposed dam. Even though he had never heard of the Senecas (Morgan 1971, 317), Morgan joined the effort, and he and colleague Barton Jones developed several alternatives to the location of the dam which would have prevented any taking of Seneca land and kept the Canandaigua Treaty intact. Morgan and Jones demonstrated that other locations would provide improved flood control for Pittsburgh and other Allegheny River communities and produce more power, but would force the relocation of more people and be more costly (Hauptman 1986, 113). Although these options were not accepted by the corps, Morgan's status was such that they could not be dismissed out of hand. Even though ultimately unsuccessful, Morgan and Jones were critical in buying time for the Senecas to rally support. Many organizations went on record as supporting the Senecas, among them the Indian Rights Association, the Indian Committees of the Philadelphia and New York Yearly Meetings, the Six Nations Confederacy, the Councils of the Cherokee and Oneida Nations, the National Congress of American Indians (NCAI), the American Civil Liberties Union (ACLU), and the American Indian Chicago Conference. Although the Annual Conference on Iroquois Research did not publicly oppose Kinzua Dam, its founder, William N. Fenton, wrote an open letter (1960) to Congressman James Haley (D–FL), chair of the House Subcommittee on Indian Affairs. This letter is probably the most poignant and precise of all the public statements about Kinzua Dam (Bilharz 1998, 56). Members of these organizations also participated in letter-writing campaigns and used other back channels to attempt to influence congressional opinion.

The stereotypical Indian in the American mind was the Plains warrior of the mid to late nineteenth century, and the Senecas adopted this image despite the fact that feathered war bonnets were far removed from the Seneca *gastoweh* with its single feather. Photographs of Longhouse leader Harry Watt and Abner Jimerson in beaded buckskins and plains war bonnets in front of the dam construction site (in Hauptman 1986, 116), although bizarre to Seneca eyes, struck a resonant chord in the general public. It had the same effect on legislators. George Heron, president or treasurer of the Seneca Nation during much of the Kinzua era, told me that when he went to Washington to lobby members of Congress dressed in his usual clothing he was roundly ignored or politely put off to an aide. Realizing the power of the Plains image, he returned wearing a war bonnet, only to find that congressmen were eager to pose for pictures with him and grant him an audience. Whether they were more receptive to what he had to say is unknown, but the manipulation of symbols was critical to gaining a hearing.

On May 24, 1957, the *New York Times* ran a brief article that reflects the myths and stereotypes used by the Senecas and the media. A picture shows Cornelius Seneca "studying" the Canandaigua Treaty at the National Archives. Seneca is wearing a Plains feather headdress and is identified as the "Chief." The article further states that the treaty was signed by George Washington. None of these is correct. The clothing is culturally and temporally wrong; Seneca was president of the Seneca Nation of Indians; the original treaty was signed by Timothy Pickering. Washington's signature, witnessed by Edmund Randolph of the Department of State, appears on the ratification statement dated January 25, 1795, following the advice and consent of the Senate. His signature, therefore, is not a pledge of his personal honor, but rather of his position as president, committing the United States to uphold the treaty.

Basil Williams (Seneca) wearing Plains style headdress, 1961. Photo courtesy of George Heron.

However, the image of Seneca was a powerful one, evoking positive images of Indians and invoking the mythology of George Washington, who never told a lie. If Washington promised that Seneca lands were to be inviolate, should Congress turn the first president into a liar by unilaterally breaking the Canandaigua Treaty?

Washington not only is important to U.S. political mythology but also plays a role in the Handsome Lake religion, founded by Cornplanter's half-brother, who was visited by representatives of the Creator on the Cornplanter Grant beginning in 1799. In his second vision, Handsome Lake was taken on a sky journey and shown heaven and hell. He encountered Washington, halfway to heaven, sitting on his porch and representing the good white man who guaranteed Indian lands at Canandaigua (Wallace 1969, 244).

Washington's signature was critical in the public relations campaign, because it brought to the foreground the issue of honesty, one issue on which the United States was criticizing the Soviet Union. Ten of twenty-three articles in the *Times* that discuss the treaty state that Washington signed it. These are, however, news service (Associated Press or United Press International) articles; the columns by Brooks Atkinson and the *Times'* own editorials never make the claim. Atkinson and the editorial writers refer to the treaty as signed during the administration of Washington or by Washington's deputy. The distinction was lost on most Americans and it was not in the best interests of the Senecas to correct the misstatements of others.

The first of eight *Times* editorials on the Senecas (four of which deal specifically with the treaty) appeared on Washington's birthday in 1961 and was entitled "As Long as the River Flows." Of course this phrase does not appear in the treaty, but again it evokes potent images of broken treaties and the belief of most Americans that treaties cannot be broken. In the same vein is the song about the Senecas and Kinzua Dam made popular by Johnny Cash, "As Long As the Grass Shall Grow" (LaFarge 1964). Cash was later adopted by the Turtle Clan in recognition of his contribution. Basil Williams, Seneca Nation president, also used Washington's birthday to again request President Kennedy to investigate the alternatives to Kinzua Dam proposed by Arthur Morgan.

The most constant national opposition to the dam was voiced by Brooks Atkinson, whose "Critic at Large" column ran daily in the *Times*. On October 25, 1962, he met with SNI president George Heron, Walter Taylor, and Sidney Carney, the Choctaw representative of the Bureau of Indian Affairs, who had also moved his family to the Allegany Reservation in order to help with the relocation. Following this meeting, although primarily a theater critic, Atkinson wrote the first of eleven columns supporting the Senecas and dealt specifically with the Canandaigua Treaty in seven of them. The titles of his articles left no doubt as to his position: "Proposed Allegheny River Dam Brings To Mind 1794 Treaty With Seneca Indians" (February 17, 1961), "Proposed Dam That Would Violate Treaty With The Senecas Poses Moral Question" (April 21, 1961), "Quakers, Too, Question Need For Breaking Seneca Treaty In Flood-Control Project" (June 9, 1961), "Construction On Kinzua Dam: A Case Of U.S. Morality Losing To Expediency: (September 5, 1961), "Kinzua Dam On Senecan [sic] Lands Breaks The Word Of Washington And Jefferson" (February 27, 1961), "Government Is Making Bland Amends To Senecas After Breaking Treaty" (July 17, 1962), "Quaker Journal Of 1794 Vividly Recalls Life In The Seneca Indian Nation" (July 30, 1964).

In addition to recruiting engineers and reporters to their cause, the Senecas and their Quaker allies also engaged in activities designed to draw attention to the Kinzua issue. In August of 1961, sixteen Quakers from New York and Philadelphia, sponsored by the Treaty of 1794 Committee, began a silent vigil at the dam site, which continued through Labor Day. They erected signs along Route 59 that said: "Kinzua Vigil. At this spot the Treaty of 1794 is being broken. An impartial study of the alternative would save it. Stop for literature." The literature included the Quaker booklet (Philadelphia Yearly Meeting of Friends, 1961) outlining the case against the dam and torn copies of the treaty. Although contemporary news reports state that few motorists stopped, the protest received important media coverage. Not surprisingly, some of the demonstrators wore Plains headdresses.

The Senecas also took the opportunity of American Indian Day, proclaimed by New York Governor Nelson Rockefeller as September 15, 1962, for a motorcade to the old Quaker school at Tunesassa, the site of the dam, and the Cornplanter monument in the cemetery on the Cornplanter Grant in Pennsylvania. The monument, given by Pennsylvania in memory of Cornplanter, represents the earliest memorial to an Indian in the United States.[3] Melvin Patterson, a Tuscarora who served as master of ceremonies, said, "From this day forward we of Indian blood will call the waters that will flood this reservation [the Cornplanter Grant] practically out of existence the Lake of Perfidy." Five days later, the *New York Times* ran a pro-Seneca editorial "The 'Lake of Perfidy'." The rally on the Cornplanter Grant included the adoption by the Senecas of Robert Haines of the Philadelphia Yearly Meeting and Rep. John Saylor (R-PA), the sole member of the Pennsylvania congressional delegation to vote against the dam. The adoption was handled by Corbett Sundown, a traditional Chief from the Tonawanda Band of Senecas. All three men donned Plains war bonnets as part of the ceremony.

Although the Pennsylvania Railroad had received $20 million in compensation for its tracks through the Allegany Reservation in the summer of 1962, it was not until January 10, 1963 that Congressman

James Haley (D–FL), chairman of the House Subcommittee on Indian Affairs, introduced House Resolution 1794 calling for compensation for the Senecas. The construction of Kinzua Dam began twenty-seven months before Congress turned its attention to the people whose lands were being taken. At the groundbreaking for the dam on October 22, 1960, Pennsylvania governor David Lawrence, a former mayor of Pittsburgh, stated "[Kinzua Dam] . . . will some day stand as a living, useful reminder of the first lesson of good government—the needs of human welfare come first" (cited in Hauptman 1986, 121). The rehabilitation funds for the Senecas were significantly higher than compensation for the tribes dislocated by the Pick-Sloan Plan. Seneca compensation was also greater than that provided to non-Indians whose lands were taken by the dam. The final compensation package for the Seneca Nation as contained in Public Law 88-533 (78 Stat. 738) was passed on August 31, 1964, and contained the following provisions: $666,285 for direct damages, $100,000 to compensate for increased costs of developing gas and oil resources, $250,000 for fees and expenses, $945,573 for all other claims, $522,775 to individual Senecas for improvements on their land, and $12,128,917 "to improve the economic, social, and educational conditions of enrolled members of the Seneca Nation." When asked to explain the difference between this compensation package and the others, anthropologist Phileo Nash, commissioner of Indian Affairs, replied "Broken promises come high" (Senate 1964, 166).

NOTES

1. For studies of Kinzua Dam from the perspectives of anthropology, political science, and history, see Bilharz (1998), Brant (1970), and Hauptman (1986).

2. The latter is a mile square tract that has no permanent residents.

3. In the summer of 1998, the Commonwealth of Pennsylvania replaced the original monument, which had been relocated, along with the Cornplanter cemetery graves, to a new site on the banks of the reservoir.

REFERENCES

Bilharz, Joy A. 1998. *The Allegany Senecas and Kinzua Dam: Forced Relocation through Two Generations*. Lincoln: University of Nebraska Press.

Brant, Roy E. 1970. "A Flood Control Dam for the Upper Allegheny River: Forty Years of Controversy." Ph.D. diss., University of Pittsburgh.

Cornplanter Tribe Asks State Archeological Group to Halt Dam Plan. 1935. *Pennsylvania Archaeologist* 5 (3): 66.

Deardorff, Merle H. Papers. MG 220. Pennsylvania StateArchives, Harrisburg.

Deardorff, Merle H., and George S. Snyderman, eds. 1956. A Nineteenth-Century Journal of a Visit to the Indians of New York. *Proceedings of the American Philosophical Society* 100 (6): 582–612.

Ericson, Jack. 2000. Personal communication (6 January).

Fenton, William N. 1960. Letter to Rep. James Haley, Chair, House Subcommittee on Indian Affairs (4 July).

Fenton, William N., ed. 1965. "The Journal of James Emlen Kept on a Trip to Canandaigua, New York, September 15 to October 30, 1794, to Attend the Treaty between the United States and the Six Nations." *Ethnohistory* 12: 279–342.

Fixico, Donald L. 1986. *Termination and Relocation: Federal Indian Policy, 1945-1960.* Albuquerque: University of New Mexico Press.

Hauptman, Laurence. 1986. *The Iroquois Struggle for Survival: World War II to the Emergence of Red Power.* Syracuse, NY: Syracuse University Press.

James, Sydney V. 1963. *A People among Peoples: Quaker Benevolence in Eighteenth-Century America.* Cambridge, MA: Harvard University Press.

Jennings, Francis, William N. Fenton, and Mary A. Druke, eds. 1984. *Iroquois Indians: a Documentary History of the Diplomacy of the Six Nations and Their League.* Microform. Reel 43. Woodbridge, CT: research publications.

Khera, Sigrid, and Patricia S. Mariella. 1982. "The Fort McDowell Yavapai: A Case of Long-Term Resistance to Relocation." Pp. 159–77 in *Involuntary Migration and Resettlement: The Problems and Responses of Dislocated People,* ed. Art Hansen and Anthony Oliver-Smith. Boulder, CO: Westview.

LaFarge, Peter. 1964. "As Long As the Grass Shall Grow." Performed by Johnny Cash, *Bitter Tears,* Columbia CS 9048.

Lawson, Michael. 1982. *Dammed Indians: The Pick-Sloan Plan and the Missouri River Sioux, 1944–1980.* Norman: University of Oklahoma Press.

Madigan, LaVerne. 1956. *The American Indian Relocation Program.* New York: Association of American Indian Affairs.

Morgan, Arthur E. 1971. *Dams and Other Disasters: A Century of the Army Corps of Engineers in Civil Works.* Boston: Porter Sargent.

Philadelphia Yearly Meeting of Friends. 1961. *The Kinzua Dam Controversy: A Practical Solution—Without Shame.* Philadelphia: Kinzua Project of the Indian Committee of the Philadelphia Yearly Meeting of Friends.

Savery, William. 1844. *A Journal of the Life, Travels, and Religious Labours of William Savery, a Minister of the Gospel of Christ, of the Society of Friends, Late of Philadelphia.* Compiled from his original memoranda by Jonathan Evans. Philadelphia: Friends' Book-Store.

Scudder, Thayer, and Elizabeth Colson. 1982. "From Welfare to Development: A Conceptual Framework for the Analysis of Dislocated People." Pp. 267–87 in *Involuntary Migration and Resettlement: The Problems and Responses of Dislocated People,* ed. Art Hansen and Anthony Oliver-Smith. Boulder, CO: Westview.

U.S. Senate. 1964. Subcommittee of Indian Affairs of the Committee on Interior and Insular Affairs. *Kinzua Dam (Seneca Indian Relocation): Hearings on S. 1836 and H.R. 1794.* 88th Cong., 2d sess.

Wallace, Anthony F. C. 1969. *The Death and Rebirth of the Seneca.* New York: Vintage.

Washburn, Wilcomb E. 1971. *Red Man's Land/White Man's Law: A Study of the Past and Present Status of the American Indian.* New York: Charles Scribner's Sons. p 65

The Right to Sovereignty

RON LAFRANCE

I'm not a Chief. In our language the literal translation for that position is "I'm holding up the tree." The man who occupies that position is still alive. His name is Louie Thompson, and he's close to ninety now. So my role is, "I'm guarding his tree," if you will.

When we deal with these issues of sovereignty and jurisdiction, I think in terms of what's happening not only up north but in all of the United States to Indian people. Some of you may remember what happened to us in Akwesasne,[1] where we came close, once again, to a civil war. I don't know if it's just us Mohawks, but it seems we're always fighting all the time about something. If we can't fight with anybody else, we'll fight with each other. We'll even argue about who we're going to fight with. Well, that's life in Indian country!

But on a more serious note, I think we, not only as Iroquois but also as we call ourselves, Haudenosaunee, are facing probably one of the most serious decades, from a political point of view, that we have ever faced in our existence. That is because we are dealing with true sovereignty and true jurisdiction over our territories.

The annual treaty commemoration is very important, partly as a yearly celebration get-together by many of our people, our friends, and our allies. In one sense it's a celebration; it's a ritual and a commemoration. It must continue year after year; otherwise, we'll forget it.

On a day-to-day basis, however, each member of the Haudenosaunee society has a responsibility. Not just the Chiefs and the Clan Mothers who sit in Council, or the spiritual leaders that sit in Council, but *you* as individual people. The translation from our language is "the men and women who hold no position." This doesn't mean that you don't have to worry about anything. On the contrary, it means *you* also have to pay attention. *You* also have to be responsible. Because it is *you* that put us in positions of authority.

I think that one of the most traumatic things happening to us today is what we're experiencing now. We are in a transition; it's probably one of the worst transitions we'll ever go through. I think it's the second major one we have gone through.

Many years ago, Kanatari:io, Handsome Lake, told us of a prophecy. The message that had been given to him was a forewarning of what was going to happen to our people if we didn't pay attention. That's all it basically was. It's not very complicated. But that's what it meant, to pay attention, not just to non-Indians but to ourselves. Because we see that right now, again, at least in Mohawk country, we're on the verge of another revolution, on the verge of another civil war. The issues are complex and are getting more and more complicated. We need to pay attention.

Most of the work that I did before was as one of the Council's runners. Now I do a lot of work in education. Education means many things. It's not just "school"; it's education about our own political systems.

I want to reference the event in Akwesasne.[2] *That* was a real fight over sovereignty. Many nations, not only the Haudenosaunee, but also many Indian nations across the country and many nations around the world supported us in our fight for sovereignty. Many of the people from urban areas came out and supported us. I remember on the cold winter nights, night after night, the men and women that were in bunkers. And you know how the weather gets at home—"Fourth of July and forty below!" (And you've got to pay attention on the Fourth of July. Otherwise you won't even sweat.)

But seriously, that was a real fight about sovereignty. The fight that is going on now[3] is not, and at the same time, it is. The issue of gambling, whatever it is under the broad title of gambling, is not an individual's right. And I know there are some people in opposition to that thinking. But that's what it's coming down to.

One of the things that those of you who study law are examining is some of the history of our people, including the issue of citizenship. On October 25, 1919, Congress passed an act that made World War I veterans automatically citizens. One of the important clauses of this act was that the Indian veterans retained all rights as tribal members. The key phrase is "property rights," that the United States has the right to buy our property. You have to think about that. Does this mean that we have the obligation to sell them our property? Or does it mean somewhere, sometime, somehow the government of not only the state of New York but also of the United States *can* take our lands again? We objected to this, but that clause is still in there, the rights of property. In 1948 and 1950, civil and criminal jurisdiction was given to the state.[4]

Somewhere in 1979, the Mohawks in Akwesasne, and I can say this, we went a little crazy. But not crazy in a crazy sense, but crazy in a positive sense, if there's such a thing. Because not only in Akwesasne but also in other places across the Six Nations, such as the Seaway,[5] they began to open up this "can of worms" about who has the right over what. Those of you who remember the "rock 'em, sock 'em" days of the 1960s know there was a great change in America. We have kept our fight going through the courts. The money-lawyers would sell us out, but still we kept going.

About three years ago I had an opportunity to visit with some of the lawyers in the Justice Department on a federal level. They said that ever since the events in Akwesasne, the Justice Department has had a hard time deciding what to do with us. The way American politics works is that (and I'm being very simple in my example) they let an issue continue until it boils, then it pops; then they go in and either arrest or support who's left standing. Finally, that becomes a precedent that is set down.

Regarding taxation, in the fall of 1983 the Taxation and Finance Department voted on a series of *proposed* (and I want to underscore *proposed)* rules and regulations regarding cigarettes and gasoline. My interpretation of that then (and our Council brought the information into Grand Council) was that the state was saying in their proposed rules and regulations that an individual Indian had the same authority as Indian government and had the same responsibility as Indian government.

Now let's step out of that for a second. Let's say you, as U.S. citizens, for example, in Rochester, each have the same authority and responsibility as the city government. What would happen? You could do anything you wanted to do, if you chose to do that. And some of our guys did just that. I'm not defending this and I'm not condoning it. I'm not against it at this point in what I'm talking about. But this is the situation. Imagine letting a pit bull run loose until it matures, biting and chewing and all that other stuff. Then all of a sudden try to put a collar on it. Or imagine a dog trying to get to a cat. You know you have to grab the dog. And when you touch it, it could cut you to ribbons. If you can subdue it, you're going to be afraid to let go, because it's going to cut you to ribbons again. So you get nailed twice.

One of the things that we have been trying to do is to say to the state of New York and the federal government that this issue cannot be resolved administratively. What does that mean? We can't sit down with a bunch of papers and rules and say, "O.K. we agree to four of these. And with five of those we don't agree." It can't work that way. That's not how our government works. We make a political solution, and then we work on the administration of that solution.

For example, the return of the wampum belts—that was a result of a government-to-government relationship. We worked out the details and the belts are back in Onondaga where they belong.[6] How they get to other communities hasn't been worked out yet. That's up to the Haudenosaunee and the Onondagas to decide. That's how it works in our system.

The state system says, "Well, let's create these make-believe proposals (and I say make-believe because *proposed* means that—make-believe, they're not real), and then we'll run them out there and see what happens." Well, we know what happens.

What does that have to do with sovereignty? We have always been raised that we have a right to do what we want on our own lands—but within reason, within some logical, rational framework. Within our society, we can do that. However, that is not the situation now. Some businesses, not all of them, but some have chosen to say, "I am going to do what I want to do because I have a *right.*"

This is where many of us differ. I think this difference is important, even if you have it in your head that you're not going to agree with my interpretation. I think it's important that you *listen*, though, and think about it. Because, again going back to what I first said, this is one of our most crucial times, so we have to stop fighting among ourselves.

If you want to talk about politics in terms of the Great Law, we do have rights as individuals. There are principles governing how those rights operate. There is a structure, whether it's the Clan Mothers, the Faithkeepers, the elders, the Council, the Chiefs' Council, or the Grand Council to deal with issues. Now, however, we are looking at individuals who are taking their own rights and making them privileges. By turning these rights into the level of privileges, they have abused their own communities. They have abused that very, very tender thread that keeps us sovereign.

Every one talks about sovereignty. This can be viewed from a very extreme but very simple point by saying, for example, that you have the right to buy anything you want to buy. Right? Basically, you can go anywhere in America, and you can buy anything you want to buy. If it's good for you, fine. If it's bad for you, you have to suffer the consequences. If you want, you can go to McDonalds and say, like the commercial says, "Give me nine million cheeseburgers." And if they cook you nine million, you've got to pay for them. And you have to eat them, or throw them away. I want to give you some extreme examples to bring some points home, because that's what's happening in our communities.

Right now we have, at least in my mind, many instant millionaires. I don't have a problem with someone becoming a millionaire. But I have a problem when that individual really harms, threatens, and endangers all of *our* rights that *our* forefathers, *your* forefathers fought and died for.

There are many forms of sovereignty. There is sovereignty of choice. There's individual sovereignty, economic sovereignty, political sovereignty, spiritual sovereignty, and educational sovereignty. These are issues of sovereignty that we must maintain for ourselves as a society. Neither New York State nor the federal government has jurisdiction over these areas.

But now the issue becomes internalized. Do we protect the individuals that are harming, for whatever reason, the rights of the community? We know communities right here in New York State that have really gone through some hard times. I sympathize because we went through some hard times in our community, too. But this is a major issue that has to be discussed, and not at the end of a gun.

This is my opinion, and I still hold this same opinion in Council. My opinion is that approval or disapproval of activities such as the ones in question must be the decision of all the people, and they must be sanctioned by the governments. Otherwise, we are going to have the same conditions again. Does this mean that I'm against anyone making a living? Does it mean, and I've heard this stated, that the Councils want us to be poor? I have never heard a Council say that. I have never heard anyone in Council say that we should be poor. Poor means many, many things. We would be crazy to advocate that. No leadership would be responsible if they believed that, and they should not be leaders if that's what they advocate. In terms of this political issue facing us now, it's very important that not only the Indian people understand, but also our non-Indian friends and allies, as the treaty says.

Let me give an example of just one little case, one incident that happened in Akwesasne not long ago. I want to work both sides of this. Some stones were thrown at one of the bingo buses. So the bingo company, or whoever runs the bingo, had the state police escort the bus to the Mohawk Bingo Palace.

At home, there are folks against the gambling issue. People get emotional about things. I don't condone the stone throwing, but the people said, "If this cannot be resolved through political or other kinds of negotiations, then we're going to resolve it." We cannot condone violence. No leader of the Haudenosaunee will ever condone violence.

You have to understand that there is a group of men who call themselves the Mohawk Security Sovereignty Force. Their public statement says that they are sworn to uphold the sovereignty of the Mohawk Nation, which is good rhetoric, but that's not the case. They are protecting the gambling businesses there, which, if it were a different situation, would be a violation of sovereignty. In one sense, it's a paramilitary invasion of our territory.

Here is what it means. The Mohawks have the *authority*, not the right—the Mohawk Nation has the authority to grant the right and privilege to all non-Mohawk citizens to participate in that activity. No one else has that right. Just because you pay your $10 to get on the bus, it does not make you a politician, it does not grant you the right to invade another person's territory.

Case in point, let's say this small town of Canandaigua was against gambling. The neighboring city says we don't care; we're going to go there and do that, we're going to have our local police escort us right into the school, and we're going to do what we're going to do there. That would be an invasion. Under any circumstance, that's an invasion.

In the earlier case, the state police were protecting the bus, but they were also invading the Mohawk Territory.

So in a very weird sense, it may look like the anti-gamblers and the Mohawk Nation are going to be siding against the Mohawk Sovereignty Security Force over bingo. But that's not the issue, that's not the case, and that's not how it's going to come down.

Now, as our friends, I don't want to make you feel guilty. This is not my purpose. But as United States citizens, our friends and allies, it's your responsibility to inform your fellow Americans of what they're doing. This is not the issue of denying your right to play bingo or slot machines. It's the issue of your taking a right and turning it into a privilege—a privilege of invading an Indian Territory.

I was reading some of the newspaper clippings from one of our communities in Canada. One person said, "No one will stop me from playing bingo in Quebec." That's true, but if the Mohawk community says no, then playing bingo is not your right, unless the Mohawks extend that right.

So it's very complicated. Now that this ruling has come down, we have to fight again. And it's more complicated. And we told the state and the federal government, "Hey, you've got to pay attention." We told them that in 1979 and 1980, "If you don't pay attention on this round, folks, these are the things that are going to happen." We almost wrote a prescription out: "If you don't pay attention, this is what's going to happen."

So they followed the prescription and it's happened. Now should we be called prophets (not *profits*, but something of another nature) or vision-seekers? No, this again is where you as friends and allies have to help us through your legislators, your congressmen, and your senators. We cannot interfere with your government. There's another belt, the Kas-wen-tha, Two Row Wampum Belt. We can advise you and give you a lot of interpretations of what we think you should do, but we can't influence you in that sense.

Here is the impact of what that decision's going to do now. Because the United States works by precedent, all it takes is one person. You know the whole thing about Humpty Dumpty. Well, this is where we're at now. You take one little thing out and that whole thing is going to come falling down. It's going to require not just the energy of those of us who have been in this for a long time, but a lot more. It's going to require a lot more education, meetings, and lectures. It's going to mean a lot more information sharing, so that you as individuals, regardless of where you are in your own consciousness about where life is at, can be brought up to speed. We all need to be sharing our true responsibilities of how we are to treat each other.

There are many more issues involved. This is just one of them. The problem is our own people—the same as with you. We have almost become civilized to the point where people say to their representatives, "Well, I voted for you. You're supposed to take care of me. *I don't have to think anymore.*" I get angry about that.

That's what is important—we've lost our ability to think about these things. We're zonked out after thirty seconds watching the television regarding local issues and a minute thirty seconds about national issues—they are that quickly resolved in our minds. But they're still there. We need to pay attention, for our people today and for the future generations.

This chapter is based on an address delivered by Ron LaFrance, then Subchief of the Mohawk Nation, at the social following the 1989 Canandaigua Treaty Commemoration held on November 11 in Canandaigua, New York. It was recorded on audiotape by Robert Gorall and made available to the editors for inclusion in this volume. It is published here posthumously with the permission of Martha LaFrance.

NOTES

1. In a recent essay, John C. Mohawk summarizes the 1979 events within the Mohawk Nation which culminated in a standoff at Raquette Point in Akwesasne: "In 1979, Akwesasne came under siege. Traditional Mohawk Chief Loran Thompson was arrested in a dispute with the rival elected system. Chief Thompson opposed the rival elected system's plan to build a fence around the Akwesasne territory, and he resisted arrest. The situation developed into a standoff in which Chief Thompson and his supporters remained at Thompson's home on Raquette Point near the western border of Akwesasne. . . .

The standoff at Raquette Point continued for approximately thirteen months. During that time, the New York State police surrounded the Mohawk enclave. Some occupants were able to ferry supplies into their camp because it was located adjacent to the St. Lawrence River which serves as the border between the United States and Canada. On several occasions, New York officials threatened invasion, but the Mohawks, including the Mohawk Warrior Society, held their ground." (Mohawk 1998: 1066–67). For a full discussion of these events see John C. Mohawk, "Echoes of a Native Revitalization Movement in Recent Indian Law Cases in New York State," *Buffalo Law Review* 46.3 (fall 1998): 1061–71.

2. The standoff at Raquette Point. See Mohawk 1998: 1061–71.

3. During the 1980s, after nearly another decade of increasing civil unrest over the establishment of casino gambling in Akwesasne, the Mohawk Nation found itself in the midst of another civil war. "Spawned by a brawl on June 6, 1989, this conflict developed into an open civil war between the various factions of Mohawks that lasted eleven months and eventually resulted in the deaths of two men" (Porter 1998: 847). For a summation of events during this decade, see Mohawk,1998: 1061–71.

4. USC Public Law 232 (1948) and USC Public Law 233 (1950) granted the state of New York criminal and civil jurisdiction over Haudenosaunee affairs by opening "the State courts to lawsuits involving Indians that arose within *Haudenosaunee* territory" (Porter 1998: 843). For a discussion of how these laws have affected Haudenosaunee governance, see Robert B. Porter, "Building a New Longhouse: The Case for Government Reform Within the Six Nations of the *Haudenosaunee*," *Buffalo Law Review* 46.3 (fall 1998): 805–945.

5. In his 1998 essay, Robert P. Porter summarizes these events: "During the late 1950s to the early 1960s, three Haudenosaunee communities—the Seneca, Mohawk and

Tuscarora—lost territory as a result of the federal and State governments' economic development efforts. The Seneca Nation lost one-third of its Allegheny Reservation—almost ten thousand acres—as a result of the federal government's condemnation action to construct the Kinzua Dam and reservoir on the Allegheny River. . . .The Mohawk community at Akwesasne lost land and had its ecosystem destroyed when the St. Lawrence power project was constructed and two heavily polluting multinational corporations—Reynolds Aluminum and General Motors—built large manufacturing facilities within a mile of their territory . . . And the Tuscarora Nation lost 500 acres of its territory due to the State's efforts to build a reservoir for the Niagara River power project. . . ." (Porter 844) For a full discussion see Porter, Robert B. "Building a New Longhouse: The Case for Government Reform Within the Six Nations of the Haudenosaunee," *Buffalo Law Review* 46, 3 (fall 1998): 805–945.

6. On October 21, 1989, twelve Haudenosaunee wampum belts were returned to the Longhouse on the Onondaga Nation. (See Mark Weiner, "Onondagas Rejoice Over Wampum Belts," *Syracuse* [New York] *Herald American/The Post Standard*, 22 October 1989, sec. A, p. 1+.

REFERENCES

Mohawk, John C. "Echoes of a Native Revitalization Movement in Recent Indian Law Cases in New York State." *Buffalo Law Review* 46, 3 (fall 1998): 1061–71.

Porter, Robert B. "Building a New Longhouse: The Case for Government Reform within the Six Nations of the *Haudenosaunee.*" *Buffalo Law Review* 46, 3 (fall 1998): 805–945.

Weiner, Mark. "Onondagas Rejoice Over Wampum Belts." *Syracuse* [New York] *Herald American/The Post Standard.* 22 October 1989, sec. A, p. 1+.

Celebration at the Chosen Spot:
THE 200TH ANNIVERSARY OF THE CANANDAIGUA TREATY
11 November 1994

a documentary essay written, transcribed, and compiled by

ANNA M. SCHEIN

"A treaty, in the minds of our people, is an eternal word. Events often make it seem expedient to depart from the pledged word, but we are conscious that the first departure creates logic for the second departure, until there is nothing left of the word."

Declaration of Indian Purpose (1961)
American Indian Chicago Conference

TREATY COMMEMORATIONS IN CANANDAIGUA

Canandaigua is derived from the Haudenosaunee word Ganundagwa[1] which means "The Chosen Spot."[2] Ganundagwa has been a place for more than a thousand years where peaceful ways of living have been forged. Near present-day Canandaigua, New York, the Peacemaker journeyed to the Seneca village of Ganondagan and met a woman who became known as the Mother of Nations. This site is referred to by the Senecas as the Town of Peace. In more recent history, it has also been a place of conflict. In 1687, the Marquis de Denonville, governor general of New France, led a military campaign which destroyed Ganondagan. In 1779, Major General John Sullivan's raid through the area destroyed more than forty Seneca and Cayuga towns. Just a few years later in 1794, Canandaigua was again the Chosen Spot for a more peaceful event—the negotiating and signing of a treaty between the Six Nations Iroquois Confederacy and the United States of America.

For more than two hundred years, citizens of the United States and the Confederacy, as well as other international visitors, have been drawn to the site of the original treaty signing. During the early part of the twentieth century, local residents remember seeing groups at the site, now marked by a large boulder known as Council Rock.[3] Former Ontario County Historian J. Sheldon Fisher recalls:

In my youth, every once in a while some of the nostalgic Indians would come there for a ceremony at the Rock. They weren't very big. It was just a gathering of the Indians. It was sporadic. It was nothing much . . . more for old times sake. (Fisher 1996)

In 1944, a two-day event was held in Canandaigua in celebration of the 150th anniversary of the Canandaigua Treaty ("Six Nations . . . " 1944, 3). Gatherings were again sporadic until large crowds returned to the Chosen Spot during the Kinzua Dam controversy. The construction of the Kinzua Dam, which flooded thousands of acres of Seneca homelands, violated the Canandaigua, or Pickering, Treaty. In Articles 2, 3, and 4 of the treaty, the U.S. government had pledged never to "claim . . . nor disturb" the Six Nations in the "free use and enjoyment" of their lands.

In 1961, Society of Friends representative Jack Preston told the crowd in attendance at the 167th anniversary of the treaty:

We came to Canandaigua . . . because we wanted to show what is happening to the solemn language of the Pickering treaty and how our government has found it convenient to forget the treaty. ("Senecas . . ." 1961, [1])

For the Senecas, the final completion of the Kinzua Dam would mark another moment in time when their communities were forever changed. A widely circulated publication issued by the Kinzua Project of the Indian Committee, Philadelphia Yearly Meeting of Friends, in 1961 summarized the Seneca Nation perspective:

In order to understand the Kinzua controversy, Americans with different cultural backgrounds have to look at the Seneca problem through American Indian eyes. In 1960 when Mr. George Heron was President of the Seneca Nation of Indians, he made the following statement to the House Subcommittee on Indian Affairs:

I appear before this Subcommittee today as an official rep-resentative of my people to express once again their unaltered opposition to construction of the Kinzua Dam. As you know, this project will flood the heart of our reser-vation homeland, which we Senecas have peacefully occupied since the Treaty of November 11, 1794, under the protection of the United States, and will force the relo-cation of more than 700 members of the Nation.

My friends from Pennsylvania seem to believe that some Senecas are willing to sell their lands. I do not know where these witnesses got their information, though I suppose every group, even an Indian nation, contains a few unhappy people who will sell out their birthright. I do know that the overwhelming majority of my people, including every Councilman and other tribal leader, both in and out of office, is trying desperately to save our reservation. The thought that we would freely give up the lands of our ancestors, which we are pledged to hold for our children yet unborn, is so contrary to the Seneca way of life that it is not even considered seriously. . . .

Now let me tell you a little bit about what the Kinzua Dam will do to my people. Our own census shows that over 700 members of the Nation or more than half the population of the Allegany Reservation will be forced to move by the reservoir. On paper, this does not seem like very many people: other lands, substitute houses can be found, say the supporters of the project. If you knew these Senecas the way I do, though, if you knew how much they love that land—the last remnant of the original Seneca country—you would learn a different story. To lose their homes on the reservation is really to lose a part of their life.

The Corps of Engineers will tell you that Kinzua Dam will flood only 9,000 out of the 29,000 acres within the Allegany Reservation. What the Corps does not say is that this 9,000 acres includes almost all of the flat lowlands and fertile riverbanks, while the remainder of the reservation is inaccessible and thus virtually uninhabitable mountainside. What the Corps does not say is that during the dry season these 9,000 acres will not be a lake but rather muck and mud flats. What a pleasant yearly reminder, what an annual memorial to the breaking of the 1794 Treaty that will be!

Lastly, I know it will sound simple and perhaps silly, but the truth of the matter is that my people really believe that George Washington read the 1794 Treaty before he signed it, and that he meant exactly what he wrote. For more than 165 years we Senecas have lived by that document. To us it is more than a contract, more than a symbol; to us, the 1794 Treaty is a way of life.

Times have not always been easy for the Seneca people. We have known and we still know poverty and discrimination. But through it all, we have been sustained by a pledge of faith, unbroken by the Federal Government.

> Take that pledge away, break our Treaty, and I fear that
> you will destroy the Senecas as an Indian community."
> (*The Kinzua Dam* . . . [1961?], 8–10)

Despite the efforts of the Seneca Nation and those U.S. organizations
which supported the Senecas' right of ownership and free use of their
lands, the decision of the United States government to build the Kinzua
Dam held firm. Many prominent U.S. citizens issued written protests of
their government's departure from the "pledged word." The following is
an excerpt from an editorial that appeared in the October 1963 issue of
Social Education:

> Within a few months the Army Corps of Engineers will close the
> gates, and the waters will begin to lap higher and higher against
> the massive wall of steel and concrete. The rising waters will
> inundate land that the Seneca Indians claimed as their own long
> before the first European set foot on the soil of the New World.
> By the end of 1964 the forest glades through which the Indians
> hunted deer, and the fertile valleys in which in more recent time
> they built their homes and raised their families, will have van-
> ished for all time beneath a man-made lake.
>   Opponents of the Kinzua Project—and there are many of
> them—have already christened the lake. "The Lake of Perfidy,"
> they call it, and with reason, for the Army Corps of Engineers,
> and behind them the government and the people they work for—
> which is all of us—had to violate a solemn pledge and callously
> break our oldest existing treaty in order to build the dam. . . .
>   The Senecas have never "chosen" to sell their land. Legally and
> morally, it belongs to them to this day. But they are few in number
> (some 150 families totaling fewer than 800 men, women, and chil-
> dren are being dispossessed), and the United States has acted in the
> name of *might*, rather than *right*, to pursue its own ends.
>   The Seneca lands on the Alleghany Reservation originally
> included 30,000 acres. When the railroads came after the Civil
> War, they secured rights of way through the reservation. These
> rights of way and roads that were built ate up perhaps 2,000
> acres. Non-Indian workers who constructed the railroads built
> squatter settlements on Indian land, and in 1875 Congress rec-
> ognized these settlements as *faits accomplis*. These non-Indian
> congressional villages—Salamanca, Killbuck, Vandalia, and Car-
> rollton—occupy about 6,000 acres, for which the residents pay a
> modest annual lease to the Seneca Nation. The Allegheny Reser-
> voir will take another 10,000 acres, and these the best land on
> the reservation. The Corps of Engineers is also taking additional

acreage for the relocation of highways, railroads, and utilities. How much, the Corps has not yet revealed, but informed guesses place it as high as 1,000 acres. Moreover, the state of New York, with the permission of the Corps, proposes to build a limited access highway through one end of the reservation.

The arithmetic of the "taking" is depressing. Out of the original 30,000 acres, guaranteed to the Senecas "forever," the Indians will be left with about 11,000 acres of land, but since 10,000 of these acres consist of swamp or rugged mountain, the habitable area remaining to the Senecas will amount to only 1,000 acres.

One would think that a government that had dealt so shamefully with a helpless people would, when confronted with the fruits of its immorality, seek to do everything within its power to make amends. Up to now, the amends have consisted almost entirely of promises. . . .

There is, of course, another solution. It would require vision of the highest order, and there is not the slightest likelihood that it will ever be mentioned, let alone get the consideration we believe it deserves.

We could, even at this late date, keep our faith and maintain our integrity by a simple order that the gates of the Kinzua Dam must never be closed. Were this order given, the massive wall of steel and concrete would be transformed into a $46 million (the appropriation to date) testimony of our faith in government under law and our belief in the inalienable rights of the individual in a free society. The cost would indeed be formidable, but we have on a number of occasions wiped out with the stroke of a pen defense installations and military programs before they were completed and at costs far higher than the $46 million already poured into Kinzua. ("The 'Lake of Perfidy'" 1963, 293, 333)

Residents of Pittsburgh, Pennsylvania, who had been experiencing devastating flood conditions since the turn of the century held a different opinion of the dam and were anxious for construction to begin. The Pittsburgh District of the U.S. Army Corps of Engineers first considered locating a dam on the upper Allegheny River in 1928 (Johnson 1978, 276). Early opposition to the proposal stopped the investigation until the area was again flooded in 1954. Dr. Leland R. Johnson summarized the perspective of the Pittsburgh communities:

In October 1954, Hurricane Hazel sent rains inland over the Pittsburgh District, causing a flood that, without the reductions made by the ten reservoirs then in operation, would have been the second greatest of record. The reservoirs lopped 8.7 feet off the 1954 flood crest at Pittsburgh and 9 feet off the crest at Wheeling, but heavy damages still occurred. The reservoirs in service in 1954 controlled about 23% of the watersheds above Pittsburgh, and water from the uncontrolled watershed areas crested at 32.4 feet on the Point gage *[sic]*, 7.4 feet above the 25-foot flood stage.

Leaders of Pittsburgh and other flooded communities began an intensive campaign in 1955 for construction of Kinzua. Further support developed in the aftermath of the March 8, 1956, flood, greatest of record at the proposed site of Kinzua Dam, which inflicted about $2 million damages on the Warren, Pennsylvania, area. President Dwight D. Eisenhower approved funding for Kinzua Dam in 1956, and Lawrence "Al" Layton and the Pittsburgh District Legal Branch started condemnation proceedings to obtain the parts of the Seneca reservations needed for the reservoir. . . .

The U.S. District Court for Western New York decided on January 11, 1957, that Congress had been fully informed about Seneca treaty rights when it approved the Kinzua project and that it intended to take lands for the project regardless of the provisions of the 1794 treaty. That decision was not without precedent. The Seneca Nation appealed through a series of courts seeking injunction against the Kinzua project all the way to the Supreme Court, which, on June 15, 1959, denied the injunction.

While the court hearings were in progress, a wave of intense public sympathy for the Senecas rippled through the news media, but people at Pittsburgh and communities downstream of the dam site fumed at the delays. Editors of the *Pittsburgh Press* said the Senecas deserved no more consideration than the 2,500 whites, ten times the number of Senecas to be relocated by Kinzua, who had been forced to move to make way for the Conemaugh project. The editors had no sympathy for the view that "Indians were so poorly treated by white men that we shouldn't take their lands now—even to save ourselves from flood disaster—as if tender solicitude now could wipe out the ancient injustices." Editors of the *Pittsburgh Post-Gazette* declared: "This project has waited long enough. Flood waters are not nearly so patient."

At the May 1957 hearings before the House Public Works Committee, Sherman P. Voorhees of the Pittsburgh Chamber of Commerce said the fact that more than a hundred people had lost their lives to Allegheny river floods since 1937 proved the need for the Kinzua project. . . . "Those of us who went through the flood of 1936," said Robert T. Griebling of Tarentum, "will never rest easy until *all* precautions have been taken." (Johnson 1978, 277–78)

Seneca Nation leaders realized that a dam was necessary to conserve water and prevent further flooding in the Allegheny Valley. However, they objected to a violation of the Canandaigua Treaty without a thorough investigation of an alternative dam site at Conewango that would have saved Seneca homelands. Throughout the Kinzua Dam controversy, continual reference was made to the "utter reasonableness of the appeal of the Seneca Nation of Indians" (*The Kinzua Dam* . . . [1961?], 1). The Society of Friends noted "the magnanimous offer of the Senecas to forego at great sacrifice further opposition to the Kinzua Dam "if and when it is shown by competent, objective evidence that a feasible alternative does not exist" (*The Kinzua Dam* . . . [1961?], 1).

On May 23, 1961, Basil Williams, President of the Seneca Nation of Indians, wrote to John F. Kennedy, president of the United States:

> In a letter written last February 22, the Seneca Nation pleaded that you order an independent investigation into the merits and comparative costs of the Allegheny River (Kinzua Dam) Project and the Conewango-Cattaraugus substitute flood control plan devised by Dr. Arthur E. Morgan. Under date of March 21, 1961, the Deputy Director of the Bureau of the Budget turned down our plea on the ground that "actions by the Congress and the Supreme Court appeared to have decided the major points at issue."
>
> We respectfully submit, Mr. President, that this reply is unworthy of a great nation. The major issue in the Kinzua Dam case is whether the United States has a moral right unilaterally to break its oldest treaty—in particular where an admittedly feasible alternative course is available. This basic ethical question is not answered for the Seneca people or for the world by saying that the Federal Government has a legal right to go back on its word. (Williams 1961)

However, President Kennedy's reply to the Seneca Nation on August 9, 1961, sealed the fate of Seneca lands:

> I fully appreciate the reasons underlying the opposition of the Seneca Nation of Indians to the construction of the Kinzua Dam on the Allegheny River. Involved are very deep sentiments over the loss of a portion of the lands which have been owned by the Seneca Nation for centuries. I therefore directed that this matter

be looked into carefully and that a report be submitted to me on the basic issues involved.

I have now had an opportunity to review the subject and have concluded that it is not possible to halt the construction of Kinzua Dam currently under way. . . .

Even though construction of Kinzua must proceed, I have directed the department and agencies of the Federal Government to take every action within their authority to assist the Seneca Nation and its members who must be relocated in adjusting to the new situation. (Kennedy 1961)

With no choice but to accept the inevitable completion of the dam, the following sentiment was expressed in the April 2, 1962, issue of the *Kinzua Planning Newsletter*:

We are saddened by the coming loss of some of our lands. It is a cruel blow to us. I believe, however, that the Great Spirit would have us strengthen ourselves, grow in wisdom and knowledge, and take comfort in the thought with courage [that] we can make the future of our Nation and ourselves bigger, better and brighter." (*Kinzua Planning* 1962, [1])

Later the same year Walter Taylor, a representative of the Society of Friends, wrote:

At the bicentennial ceremonies in Canandaigua, New York, commemorating the Pickering Treaty of 1794, what story will be told of the Seneca response to broken promises. Will there be a Seneca Nation of Indians? Will there remain a unique heritage, however modified by circumstances? Will the history of the next thirty-two years justify Seneca pride in the Nation's astonishing capacity to survive and flourish in spite of devastating threats to its existence? Will the Iroquois, who have contributed so much to the society which defeated and absorbed them, play a significant role in the world-wide struggle to master the Space Age without extinguishing the human race in the process? ("Editorial" 1962, 7)

In the wake of Kinzua, Seneca Nation leaders realized the importance of maintaining public awareness of the Canandaigua Treaty in preventing future violations. They asked J. Sheldon Fisher, then Ontario County historian, to keep the remembrance of the treaty alive. He gave his word to the Senecas that he would do so. Decades before the Canandaigua Treaty would receive broader international attention, Fisher recognized the significance of the document. Fisher was general chairman of the arrangements for the 1961 treaty commemoration. With his leadership, treaty commemorations became an annual event in Canandaigua.

In 1962, more than three hundred gathered at Council Rock. The following year a re-enactment of the Pickering Treaty and a pageant written by Fisher depicting Indian history were performed before a crowd of a thousand people. From 1964 to 1967, members of the Six Nations Confederacy boycotted treaty celebrations in Canandaigua as the completion of the Kinzua Dam and flooding of Seneca lands became a reality. In 1965, "only the historians of this city and Ontario County paused yesterday to recall the signing here on Nov. 11, 1794, of the famed Pickering treaty" (Van Iseghem 1965, 2B). In 1967 although no Iroquois were present, a message was read from Sachem Freeman Johnson: "As you gather at the Pickering Treaty rock my heart is heavy with sadness. I am reminded that the nation's oldest treaty between the U.S. and the Six nations is no longer honored." (Gorall [1994?], 81)

Confederacy representatives returned to the Chosen Spot in 1968 and joined Fisher and other local residents at Council Rock. In the years which followed, those who actively participated with Fisher and Ellis included Harry Logan, Rodney Johnson, Jane Rode LeClair, Chief Corbett Sundown, Chief Leon Shenandoah, Faithkeeper Oren Lyons, Lee Lyons, Barney and Carol Jimerson, Lillian and Douglas A. Fisher, Jackie Platt, Don Moore, Barbara Bethmann, Marion Miller, Julian and Ann Galban, Robert and Muriel Gorall, G. Peter Jemison, Clayton Logan, Chief Irving Powless Jr., Chief Bernard Parker, Chief Jake Swamp, and Chief Leo Henry.

Attendance at commemorations ranged from gatherings of only a few people to crowds of several hundred. Some years, faithful supporters braved cold, icy winds and heavy rains and snows to observe the treaty anniversary of November 11 (Gorall [1994?], 79–96). Still the spirit of peace grew. During these years the Chosen Spot became an annual meeting place where friends gathered to respect a pledged agreement between nations. It was a place where grief, anger, disappointment, and hope were openly expressed. Victories were celebrated, such as the establishment of Ganondagan as a New York State Historic Site in 1984. Current issues which would again threaten peace between the United States and the Six Nations were also discussed.

The return of twelve wampum belts to the Six Nations Confederacy in 1989 was celebrated that year at the annual Canandaigua Treaty commemoration. The return of other belts to the Confederacy remains "unfinished business," as Tadodaho Leon Shenandoah remarked at the social following the 1989 treaty celebration:

I've been sitting over there listening. And while I'm listening, many things are coming to my mind, things about our treaty belts and everything. And we got the Two Row Wampum yet that we have to bring back.

And this is what I got to thinking. You know, I go around, I have many titles. One is Tadodaho, Spritual Leader, Chief of Chiefs, Chief of the Six Nations, Activist. But nobody ever calls me my real name. My real name before I got the title, before I got to be a Six Nations chief is *Gia Wha Gen Hiadeh,* which fits the title I think. It means "unfinished business." When I came to be a Six Nations Chief, a lot of this was unfinished. So from there, I went on.

That's why I got to thinking. I'm trying to get back our Two Row Wampum. Will it be that we won't get it back until we get another Tadodaho with the right name? Because I'll leave here with unfinished business. But we are trying to get that back which we call, like we say, "the main thing," that's one of the main belts that we got to get back. It's like saying, "That's the granddaddy of all, all the treaty belts." And I don't know when we're going to get it back. (Shenandoah 1989)

The moving remarks by Seneca Faithkeeper Geraldine Green at the 1989 treaty commemoration social reveal what the return of the twelve wampum belts meant to the Haudenosaunee:

We really are a complex people. There are so many things that need to be discussed and brought out in the open for the younger people to learn so that they can learn their identity. There are so many who have become urban Indians and have forgotten . . . what their identity is.

Now, Irv[4] talked about the coming back of the Guswenta, that's how I like to refer to them. I was not able to attend that ceremony because there was another happening that day. . . . So I can just imagine of the emotion that he talked about when the wampums came back. Because those are the true concepts of how we are, of our way of life. And I don't believe you have to be one of us to know, if you only understood what that means to us. I was emotional that day just imagining them coming back. I didn't need to be there. I was just as emotional as some of those people were because this has been an ongoing effort through all the Haudenosaunee territories. For all these years, it has been the wish of some of my elders who are no longer with me.

They would always say, "Perhaps you will see the day when they come back."

And then they would go on and explain the meaning of those beads. It is those beads that were woven into the many different designs some of you have seen. Our ancestors wove the concepts of our way of life. And to sit back and see how they were treated. Perhaps one of the best examples that you can relate to would be by saying how the government has done away with the middle class people, if you know what I mean.

And there were many things that our ancestors offered to your ancestors that came here to this country. But [it] was government to government.

And it has always been said, "If the government misuses those concepts of our way of life, get them back and then offer it to the people. Talk with them. Communicate. Show them how we are, what we're about who live here on this Turtle Island."

So really, in a way I'm very glad that we got them back, because we got all of those concepts back. And secondly, it is a lot of hard work . . . For there is so much work I do not know where to begin. There is just so much. But nevertheless, I have committed myself ever since I was asked to be one of the spiritual leaders . . . At that time when I was asked, that's when I decided to commit myself to a lifetime of work for my people.

Now when a Haudenosaunee says "my people," he means all of the Haudenosaunee. And it goes beyond that to all four different colors of the people made by the Creator. So that they can live in peace. So it is a big responsibility. Perhaps some of you don't know about it, but it is really a heavy job on our shoulder, and yet we must be very careful not to be above anybody for we *are* created equal. And that is what that means. It just means that some of us have heavy jobs put on our shoulders, which doesn't necessarily mean that we are above anyone else.

Each Fire has a different job. And they must be ever vigilant to make sure they do their particular job. For when all of those Fires get together, we become whole. And each time we do that, we come together, we draw strength from one another and become ever stronger again. And that is where your whole bunch of words, shall I say, that "people need people." And we need each other. We draw strength from one another.

So on that day when you leave, we become just male and female Haudenosaunee people, ever before we are stripped of who we are and our jobs and our titles. For the Creator when he calls you back does not consider what your title is. It is enough that you have finished your job here on earth, which is the reason why He sent you here in the first place.

Now, there was mention about this cloth which still is alive as a result of the signing of this treaty. Well, just last week I went down and collected a half a yard of unbleached muslin. That isn't even enough to make one panel on my window. It might make four potholders. But nonetheless, I went down and claimed it, keeping that Canandaigua Treaty alive and what it stands for. If it gets down to an eighth of a yard, I will stand there and collect it. (Green 1989)

The 1794 Canandaigua Treaty Commemoration Committee was formed in 1984 by many long time supporters of the treaty. The purpose of the committee was to continue to maintain awareness of the treaty through a program of public education. Planning efforts for the 200th anniversary of the Canandaigua Treaty began in 1984 and continued for a decade. In 1985 and for the next eight years, the committee unsuccessfully petitioned the U.S. Postal Service to issue a commemorative postage stamp for the bicentennial treaty celebration.

Hundreds of local officials and residents continued to attend annual treaty commemorations in Canandaigua. Noticeably absent, however, were U.S. state and national officials. On the eve of the 200th Anniversary Canandaigua Treaty Commemoration, there was an unprecedented effort to publicize the upcoming event as widely as possible.

THE YEAR 1994: EDUCATING "OUR WHITE BROTHERS"

At the social at the Canandaigua Academy on the evening of the 200th anniversary of the Canandaigua Treaty, Chief Irving Powless Jr., Onondaga Nation, remarked:

1994 has been a year of education to our white brothers. We have spent the year lecturing at various learning institutes from elementary schools on into the colleges. I have attended Cornell, Colgate, Finger Lakes Community College, [and] Onondaga Community College, informing our white brothers about the meanings of the treaties. Fundamentally, all of the treaties that we have or made, at Fort Stanwix, Fort Harmar, and the Canandaigua Treaty, are all based on the first treaty that was made in 1613, the Guswenta, the Two Row Wampum Belt, which depicts how we shall travel down through life together in harmony with each other and with nature, looking out for the future generations. (Powless 1994)

In June 1994, Vernon Jimerson, chair, and G. Peter Jemison, co-chair of the 1994 Canandaigua Treaty Commemoration Committee, flew to Washington, D.C., to invite U.S. congressional representatives to attend the 200th anniversary treaty celebration. President Bill

Clinton was invited to attend. "The president's assistant, Ricki L. Seidman, wrote in a Sept. 26 letter to Louis Clark, Bristol Historical Society president, that Clinton could not attend the celebration" (Tarr 1994, 3A). Local officials and citizens continued to write to Clinton, still hopeful he would come.

On September 25, 1994, an article about the 200th anniversary of the treaty appeared in the *New York Times*. The article announced the arrival of treaty cloth from the U. S. government "at the upstate tribal grounds 12 days ago, on time and true to an exceptional 200-year-old treaty, just the way George Washington intended" (Clines 1994, 39).

On October 3, J. Sheldon Fisher and his wife and son visited the National Archives in Washington, D.C., to obtain a photograph of the U.S. government copy of the treaty. A life-sized enlargement of the photograph was compared with the Six Nations copy of the treaty displayed at the Ontario County Historical Society. The language of the two handwritten documents was exactly the same.

Later the same month, Seneca Vernon "Barney" Jimerson, chair of the 1994 Canandaigua Treaty Commemoration Committee, traveled to Salem, Massachusetts, to honor Timothy Pickering, the sole U.S. commissioner at the Canandaigua Treaty negotiations. Jimerson gave the following account of his visit:

> My wife, Carol, and I went to Gloucester, Massachusetts, the weekend of October 15, 1994. Carol's cousin Inda Gill and our friend Armand Sindoni live there. Before we went, we had made arrangements to visit the gravesite of Timothy Pickering. We had called the newspaper. They suggested to do it on Monday, October 17, and said they would have a reporter there. So we did.
>
> Gloucester is the oldest American fishing colony and fishing seaport. It still has some fishing businesses and is a summer tourist attraction with its seascape and artist colonies. When we started out on Monday to go to Salem, we had breakfast with Inda and Armand. They joined us because we had talked about the Canandaigua Treaty and making the trip. They wanted to see the gravesite. We had breakfast in Rockport and afterward stopped at a small florist's for the flowers. I talked with the florist about what I was doing and what I wanted.
>
> And he said, "Anyone who comes all this way to do an honor to Timothy Pickering, I'll give you the flowers for free."
>
> Of course, I thanked him. I thought that was pretty nice of him.
>
> When we got to Salem, I had to ask for directions. But we finally met with the reporter and went to the Pickering House.

Sarah Pickering, descendant of Timothy Pickering, and Vernon Jimerson at Timothy Pickering gravesite, Salem, Massachusetts, October 1994. Photo © Armand Sindoni.

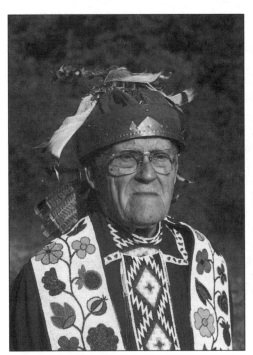

J. Sheldon Fisher,
Former Ontario County Historian.
Photo © Helen M. Ellis.

Vernon "Barney" Jimerson (Seneca).
Photo © Helen M. Ellis.

And it happened that Sarah Pickering, the President of the Pickering Foundation, was there. So we told her what we were doing. She had only about an hour to spend with us.

We visited the tomb of Timothy Pickering and even had time to go inside the house. We saw a letter to Timothy Pickering from the then President George Washington. There were other things that would have been interesting to see but we didn't have the time.

The reason I went to Salem was to promote interest in Pickering's accomplishment and to honor him. I thought it would be a way from someone from the Six Nations to say "thank you" after all these two hundred years.

To me, the Canandaigua Treaty is proof that *peace and friendship* will last a long time with compromise. What made it so great was that it was made by the great minds and hearts of great men who were wise to know that it should be that way. I would like the whole world to know about the treaty. Maybe there wouldn't be so much fighting. (Jimerson 1996)

A few days later, the following editorial by Managing Editor Nelson K. Benton III appeared in the Salem, Massachusetts, *Evening News*:

A member of the Seneca Nation, Vernon Jimerson, stopped in at Recreation Director Larry McIntire's office in the former Salem Willows fire station the other day to ask for directions to the Pickering House.

According to McIntire, the Native American leader from upstate New York had apparently followed the signs for Pickering Wharf figuring the house bearing the same name must be someplace nearby. He soon discovered, however, that there are a number of sites in Salem that bear the Pickering name, and rightly so.

In fact, the reason for Jimerson's visit was to honor one of the most prominent of the Pickerings—Timothy—who served as secretary of state under George Washington and John Adams.

A Recreation Department employee led the visitor to Broad Street where, across from the family homestead, Timothy Pickering is buried. There Jimerson placed a bouquet of flowers on the gravesite of the Salem man who 200 years ago next month negotiated a treaty with the Seneca, Mohawk, Oneida, Onondaga, Cayuga, and Tuscarora tribes that is still honored today.

Every year, members still receive the annual payment, including several thousand yards of muslin cloth, promised under the terms of the 1794 agreement giving the people of the fledgling nation Pickering represented access to the western frontier across Indian lands.

United States flag and Ontario County flag at Ontario County Courthouse, Canandaigua, New York. 200th Anniversary of the Canandaigua Treaty, November 11, 1994. Photo © Anna M. Schein

In this age of fleeting commitments in everything from business dealings to marriages, this is an achievement that ought to be celebrated not only by the Senecas and other tribes, but by the citizens of Salem.

The official observance of the 200th anniversary of the Canandaigua Treaty will take place on Nov. 11 in Canandaigua, New York, and is expected to attract several thousand people.

But the fact that two centuries later people still remember and honor a man—a son of Salem—who negotiated in good faith and could be counted on to keep his word, is something that ought to be impressed on every student in the city's public schools. It's a lesson that ought not be forgotten. (Benton 1994, 6)

In early November, several events were held to further publicize the upcoming celebration. On November 1, Seneca G. Peter Jemison spoke in Henrietta, New York, about the treaty and the two hundred-year anniversary. A daylong festival of storytelling for children by Seneca-Cayuga Charlene Winger-Bearskin, crafts, and a symposium for adults was sponsored by the Ontario County Historical Society in Canandaigua. Seneca historian John Mohawk spoke at Finger Lakes Community College on November 9, 1994.

The 1794 Canandaigua Treaty Commemoration Committee completed final preparations for the grand celebration. The City of Canandaigua stood ready to welcome all who would return once more to the Chosen Spot for the 200th anniversary of the Canandaigua Treaty.

＊　　＊　　＊

The 200th Anniversary of the Canandaigua Treaty

In the quiet of the morning on November 11, 1994, Seneca Vernon Jimerson, chair of the 1994 Canandaigua Treaty Commemoration Committee, and Mohawk Art Cook placed a Two Row Wampum Belt floral arrangement at Council Rock. By noon, hundreds walked through the city, stopping at vendors' craft stands on their way to the Ontario County Courthouse. A few hours later, thousands lined Main Street awaiting the parade of Nations. Seneca G. Peter Jemison, master of ceremonies for the commemoration, recalls the spirit of the moment as the parade began:

Crisp fall air, clear blue sky, and bright sunshine lent to the beauty of the 200th Anniversary of the Canandaigua Treaty. With Haudenosaunee spirits high and the people dressed in their finest *On:gweh'onh:weh:ka:a asyon'yasha'* Indian outfits the parade began.

From the West Gibson Street Elementary school marchers proceeded to North Main Street in Canandaigua, New York, turned right and headed south to meet federal officials as well as state and local leaders who gathered to mark this historic occasion. Hundreds of cameras began clicking at once, and those lining the route broke into spontaneous applause. Looking down Main Street, I saw the tops of the American flags as the marchers coming from South Main began to reach the crest of the hill. The hair on the back of my neck stood up; the spectacle was dazzling and I was filled with joy. The day we had been carefully planning for a year was at hand.

We proceeded to a point near the front of the Ontario County Court House where a facsimile made of plywood depicting the *Guswenta,* our Two Row Wampum Belt, was laid across the street. Jay Claus, Tuscarora Nation, was designated as the Runner for the Six Nations; he carried an Eagle Staff and was dressed in a buckskin outfit and *gustoweh.* He met at the site of the Two Row Belt with Jeff Gleason, a Canandaigua Boy Scout.

Jay gave three whoops to announce their rendezvous. The Eagle Staff was presented to the young Scout which he solemnly carried to the official Federal representative, Louise Slaughter, Democratic member of the House of Representatives. She in turn led the Federal contingent to the appointed place where they joined with the Haudenosaunee delegation led by Tadodaho Chief Leon Shenandoah.

Together they proceeded up the front walk of the Courthouse towards the portico for the ceremonies which followed. By now non-Native friends were participants as well. (Jemison 1995, 55)

Compiler's note: Here begins the transcript of the 200th Anniversary Canandaigua Treaty Commemoration. Compiler's notes appear in italics. The speakers' public addresses have been edited slightly for this written version and include only the substantive portion of their remarks. This transcript was prepared from a personal audio tape and the video entitled: **1794 Canandaigua Treaty Commemoration Committee Hosts the Canandaigua Treaty [Also Known As] the Pickering Treaty: The Two Hundredth Anniversary, Canandaigua, New York, November 11, 1994,** *produced by Finger Lakes TV, 1994.*

G. Peter Jemison, Seneca Nation
Master of Ceremonies

OPENING REMARKS AND ACKNOWLEDGMENTS

I would like to thank each and every one of you for coming today to join
with us here to commemorate this treaty, 200 years old, still in place,
still a binding agreement, creating peace and friendship between our
people. My name is Peter Jemison and I serve as the Co-Chairman of the
1794 Canandaigua Treaty Commemoration Committee. I would invite
those who were in the parade to come forward and join us here in front.
With the federal delegation, we have a Color Guard, an Army National
Guard, 10th Mountain Division, Headquarters Company, 2nd Battal-
ion, 108th Infantry Regiment.

I want to acknowledge those who have gathered here with us. Here
in front, holding our George Washington Belt[,] is Emerson Webster of
the Tonawanda Band of Seneca, a Seneca Chief. And to his right is Chief
Leo Henry of the Tuscarora Nation. This is the Washington Covenant
Belt which we associate with this Treaty of Canandaigua between the
United States government and our Six Nations Haudenosaunee people.

I want to acknowledge the runner who came from the Six Nations
side, Jay Claus. As he said to me, "It's a great honor to be able to be the
runner to carry our Eagle Flag for our Native American people." And
Jeff Holland, who represented the U.S. side, I want to thank Jeff Holland
who was the runner for the federal side.

And now, I'm going to mention these leaders who are here to my
right. Then, I'm going to do as we do traditionally, that which comes
before all, we give a Thanksgiving. And we're fortunate again today that
we have with us Clayton Logan, who will take care of what we call our
Gannönyoh.

So first, I'd like to acknowledge Irving Powless, the Chief of the
Onondaga Nation. I want to acknowledge next, Chief Oren Lyons,
Stanley Buck, Seneca Chief, and behind him, Stuart Patterson.

Now, I'd like to ask the gentlemen in the audience to remove their
headgear, to remove their hat. We're going to ask Mr. Clayton Logan to
come and give a Gannönyoh. He's going to give first a translation in
English and then a Seneca version of that Gannönyoh.

*The transcription of the Thanksgiving Address as spoken by Clayton
Logan opens this volume and appears immediately following the Introduction by G. Peter Jemison.*

And now we have one other formal part. Subchief Jake Swamp, of the
Kahniakehaka Nation, the Mohawk Nation, is going to address the

Edge of the Woods speech to the United States official representative Louise Slaughter, representing the 28th district in the Congress of the United States.

The transcription of the Edge of the Woods as spoken by Chief Jake Swamp opens this volume and appears immediately following the Thanksgiving Address by Clayton Logan.

LOUISE M. SLAUGHTER
Congress of the United States, 28th District, New York

To the Sachems, Chiefs, and people of the Haudenosaunee, I bring greetings from the President of the United States:

> Warm greetings to everyone gathered in Canandaigua, New York, to commemorate the 200th anniversary of the Canandaigua Treaty between the Six Nations Iroquois Confederacy and the United States of America.
>
> This momentous occasion comes during an important chapter in our nation's history—a chapter in which the federal government is keeping faith with Native Americans. Last April, I was pleased to sign a memorandum on government-to-government relations renewing our support for self-governance and our commitment to a stronger partnership between our nations. In this same spirit, we join together to celebrate our diverse cultures and common history.
>
> Since 1794, the historic Canandaigua treaty has been a symbol of our relationship, which today remains unique and enduring. As the Treaty's First Article states, "peace and friendship are hereby established, and shall be perpetual . . ." Working together, we can usher in a great new era of understanding, cooperation, and respect among our people. In the spirit of the Treaty, we continue to listen and learn from one another and look forward together to a brighter future for all people.
>
> Best wishes for a wonderful anniversary celebration.
>
> William Jefferson Clinton
President of the United States

It is a singular honor for me, as a member of Congress of the United States, to be with you today to celebrate the oldest document of its kind in United States history. Peace has been perpetual. Our chains of friendship have sometimes been strained. Encroachments have been made on lands. But every time, the treaty held.

To the sixty thousand members of the Confederacy, I express my government's gratitude and my own, that they have kept the treaty intact. The United States will do no less. We affirm our intention to respect the sovereignty of one another and pledge not to interfere in the government affairs of the other. Let us continue to live in peace and friendship as two sovereign nations according to the articles of the Canandaigua Treaty. And may our peace and friendship be perpetual.

G. Peter Jemison, Seneca Nation
Master of Ceremonies

Many people over the years have helped to maintain this important treaty between our people. One of those that we must acknowledge as playing a long and continuing role in the remembrance of this treaty is the venerable historian from the town of Victor. I'd like to call forward Mr. J. Sheldon Fisher, who will read part of the preamble to the Pickering Treaty as well as some of the pertinent articles.

J. SHELDON FISHER
Ontario County Historian, 1960–66

I want to call your attention to the Ontario County flag. When I became County Historian, I thought it was a good opportunity to officially recognize the Haudenosaunee, the People of the Longhouse, who once lived here. And so I used the white pine tree, which has five needles for the Five Nations, and the colors from the two men who bought Western New York from the Indians, Oliver Phelps and Nathaniel Gorham.

Now October 3, my wife, my son, Doug, [and I] went down to Washington so he could be sworn as a lawyer to practice before the opening of the United States Supreme Court. And that gave us a chance to go over to the National Archives and search out that original treaty, because so few white people have ever seen it. And so down here in front, we have a photograph of that in color. This is the one, as we saw it.

And when I went in there, I remarked, "This is like getting into Fort Knox!"

The man said, "It's worse!"

So, it's well protected. Now, this treaty:

> [*Article 6.*] In consideration of the peace and friendship hereby established, and of the engagements entered into by the Six Nations; and because the United States desire, with humanity and kindness, to contribute to their comfortable

support; and to render the peace and friendship hereby established strong and perpetual, the United States now deliver to the Six Nations and the Indians of other nations residing among, and united with them, a quantity of goods, of the value of ten thousand dollars. And for the same considerations, and with a view to promote the future welfare of the Six Nations, and of their Indian friends aforesaid, the United States will add the sum of [three thousand dollars to the one thousand five hundred dollars heretofore allowed them by an article ratified by the President, on the twenty-third day of April, 1792, making in the whole] four thousand five hundred dollars; which shall be expended yearly, forever, in [purchasing] clothing, domestic animals, implements of [husbandry] . . .

[Note.] In witness whereof, the said Timothy Pickering, and the sachems and the war chiefs of the said Six Nations have hereunto set their hands and seals.

Done at Canandaigua, in the State of New York, the eleventh day of November, in the year one thousand and seven hundred and ninety-four.

[Ratification by George Washington] Now know ye that I, having seen and considered the said Treaty, do by, and with the advice and consent of the Senate of the United States, accept, ratify, and confirm the same, and every article and clause thereof. In testimony whereof, I have caused the seal of the United States to be hereunto affixed, and assigned with the same with my hand, here in the City of Philadelphia, the twenty-first day of January in the year of our Lord, one thousand seven hundred and ninety-five, and in the nineteenth year of the sovereignty, and independence of the United States.

Signed by George Washington. And you can see his signature there.

G. Peter Jemison, Seneca Nation
Master of Ceremonies

Now it is my great pleasure to ask the Tadodaho of our Haudenosaunee people to come forward and to give his message to you today.

CHIEF LEON SHENANDOAH
Tadodaho, Haudenosaunee Six Nations Confederacy

Thank you. You are well. I know it's been a long time that we've been waiting for this day, this treaty that was made in 1794. I've always thought back, at that time, my people and other people must have been a hearty people to stand this cold weather. And I'm sure they didn't get here by cars. They had to travel by canoe. And it's been a long journey for them to get here.

At that time, when they were making the treaty,[5] they were trying to decide, how to, where to write the things. They wanted to use wood. But they thought if they wrote it on the wood, then it would rot. Then they thought they would use paper, but that also would rot. Then they mentioned about iron. But they thought that would get rusty.

So the Six Nations decided to make a wampum, a Two Row Wampum, with the United States canoe on one side and the Six Nations on one side. And if you turn that wampum, they would never meet.

So the question came, was that, "What if," the government said, "what if your people will want to get in our canoe?"

"Well," [the Chief] says, "if they do, then they'll have to follow your way of life."

"And supposing my people try to get in your canoe?"

And the chief says, "No, I doubt that they would want to come in our canoe."

So they decided that the United States would write their treaty on a paper. And the Six Nations made their wampum, the Two Row Wampum, which will never meet or cross over.

So to this day, as of this day, we are still getting our treaty cloth, which means that they are now, they are honoring the treaty. They're still honoring the treaty. So we are still getting our cloth.

After the treaty was made, there were a lot of other treaties that were made, some about the boundary lines. And there's three or four treaties that I know are very important.

But also, that we are also honoring the United States for holding on to the treaty and upliving. This day, I know you've been standing out there a long time. And it's not really that warm. At least, I'm not the one that's warm.

But what I wanted to say was that we hope, nobody knows how long it's going to last. But five years after they made this treaty, a message came from the man above telling what's going to happen in the future.[6] But that future, there are some that are here now. But there are some that hasn't happened yet. But it will get here later.

So I could stand here about another couple hours and tell you what's coming in the future, how it's going to happen. But I think I'll just leave that until later.

G. Peter Jemison, Seneca Nation
Master of Ceremonies

At that meeting 200 years ago when this treaty was made, the Quakers were present. They were invited by the Seneca people, because they were people of peace. And they came here to observe the treaty proceedings and to be sure that the language in each of these treaties, as it was written, was consistent with what we understood, so that our agreements would be firm. And we have with us a Quaker Representative today.

LOIS KUTER, CLERK OF THE INDIAN COMMITTEE
Philadelphia Yearly Meeting of the Society of Friends

I am here with Alice Long and Dan Long, and we bring you greetings from the Indian Committee of the Philadelphia Yearly Meeting of the Society of Friends.

Just three weeks ago, we celebrated the 350th birthday of William Penn in Philadelphia. Although not perfect, this Quaker founder of Pennsylvania tried to create a society where all could live in peace with each other. In a letter to the Lenape he wrote, "Now I would have you well observe that I am very sensible of the unkindness and injustice towards you by the people of these parts of the world. But I am not such a man. I have great love and regards towards you and desire to win and gain your love and friendship by a kind, just and peaceable life."

In the last decade of the 18th century when the capital of the United States was located in Philadelphia, Quakers were able to petition on behalf of the Indians who came to present grievances to the President and Congress. And it was not uncommon in this period for delegations of Quakers to be called upon by Indians to witness treaty conferences.

Such was the case in 1794 as you heard. As a report that was made after the trip when Friends got back to Philadelphia stated:

Many are the difficulties and sufferings to which the Indians are subjected, and their present Situation appears loudly to claim the Sympathy and Attention of the members of our religious Society and others who have grown numerous and opulent on the former Inheritance of these poor declining People; we cannot but believe some mode may be fallen upon of rendering them more essential service than has yet been adopted. (Kelsey 1917, 91–92)

That mode to be created was the Indian Committee of Philadelphia Yearly Meeting.[7] And as you mark the 200th Anniversary of the Canandaigua Treaty, next year we will mark the 200th Anniversary of the Indian Committee. In looking back over 200 years, one can see that some of the essential service the Committee tried to render the Six Nations was not always very welcome. The new farming practices that we tried to use to help you civilize (although you were already civilized) was a case in point. We would like to hope that our efforts to help with the Kinzua Dam, to prevent the relocation of people, was more welcome even though it was unsuccessful.

Today the Indian Committee tries to continue the work first started by William Penn, to win and gain the love and friendship of Native Peoples by learning from you, by working with you to create a kind, just and peaceable world. And it's in this spirit that we present a small token of our friendship. This is a tapestry that was created specifically for the 350th Anniversary of William Penn.

G. Peter Jemison, Seneca Nation
Master of Ceremonies

We have representatives who have joined us of some of our Congressmen. And I'd like to, at this time, invite to the microphone Kraig Siracuse from the office of Alfonse D'Amato.

KRAIG SIRACUSE
From the Office of Senator Alfonse M. D'Amato, State of New York

The address delivered by Kraig Siracuse from Senator Alfonse D'Amato was entered into the **Congressional Record** *in December 1994.*

Good afternoon. I'm here on behalf of Senator D'Amato, who sends his best regards.

We are here today gathered to recognize one of the oldest and most respected treaties ever written in New York State. The Canandaigua Treaty of 1794 signed between the United States and the people of the Six Nations of Indians established a firm and permanent friendship which has lasted two hundred years. In recognizing this treaty, we also recognize the many great things accomplished all over New York State through the team work of the Haudenosaunee and the descendants of all those who settled in New York State. Together our state has grown and prospered, always respecting the rights of all who live within our borders.

The Treaty of 1794 served as a model for the entire United States. The friendship that it recognized on paper has grown into a bond which knows no separation. The American Frontier had seen much bloodshed. People from all over the globe came to America to escape injustice and begin new lives free of oppression. As the fight for expansion raged on in the West, the people of the Six Nations of Indians worked with their new neighbors to establish what would serve all in the United States as a model of peace and understanding based on trust and respect.

The first Article of the treaty proclaims the underlying theme of the entire agreement—peace and friendship. That friendship has remained for two hundred years, and continues to grow as we work together.

The second through fourth Articles establish the recognized boundaries between the United States and the Haudenosaunee. The focus is mutual respect and an understanding that the United States, having acknowledged what lands belong to the Six Nations "will never claim the same, nor disturb the Six Nations people or their Indian friends in the free use of and enjoyment thereof."

The last Article of the Canandaigua Treaty, Article number seven, incorporates the spirit of cooperation and the sense of justice which both signatories held so sacred. Article seven establishes "that, for injuries done by individuals, on either side, no private revenge or retaliation shall be made by the party injured, to the other, but, instead thereof, complaint shall be made by the party injured, to the other."

The celebration of the Canandaigua Treaty of 1794 is a celebration of friendship and cooperation. This day is important because it commemorates that great spirit of friendship which keeps our separate communities together. I congratulate the people of Canandaigua and the Haudenosaunee.

G. Peter Jemison, Seneca Nation
Master of Ceremonies

From Congressman Bill Paxon's office from the New York 27th District, his staff assistant, John R. Haldow:

JOHN R. HALDOW
Office of L. William Paxon, House of Representatives,
27th District, State of New York

Bill's sorry he couldn't be here personally today as a representative of Canandaigua in the Congress. It's a very special day not only for Canandaigua but for the United States. The Canandaigua Treaty represents two hundred years of friendship and peace between the nations of the Six Nations of Indians and the United States of America. And we look forward to another two hundred years of continued peace and friendship. We thank you very much for allowing us to be part of the program.

G. Peter Jemison, Seneca Nation
Master of Ceremonies

Representing the State of New York is the Secretary of State from New York State, Gail Shaffer.

GAIL SHAFFER
Secretary of State, State of New York

It is truly an honor to be here today on behalf of Governor Cuomo and all the people of the State of New York to honor and rededicate ourselves to this special treaty. It is also an occasion to pay tribute on behalf of all New Yorkers to the great Haudenosaunee Nation, to their wonderful leaders with whom we have worked over the years. We're very honored, too, to have Congresswoman Slaughter here, and also, Assistant Secretary Ada Deer, and the Mayor of Canandaigua. You notice in the true matriarchal tradition of the Iroquois, there are many women involved here today.

If you will permit me to make a couple of personal observations, because I will be winding up my service as Secretary of State in about seven weeks. And in my twelve years as Secretary of State, I must say that one of the great privileges has been to work with the Iroquois and to learn so much from them. Some of my most treasured memories will be of those occasions of meeting in the Longhouse to discuss issues of equity that involved the State of New York and the Haudenosaunee, to work for the return of the wampum to the Longhouse, which after eight long years we finally did accomplish, to be there at the celebration of the 200th Anniversary of the Fort Stanwix Treaty, and now here today for this very special commemoration of two centuries of peace and friendship represented by the Canandaigua Treaty.

We are particularly honored by the presence of Chief Shenandoah and all the other leaders of the Haudenosaunee. And I want to say how very much I will treasure all the memories I have of working with you, particularly wonderful people like Oren Lyons, a very special friend, and Irving Powless, and so many others.

We have so much to learn in our own culture from the Iroquois. There is already so much that we have borrowed in our own culture, particularly the Federalist concept in our own constitution which has been one of the strongest pillars of our democracy. That was borrowed from the Haudenosaunee. And also the values that they have taught us and symbolized in their actions of treasuring Mother Earth and being true stewards of the values of environmental caring. They have a saying among Native Americans that we do not inherit the Earth from our ancestors, we borrow it from our children. That is the kind of attitude we have learned from them.

I had the privilege only two weeks ago of being in New York City with Senator Moynihan for the dedication of the new Museum of the American Indian of the Smithsonian Institution, the first branch in New York being commemorated, and the Washington museum will be completed by the year 2000. This museum will be a wonderful resource for all Americans to teach all of us, Native Americans and others, of the wonderful traditions of this living culture of Native Americans throughout our country. When we dedicated the museum, Senator Moynihan alluded to the importance of the Pickering Treaty on that occasion.

It is a treaty which embodies, as the words of the treaty say, "humanity and kindness," and a permanent and perpetual and strong friendship and peace among our peoples. We know that the great strength of America has been our pluralism and our mutual respect for each other's rights and values in this wonderful mosaic of many cultures that is represented in America more than anywhere else on the Earth. But the great irony of our history has been that when it has come to our relationship with our Native American brothers and sisters, we have not always lived up to those ideals of freedom and equal opportunity. We are on a journey, hopefully, of reaching that greater equity as we continue to work together.

And as this treaty embodies the spirit of peace and of friendship, it is important to remember that peace does not merely mean the absence of war, but the presence of justice. And that is what we all must dedicate ourselves to today.

It is my great honor on behalf of the Governor to present a citation from the people of the State of New York to Chief Shenandoah. And I will read it as follows:

November 11, 1994 marks the 200th Anniversary of the Treaty of Canandaigua which firmly established perpetual peace and friendship between the United States and the Six Nations of the Iroquois. The Treaty commemorates an historic and significant relationship between the Iroquois Confederacy and the United States government.

Many Indians who reside within the boundaries of New York State have retained their language, their religion, their traditional government of chiefs and clan relationships. Indian people, including the Iroquois and Algonquin, indigenous to this state, continue to play a prominent role in the culture and economy of New York State.

The State of New York aspires to seek greater knowledge, understanding, and trust in carrying out its unique government-to-government relationships with Indian nations within our borders. I urge all citizens to celebrate and study the history and traditions of Native People during this special day.

Now, therefore, I, Mario Cuomo, Governor of the State of New York, do hereby confer this special citation upon the people of the Six Nations of the Iroquois in New York State.

And I will present this to Chief Shenandoah. It is an honor to be with you. And we also have a reproduction of the George Washington Wampum.

And I'd like to conclude by mentioning one of those very special memories I will keep with me forever. The Iroquois, some years ago, honored me with honorary membership in the Six Nations and gave me the name of *Goyodadogoot*. So, as Goyodadogoot, which they tell me means Outstanding Truth, I will take you in my heart in whatever I go forward in from here.

G. Peter Jemison, Seneca Nation
Master of Ceremonies

Now I'd like to call forth Chief Bernie Parker of the Tonawanda Band of Seneca. It is in the original territory of the Seneca people that we are today. This is where we come from, those of us who refer to ourselves as Onöndawahgah. And so it's a fitting place that we here have the message from one of those who is charged with Keeping the Western Door.

CHIEF BERNARD PARKER
Tonawanda Band of Seneca

Honored guests that are standing up here addressing you today and all of you people:

You are all honored guests today because we come here to honor and acknowledge this 200-year-old Canandaigua Treaty. I'm proud of you for that fact, to see so many people here today, and especially the young ones who will carry this responsibility on into the next generation. We have always taught among our people to make the decisions for the seventh generation. And if there is anything that we can carry on in the future, let's pass the responsibility of polishing this covenant chain in our treaty relationships. That is the most important message that I can give you today.

And I know we've all been standing here for a long time. And somewhere in this wind, I think I smell some fry bread. Clayton gave us the good words of our Thanksgiving. The Sun has given us brightness this

day. It's just been a pleasure and I'd like to thank everybody here for coming and participating. That's all I have to say at this time.
Da'ne'ho'.

G. Peter Jemison, Seneca Nation
Master of Ceremonies

Our next speaker is Ada Deer of the Menominee Nation. She's Assistant Secretary for Indian Affairs, United States Department of the Interior.

ADA DEER, MENOMINEE NATION
Assistant Secretary for Indian Affairs, U.S. Department of the Interior

Honored Chiefs, Sachems, Members of the Haudenosaunee, Fellow Citizens:

I am deeply honored and pleased to share with you in this celebration of the 200th Anniversary of the signing of the Canandaigua Treaty. As I sat here listening to the moving words of the previous speakers, many thoughts came to my mind. And I want to share some of these with you.

I stand here in my official capacity as the Assistant Secretary for Indian Affairs in the Department of the Interior. I am also a Native person of this country. And as I listened to the Society of Friends, the Quakers, I thought about the generations that preceded me in my family. My mother is [of] English, Scotch, and Irish descent. My father is a member of the Menominee Tribe. I'm also an activist and a social worker. And I want to make special note of the Society of Friends. As citizens they have stood for peace, justice, and equality, for many, many years, not only in this country but across the world. I have from my mother's side of the family, members of the Society of Friends. And so, I have many strands here embodied today in my person.

I feel the weight of history on my shoulders as I work every day to do my best to carry out the duties and the obligations of this country toward American Indians and Alaska Natives. And I'm strengthened by the courage, the vision, the dedication of the people on all sides of my family. I share this with you to help you think about your family and your connections. We are all connected. We are all people on the planet. The Haudenosaunee knew this. The Native Peoples practice this. It is an important aspect of all of our lives. So we are all connected. And as you look across here today, we see people from the Federal government, the state government, the city government, the citizens, friends, we are all connected.

And it is important to know the history of our country. It is important to celebrate this particular occasion. Treaties are the supreme law of the land. Our constitution is a living document. And we are all here to remember and to commemorate that.

Today, and in the months and years to come, we all face difficult choices on issues of mutual concern. The federal government as a whole, the State of New York, and people of the Six Nations all must honestly confront the issues of sovereignty, law, and political development which are inherent in the provisions of the Treaty of Canandaigua. That is the relationship of the treaty to us here today, and that is the relationship which we will continue to foster with all of you, as we all carry out our joint and mutual responsibilities. We must continue to build up the partnership of mutual respect and cooperation which is inherent in the treaty. That is why I am here today to again give you the treaty cloth as representatives have in the past.

We must confront the dilemma of balancing traditions and governing practices to meet the challenges of an ever changing world. The Two Row Wampum, the two canoes in the ocean of life, need not go in opposite directions. Some may prefer one canoe over the other, but the current may take us all in the same direction.

One of the signers of this treaty which we honor today was Handsome Lake. Within five years of the treaty signing, he had his vision, which set out the beginning of his religious and personal odyssey. Each of us today must rededicate ourselves to inspire our people, as he sought to inspire the Haudenosaunee. We should all participate in this renewal.

We must explore the opportunities for economic development which will include all the members and leaders of the Haudenosaunee who want to participate. Because of these challenges, each of us must persevere to observe and uphold the rule of law, educate and enlighten our constituencies of the great laws, and carry out the vision for the seven generations.

So as a continuing commitment of this country in honoring the treaty, I am now going to present to Chief Leon Shenandoah this muslin: Chief, it is my honor and pleasure to present this muslin to Chief Shenandoah as a perpetual honoring and observation of the treaty of this country.

CHIEF LEON SHENANDOAH
Tadodaho, Haudenosaunee Six Nations Confederacy

I think I mentioned the vision, or the message, that came from Handsome Lake. In that message that he got, it says "You must, all leaders, must think seven generations ahead, even those little ones that's still coming from under the ground. That they, too, must enjoy what we are enjoying today."

G. Peter Jemison, Seneca Nation
Master of Ceremonies

It was not mentioned earlier that the message that was read from Mr. D'Amato will be entered into the *Congressional Record* when the Congress convenes again in December. I wanted to acknowledge that. And now, I'm going to call upon Craig J. Doran, the New York State Assemblyman of the 129th District.

CRAIG J. DORAN
New York State Assemblyman, 129th District

Distinguished leaders of the Six Nations and distinguished government leaders, and ladies and gentlemen of the Finger Lakes and of New York State:

I can't express with words what an honor it is for me to have the opportunity to participate in the commemoration of such an important occasion in not only the history of Canandaigua and the history of Ontario County, but the history of our nation. I grew up in this community and know of the rich traditions and history that are so important to those of us in this area. Many times, as a child, I walked by the Council Rock that's right over here and read the plaque. And I've been to the Historical Society on several occasions and read the treaty. But it wasn't before today, as I stood on Main Street and watched the members of the Iroquois Confederacy and the members of the government contingency here meet on Main Street in a very symbolic gesture, that I realized how the treaty represents so much of the tradition that is important to all of us.

I would ask all of you to remember today that not only do we commemorate an important moment in our history, but we are also making history as we speak. And I think that is so important for all of us to remember, particularly those of us who are here who have the responsibility of representing you in government. I think we should utilize this opportunity not only to remember the great men and women of the Iroquois Confederacy and the great men and women of the United States that two hundred years ago overcame, what I am sure seemed to them to be, insurmountable obstacles to make peace.

And I would ask all of you to join me in not only commemorating history, but in making history today by recommitting ourselves to those traditions of character and stamina. Let us recommit ourselves to the values that have made both of our nations great and move forward, so that we can do justice to the history that has been established for us today.

Peace is so important to all of us. It's truly the foundation of everything that we do. And if Mr. Jemison doesn't mind, I'm going to borrow a quotation that I read in a recent newspaper article, "Peace is a concept that has to be renewed in people's minds over and over again." So whether we're young children, adults, grandparents, or great grandparents, fathers, mothers, I ask that we all take this opportunity to remember those that have made this moment today and to recommit ourselves to bringing peace forth whether in our communities, in our families, in our state, or in our nation. Again, I thank all of you for giving me the opportunity to participate in this moment. And I wish you much happiness in your celebration.

G. Peter Jemison, Seneca Nation
Master of Ceremonies

Among us, there are many veterans. Perhaps they, better than any of us, can appreciate what we come together to acknowledge: peace and friendship. I want to recognize the Color Guard of the Oneida Nation of Wisconsin who has joined us. I also want to acknowledge the Vietnam veterans from Ontario County that have also joined us here today. They have helped to maintain that peace that we all live in. And the many other veterans that are out there today, I want to acknowledge them also on this particular day.

None of this would be possible without the work of the 1794 Canandaigua Treaty Commemoration Committee. Those individuals who are members of that Committee have worked very hard for more than ten years for this occasion. And for the last year, they have given untold amounts of time to make this day happen the way that it has happened. I'd like to ask some of the members of the Committee that may be present and nearby me to come up toward the front of this area here. Would you please join me in giving a thanks, a hearty thanks to all those who have worked so hard as members of the Canandaigua Treaty Commemoration Committee.

I know that there are others who may not be present at this time. But these are the members of the Canandaigua Treaty Commemoration Committee. There's Vernon and Carol Jimerson, Debra Glor, Douglas Fisher, Sheldon Fisher, Robert and Muriel Gorall, Robert Abraham, Arthur Cook, Ed Schmitt, Peter Gerbic, Jerry Fulmer, Ivan Hermanet and his wife, and there's also here Carl Brant. Jane LeClair is certainly an important member. She'll have a role to play here in just a moment. These are some of the members of our Canandaigua Treaty Committee. There are others who are not here right now.[8]

Now I want to acknowledge also that there are others who have made this possible today. And certainly not the least of which is the City of Canandaigua. The City of Canandaigua opened its arms and did everything possible.

When we asked, "Could this be done?"

Their answer was, "Yes, we'll do it for you."

When we turned to Ontario County—the same thing. The cooperation of the City of Canandaigua and Ontario County, I really want to acknowledge at this moment and thank each and every one of them. And now, if I may, I'd like to bring forth the Mayor of the great City of Canandaigua, Ellen Polimeni.

ELLEN POLIMENI
Mayor, City of Canandaigua, New York

This is indeed a very special occasion. It is of special significance to the Haudenosaunee, for they are returning to a sacred spot in their history. It is very special to the people of Canandaigua, because we are privileged to welcome as our guests today all of the elders, all of the Native Americans from other groups, and also all of our residents, Federal officials, state officials, and county officials to take part in this very significant commemoration.

Two hundred years ago today, there met on this spot another group of Native Americans and settlers on a day not quite so pleasant as this. One of the participants wrote in his journal that it was a cold day with several inches of snow on the ground. So I believe today we're blessed. The group that gathered for this momentous occasion stood near an oak tree which later became known as the Treaty Oak. That oak tree stood 96 years past the signing of the Canandaigua Treaty. When it was cut down about 104 years ago, the residents, realizing the significance of this tree, used the wood to make several artifacts: canes, candleholders, and others. And many of those are still within the community.

We, as a people, respect those who keep their word. And I'm told by Native Americans that they, too, deeply respect those who keep their word. It is that mutual respect which has enabled this treaty to endure for 200 years. It is certainly an example which all nations might follow.

On behalf of the City of Canandaigua, I welcome you here today for the 200th Anniversary. But I not only welcome you; I extend a pledge to you that we will join you each year to commemorate this treaty and to reconfirm the loyalty and friendship that exists between us. May it grow stronger as the years pass.

G. Peter Jemison, Seneca Nation
Master of Ceremonies

This year we produced a poster to commemorate the Canandaigua Treaty. The work that went into this poster was done by Jeff Marinelli. He donated this work to us. I want to acknowledge Maranatha Printing who went out of their way to make it possible to get this poster to us. We have this commemorative poster available. I'd like to present one of these framed posters to Louise Slaughter who is here as the U.S. official representative.

Now I want to mention a couple of other things. There is an exhibition devoted to the Canandaigua Treaty at the Ontario County Historical Society. There's also an exhibit of contemporary Haudenosaunee artists. The title of the exhibit is "Our Spirit Grows."

I want to acknowledge our elders who have remained here with us, who have joined us here today and stayed with us through this afternoon as it has cooled off.

Now I would like to bring the Chairman of the Ontario County Board of Supervisors, Mr. Ray Berend to the microphone.

RAY BEREND
Chairman, Ontario County, Town of Bristol, Board of Supervisors

Good afternoon, ladies and gentlemen, People of the Longhouse. It gives me a great deal of pleasure to welcome you here today in front of the County Courthouse to commemorate the 200th Anniversary of the treaty between the United States of America and the Six Nations of the Iroquois Confederacy.

The historic Council Rock marks the location where our ancestors met, negotiated, and signed a treaty of enduring friendship and peace. Many days of preparation took place before the ceremonies and signing on November 11, 1794.

The 1794 Canandaigua Treaty Commemoration Committee has worked for ten years to bring this [event] to the citizens of the Haudenosaunee and the United States. Through the act of celebration, the ceremonies in connection with the historic occasion serve to make us aware of our early history and its importance to generations of citizens. Again, welcome to Ontario County. Thank you for joining us in the celebration of the 200th Anniversary of the Pickering Treaty.

G. Peter Jemison, Seneca Nation
Master of Ceremonies

Now over at the Treaty Rock, joining Jane LeClair are some of our Native American children. What we acknowledge when we go to the Treaty Rock are all of those that have helped to commemorate and to maintain this treaty over the many years that the Canandaigua Treaty Committee has met here in Canandaigua, New York. If those children who would like to lay flowers would begin to move toward the Treaty Rock.

This gives me an opportunity to mention that tomorrow morning beginning at 10:00 a.m. there is a symposium at the Canandaigua high school. And that symposium will be an opportunity for us to discuss the significance of this treaty. We've entitled it "1794–1994: Polishing the Rust from the Chain."[9] Those who will be speaking include Ada Deer, Assistant Secretary for Indian Affairs. "Treaty Making from a Federal Perspective" is the title of her presentation. Then next is Paul Williams, who is attorney for the Six Nations Chiefs at Grand River, "Treaty Making: The Legal Record." The next presenter will be Daniel Richter from Dickinson College. He's Associate Professor of History. The title of his presentation is "The United States and the Canandaigua Treaty." Following a break for lunch, there will be a presentation by Dr. Robert Venables, Senior Lecturer, Department of Rural Sociology, American Indian Program, Cornell University. The title of his presentation is "Sovereignty, Land, and Taxes: The Legal and Historical Context of the Treaty of Canandaigua." And then following that will be Oren Lyons, Faithkeeper of the Turtle Clan, Onondaga Nation, Professor of Native American Studies, American Studies Department, SUNY Buffalo. And his is "A View from the Six Nations of the Canandaigua Treaty."

Jane LeClair then spoke as children laid flowers on Council Rock. Her remarks were inaudible on the videotape. Jane later supplied the text of her ceremony. Following is her supplied text:

> Today we come together to
> recall the signing of the Great Treaty
> at the "Chosen Spot,"
> Canandaigua, New York, in 1794.
> May our children be inspired
> to continue this commemoration
> to honor their ancestors, to honor their elders
> and to pass this beautiful ceremony to future generations.
>
> We hope and pray,
> May the United States and the Six Nations

continue to honor each other
for all time through
the 1794 Canandaigua Peace Treaty preservation.

May all children only know peace.

A red rose is placed upon Treaty Rock
in memory of the people of the Six Nations
who signed the 1794 Treaty in good faith.

We remember those who have gone on to the Spirit world.
(LeClair 1996)

G. Peter Jemison, Seneca Nation
Master of Ceremonies

Joining me here at the podium are Oren Lyons and Arvol Looking Horse from the Lakota Nation. And I would like to acknowledge and have Oren speak further on that.

OREN LYONS
Faithkeeper, Onondaga Nation

I'm very pleased to see Arvol here as a representative of the Oglalas and the Lakota Nation. As you may or may not know, in 1973 when they had a great deal of trouble in his nation, the Haudenosaunee went in force. And we met with Chief Fools Crow here at Onondaga and we sent people to his nation to help bring peace to a very troubled time and place. And so we struck a treaty at that time with the Lakota people, of peace and friendship and mutual respect.

I'm very pleased to see that Arvol Looking Horse has made it here from there. This is Arvol.

ARVOL LOOKING HORSE
Lakota Sioux Nation

On behalf of our people, the Lakota, Dakota, Nakota Sioux Nation, it's an honor to come and be part of this gathering, of nations of all nations, upon Mother Earth. I didn't come by myself. I came with Ernest Sundown from Bighead Reservation, Saskatchewan, Canada. I'd like to thank them for coming with me and some of the people from Six Nations.

We think about our children, the time of peace, and peace gatherings throughout the world. We made a trip to Baghdad in 1990. We took a pipe of peace. And one of our elderly people, she's a well-respected elder from Rosebud Reservation in South Dakota, she made a prayer song on behalf of what is called "mending the sacred hoop" and world peace and harmony.

So I'd like to sing and leave you with this prayer song.

May peace be with you.

G. Peter Jemison, Seneca Nation
Master of Ceremonies

The concluding part of our ceremony is going to take place around the corner, where we have planted a white pine, the Tree of Peace, the symbol of our Confederacy. So those of you who would like to join Mr. Clayton Logan, he will be around to my far left at the Tree of Peace.

For those of you who will be joining us for this evening, we will be concluding our day at the Canandaigua Academy, otherwise known as the high school here in Canandaigua.

I want to thank each and every one of you for joining us here today. It's been a beautiful day. It's been a great day.

Da'ne'ho'.

Here ends the transcript of the 200th Anniversary of the Canandaigua Treaty Celebration.

*   *   *

That evening at the social held at the Canandaigua Academy, Chief Bernard Parker, Tonawanda Band of Seneca, reflected upon the day:

> For myself, as one of the leaders of the Iroquois Confederacy, it was a good feeling to take part in an event such as this and to see so many people, both young and old experience the treaty relationship that we have among one another.
>
> One of the points that I wanted to make, and I hope we make today, is that the polishing of the covenant chain process is for all of us to carry out and to carry on into the future generations. It's a huge responsibility for all of us. And hopefully, we can all go away and share our experience with our friends and relatives all over the United States, because it is a global message. And it's a standard that we should all bear for all the future generations to come. Our responsibility is to them.

So today, we took care of yesterday. Tomorrow, we're going to take care of the future. So, carry these messages forward from these treaty relations (Parker, 1994).

THE CLOSING

At the end of symposium the following day, Chief Jake Swamp, Mohawk Nation, was asked to give the Haudenosaunee traditional closing for the gathering. Before doing so, Jake spoke on behalf of his people:

> First, I'd like to mention how good I feel being here today in honoring the treaty that was made two hundred years ago, and maybe, at the same time mention that some of our people in those times were not able to be present. But we know they were there, a few of them that were able. In that time they were in a very bad situation as a result of the Revolutionary War. It happens all the time. Even at this gathering, I'm not really certain about the nations that were present. But the fact is, we are here today still. We are present here two hundred years later. And that is a fact of life.
>
> Yesterday we cleared the eyes, ears, and the throat. And our vision is very clear when it comes to the rights of our people. Health, education, and welfare are embodied in the framework of the Canandaigua Treaty. And at the same time we have many grievances, grievances that can be taken care of by the stroke of a pen.
>
> We are few in number. And our hopes and dreams of the future are for our people to come back together as a family. We have been estranged for quite some time by various governments surrounding us; by governments that we made agreements, solemn agreements with, who promised to take care of our health, education, and welfare with no restrictions. But today we are faced with problems.
>
> What does the welfare of our people mean? It means security in our communities, that our minds are at peace, that if we suffer as a result of something, the United States is obligated to come to our aid. When I look around and review the last two hundred years, our lands have shrunk almost to nothing. Inside of those boundaries that were not supposed to be violated were vast resources that used to be there: mineral, timber, water.
>
> If the United States feels that they have a trust responsibility with the people that they have assigned to be within our jurisdiction, then they should not allow the Internal Revenue Service's

laws to usurp the rights that we have. We have many people in our community today who are suffering because of the laws of taxation. That was already provided for in the United States Constitution; no Indians are supposed to be taxed. These are some of the issues that our leaders continue to think about.

We are moving ahead. We are not going to be brushed aside. We will continue to prevail. We just built a new Longhouse. Almost two thousand people came to celebrate that event. And if I am right in my estimation, the Longhouse that we have just built should last us at least another one hundred and fifty years before there's a need to build another.

I hope that the message is taken back so that in our community, all of the people's needs can be taken care of, not just a select few. I didn't know that you had to be poor, be barely existing before you receive help. It seems like that's where they're pushing us to be, in poverty. Then we can receive help.

And so our rights have been hijacked. And we need to put things back in order. And with the help of the United States people, please tell your government to put it back where it belongs. (Swamp 1994)

Chief Jake Swamp continued with the traditional closing of the gathering:

Thank you for honoring me again. I'm always willing to do this when it comes to bringing minds together in the Spirit:

> As we came here,
> we came from long distances.
> And we came
> from many different directions.
>
> At the beginning of time,
> at the beginning of the world,
> there were Four Sacred Spirit Beings
> assigned to watch over the human family.
>
> So we look to them today
> to guide us home,
> to be safely arriving back to our homes
> where we came from,
> so that we may find our loved ones
> safe and sound when we arrive,
> who await our return.

And so that is the request that we make. And I would like to thank the speakers and all the people that came. You came because you care. And we hope that this caring attitude will transcend to our youth whom we need so badly. We need to empower our youth so that they can work hard to find the answers to our problems of the future. (Swamp 1994)

NOTES

1. From a telephone interview with Chief Irving Powless Jr., on 23 June 1998.

2. Known also to some residents of Canandaigua as "The Chosen Place"; reported in the Canandaigua *Daily Messenger* in 1944 as "The Chosen Spot" ("Six Nations Indians . . ." 3).

3. The boulder known as Council Rock was donated to Ontario County by Dr. Dwight R. Burrell in 1902. Letters recording Dr. Burrell's gift were recorded in the *Proceedings of the Board of Supervisors of Ontario County, New York*, 1899/1905:157, 299–300 as follows:

(1) Burrell, Dwight R. Letter to Board of Supervisors of Ontario County, 2 Dec. 1901. *Proceedings of the Board of Supervisors of Ontario County, New York*, 1899/1905:157.

Dr. Dwight R. Burrell appeared before the Board and submitted the following proposition:

December 2nd, 1901.

To the Board of Supervisors of Ontario County:

Gentlemen:-

Having been informed that the original square in this village is under your jurisdiction as county officials, I appear before you to request permission to carry out a project contemplated by me for several years. You are aware that attaches to this spot a fact of historic interest and importance, yet unknown to many of our citizens and to the passserby. Here was held the last great Council of the Six Nations, which resulted in the signing of a treaty, November 11, 1794. The United States was represented by a single commissioner, Col. Pickering, appointed by Washington. He was materially assisted by Gen. Israel Chapin and by four Friends from Philadelphia, William Savery, David Bacon, John Parrish and James Emlin [sic], who attended at the earnest solicitation of the Indians, and with the hearty approval of the President.

The most distinguished Indians in the Council were Farmer's Brother, Red Jacket, Cornplanter, Little Beard, Saragaressa, Clear Sky, Fish Carrier, Big Sky, and Little Billy, some of whom were personally known to citizens we met on these streets not many years ago.

I request permission to place upon this square, at a spot selected by you and me, a granite boulder, hewn only by the ages, and weighing about thirty tons. If such permission is granted, the boulder will be moved this winter, properly set in the spring, and when marked by a bronze plate suitably commemorating the event mentioned, presented to the County. My only stipulation is, that it shall always stand as when presented, *alone*, with no planting about it and no ornament or figure upon it to detract from its grim dignity.

Very respectfully yours,

Dwight R. Burrell

(2) Burrell, Dwight R. Letter to Henry P. Hewitt, 20 May 1903. *Proceedings of the Board of Supervisors of Ontario County, New York*, 1899/1905:299. The clerk then read the following letter:

> Brigham Hall Hospital,
>   Canandaigua, N.Y.
> May 20, 1903.
>
> Mr. Henry P. Hewitt,
>   Chairman of the Board of Supervisors.
>   of Ontario County, West Bloomfield, N.Y.
> Dear Sir:-
>
> It is my pleasure to inform you that the tablet commemorating "THE LAST GENERAL COUNCIL OF THE UNITED STATES WITH THE IROQUOIS CONFEDERACY" has been attached to the boulder you permitted me to place upon the Public Square here, and will be uncovered in the early morning of Decoration Day. Permit me to present to Ontario County, through you its representative, this monument to an event of National importance the signifiance of which we of this day can hardly appreciate. By your acceptance, it becomes the tribute of Ontario County and ceases to be that of an individual. Permit me also to ask that upon the minutes of the Board of Supervisors, record may be made of the gift and its acceptance, and of my request that the monument may always stand as now, alone in its grim dignity.
>
> Very respectfully yours,
> Dwight R. Burrell

(3) Hewitt, Henry P. Letter to Dwight R. Burrell, 28 May 1903. *Proceedings of the Board of Supervisors of Ontario County, New York*, 1899/1905: 300. The Clerk at the request of the Chairman, then read the following letter of acceptance:

> May 28, 1903.
>
> Dr. Dwight R. Burrell,
>   Canandaigua, N.Y.
> Dear Sir:-
>
> Permit me, in informally accepting for the Board of Supervisors of Ontario County, your gift of the sturdy monument bearing the tablet in commemoration of "THE LAST GENERAL COUNCIL OF THE UNITED STATES WITH THE IROQUOIS CONFEDERACY," to thank you most heartily on behalf of the Board and through them, for the people whom they have the honor of representing, for the great interest and public spirit which you have manifested in this work.
>
> Believing that this record of commemoration will increase in historical value, as the coming generations succeed each other, I remain,
>
> Most respectfully yours,
> Henry P. Hewitt, Chairman

4. Chief Irving Powless, Jr., Onondaga Nation.

5. A reference to the 1613 Two Row Wampum treaty between the Haudenosaunee and Dutch colonizers of America. (*See* Hill 1990: 21–30.)

6. The vision of Sēdwāgo'wane Ganio dai'io or Handsome Lake. (*See* Parker1990.)

7. The Committee "was composed of 29 Friends as follows: John Parrish, John Elliott, John Spencer, jun., Anthony Johnson, John Stapler, Oliver Paxson, Joseph

Trimble, James Emlen, Isaac Coates, Amos Harvey, Warner Mifflin, Samuel Howell, John Smith, Benjamin Clark, Benjamin Swett, John Hunt (of Evesham), James Cooper, Mark Miller, Wm. Hartshorne, Richard Hartshorne, Thos. Wistar, Joseph Sansom, Wm. Savery, John Biddle, Thomas Harrison, Henry Drinker, Joseph Sloan, John Pierce, John Hunt (of Darby). This committee met Oct. 4, 1795, the day after its appointment, and organized with Thomas Wistar as Clerk and John Elliott as Treasurer. Phila. Y.M. Indian Comm., MS. *Minutes*, 1:3" (Kelsey 1917, 92).

8. The 1794 Canandaigua Treaty Commemoration Committee, 1994 Committee Members were Tadodaho Leon Shenandoah, Onondaga; Chief Bernard Parker, Seneca; Jerry Fulmer; Robert Abraham; Carl Brant, Mohawk; Marcheta Davidson, Seneca; J. Sheldon & Lillian Fisher; Peter Gerbic; Robert & Muriel Gorall; Ivan & Gale Hermanet; Debra Glor; Charles Fordham, Sr.; Al Klos; Douglas A. Fisher, Esq.; Ed Schmitt; G. Peter Jemison, Seneca; Vernon Jimerson, Seneca; Carol Jimerson; Jane LeClair; Clayton Logan, Seneca; Jeanette Miller, Mohawk; Jackie Platt; Barbara Smoke, Mohawk; Leah Smoke, Mohawk; and Arthur Cook, Mohawk. (See *Canandaigua Treaty Commemoration: November 11, 1794–1994*, n.p. [1994]).

9. Many of the papers delivered on November 12, 1994, have formed the basis of several chapters in this volume.

REFERENCES

Benton, Nelson K., III. 1994. "Timothy Pickering Left Us a Legacy Worth Learning." Salem, Mass. *Evening News* (21 October): 6.

Burrell, Dwight R. 1901. Letter to Board of Supervisors of Ontario County (2 December). *Proceedings of the Board of Supervisors of Ontario County, New York.* 1899/1905: 157.

_____. 1903. Letter to Henry P. Hewitt (20 May). *Proceedings of the Board of Supervisors of Ontario County, New York.* 1899/1905: 299.

Canandaigua Treaty Commemoration: November 11 1794–1994. [1994]. N.p.:n.p.

Clines, Frances X. 1994. "Peace Prevails In an Offering of Simple Cloth." *New York Times* (25 September): 39.

"Editorial." 1962. *The Kinzua Planning Newsletter.* 1.10 (24 August): 7.

Fisher, J. Sheldon. 1996. Personal interview (16 August).

Gorall, Robert. [1994?]. "A Brief History of Canandaigua Treaty Commemoration, (1963–1987)." With input by Jane Rode LeClair. *The Iroquoian.* 23/24: 79–96.

Green, Geraldine. 1989. Address at the 1989 Canandaigua Treaty Commemoration Social. Audiotape. Rec. by Robert Gorall (11 November).

Hewitt, Henry P. 1903. Letter to Dwight R. Burrell (28 May). *Proceedings of the Board of Supervisors of Ontario County, New York.* 1899/1905: 300.

Hill, Richard. 1990. "Oral Memory of the Haudenosaunee: Views of the Two Row Wampum." *Northeast Indian Quarterly.* 7.1 (spring): 21–30.

Jemison, G. Peter. 1995. "The Canandaigua Treaty Commemoration." *Akwesasne Notes.* 1.1 (Apr./May/June): 55.

Jimerson, Vernon. 1996. Letter to the author (17 May).

Johnson, Leland R. [1978]. *The Headwaters District: a History of the Pittsburgh District, U.S. Army Corps of Engineers.* N.p.: [Pittsburgh District, U.S. Army Corps of Engineers; U.S. Government Printing Office].

Kelsey, Rayner Wickersham. 1917. *Friends and the Indians, 1655–1917.* Philadelphia: Associated Executive Committee of Friends on Indian Affairs.

Kennedy, John F. 1961. Letter to Basil Willliams (9 August). Ms. White House Name File. Folder "Williams—Barbara". Box 3013. John Fitzgerald Kennedy Library, Boston, Mass.

The Kinzua Dam Controversy: A Practical Solution—Without Shame. [1961?] N.p.: Kinzua Project of the Indian Committee, Philadelphia Yearly Meeting of Friends.

The Kinzua Planning Newsletter. 1962. 1.5 (April 1): [1].

"The 'Lake of Perfidy'." 1963. Editorial. *Social Education.* 27.6 (October): 293, 333.

LeClair, Jane R. 1996. Letter to the author (29 June).

Parker, Arthur C. 1990. *The Code of Handsome Lake, the Seneca Prophet.* Ontario: Iroqrafts.

Parker, Bernard. 1994. Remarks at the 1994 Canandaigua Treaty Commemoration Social. *1794 Canandaigua Treaty Commemoration Committee Hosts the Canandaigua Treaty [Also Known As] The Pickering Treaty: The Two Hundredth Anniversary, Canandaigua, New York, November 11, 1994.* Videotape. Prod. Finger Lakes TV. Program Dir.: Dave Conyer. FLTV.

Powless, Chief Irving, Jr. 1994. Remarks at the 1994 Canandaigua Treaty Commemoration Social. *1794 Canandaigua Treaty Commemoration Committee Hosts the Canandaigua Treaty [Also Known As] The Pickering Treaty: The Two Hundredth Anniversary, Canandaigua, New York, November 11, 1994.* Videotape. Prod. Finger Lakes TV. Program Dir.: Dave Conyer. FLTV.

_____. 1998. Telephone interview (23 June).

"Senecas Protest Kinzua Dam Plan." 1961. Canandaigua, N.Y. *Daily Messenger* (13 November): [1].

1794 Canandaigua Treaty Commemoration Committee Hosts the Canandaigua Treaty 1994. *[Also Known As] The Pickering Treaty: The Two Hundredth Anniversary, Canandaigua, New York, November 11, 1994.* Videotape. Prod. Finger Lakes TV. Program Dir.: Dave Conyer. FLTV.

Shenandoah, Leon. 1989. Address at the 1989 Canandaigua Treaty Commemoration Social. Audiotape. Rec. by Robert Gorall (11 November).

"Six Nations Indians Complete Plans for Treaty Anniversary." 1944. Canandaigua, N.Y. *Daily Messenger* (9 November): 3.

Swamp, Jake. Address. 1994. "1794–1994: Polishing the Rust from the Chain." Symposium (12 November) Canandaigua, N.Y. Videotape.

Tarr, Joe. 1994. "Pickering Party Hopes to Include President." Canandaigua, N.Y. *Daily Messenger,* (4 October): 3A.

Van Iseghem, Marge. 1965. "Indian Treaty Memorial Held Without Red Men." Rochester, N.Y. *Democrat and Chronicle* (12 November): 2B.

Williams, Basil. 1961. Letter to John F. Kennedy (23 May). Copy. Kinzua Dam Vertical File, Seneca Nation Library, Allegany Branch, Salamanca, N.Y.

Appendix
COUNCIL FIRE AT CANANDAIGUA: SELECTED HISTORICAL SOURCE DOCUMENTS

compiled and with introductory notes by
ANNA M. SCHEIN

Contents

1794: TREATY NEGOTIATIONS IN CANANDAIGUA

Knox, Henry. Letter to Israel Chapin. 25 July 1794. B. V. O'Reilly Papers. Volume 10. New York Historical Society, New York, NY.

Chapin, Israel. Address to the Chiefs of the Six Nations at Buffaloe Creek. 15 Aug. 1794. B. V. O'Reilly Papers. Volume 10. New-York Historical Society, New York, NY.

Savery, William. The Canandaigua Treaty Excerpt from the Journal. Ms. Magill Library, Haverford College, Haverford, PA. In *A Journal of the Life, Travels, and Religious Labors of William Savery, a Minister of the Gospel of Christ, of the Society of Friends, Late of Philadelphia.* Compiled from his original memoranda by Jonathan Evans. Stereotype ed. Philadelphia: For sale at Friends' Book-store, [1837]: 88–155.

1795: TEXT OF THE CANANDAIGUA TREATY

United States. Congress. *American State Papers: Documents, Legislative and Executive, of the Congress of the United States . . .* Selected and Edited under the Authority of Congress. Volume 4. (Class II. Indian Affairs. Volume 1). 3d Congress, 2d Session, No. 58. Washington: Gales and Seaton, 1832: 544–45.

Pickering, Timothy. Letter to the Governor of Pennsylvania. 27 Jan. 1795. Ms. (letter only) Record Group 26, Executive Correspondence, Pennsylvania State Archives, Harrisburg. Letter and treaty published in Linn and Egle, eds., *Pennsylvania Archives.* Second Series, Volume 6. Harrisburg: State Printer, 1874–90, 799–804.

1795: RATIFICATION OF THE TREATY BY GEORGE WASHINGTON

Washington, George. Ratification of Treaty of Peace With Indians. 22 Jan. 1795. Ms. Aboriginal Peoples in the Archives. Private Papers. 181. F 47. Simcoe Family Papers. Archives of Ontario, Toronto. In Cruikshank, E. A., ed. *The Correspondence of Lieut. Governor John Graves Simcoe, with Allied Documents Relating to his Administration of the Government of Upper Canada.* Volume 3. Toronto: Ontario Historical Society, 1925, 263–64.

Pickering, Timothy. Letter to the Six Nations. 31 Mar. 1795. Ms. Aboriginal Peoples in the Archives. Private Papers. 181. F 47. Simcoe Family Papers. Archives of Ontario, Toronto. In Cruikshank, E. A., ed. *The Correspondence of Lieut. Governor John Graves Simcoe, with Allied Documents Relating to his Administration of the Government of Upper Canada.* Volume 3. Toronto: Ontario Historical Society, 1925, 339–40.

STATEMENT OF METHOD:

In transcribing the source documents in this appendix, the following methods were used. The spelling of a word in the source document was retained although the word is spelled differently in modern English. Where a spelling in the source document could be interpreted as a transcription or printing error, [sic] appears after the word. In cases where a misspelling or mark of punctuation may result in a misunderstanding of the text, the compiler has supplied the correction in brackets. Words which were underlined in the source document appear in italics.

The format of these documents duplicates the appearance of the original source texts within the limits of modern word processing technology with one exception: to achieve overall unity in this volume, the publisher has made punctuation, indention, and paragraph parsing changes to the quoted portions of the William Savery journal.

Scholars who access manuscript materials for their research know there are slight variations from one copy of a source document to another. These often result from the following: human fallibility in transcription, the transcriber's explicit changes made to the source text, the transcriber's changes to the text which are not explained, and, in the case of published versions, the changes made by the publisher to the transcriber's copy.

There are multiple copies of many of the source documents in this appendix in U.S. and Canadian archives. By using standard bibliographic reference utilities, the location of these copies can easily be determined. As with any legal or scholarly research, an examination of all of the extant versions of a document will result in the most complete archival representation of a text.

1790: Appeal of the Senecas to George Washington

The 1794 Canandaigua Treaty was negotiated between the Six Nations Confederacy and the United States of America just twenty-two years after the United States had become a sovereign nation. During the first two decades of independence, the United States was recovering from the Revolutionary War and, at the same time, struggling to establish a federalist concept of government.

Political tension mounted between the United States and the Six Nations during the postwar period. U.S. citizens and individual states continued to secure large tracts of Six Nations lands without adequate compensation. In addition to these individual actions, many of the treaties signed between the two nations from 1777 to 1790 are reported to have been unfairly negotiated and not in the best interest of either nation.

In 1790, the United States took several steps to stop state and independent land transactions, including the enactment of the Non-Intercourse Act. With this act, a U.S. government policy was established to resolve issues which arose between the United States and Indian nations at the federal level. The Non-Intercourse Act influenced the language and intent of future treaties between the United States and the Six Nations, including the 1794 Canandaigua Treaty.

The effect of this policy on intergovernmental relations between the two nations is evident in the following set of documents. Included here are three addresses by Seneca Chiefs Cornplanter, Half Town, and the Great Tree to President George Washington in 1790 and 1791. The Senecas appealed to the president to restore and secure their lands to them. The first two addresses were answered by the president; the third by U.S. Secretary of War Henry Knox. Excerpts from these documents have been quoted in various publications to illustrate the strained relations between the two nations just a few years before the 1794 Canandaigua Treaty.

CORNPLANTER, HALFTOWN, AND THE GREAT TREE. ADDRESS TO GEORGE WASHINGTON. 1 DEC. 1790.

Transcription of address only (no bibliographic notes or references) as published in
Washington, George. *The Papers of George Washington*. Ed. Dorothy Twohig et al.
Presidential Series, Volume 7. Charlottesville: UP of Virginia, 1998, 7–13.

From the Seneca Chiefs

[1 December 1790]

To the great Councillor of the thirteen fires.

The Speech of the Corn-planter, Half-town, and the Great-Tree chiefs of the Senecca Nation.

Father

The voice of the Senecca Nation speaks to you the great Councillor, in whose heart, the wise men of the thirteen fires, have placed their wisdom. It may be very small in your ears, & we therefore entreat you to harken with attention. For we are about to speak of things which are to us very great. When your army entered the Country of the Six Nations, we called you the Town-destroyer and to this day, when that name is heard, our women look behind them and turn pale, and our children cling close to the neck of their mothers. Our Councillors and warriors are men, and can not be afraid; but their hearts are grieved with the fears of our women & children, and desire, that it may be buried so deep, as to be heard no more. When you gave us peace we called you father, because you promised to secure us in the possession of our Land. Do this and so long as the Land shall remain that beloved name will live in the heart of every Senecca.

Father,

We mean to open our hearts before you, and we earnestly desire, that you will let us clearly understand, what you resolve to do. When our chiefs returned from the treaty of fort Stanwix, and laid before our Council what had been done there our Nation was surprised to hear, how great a Country you had compelled them to give up, to you, without paying us any thing for it. Every one said your hearts were yet swelled with resentment against us for what had happened during the war: but that one day you would reconsider it with more kindness. We asked each other what we had done to deserve such severe chastisement.

Father,

When you kindled your thirteen fires separately, the wise men that assembled at them told us you were all brothers, the children of one great Father who regarded also the red people as his children. They called us brothers and invited us to his protection. They told us he resided beyond the great waters where the sun first rises: that he was a King whose power no people could resist, and that his goodness was bright as that sun. What they said went to the bottom of our hearts: We accepted the invitation and promised to obey him. What the Senecca Nation promise they faithfully perform: and when you refused obedience to that King he ordered us to assist his beloved men in making you sober. In obeying him we did no more than you yourselves had lead us to promise. The men who claimed this promise said that you were children and had no Guns that when they had shaken you, you would submit. We harkened to them and were deceived until your army approached our towns. We were deceived but your people in teaching us to confide in that King, had helped to deceve us and we now appeale to your hearts. Is the blame all ours?

Father,

When we saw we were deceived and heard the invitation which you gave us to draw near to the fire you had kindled and talk with you concerning peace we made haste towards it. You then told us we were in your hand & and that by closing it you could crush us to nothing; and you demanded of us a great Country as the price of that peace you had offered us; as if our want of strength had destroyed our rights. Our Chiefs had felt your power & were unable to contend against you and they therefore gave up that Country. What they agreed to has bound our nation. But your anger against us must by this time be cooled, and altho' our Strength has not encreased nor your power become less we ask you to consider calmly were the terms dictated to us reasonable and just?

Father,

Your commissioners when they drew the line which separated the land then given up to you, from that which you agreed should remain to be ours did, most solemnly promise, that we should be secured in the peaceable possessions of the lands which we inhabited, East, & North, of that line. Does this promise bind you?

Hear now we entreat you, what has since happened, concerning that Land. On the day on which we finished the treaty at fort Stanwix, commissioners from Pensylvania, told our chiefs, that they had come there to purchase from us, all the Lands belonging to us within the lines of their State, and they told us that their line would strike the river Susquehanna below Tioga branch. They then left us to consider the bargain 'till the next day. On the next day we let them know, that we were unwilling to sell all the Lands within their State, and proposed to let them have a part of it which we pointed to them in their map.

They told us they must have the whole: That it was already ceded to them by the great King at the time of making peace with you, and was *their own*. But they said they would not take advantage of that, and were willing to pay us for it after the manner of their Ancestors. Our chiefs were unable to contend at that time, & therefore they sold the Lands up to the line which was then shewn to them as the line of that State. What the Commissioners had said about the land having been ceded to them at the peace our Chiefs considered only as intended to lessen the price, & they passed it by with very little notice; but since that time we have heard so much of the right to our lands which the King gave when you made peace with him that it is our earnest desire you will tell us what they mean.

Father,

Our nation empowered John Livingston to let out a part of our lands on rent. He told us he was sent by Congress to do this for us and we fear he has deceived us on the writing he obtained from us: For since the time of our giving that power, a man of the name of Phelps has come among us, and claimed our whole Country northward of the line of Pensylvania under purchase from that Livingston to whom he said he had paid twenty thousand dollars for it. He said also he had bought likewise from the Council of the thirteen fires, and paid them twenty thousand dollars more for the same. And he said also that it did not belong to us for that the great King had ceded the whole of it when you made peace with him. Thus he claimed the whole country North of Pensylvania and west of the Lands belonging to the Cayugas. He demanded it: He insisted on his demand and declared that he would have it all. It was impossible for us to grant him this and we immediately refused it. After some days he proposed to run a line at a small distance Eastward of our western boundary which we also refused to agree to. He then threatened us with immediate war if we did not comply. Upon this threat our Chiefs held a Council and they agreed that no event of war could be worse than to be driven with our wives & children from the only Country which we had any right to, and therefore weak as our nation was, they determined to take the chance of war rather than submit to such unjust demands, which seemed to have no bounds. Street the great trader at Niagara was then with us having come at the request of Phelps, and as he always professed to be our great friend we consulted him on this subject; He also told us, that our Lands had been ceded by the King and that we *must* give them up.

Astonished at what we heard from every quarter, with hearts akeing with compassion for our women and children, we were thus compelled to give up all our Country North of the line of Pensylvania, and East of the Chenesco river up to the forks, and East of a South line drawn from that fork to the Pensylvania line. For this Land Phelps agreed to pay us Ten thousand dollars in hand and one thousand dollars a year for ever. He paid us two thousand & five hundred dollars in hand part of the Ten thousand, and he sent for us last Spring to come and receive our money; but instead of paying us the remainder of the Ten thousand dollars, and the one thousand dollars due for the first year, he offered us no more than five hundred dollars, and insisted he had agreed with us for that sum only to be paid yearly. We debated with him six days during all which time he persisted in refusing to pay us our just demand; and he ins[is]ted that we should receive the five hundred dollars, and Street from Niagara, also insisted on our receiving the money as it was offered to us. The last reason he assigned for continuing to refuse paying us was, *that the King had ceded the lands to the thirteen fires* and that he had bought them from you and *paid you for them.*

We could bear this confusion no longer, & determined to press thro' every difficulty, and lift up our voice that you might hear us, and to claim that security in the possession of our lands which your commissioners so solemnly promised us, and we now entreat you to enquire into our complaints and redress our wrongs.

Father,

Our writings were lodged in the hands of Street of Niagara, as we supposed him to be our friend; but when we saw Phelps consulting with Street, on every occasion, we doubted of his honesty towards us, and we have since heard, that he was to receive for his endeavors to deceive us, a piece of land ten miles in width west of the Chenesco river, and near forty miles in length extending to lake Ontario; and the lines of this tract have been run accordingly tho no part of it is within the bounds which limit his purchase. No doubt he meant to deceive us.

Father,

You have said that we are in your hand, and that by closing it, you could crush us to nothing. [A]re you determined to crush us? If you are, tell us so that those of our nation who have become your children & are determined to die so, may know what to do: In this case, one chief has said, he would ask you to put him out of pain; Another who will not think of dying by the hand of his father, has said he will retire to the Chataughque, eat of the fatal root, and sleep with his fathers in peace.

Before you determine on a measure so unjust, look up to the God who made us, as well as you, we hope he will not permit you to destroy the whole of our nation.

Father,

Hear our case. [M]any nations inhabited this Country, but they had no wisdom, and therefore they warred, together. The six Nations were powerful & compelled them to peace: The Lands for a great extent were given up to them, but the nations which were not destroyed, all continued on those Lands and claimed the protecti[on] of the six Nations, as the brothers of their fathers. They were men and when at peace had a right to live on the Earth. The French came among us and built Niagara. They became our fathers, and took care of us. Sr William Johnson came and took that Fort from the French; he became our father and promised to take care of us and did so until you were too strong for his King. To him we gave four miles round Niagara, as a place of Trade. We have already said how we came to join against you. We saw that we were wrong: we wished for peace. You demanded a great Country to be given up to you. It was surrendered to you as the price of peace and we ought to have peace, and possession, of the little Land which you then left us.

Father,

When that great Country was given up, there were but few Chiefs present, and they were compelled to give it up. And it is not the Six nations only, that reproach those Chiefs, with having given up that Country; the Chipaways and all the nations who lived on those lands westward, call to us & ask us brothers of our fathers where is the place which you have reserved for us to lie down on.

Father,

You have compelled us to do that which has made us ashamed. We have nothing to answer to the children of the brothers of our fathers. When last Spring they called on us to go to war to secure them a bed to lie upon, The Seneccas entreated them to be quiet until we had spoken to you: but on our way down we heard, your army had gone to the Country which those nations inhabit: and if they meet together the best blood on both sides will stain the ground.

Father,

We will not conceal from you, that the great God, and not m[a]n has preserved the Corn planter from his own nation: for they ask continually, where is the Land which our children and their children after them are to lie down on?

You told us say they, that the line drawn from Pensylvania, to lake Ontario, would mark it for ever on the East, and the line running from Beaver Creek, to Pensylvania, would mark it on the west, and we see that it is not so. For first one, and then another, come and take it away, by order of that people, who promised to secure it to us. He is silent for he has nothing to answer.

When the Sun goes down, he opens his heart before God, and earlier than that Sun appears again upon the Hills, he gives thanks for his protection during the night, for he feels, that among men become desperate by their danger, it is God only that can preserve him. He loves peace, and all he had in store he has given to those who have been robbed by your people, lest they should plunder the innocent to repay themselves: the whole season which others employed in providing for their families, he has spent in his endeavour to preserve peace. And at this moment his wife and children are lying on the Ground in want of food. His heart is in pain for them; but he perceives that the great God will try his firmness in doing what is right.

Father,

The Game which the great Spirit sent into our Country for us to eat, is going from among us: We thought he intended we should till the ground as the white people do, and we talked to one another about it. But before we speak to you of this, we must know from you, whether you mean to leave us, and our children, any land to till. Speak plainly to us concerning this great business. All the Lands we have been speaking of belonged to the Six Nations: no part of it ever belonged to the King of England, and he could not give it to you. The Land we live on our Fathers received from God, and they transmitted it to us, for our Children and we cannot part with it.

Father,

We told you we would open our hearts to you. Hear us once more.

At fort Stanwix we agreed to deliver up those of our people, who should do you any wrong, that you might try them, and punish them according to your Law. We delivered up two men, accordingly. But instead of trying them according to your Law, the lowest of your people took them from your magistrate, and put them immediately to death. It is just to punish murder with death, but the Seneccas will not deliver up their people to men, who disregard the treaties of their own nation.

Father,

Innocent men of our nation are killed one after another, and of our best families: But none of your people who have committed the murders have been punished. We recollect that you did not promise to punish those who killed our people, and we now ask, Was it intended that your people should kill the Seneccas, and not only remain unpunished by you: but be protected by you against the next of kin?

Father,

These are to us very great things. We know that you are very strong and we have heard that you are wise; and we wait to hear your answer to what we have said that we may know that you are just.

Signed at Philadelphia the first day of December. 1790.

	his
Present at signing	Corn X planter
Joseph Nicolson	mark
Interpreter	his
T.J. Matlack.	Half X Town
	mark
	his
	Great X Tree
	mark

WASHINGTON, GEORGE. REPLY TO 1 DEC. 1790 ADDRESS OF CORNPLANTER, HALFTOWN, AND THE GREAT TREE. 29 DEC. 1790.

Transcription of address only (no bibliographic notes or references) as published in Washington, George. *The Papers of George Washington.* Ed. Dorothy Twohig et al. Presidential Series, Volume 7. Charlottesville: UP of Virginia, 1998, 146–50.

To the Seneca Chiefs

[Philadelphia, 29 December 1790]

I, the President of the United States, by my own mouth, and by a written speech signed with my own hand, and sealed with the seal of the United States, speak to the Seneka Nation, and desire their Attention, and that they would keep this speech in remembrance of the friendship of the United States.

I have received your Speech with satisfaction, as a proof of your confidence in the justice of the United States—and I have attentively examined the several objects which you have laid before me, whether delivered by your Chiefs at Tioga point in the last month to Colonel Pickering, or laid before me in the present month by the Cornplanter and the other Seneka Chiefs now in Philadelphia.

In the first place I observe to you, and I request it may sink in your minds, that it is my desire, and the desire of the United States that all the miseries of the late war should be forgotten and buried forever. That in future, the United States and the six nations should be truly brothers, promoting each other's prosperity by acts of mutual justice & friendship.

I am not uninformed that the six nations have been led into some difficulties with respect to the sale of their lands since the peace. But I must inform you that these arose before the present government of the United States was established, when the separate States, and individuals under their authority, undertook to treat with the Indian tribes respecting the sale of their lands.

But the case is now entirely altered—the general government only has the power to treat with the Indian nations, and any treaty formed and held without its authority will not be binding.

Here then is the security for the remainder of your lands—No state nor person can purchase your lands, unless at some public treaty held under the Authority of the United States. The general Government will never consent to your being defrauded—But it will protect you in all your just rights.

Hear well, and let it be heard by every person in your nation, that the President of the United States declares, that the general government considers itself bound to protect you in all the lands secured to you by the treaty of Fort Stanwix, the 22d of October 1784, excepting such parts as you may since have fairly sold to persons properly authorized to purchase of you.

You complain of John Livingston and Oliver Phelps have obtained your lands, assisted by Mr. Street of Niagara, and they have not complied with their agreement.

It appears, upon enquiry of the Governor of New York, that John Livingston was not legally authorized to treat with you, and that every thing he did with you has been declared null and void, so that you may rest easy on that account.

But it does not appear from any proofs yet in possession of government, that Oliver Phelps has defrauded you.

If, however you should have any just cause of complaint against him, and can make satisfactory proof thereof, the federal Courts will be open to you for redress, as to all other persons.

But your great object seems to be the security of your remaining lands, and I have therefore upon this point, me[a]nt to be sufficiently strong and clear.

That in future you cannot be defrauded of your lands—That you possess the right to sell, and the right of refusing to sell your lands.

That, therefore, the sale of your lands in future, will depend entirely upon yourselves.

But that when you may find it for your interest to sell any parts of your lands, the United States must be present by their Agent, and will by [be] your security that you shall not be defrauded in the Bargain you may make.

It will, however, be important, that before you make any further sales of your land, that you should determine among yourselves, who are the persons among you that shall give sure conveyances thereof as shall be binding upon your nation, and forever preclude all disputes relative to the validity of the sale.

That besides the before mentioned security for your land, you will perceive by the law of Congress, for regulating trade and intercourse with the Indian-tribes, the fatherly care the United States intend to take of the Indians. For the particular meaning of this law, I refer you to the explanations given thereof by Colonel Pickering at Tioga, which with the law, are herewith delivered to you.

You have said in your Speech that the game is going away from you, and that you thought it the design of the great spirit, that you should till the ground. But before you speak upon this subject, you want to know whether the United States meant to leave you any land to till?

You know now that all the lands secured to you by the treaty of Fort Stanwix, expecting [excepting] such parts as you may since have fairly sold are your's, and that only your own Acts can convey them away—speak therefore your wishes on the subject of tilling the ground. The United States will be happy to afford you every assistance in the only business which will add to your numbers and happiness.

The murders that have been committed upon some of your people, by the bad white men, I sincerely lament and reprobate—and I earnestly hope the real murderers will be secured and punished as they deserve. This business has been sufficiently explained to you here by the Governor of Pennsylvania, and by Colonel Pickering on behalf of the United States, at Tioga.

The Senekas may be assured, that the rewards offered for apprehending the murderers, will be continued until they are secured for trial, and that when they shall be apprehended, that they will be tried and punished as if they had killed Whitemen.

Having answered the most material parts of your speech, I shall inform you, that some bad Indians, and the outcast of several tribes who reside at the Miamee Village, have long continued their murders and depredations upon the frontiers laying along the Ohio. That they have not only refused to listen to my voice inviting them to peace, but that upon receiving it, they renewed their incursions and murders with greater violence than ever. I have therefore been obliged to strike those bad people, in order to make them senisble of their madness. I sincerely hope they will harken to reason, and not require to be further chastised. The United States desire to be the friends of the Indians, upon terms of justice & humanity—But they will not suffer the depredations of the bad people to go unpunished.

My desire is that you would caution all the Senekas and six nations to prevent their rash young men from joining the Miamee Indians. For the United States cannot distinguish the tribes to which bad Indians belong, and every tribe must take care of their own people.

The merits of the Cornplanter and his friendship for the United States are well known to me and shall not be forgotten—And as a mark of the esteem of the United States, I have directed the Secretary of War to make him a present of Two hundred and fifty dollars, either in money or goods, as the Cornplanter shall like best—And he may depend upon the future care and kindness of the United States—And I have also directed the Secretary of War to make suitable presents to their other Chiefs present in Philadelphia—and also that some further tokens of friendship to be forwarded to the other Chiefs now in their nation.

Remember my words, Senekas, continue to be strong in your friendship for the United States, as the only rational ground of your future happiness—and you may rely upon their kindness and protection.

An Agent shall be soon appointed to reside in some place convenient to the Senekas and six nations—He will represent the United States—apply to him on all occasions.

If any man brings you evil reports of the intentions of the United States, mark that man as your enemy, for he will mean to deceive you, and lead you into trouble. The United States will be true & faithful to their engagements. Given under my hand, and the Seal of the United States at the City of Philadelphia, this twenty ninth day of December, in the year of our Lord One thousand seven hundred & ninety one[sic], and in the fifteenth year of the sovereignty & Independence of the United States.

G. Washington

CORNPLANTER, HALFTOWN, AND THE GREAT TREE. SECOND ADDRESS TO GEORGE WASHINGTON. 10 JAN. 1791.

Transcription of address only (no bibliographic notes or references) as published in Washington, George. *The Papers of George Washington.* Ed. Dorothy Twohig et al. Presidential Series, Volume 7. Charlottesville: UP of Virginia, 1998, 218–21.

From the Seneca Chiefs

Father,   Philadelphia, 10th January, 1791.

Your speech written on the great paper, is to us, like the first light of the morning to a sick man, whose pulse beats too strongly in his temples, and prevents him from sleep: He sees it and rejoices, but he is not cured.

You say, that you have spoken plainly on the great point: That you will protect us in the lands secured to us at Fort Stanwix, and that we have the right to *sell* or to *refuse* to sell it. This is very good. But our nation complains, that you compelled us, at that treaty, to give up too much of our lands: We confess that our nation is bound by what was there done, and, acknowledging your power, we have now appealed to yourselves, against that treaty, as made while you were too angry at us, and therefore, unreasonable and unjust: To this you have given us no answer.

Father,

That treaty was not made with a single State, it was with the thirteen States: We never would have given all that land to one State. We know it was before you had the great authority and as you have more wisdom than the Commissioners who forced us into that treaty, we expect, that you have also more regard to justice, and will now, at our request, reconsider that treaty, and restore to us a part of that land.

Father,

The land which lies between the line running South from Lake Erie to the boundary of Pennsylvania, as mentioned at the treaty of Fort Stanwix, and the Eastern boundary of the land which you sold and the Senekas, confirmed to Pennsylvania, is the land on which Half Town, and all his people live, with other chiefs who always have been, and still are disatisfied with the treaty at Fort Stanwix: They grew out of this land, and their fathers fathers grew out of it, and they cannot be persuaded to part with it: We therefore intreat you to restore to us this little piece.

Father,

Look at the land which we gave you, at that treaty, and then turn your eyes upon what we now ask you to restore to us, and you will see that what we ask you to return, is a *very little piece*. By giving it back again, you will satisfy the whole of our nation: the chiefs who signed that treaty, will be in safety; and peace between your children and our children, will continue so long as your land shall join to ours. Every man of our nation will then turn his eyes away from all the other lands which we then gave up to you, and forget that our fathers ever said that they belonged to them.

Father,

We see, that you ought to have the path at the carrying place from Lake Erie to Niagara, as it was marked down at Fort Stanwix, and are all willing it should remain to be yours. And if you desire to reserve a passage through the Conewango, and through the Chetaughque lake, and land for a path from that lake to lake Erie, take it where you best like. Our nation will rejoice to see it an open path for you, and your children, while the land and water remain: But let us also, pass along the same way, and continue to take the fish of those waters, in common with you.

Father,

You say that you will appoint an agent to take care of us. Let him come, and take care of our trade, but we desire he may not have any thing to do with our lands; for the agents which have come among us, and pretended to take care of us, have always deceived us whenever we sold lands; both when the king of England, and when the States have bargained with us. They have, by this means, occasioned many wars, and we are, therefore, unwilling to trust them again.

Father,

When we return home, we will call a great council, and consider well how lands may be hereafter sold by our nation, and when we have agreed upon it, we will send you notice of it. But we desire, that you will not depend on your agent for information concerning land: For after the abuses which we have suffered by such men, we will not trust them with any thing which relates to land.

Father,

We will not hear lies concerning you, and we desire that you will not hear lies concerning us; and then we shall certainly live at peace with you.

Father,

There are men who go from town to town, and beget children, and leave them to perish, or, except [expect] better men take care of them, to grow up without instruction. Our Nation has looked round for a father, but they found none that would own them for children, until you now tell us, that your courts are open to us, as to your own people!

The joy which we feel at this great news, so mixes with the Sorrows that are passed, that we cannot express our gladness, nor conceal the remembrance of our afflictions: We will speak of them at another time.

Father,

We are ashamed that we have listened to the lies of Livingston, or been influenced by threats of war by Phelps, and would hide that whole transaction from the world, and from ourselves, by quietly receiving what Phelps promised to give us for the lands they cheated us of: But as Phelps will not pay us, even according to that fraudulent bargain, we will lay the whole proceedings before your court. When the Evidence which we can produce, is heard, we think it will appear, that the whole bargain was founded on lies, which he placed one upon another; that the goods which he charges to us, as part payment, were plundered from us: that if Phelps was not directly concerned in the theft, he knew of it at the time, and concealed it from us; and that the persons we confided in, were bribed by him to deceive us in the bargain: And if these facts appear, that your court will not say that such bargains are just, but will set the whole aside.

Father,

We apprehend that our evidence might be called for, as Phelps was here, and knew what we have said concerning him, and as Ebenezer Allen knew something of the matter, we desired him to continue here. Nicholson, the interpreter, is very sick, and we request that Allen may remain a few days longer as he speaks our language.

Father,

The blood which was spilled near Pine Creek, is covered, and we shall never look where it lies. We know that Pennsylvania will satisfy us for that which we spoke of to them, before we spoke to you. The chain of friendship will now, we hope, be made strong as you desire it to be: We will hold it fast, and our end of it shall never rust in our hands.

Father,

We told you what advice we gave the people you are now at war with; and we now tell you, that they have promised to come again to our towns next spring: We shall not wait for their coming, but set out very early, and show to them what you have done *for us*, which must convince them that you will do *for them*, every thing which they ought to ask. We think they will hear and follow our advice.

Father,

You gave us leave to speak our minds concerning tilling the ground. We ask you to teach us to plow and to grind corn: to assist us in building saw-mills, and supply us with broad axes, saws, augers, and other tools, so as that we may make our houses more comfortable and more durable; that you will send smiths among us, and above all, that you will teach our children to read and to write, and our women to spin and to weave. The manner of your doing these things for us, we leave to you, who understand them; but we assure you, that we will follow your advice, as far as we are able.

Present at signing,

Joseph Nicholson, interpreter.

Ty Matlack.

his
John X Dechart,
mark.

his
Jem. X Hudson,
mark.

his
Corn X Planter.
mark

his
Half X Town.
mark.

his
Great X Tree.
mark.

WASHINGTON, GEORGE. REPLY TO 10 JAN. 1791 ADDRESS OF CORNPLANTER, HALFTOWN, AND THE GREAT TREE. 19 JAN. 1791.

Transcription of address only (no bibliographic notes or references) as published in Washington, George. *The Papers of George Washington.* Ed. Dorothy Twohig et al. Presidential Series, Volume 7. Charlottesville: UP of Virginia, 1998, 252–53.

To the Seneca Chiefs

Brothers!   Philadelphia, January 19, 1791.
I have maturely considered your second written speech.

You say your nation complain that at the Treaty of Fort Stanwix, you were compelled to give up too much of your lands. That you confess your nation is bound by what was there done, and acknowledging the power of the United States, that you have now appealed to ourselves against that treaty, as made while we were angry against you, and that the said treaty was therefore unreasonable and unjust.

But while you complain of the treaty of Fort Stanwix in 1784, you seem entirely to forget that you yourselves, the Cornplanter, Half-Town and Great-Tree, with others of your nation, confirmed by the Treaty of Fort Harmar upon the Muskingum, so late as the 9th of January 1789, the boundaries marked at the Treaty of Fort Stanwix, and that in consequence thereof you then received goods to a considerable amount.

Although it is my sincere desire in looking forward to endeavour to promote your happiness by all just and humane arrangements; yet I cannot disannull treaties formed by the United States before my administration, especially as the boundaries mentioned therein have been twice confirmed by yourselves.

The lines fixed at Fort Stanwix and Fort Harmar, must therefore remain established.

But Half Town and others who reside upon the land you desire may be relinquished, have not been disturbed in their possession, and I should hope that while they continue to demean themselves peaceably, and to manifest their friendly dispositions towards the people of the United States, that they will be suffered to remain where they are.

The Agent who will be appointed by the United States will be your friend and protector. He will not be suffered to defraud you, or to assist in defrauding you of your lands, or of any other thing, as all his proceedings must be reported in writing, so as to be submitted to the President of the United States.

You mention Your design of going to the Miami Indians, to endeavour to persuade them to peace—By this humane measure you will render those mistaken people a great service, and probably prevent their being swept from off the face of the earth—The United States require only that those people should demean themselves peaceably. But they may be assured that the United States are able, and will most certainly punish them severely for all their robberies and murders.

You may, when you return from this city to your own Country, mention to your Nation my desire to promote their prosperity, by teaching the use of domestic animals, and the manner that the white people plough and raise so much corn—And if upon consideration it would be agreeable to the Nation at large to learn these arts, I will find some means of teaching them at such places within their Country as shall be agreed upon.

I have nothing more to add, but to refer you to my former speech, and to repeat my wishes for the happiness for the Seneka Nation. Given under my hand, and the Seal of the United States, at Philadelphia, this nineteenth day of January 1791.

Go: Washington
By the President
Th. Jefferson

CORNPLANTER, HALFTOWN, AND THE GREAT TREE. THIRD ADDRESS TO GEORGE WASHINGTON. 7 FEB. 1791.

Transcription of address only (no bibliographic notes or references) as published in Washington, George. *The Papers of George Washington*. Ed. Dorothy Twohig et al. Presidential Series, Volume 7. Charlottesville: UP of Virginia, 1998, 322–23.

From the Seneca Chiefs

Father. Philadelphia february 7: 1791

No Seneca ever goes from the Fire of his Friends, untill he has said to him, I am going: We therefore tell you, we are now setting out for our own Country.

Father,

We thank you from our hearts, that we now know that there is a Country that we may call our own, on which we may lie down in peace. We see that there will be peace between your Children and our Children, and our hearts are very glad. We will perswade [*sic*] the Wyandots, and other Western Nations to open their Eyes, and look towards the Bed which you have made for us, and to ask of you a bed for themselves, and for their Children, that will not slide from under them: We thank you for your presents to us, and rely on your promise to instruct us in raising Corn as the white people do; The sooner you do this the better for us; And we thank you for the Care which you have taken to prevent bad people, coming to trade among us; if any come without your leave, we will turn them back; and we hope our Nation will determine, to spill all the Rum, that shall here after be brought to our Towns.

Father,

We are glad to hear that you determine to appoint an Agent, that will do us Justice, in taking Care that bad men do not come to trade among us but We earnestly entreat you will let us have an Interpreter in whom We can confide, to reside at Pittsburgh; To that place our people and other nations will long resort; there we must send what news We hear, when we go among the western nations, which we are determined shall be next Spring. We know Joseph Nicholson he speaks our language, so that we clearly understand what you say to us. And depend upon what he says; if we were able to pay him for his Services we wou'd do it, but when We gave him land for pay, it has not been confirmed to him, and he will not serve us any longer, unless you will pay him; let him stand between us and you. [W]e entreat you.

Father,

You have not asked of us, any Surety for peace, on our part, but we have agreed to send nine Seneca boys to be under your Care for Education; tell us at what time you will receive them, and they shall be sent at that time. This will assure you, that we are indeed at peace with you, and determined to continue so; if you can teach Them to be wise and good men, we will take Care, that our nation shall be willing to be instructed by them.

Signed in the presence of
Joseph Nicholson interpreter
Thomas Proctor
Timothy Matlack.

KNOX, HENRY. REPLY TO 7 FEB. 1791 ADDRESS OF CORNPLANTER, HALFTOWN, AND THE GREAT TREE. 8 FEB. 1791.

Ms. Volume 60: 30–31. The Pickering Papers. Massachusetts Historical Society, Boston.

[The Reply of the Secretary of War to Cornplanter's third Speech to the President of the U.S.]

The Subscriber, the Secretary of War has submitted your Speech of yesterday to the President of the United States who has commanded him to assure you of his good wishes for your happiness, and that you may have a pleasant journey to your own Country.

The Governor of the Western territory will appoint you an interpreter whenever one shall be necessary—The President of the United States does not choose to interfere on this point.

The President of the United States think[s] it will be the best mode of teaching you how to raise corn by sending one or two sober men to reside in your Nation, with proper implements of husbandry—it will therefore be proper that you should upon consultation appoint a proper place for such persons to till the ground. They are not to claim the land on which they shall plough.

The President of the United States also thinks it will be the best mode of teaching your children to read and write to send a School master among you, and not for you to send your children among us, he will therefore look out for a proper person for this business—

As soon as you shall learn anything of the intentions of the Western Indians, you will inform the Governor of the Western territory thereof or the commanding Officer at Fort Washington, in order to be communicated to the President of the United States—

Given at the War Office of the United
States, this Eighth day of February
in the year of our Lord one thousand
seven hundred & ninety one—
(sign'd) H. Knox
Secy. of War

1794: Councils at Buffaloe Creek

During the last decade of the eighteenth century, councils between the United States and the hostile Western Indian nations were unsuccessful in lessening the threat of war. Recent victories in battle against the U.S. Army made the Western nations confident that they could stop the westward expansion of the United States.

From April to July 1794, a series of councils were held between U.S. commissioners and the Six Nations at Buffaloe Creek. The continual dissatisfaction of the Six Nations with disputed boundary lines and U.S. treaty process is apparent from the council proceedings. The record also reports frequent Six Nations' meetings with the hostile Western Indians. From these meetings there was an emerging interest in forming an alliance among all Indian nations. The United States feared certain defeat if the Six Nations joined with the Western Indians in a war against the United States.

SIX NATIONS. REPLY TO ADDRESS BY GENERAL KNOX AS DELIVERED BY GENERAL CHAPIN. 10 FEB. 1794 AT THE COUNCIL AT BUFFALOE CREEK. 21 APR. 1794.

Ms. Aboriginal Peoples in the Archives. Private Papers. 181. F 47. Simcoe Family Papers. Archives of Ontario, Toronto. In Cruikshank, E. A., ed. *The Correspondence of Lieut. Governor John Graves Simcoe, with Allied Documents Relating to his Administration of the Government of Upper Canada*. Volume 2. Toronto: Ontario Historical Society, 1924, 214–16.

FROM THE SIX NATIONS TO GEN. KNOX.

Reply of the Six Nations assembled in Council at Buffaloe Creek the 21st April, 1794, to a Speech from General Knox, Secretary of War for the United States, delivered by General Chapin on the 10th of February last, as Interpreted by Jasper Parish, one of the Interpreters for the United States.

21st April, 1794.

Clear Sky, an Onondaga Sachem, spoke as follows.
General Chapin:
We are happy to see that you are arrived safe at our Council fire, and that it has pleased the Great Spirit above to preserve you in good health.
We are also happy in seeing you Colonel Butler, as the Representative of the English.

Captain Brant then arose and spoke.
Brothers:
You of the United States listen to what we are now going to say to you, likewise you the representative of the English.
Brothers: We are happy to see you Colonel Butler and you General Chapin setting side by side, with the intention of hearing what we have to say, we wish that no business should be transacted by us the Six Nations unless it be done openly and above board.

Brother: You of the United States make your mind easy on account of the long time your President's word has been under our Consideration, when we received them we observed to you as it was a business of the utmost importance, of course would require a serious reflection and length of time to be considered of which we have done.

Brother: The answer you brought us from Congress is not agreeable to our expectation, this is the reason we have so long delayed answering it, the business would have been done with expedition, had the United States in any wise approved of our proposals, we should then have been able to have accepted your invitation and would have collected our associates, and repaired to the Venango, the place proposed by Congress for meeting us.

Brother: We are sorry that it is out of our power now to attend, were we even to go, your Commissioners would conduct all business as they should think proper, this has been too much the case at every Treaty held with you.

Brother: At the first meeting you had with us (after the conclusion of the war between you and Great Britain) at Fort Stanwix, your Commissioners settled every thing as they thought would best suit them and be most conducive to their own interest, they pointed out a division line and at once confirmed the same, without waiting to have our opinion of it, and whether it would be approved by us or not, holding out that our Country was ceded to them by the King of England, this language confused the minds of our Chiefs and deterred them from making any reply. They [are] still saying if we did not consent to their proposals that their Warriors were at their back and that they well knew we should receive no protection whatever from the King of England, such has been the Language held out by your Commissioners at every Treaty held with us at Fort McIntosh at Rocky River, and in short at every place we have ever met you to transact business.

Brother: Such has been your proceedings with us from time to time, such the ideas held out to us, owing to which Peace has not been established, but much mischief been done to the southward as you well know.

Brother: Ever since the conclusion of your war with the English, we the Six Nations have exerted ourselves to keep Peace, we look'd upon it that it would be for the interest of you the United States, as well as for ours. The confederate Nations were advised by us to request a conference with you, in order that steps might be taken to bring about a peace, between the States and the Western Brethren. This request was made and congress appointed Muskingum, as the place, which from its central situation we agreed to, we there proposed a Boundary line, but your Governor St. Clair did not think proper to approve of it. The Wyandots, some Delawares and a few others, not authorized by our Confederacy to transact any business, went at this time and confirmed a line as claimed by you, although no part of those lands was their property, nor the property of any individuals but common to all Indian Nations.

Brother: This was fully explained at our council held at Lower Sanduskie, (long previous to the last recited transaction) for the purposes of forming our confederacy and adopting such rules as would be beneficial to all Indian Nations, our attendance to the Westward therefore has been frequent, to arrange matters for the mutual welfare of all the Nations of our own Colour umbrage has been taken at this (attendance) by the United States who supposed we went thither to take an active part in the war, with our Brethren against them but this has never been the case.

Brother: You must be fully convinced from our steady perseverance, that we were truly desirous of a Peace being established, this your Commissioners must have seen during the last Summer, the exertions we the Six Nations have made towards accomplishing this desirable object, has made the Western nations rather dubious, as to our sincerity, after we even knew their Sentiments on this head we were still not discouraged but proceeded as we before had done, in what to us appeared reasonable and right, last fall we pointed out steps to be taken by Congress and sent them forward by you, which we expected would have proven satisfactory, but to our great disappointment did not, had our advice taken place we should then have more than ever exerted ourselves, in order that our offers should be confirmed by our confederacy, and strictly adhered to, from our offers being rejected we are again placed in a similar situation to what we were when we first entered on the business.

Brother: You must recollect the number of Chiefs who have waited on Congress at divers times, they have pointed out means to be taken, and held out the same Language uniformly at one time as another which was, that you should in part withdraw your Boundary line and claims to our Land, had you done this Peace would have taken place.

Brother: We have bore every thing patiently for a long time past, we have done every thing we consistently could, with the welfare of our Nations in General notwithstanding the many advantages that has been taken of us by individuals making purchases of our Lands, whose fraudulent conduct towards us, Congress has never thought proper to enquire into, that we might be rectified and our minds made easy, our patience is now worn out, you see the difficulty we labour under and that it is impossible for us to rise from our seats, to attend your Council agreeable to the invitation we have received, the boundary line pointed out we think is a just one, and with which you might be well satisfied, without claiming any of our Lands west of that line. The Trifle that has been paid by Congress, can be no object in comparison to what Peace would be.

Brother: We are of the same opinion with the People of the United States, you call yourselves free and independent, we as the Ancient inhabitants of this Country and sovereigns of the soil, say that we are equally as free as you, or any other nation, or nations under the sun, this Country was gave to us by the Great Spirit above, we wish to enjoy in peace and that we may have an open passage along the Lake within the line we pointed out.

Brother: The great exertions we have made for this number of years in endeavouring to accomplish Peace between you and our Western Nations which we have unfortunately not been able to bring about, our patience is now exhausted and we are discouraged from persevering any longer. Therefore throw ourselves under the protection of the Great Spirit above who we hope will order all things for the best. We tell you our patience is exhausted still we wish for Peace, and whenever persons duly authorized, come here with full powers to proclaim the pleasing sound we shall be ready to pay attention.

(Here a large Belt was returned which accompanied the message from General Knox.)

Endorsed:—Reply of the Six Nations to a speech from General Knox, 21st. April 1794.

PROCEEDINGS OF A COUNCIL HELD AT BUFFALOE CREEK.
18 JUNE 1794.

Ms. Aboriginal Peoples in the Archives. Private Papers. 181. F 47. Simcoe Family Papers. Archives of Ontario, Toronto. In Cruikshank, E. A., ed. *The Correspondence of Lieut. Governor John Graves Simcoe, with Allied Documents Relating to his Administration of the Government of Upper Canada.* Volume 2. Toronto: Ontario Historical Society, 1924, 272–77.

PROCEEDINGS OF A COUNCIL HELD AT BUFFALOE CREEK
JUNE 18TH, 1794.

PRESENT

Captain Brant,	Genl. Chapin,	
Capt. Johnson,	Mr. Colt,	for the
Interpreter,	Mr. Jones,[1]	U.S.

With the Chiefs of the Six Nations,
The Chiefs having assembled,
O'Bale, spoke as follows;
Brothers:
We are thankful that you have attended the call of the Six Nations and that you have been preserved by the Great Spirit, (here he addressed the following Speech to the President of the United States.)

Brothers: I have for a long time aimed at the good of both parties, I have paid you different compliments as that of Brothers, Fathers and now I call you Friends. We were pleased when we heard that you was appointed to the Chief command of the United States.

The Great Spirit has so ordered that every Nation shall have some One to be their Head, you are to look over your people and settle all difficulties, and we the Six Nations expect that you will not be unmindfull of us but see that we have justice done us, as well as to your own people.

Brothers: We the Six Nations now call upon you we pay no attention to what has been done, heretofore by Congress, their proceedings we Consider as unjust, we wish for nothing but Justice and hope that will take place.

Brothers: You wish to be a free people in this Country, from the other side of the Water, and live here, and why should we not, we whose Forefathers have lived and died here and always had possession of this Country.

Brothers: We the Six Nations have determined on the Boundary we want established, and it is the warriors who now speak.

Brothers: You have the map on which the boundary is marked, which we want established.

Brothers: We want room for our children it will be hard for them to have no Country to live in after we are gone.

Brothers: It is not because we are afraid of Dying, that we have been so long trying to bring about a peace, we now call upon you for an answer as Congress and their Commissioners have often deceived us, and if these difficulties are not removed the consequences will be bad.

Eight Strings Wampum Black & White,

Brothers: We have opened this fire place for two kinds of business, we wish you to listen to them with attention.

Brothers: We are in distress; a number of our warriors are missing and we know not what has become of them, but suppose they have been killed by the Americans.

Brothers: Last Fall an Indian Chief of the name of Big Tree went to the American Army in a friendly manner and we have since been informed that he was killed by them.

Brothers: The other day a very unfortunate circumstance happened, one of our Nephews of the Delaware Nation was killed at Venango, by a party of warriors, and who were sent to Presqu'Isle without any notice whatever having been given us.

Brothers: You must be sensible, that it is very hard to have a man killed in time of peace, one who sat easy and peaceably in his seat, you certainly would complain if we were to treat your people in the same manner.

Brothers: It has been customary when one person has killed another that those who has done the injury go to the injured party and make satisfaction.

Brothers: We told you that we had two series of business to attend to we hope you will attend to them both.

Brothers: The establishing a garrison at Presqu' Isle may occasion many accidents, as the Southern Indians may do injury, and we may be blamed without a cause.

Ten Strings Wampum Black,

O'Bale the speaker then addressed himself to General Chapin, as follows:

Brother: When we sent for you it was because we placed great dependence in you, we expected you would not fail to do every thing in your power to assist us.

Brother: We expect that you will exert yourself in removing these people off our lands we know very well what they are come on for and we want them pushed back.

Brother: We now wish that you and Mr. Johnson would go together and move these people back over the line, which we have marked on the Map.

Brother: If these people move off immediately we shall look upon them as friends, if not we shall consider them as no friends.

Brother: We expect that you and Mr. Johnson will go together on this business and we shall send ten warriors to attend you, and we shall expect word to us when we return.

Six Strings Wampum.

To this Speech Genl. Chapin returned the following answer.

Brothers: I have heard the speeches which you have delivered with great attention, and have thought seriously on what you have communicated to me, you have requested Mr. Johnston and myself to go to Presqu' Isle, as I wish to do every thing in my power both for the United States and the indians I shall comply with the request.

Brothers: I can do no more to these people then to give them my advice it is not in my power to drive them away.

Brothers: You must be sensible that I am obliged to look to the interest of the States and the Indians, and consider myself accountable to both for whatever I do, and you may depend that whenever I return I shall give you a just account of what takes place.

Brothers: This business is of a serious nature and is really a matter of importance to both parties, you may rest assured that the President is your friend, and that he will pay attention to what you have laid before him.

Brothers: You observed that you would send ten warriors to accompany me, I request you will send Chiefs likewise.

Brothers: The business that you desire me to do is what I had little thought of I am unprepared for the journey, but as I have informed you that I would go I shall set out immediately.

Brothers: The speeches you have delivered for the President shall be sent on as soon as convenient and you may shortly expect to receive an answer.

Mr. Johnson and General Chapin with sixteen Chief Warriors proceeded to Fort Le Boeuf where they arrived the 26th of June.

27th. The foregoing speeches to the President as well as the request of the Six Nations were delivered in Council to Mr. Ellicott and the Officer Commanding there, to which they returned the following answer.

Brothers of the Six Nations:

Your Brothers of Pennsylvania have always been attentive to the wishes of the indians, especially to that of the Six Nations and are happy to meet with them in peace and unity.

Brothers: By the Peace of 1782 the King of Great Britain ceded to your Brethren of Pennsylvania all the lands which they claim but from a regard to justice and considering you as the real owners of the soil, could not consider themselves as entitled to it until fairly purchased from yourselves.

Brothers: The lands which you have requested us to move off of, have for several years been purchased by your Brothers of Pennsylvania from the Six Nations and the lines bounding the same were opened and marked with their consent and approbation. The Purchase North, of the North boundary of Pennsylvania, West of Canewango River, Lake Chataque and the path leading from thence to Lake Erie and South of the said Lake was made of your Chiefs at Fort Harmar by General Butler and General Gibson and the money and goods was punctually paid to them.

Brothers: Your Brethren of Pennsylvania have fairly and openly made the purchase of all the lands to which they lay claim, and having sold these lands to such people as chose to settle and work them they think it now their duty to protect such settlers from the depredations of all such persons as may molest them.

Brothers: The present military preparations of your Brethren of Pennsylvania are intended to protect their citizens against the hostile indians only, not supposing any protection necessary against the Six Nations whom they consider as their Friends and Allies.

Brothers: The line which you have marked on the Map will take back from your Brothers of Pennsylvania a large tract of land which they have purchased from you. We cannot therefore consistently with our duty remove from those lands unless directed by the Great Council of our people, to whom we shall immediately send your message.

Brothers: We shall be sorry that our continuing on the lands which you have sold to your Brethren of Pennsylvania should be the cause of any uneasiness or why we should not be considered by you as Friends.

Brothers: Your Brethren of Pennsylvania are a generous people, they have never wished for more than they were willing to pay for and have never attempted to take what did not belong to them. They will be glad to meet you at all times and afford relief to the weak and hungry of your people who may take the trouble to come and see them at this place, in the mean time as we are ordered here by the Great Council your Brothers of Pennsylvania we cannot consistent with our duty remove from hence, until orders come from them for that purpose, your message however shall be immediately forwarded by express to them for their Consideration.

FORT LE BOEUF, 26th June 1794,   (Signed)   ANDREW ELLICOTT,
(Signed) THOMAS NESBIT,   C. DENNY,
      Secretary.   Capt. State Troops.

---

1. Horatio Jones, 1763–1836, born at Downington, Pa.; a prisoner with the Six Nations, 1781–84; adopted by a Seneca woman, a sister of Cornplanter; interpreter for the United States, 1789–1803; died at Genesee, N.Y.

General Chapin and Mr. Johnson with the Chief Warriors having returned to Buffaloe Creek, met the Chiefs in Council on the 4th July, when after relating the answer of the people at Fort Le Boeuf and the usual compliments had passed, O'Bale a principal Seneca Chief addressed the following speech to General Washington.

Brother:

I now call you Friend, attend to the voice of the Six Nations who have been united and loved each other since the beginning of the World. We have assembled here on account of the transactions near Presqu' Isle, and we have received an answer to the message we had sent, the answer from the people at Fort Le Boeuf hints upon every thing that has taken place since the peace, the greatest part of what they have told us is not true, they have related some of their former deceptions, they have told me that they had given me Land, but to compleat my wishes, I desire that all the Six Nations may have Lands, I depend upon you Genl. Washington to grant our requests, and make our mind easy, for many reflections are thrown upon me by the Six Nations, I am almost determined to rise from my Berth and die with them.

Brother: We know what we have received from the United States from time to time, we have fully considered the Muskingum Boundary, and we are determined it shall remain, if you establish this line, I think we shall be about even.

Brother: If you do not comply we shall determine upon something else, you know that we are a free people, and that the Six Nations are able to defend themselves. We are determined to maintain our freedom.

Brother: Do not imagine that our minds are corrupted by other people, the only thing that can corrupt them will be a refusal of our Demands.

Brother: If our request is not granted I wish that my son may be sent with the Answer and tell me which side he means to join for he is at liberty to do as he likes.

Brother: We request that you will send a speedy answer to our speeches and that the messenger may come to our Council fire at this place.

Eight Strings Wampum Black & White.

The speaker then addressed Genl. Chapin.

Brother: You who stand between the Indians and the United Sates, we request that you will give every assistance in your power to forward this business. You find us as determined as ever upon the line between us and the United States, we put confidence in you and request that you will forward our Determination to the people at Fort Le-Boeuf and desire them not to move forward.

GENL. CHAPIN'S ANSWER.

Brothers: I am happy the Great Spirit has preserved us to meet again in Council, I have heard with attention the Speeches you have made and have committed them to writing, they have since been explained to you that you might see there was no Deception.

Brothers: I must give it as my opinion that Genl. Washington is a firm friend to the Six Nations and that he will not by any Means see them Wronged.

Brothers: I am happy to hear that you look upon yourselves as free, Independent people that is the Case with the United States, they are free and independent and wish to take you by the hand as Brothers. It seems now that there is some dispute but the only way to have it settled is to come together face to face and talk the matter over *Cordialy.*

Brothers: I shall now return home and will forward your speeches to Genl. Washington as soon as possible in the mean time I hope you will set easy on your seats until you hear General Washington's Voice.

Brothers: I always consider myself Accountable to the indians as well as the United States, I aim the good of both parties and you may rest assured that nothing in my power shall be wanting to Assist, I shall prepare a Copy of your determination to be sent on to Le Boeuf provided you send runners for that purpose.

GENL. WAYNE'S SPEECH.

To all the Sachems Chiefs and Warriors of the Six Nations.

Brothers: We have all to lament the unfortunate death of Capt. Big Tree, who put an end to his own existence about two months since, I made every enquiry into the cause of his death, and ordered thirteen of my warriors to examine the Body, and give me their opinion in writing under their hands and Seal which I now send to you by our friend Mr. Rosecrantz.

A few days after his arrival three Delawares arrived at this Cantonment with a flag and message from the hostile indians proposing to me to fix upon a time and place for holding a treaty in order to agree upon the terms on which peace should be made, I now send you a Copy of that message together with my answer which will be delivered to you by Mr. Rosecrantz.

Capt. Big Tree was present and heard the message from the hostile Indians to me, and my answer to the Message.

I then made this short speech to the Delaware messengers;

Nephews, I call you, because you have always acknowledged the Six Nations your Uncles. I am pleased to find that your pride is lowered and that you begin to come to your reason you were too proud last Summer to listen to the Commissioners of the Thirteen fires and your Uncles.

I will only just inform you that the Voice of the Thirteen fires is the voice of the Six Nations, therefore tell your Chiefs and Warriors to listen to the Voice of their Great Chiefs tell them immediately to comply with his Demands and to deliver up all the prisoners within the course of thirty days, and not to neglect if they wish to see their Children grow up to be men and Women.

That same night Capt. Big Tree had some angry talk with the Delawares; whether he had eat or drank with them afterwards, or whether they gave him something that put him out of his reason afterwards, I cannot tell, but certain it is that from that time to the moment of his death he was melancholy and deranged until the last moment of his death when stabing himself with his own knife.

Brothers: I have now told you every thing that has taken place and all that was said to and with the Hostile Indians, since which I have not heard nor seen any thing further from them, except that they murder our people and steal our Horses whenever they have an opportunity so that all prospect of peace is now done away I have therefore every reason to believe that the only object the hostile Indians had in view was to reconnoitre our situation and to see our numbers and to gain time to collect their warriors from their different hunting camps in order to fight us and continue the War.

Brothers: I was informed by Capt. Big Tree that many of your people had died last Summer in consequence of something you had eat, when at the Council with the hostile Indians at the Rapids of the Miami of the Lake and that my friend and Brother the New Arrow is amongst the Dead and that my good friend Capt. O'Bale was also near dying for which my heart has been sorry, this mode of making War is cowardly and base and Capt. Big Tree was determined to have revenge had he lived this they well know and are glad that He is dead.

Brothers: I have sent cloathing [sic] for the wife and daughter of Capt. Big Tree by Mr. Rosecrantz and a suit of mourning to his two Brothers and a Rifle to each.

I have also ordered the Commanding Officer of Fort Franklin to build a house for them and to give them plenty of provisions and every thing they may want and to provide for and take care of them.

(Signed) ANTHONY WAYNE.
Major General and Commander in Chief of the
Legion of the United States.
GREENVILLE, 26th March, 1794.
Per Tr. Copy taken by Mr. Johnson.[1]

Endorsed:—COUNCIL, 6 NATIONS, Buffaloe Creek, June & July 1794.

1. William Johnston.

1794: Treaty Negotiations in Canandaigua

Immediately following the councils at Buffaloe Creek, President George Washington invited the Six Nations to treat in Canandaigua on the eighth[1] of September 1794. The negotiations would be somewhat delayed, however, until all of the representatives from the Six Nations arrived in Canandaigua in mid-October. After lengthy negotiations, a treaty was successfully negotiated and signed on November 11, 1794.

KNOX, HENRY. LETTER TO ISRAEL CHAPIN. 25 JULY 1794.
B. V. O'Reilly Papers. Volume 10. New-York Historical Society, New York, NY.

> War department
> July 25th 1794

Sir,

I have the honor to acknowledge the receipt of your letters from La Boeuf dated the 26th ultimo and from Canandaigua dated the 9th instant—

It would appear Sir, that you have endeavored to the utmost of your power to avert the storm, and your exertions are noticed with pleasure.

Your ideas of a Conference are adopted. This is to be held at Canandaigua the 8th of September; Colonel Pickering will be the Commissioner to be assisted by you in all respects.

You are therefore immediately to notify the Six Nations of Indians that their father the President of the United States is deeply concerned to hear of any dissatisfaction existing in their minds against the United States and therefore invites them to a conference to be held at Canandaigua the eighth day of September next ensuing for the purpose of amicably removing all causes of misunderstanding and establishing permanent peace and friendship between the United States and the Six Nations.

I hope Colonel Pickering will be able to be with you on the 8th but his great arrangements of the post office being to be made about the first of the Month it is doubtful whether he will be punctual to the time affixed. But if the Indians should be assembled you will endeavor to render them as tranquil as possible until his arrival. He will be particularly instructed on all points which may probably arise at the Conferences. As to any Quakers attending, we have no command over them, but it may be mentioned to them.

Colonel Pickering will have a quantity of Goods to distribute. These will be forwarded by the way of Albany.

You will make arrangements for an adequate supply of provisions and suitable accommodations which it has been conceived to be more abundant at Canandaigua than elsewhere in the Vicinity. In order to enable you to comply with this instruction, I transmit you by Mr. Jasper Parrish One thousand five hundred dollars and five thousand of Wampum.

> I am Sir with
> Great esteem your
> most obedient & humble
> Servant
> H. Knox

Gen. Israel Chapin

CHAPIN, ISRAEL. ADDRESS TO THE CHIEFS OF THE SIX NATIONS AT BUFFALOE CREEK. 15 AUG. 1794.

B. V. O'Reilly Papers. Volume 10. New-York Historical Society, New York, NY.

To the Head Chiefs Sachems and Warriors of the Six Nat.

Brothers—   Having this day Rec.d a return from the President of the United States Respecting your Speech Delivered me at Buffaloe Creek and forwarded by Mr. Parrish, The President our Father having taken into Consideration the Cause of Your uneasiness Respecting the Settlement at Presqu'isle &c. and being Deeply Concerned for the wellfare of the Six Nations, and that a good understanding might exist between them and the United States, immediately entered into measures which he thought best Calculated to promise[?] an amiable agreement between both parties. And he now takes this opportunity to endeavor to Satisfy your minds and give you a right understanding in all things whereby you make your minds uneasy. He invites you all to assemble in a Treaty to be holden in Canandaigua on the tenth of September next, and has ordered Commissioners to attend said Conference, and an adequate supply of Provisions &c will be procured for you. and I hope and believe that we Shall determine on Something which will give general Satisfaction to Both Parties.

It is not in my Power to give you this information Personally on account of Sickness in my Family. I have sent my son to you with Strings of wampum to your Chiefs, for you to forward information to your Villages. And much request your attention in Business, As the President of the United States is Desirous your minds should be made easy, and for you to remain quiet on your Seats. Wishing you to notify all your Villages to attend the Treaty in your Neighborhood, as will Capt. Obeel and his People.

Israel Chapin Jun'r
In behalf of his Father

Coppy
Augt. 15th—1794
Copy of a Speech Del.d at Buffaloe
August 16—94—

---

1. The eighth of September is the date in the Knox letter to Chapin; the tenth of September is the date in the Chapin address to the Chiefs of the Six Nations.

THE SAVERY JOURNAL: THE CANANDAIGUA TREATY EXCERPT
Reprinted from
A Journal of the Life, Travels, and Religious Labors of William Savery,
a Minister of the Gospel of Christ, of the Society of Friends,
Late of Philadelphia
Compiled from his original memoranda by
Jonathan Evans

There were four Quaker representatives who attended the 1794 treaty negotia-
tions in Canandaigua: William Savery, James Emlen, David Bacon, and John
Parrish. Three of the four, Savery, Emlen, and Bacon kept journals during the
council proceedings; these handwritten documents have been archived as part of
the public record and survive as an important part of the treaty literature. An
excerpt from the William Savery journal is reprinted here to give the reader a sense
of the daily progress made during the long negotiation process. As William N.
Fenton comments below, the Savery journal is referenced most often; however,
Emlen's journal offers some unique commentary upon the treaty proceedings:

> John Parrish and William Savery (1750–1804) had earlier attended the
> abortive treaty at the Maumee Rapids; David Bacon and James Emlen
> (1760–97) were neophytes at Canandaigua. William Savery spoke for the
> four and was the most literate: his journal, printed afterward in Philadel-
> phia and London (1837), has been the sole resource for previous writers.
> Bacon's diary (Haverford College Library, ms.) describes Indian customs;
> Emlen's journal (New York State Library) ranks next to Savery's in
> quality and coverage (Fenton 1965). Emlen was a better observer of
> natural phenomena than Savery, but his account skips the last ten days of
> the treaty proceedings. Savery evidently wrote from his own notes and the
> combined journals of the other three (Fenton 1998).

Below is the Canandaigua Treaty excerpt from the Savery journal, reprinted
from Chapter II of **A Journal of the Life, Travels, and Religious Labors of**
William Savery, a Minister of the Gospel of Christ, of the Society of Friends, Late
of Philadelphia, *compiled from his original memoranda by Jonathan Evans*
(Philadelphia, [1837]).[1]

Joins another Deputation to an Indian Treaty—Address from Friends to the
Indians—Journey from Philadelphia to the western part of N. York—Hard fare
in the Wilderness—Canandaigua—Interview with Oneidas—Jemima Wilkinson
and her followers—Oneida Council—Col. Pickering—Council of the Six
Nations—Speeches of Indian Chiefs—Red Jacket—Cornplanter—Interference of
British Agent—Number and Possessions of the Six Nations—Speech of Col.
Pickering—Remarkable Spring—Speech of Red Jacket to the Friends—Red
Jacket's reply to Col. Pickering—Another Speech by the Commissioner—Reply
to Red Jacket—Interruptions to closing the Treaty—Efforts of Friends to com-
pensate the Indians formerly owning the land about Hopewell, Va.—Speech of
Cornplanter—Reply of Commissioner—Treaty signed—Address of the Indians

to the Friends—Start for Home—Difficulties of the Journey—Arrival in Philadelphia—Reflections respecting the Indians—Visit to Virginia Yearly Meeting—Remarkable Service in Richmond—Return Home.

In the Eighth month, 1794, the Meeting for Sufferings was informed through the officers of government, that a treaty was shortly to be held at Canandaigua, in the State of New York, between commissioners appointed on behalf of the United States, and the chiefs of the Six Nations; and that they were particularly solicitous Friends should attend it—the government also encouraging their doing so.

After seriously deliberating on this important movement, four Friends, viz: David Bacon, John Parrish, William Savery, and James Emlen, under an apprehension that it was their religious duty, offered themselves for the service, and being approved by the meeting, were furnished with a number of articles, as presents for the Indians, and with the following address, viz:

The people called Quakers, in Pennsylvania, New Jersey &c., by their representatives assembled at Philadelphia, the 9th of Ninth month, 1794:

To our brothers, the Indians of the Six Nations, who have appointed to meet at Canandaigua, in order for the promotion of lasting peace; BROTHERS,

We are always glad when we have an opportunity of hearing from you, our old friends, and using our endeavors in promoting the good work of peace.

Brothers,—We understand the President of the United States has proposed holding a treaty with you, by his commissioners. Our religious profession has always led us to promote so good a work; and having been informed that the President of the United States, as also your nations, are willing and desirous we should be at the treaty, we have therefore authorized our beloved friends, David Bacon, John Parrish, William Savery, and James Emlen, to attend the said treaty for us; on whose behalf we make known to you, that they are our friends, whom we greatly love, being true men, whose love is so great to their Indian brethren, the old inhabitants of this land of America, that they are willing to come to see you, with desires to do you good.

Brothers,—We meddle not with the affairs of government; but we desire to do all we can to preserve and promote peace and good-will among all men.

Brothers,—Our grandfathers and friend Onas, were careful in their day to preserve peace and love with their brothers, the Indians:—We, their children and successors, endeavor to do the same, and are happy when we can prevail on the people to be kind, and do good and not evil to one another.

Brothers,—We pity the Indians, as well as the white people, when they are brought into suffering and distress, and would do them all the good in our power.—We hope the Great and Good Spirit will put it into the hearts of the great men of the United States and your great men, to adjust and compromise all their differences.

Brothers,—We hope you will receive kindly our friends and brothers, David Bacon, John Parrish, William Savery and James Emlen. We have put under their care a small token of love for you, as the descendants of the first inhabitants of this land of North America, whom our forefathers found here after they had crossed the great water. Desiring that the chain of our friendship may be kept bright, we bid you farewell.

Signed by forty-four Friends.

The benevolent and sympathetic mind of our beloved friend, was so deeply interested for this injured people, that though he had endured so much in the late painful and hazardous journey to Detroit, yet he could not withhold his aid, when another attempt was to be made for adjusting the many grievances of his red brethren, and, if possible, settling the terms of a lasting peace. He has left the following narrative of the undertaking, viz:

Left Philadelphia in company with my friends, David Bacon, John Parrish, and James Emlen, the 15th of ninth month, 1794; being accompanied by several Friends to Germantown, where we took an affectionate leave of them. Nothing from without affords so great consolation and strength in undertaking such arduous journies, as a sense that we are favored with the precious unity and affectionate concern of our near connections and brethren. This, to me, has been a comfortable reflection, and softens the trials I have felt at leaving my home at this time, especially as the Yearly Meeting is near at hand.

Having got on the Blue mountains the 18th, we proceeded a short distance when it began to rain, and increased till our clothes were wet through; but after riding several miles, we stopt at a house, got some refreshment, dried our clothes and rode to Cattawissa. Neither the land nor the appearance of the country round this place appears very attractive.

19th. Riding through a better country on the west side of the Susquehanna, we stopped at a place where they at times entertain travellers, and expected to dine; but they having neither feed for our horses, bread nor meat, we rode two miles further and dined upon bread, the people having neither meat nor milk.

20th. Got to the house of a Friend at Loyalsock. Before I alighted from my horse I felt unwell, and immediately went to lie down. A fever coming on, I was very sick until evening, and began to doubt the propriety of going on, yet was glad that my indisposition was not the cause of detaining my friends, for it rained too hard to travel, until near night.

21st. Being much recruited I went on, and after crossing the Lycoming eight times, proceeded over an exceedingly stony and miry path through the woods; we thought the road very long and tiresome, both to ourselves and the horses. At dark we heard the barking of a dog, which rejoiced us; but it proved to be at a place called the Blockhouse, a poor shelter indeed. We were now convinced of our neglect in not providing ourselves with necessary stores when we had the opportunity; such as sugar, tea, meat, bread, &c., for this family had nothing for us but a little flour, which the woman in a very dirty manner kneaded up in the fat of an elk, shot some days before. Our lodging and fare were truly uncomfortable. I could but admire how very few, even of what are called the necessaries of life, supported this family; the children, however, have a far more healthy appearance than is common in luxurious and populous cities; and having near thirty miles to send for salt, sugar, flour and other necessaries, a girl about fourteen, and a boy about thirteen years of age, generally performed the journey alone, sometimes lying all night in the woods. We had to lie on the floor, with the house open on all sides; yet were content, though we slept but little.

22nd. Our horses being tied up all night without either hay or pasture, we fed them with some oats and rode about ten miles over an exceedingly bad path, the most difficult we had yet seen. Stopping a short time on the banks of the Tioga at the house of a new settler, we procured some feed for our horses, and a small piece of meat for ourselves. The country so abounds with wild game, bears, deer, elk, foxes and wolves, that it is difficult to keep hogs or sheep.—There being no taverns, all the farm-houses take in travellers and charge very high for poor fare.

24th. We got to an Indian cabin on the bank of the river which runs by the town of Bath, and twelve miles further reached a sort of public house, having rode the whole of this day through the woods.

On the 25th, we arrived at Canandaigua, in the afternoon, where Colonel Pickering and General Chapin were holding a conference with the Oneida Indians. Having welcomed us, they directed us to the lodgings prepared for us.

26th. Attended a second conference with the Oneidas, which chiefly consisted in a relation of what had befallen them since the last treaty. They informed us, that as we were now met again, they hoped we should discuss all the necessary objects of the treaty with candor and freedom, and for that purpose they now unstopped our ears that we might hear, and opened our throats that we might speak freely. To this Colonel Pickering expressed his wish to conduct the business with the unreserved candor they desired, and that he also opened their ears and unstopped their throats.

27th. Seeing some persons in the garb of Friends, they informed us they lived about five miles beyond this, and being glad to see us, invited us to their houses.

28th. First-day, having appointed a meeting, to begin at eleven o'clock, it was largely attended by the people, and a considerable number of Indians, so that the house could not contain the whole. Appointed another at four o'clock in the afternoon, both of which were to satisfaction, and we believe to the people generally. There is no public worship maintained within many miles of this place.

30th. Abraham Lapham came to our lodgings, and conducted us to his house, where we were kindly received, and spent a pleasant day. This country has two great disadvantages attending it, the scarcity of springs and rivulets, and the unhealthiness of the climate in its present unculti-vated state, yet it is settling very fast, the land being very fertile; but as the Indians are all around, and the settlements of the whites very thin, there still is some danger to be apprehended. The first settlers have passed through great difficulties, having near one hundred miles to go to mill, and struggling under many privations to procure a living for their large families; some have staid for many weeks under the shelter of bark and bushes before they could erect a hut.

Tenth month, 2d, fifth-day. Six of the Indians, each of them brought in a deer, and one of them made us a present of a piece, signifying that he gave it to us for Jesus Christ's sake, who had made us brethren.

First-day, 5th of the month. The weather not being very favorable, the meeting was not so large as last First-day, nor so satisfactory. The Indians were remarkably sober, making but little noise; the Oneidas pay some regard to the First-day of the week.

7th of the month. Went to Judge Potter's, and being kindly received stayed all night. The Judge is a respectable man, but having some years back been induced to entertain a favorable opinion of Jemima Wilkin-son and her doctrines, he and several others came with her into this country, and took up forty-one thousand acres of excellent land near the west side of Seneca lake, at four pence per acre. But the good under-standing of the Judge not suffering him to remain a dupe to the delusions of an assuming, presumptuous woman, he has for some time past thrown off the shackles, and is now no more accounted one of her fra-ternity. He said he believed her whole scheme was for self-interest and aggrandizement; he himself having suffered by her in a pecuniary point of view, but had now asserted his right to a part of the land occupied by these people, and forbade their making use of it. After breakfast we went to see Jemima, and found her about three miles from Potter's, in a sequestered, romantic place, suited to her genius. The family appeared to consist of ten or twelve persons, one of whom being acquainted with us, welcomed us in; another was a man far gone in a consumption, who had left his wife at some miles distance and brought so much of his little property with him, as to reduce her to great difficulty in getting a sub-sistence. His design appears to be to spend his last breath under Jemima's benediction, assuring us he was very easy about his soul. O, wretched infatuation! that can break the most solemn ties of God and nature, yet flatter its votaries that they are the favorites of heaven.

Here are several hovels adjacent, which are the residences of women who have forsaken husband and children; and also of men who have left their families, to become what they now literally are, hewers of wood and drawers of water to an artful and designing woman. One young woman who had been with them several years, told me the women fre-quently washed Jemima's feet and wiped them with the hair of their heads. Asking for the rest of the family, Rachel Malin stepped into Jemima's room and invited her out. She was attired in a loose gown or rather a surplice of calico, and some parts of her dress were quite masculine; she accosted us with a look of importance, and called me by name. The conversation becoming of a religious nature, she said much in a kind of prophetic manner. So great was her volubility, that we were obliged to interrupt her in order to express our disapprobation of the exalted character she gave to her own mission, and that it savored strongly of pride and ambition to distinguish herself from the rest of mankind by the appellation of the Universal Friend. Some other remarks were made to check her rhapsodies, but her assurance, and artful manner of leading off from a subject which she did not relish, rendered our efforts abortive. We were, however, not disappointed, for it cannot be expected that any power but that which is Divine, can bring her to a state of reason or of Christianity. This people have a meeting-house, and some of the scattered neighbors meet with them on First-days, but it appears they are declining fast; and both reason and religion inform us, that their fall is at no great distance, and perhaps the last days of this deluded woman may be spent in contempt, unless her heart becomes humbled and contrite, and the mercy of the Lord be eminently manifest to pity and spare her. Some credible persons resident in the neighborhood informed us, that Jemima had asserted, and it was believed by her credulous disciples, that the prophet Elijah had taken possession of the body of one James Parker and spoke through his organs; and that the prophet Daniel, in like manner, inhabited the body of Sarah Richards, another of her followers; but the prophet Elijah, (James Parker,) and she having afterward disagreed and separated, and Sarah Richards having died, they are now deprived of their counsel.

9th. The Senecas are very slow in coming to attend the treaty, and the lesson of last year is to be learned over again; this is patience, which will always be needed by those who attend Indian treaties.

11th. Colonel Pickering having called on David Bacon and myself, we attended him to the Oneida camp, where an interesting council was held, in which Captain John, an Indian sachem, and Peter the chief warrior, were the speakers. Colonel Pickering made a very suitable speech, informing them that he had heard of divisions among them, and if they would inform him of the cause of them he should be happy in using his endeavors to settle them. Captain John then informed us in a long speech of many things which had occasioned uneasiness in their nation, principally in relation to the manner wherein they had several times suffered in the sale of their lands; and lately by leasing to Peter Smith one-third of the land they had reserved, being a tract of four miles wide and twenty-four miles long, which they had leased to him for twenty-one years, at two hundred dollars per annum. This had occasioned great dissatisfaction between the sachems and the warriors, the warriors protesting against the lease; that the two parties, whilst the land was surveying, faced each other in arms, and had not the surveyors desisted, it might have proved destructive to the nation, and they were yet divided into parties. He began by observing, that we were all in the presence of the Great Spirit, and he knew that he could not conceal anything from Him, and as he was now surrounded by his brethren, he should speak uprightly and withhold nothing. He spoke nearly an hour, and delivered to Peter, the chief warrior, five strings of wampum, which Colonel Pickering gave into his hand as he closed his speech. He then desired, if the warriors had heard anything that was not true, they would point it out. Peter, after reminding Colonel Pickering of the advice which he gave them at Newtown in the last treaty, said he found no fault with what the sachems had said, but desired that if they had gone out of the path they were recommended to walk in when at Newtown, which he suspected they had, the colonel would put them right again.

Colonel Pickering told them he believed they had, but as it was a matter of great importance, he desired to consider it until the day after to-morrow, that he might prepare an answer. The conference held three hours, after which Colonel Pickering acknowledged that both private persons and the governor of New York had given great occasion for their complaints. Smith's lease contained sixty-one thousand four hundred and forty acres. In the evening John Parrish and James Emlen returned from the encampment of the Senecas at Gennessee river, about twenty-six miles distant, bringing an account that there were about five hundred of them at that place.

12th. Understanding a person expected to occupy our former place of meeting, we concluded to prepare the house where we lodge for holding a meeting. Friends who are settled in the neighborhood, and several others, with a number of the Indians coming in, we had a solid favored opportunity. Some who had expected us at the school-house as usual, came after that meeting was over, and said that they had been disappointed in not finding us there, but thought that for the future they should come to our lodgings on a First-day morning to know where the meeting was to be held. In the afternoon we went at four o'clock to the Oneida camp, having previously informed the chiefs of our intention of a meeting there, the interpreter being with us. We found some collected in the woods where many trees were felled, which served as seats, and one of the chiefs went round the camp, vociferating a certain sound used as a signal for them to assemble, which they did in large numbers. The curiosity of the white people being raised, and some coming from other motives, we had a large and good meeting, which held till near sunset; both whites and Indians were quiet and behaved decently; as many of the Indians had received some notion of the Christian religion from missionaries, and were desirous to begin the service with singing of hymns or psalms, and we not thinking it would be best to object to their wishes, they appeared very devout, and I thought that the melody and softness of their voices in the Indian language, and the sweetness and harmony that attended, exceeded by far anything of the kind I had ever heard among the white people. Being in the midst of the woods, the satisfaction of hearing these poor untutored people sing, with every appearance of devotion, their Maker's praise, and the serious attention they paid to what was delivered to them, conspired to make it a solemn meeting, long to be remembered by me. We left them in much love and sympathy, rejoicing in the midst of the wilderness that the Lord is indeed everywhere.

13th. Ruminating on the state of the Oneida Indians, who are said to be more civilized and better instructed in religion than any others, it is natural to inquire what influence it has had on their manners and morals, which, from anything I can discover, has yet been very small. It is true, they generally cultivate a small portion of land, and for that reason are less exposed to absolute want than other Indians: they have also heard of Jesus Christ through their missionary, and have been taught to sing psalms and hymns in their own soft and engaging language; but it appears to me that the great body of the nation have received the Gospel in word only, and not in power. It has therefore had but little influence on their conduct; and a few excepted, they appear to remain enslaved to all the vices common to the other Indians; yet I think the way is gradually preparing when some more enlightened and spiritual men than have yet been their teachers, men who will unite example with precept, may be sent among them with a good effect.

Colonel Pickering having called on us again, we went with him to the camp, where the chiefs and warriors being assembled, he delivered a long written speech, containing suitable advice for reconciling the differences in the nation, and also as a rule for their conduct in future respecting their lands, which appeared well calculated to prevent the frauds and impositions of designing men. They heard all patiently, and then desired us to withdraw a few minutes while they consulted among themselves. Being again called in, Captain John said they were in hopes that Colonel Pickering would have informed them whether the sachems or warriors had been wrong, for it would not have hurt the sachems if they had been so told plainly. The advice to them had been very long, and he could not retain all parts of it, but he recollected they were told that Peter Smith, agreeably to our laws, was not only subject to have his bargain made void, but also liable to pay a fine of a thousand dollars and suffer a year's imprisonment; the two latter they hoped would not be inflicted, as it was not their wish. He also noticed what was said concerning our government and laws, saying, the Indians had also their mode of law, which had been handed down by their forefathers; and one of their customs was, for the sachems only to sit in council on civil affairs; but of late, their warriors appeared jealous of them, and had intruded into matters contrary to the ancient customs of Indians; hence we might see, that when they were about to answer the commissioner, Peter the chief warrior had gone off and took the warriors with him, which indicated his being displeased; and he thought he would show it either during the present council-fire, or afterwards. Indeed, he apprehended that Peter was aspiring to be something more than the nation was willing he should be, and aimed at being the chief sachem. He then told us in very drolling style, the manner of the white people persuading them out of their lands, even some who had not half the understanding naturally, that was possessed by some of their chiefs, but they were skilled in dissimulation and acquainted with the propensities of the Indians. They agreed to take the advice given them and wished it again repeated.

Colonel Pickering told them, he would use his influence to have their lands, which Peter Smith had taken upon lease, restored to them, and that after they were restored, if that could be obtained, he wished them still to offer them upon lease, and to take the assistance of some judicious men that might be appointed by government; they might then lease them in three hundred separate farms, with certain stipulations that the land and timber should not be ruined, &c. The consequence of this would be, that in twenty-one years, there would be so many improved farms in their possession, which would result in a great accumulation of wealth to the Oneida nation. He concluded by promising to return by the Oneida castle, as he went home, where he would repeat his advice to them, that they might not forget it; and told them they had reason to rest peaceably and quietly, though it should not even be in the power of government to reclaim the lands which Smith had got upon lease; for they should consider that a great estate was still in their possession, if the best use was made of it: whereupon the council broke up.

14th of Tenth month. The party of Senecas, headed by the Farmer's Brother, Little Billy, &c., having arrived, last evening, within four miles, were expected this forenoon; but having to paint and ornament themselves before their public entry, they did not arrive till three o'clock this afternoon. The Oneidas, Cayugas, and Onondagoes, were drawn up, dressed and painted, with their arms prepared for a salute before General Chapin's door. The men able to bear arms marched in, assuming a good deal of importance, and drew up in a line facing the Oneidas, &c; Colonel Pickering, General Chapin, and many white people being present. The Indians fired three rounds, which the other Indians answered by a like number, making a long and loud echo through the woods. Their commanders then ordered them to form a circle around the commissioner and General Chapin; then sitting down on the ground, they delivered a speech through the Farmer's Brother, and returned the strings of wampum which were sent them, when they were requested to come to the treaty. Colonel Pickering answered them in the usual complimentary manner, and ordered several kettles of rum to be brought; after drinking which, they dispersed, and went to prepare their camp. Each chief delivered in a bundle of sticks, answerable to the number of persons, men, women, and children, under his command, which amounted to four hundred and seventy-two. They made a truly terrific and warlike appearance.

16th. About three o'clock this afternoon, Cornplanter and his party of Senecas arrived, amounting to about four hundred. They drew up in three sides of a square, the Oneidas, Onondagoes, &c., facing them; each fired three rounds, and performed some manoeuvres; all in full Indian dress, and painted in an extraordinary manner. Then encircling the commissioners and us, they exchanged a short speech of congratulation, and as it rained, the rum was soon brought, and the company dispersed. There are now about sixteen hundred Indians assembled. Last night one Indian stabbed another, who, although not yet dead, is unlikely to continue long.

17th. Sixteen hundred Indians are around us, many of them very noisy night and day, dancing, yelling, and constantly intruding upon us to beg for rum, &c., but we uniformly resist their importunities for strong drink. The attendance at Indian treaties is a painful task, wherein resignation is highly necessary. May it be granted. They kill plenty of venison, and sell it for three half-pence, or less, per pound. Whilst at our present place of abode, I sat in company with an Indian Queen, who had a small child in one of their kind of cradles, hung with about one hundred small brass bells, intended to soothe the child to rest.

18th. This morning Cornplanter, Farmer's Brother, Red Jacket, Little Beard, and a number more of the Seneca chiefs, came to our lodgings to hold a conference, the interpreter being with them. Cornplanter congratulated us upon our safe arrival among them, and acknowledged the kindness of General Washington in informing Friends of the request of the Indians, that they should attend the treaty. He then opened the business, which more particularly occasioned their present visit. This was to answer a request made to them a year or two past by Friends at Philadelphia, that they might make inquiry after the Indians, or their descendants, who formerly lived about Hopewell, in Virginia.* He said that they had conferred together on the subject several times, and believed they had come to the knowledge of the original owners of that land, two of whom, ancient men, were now present, who said their people were once settled about Conestogo, and that they remembered well the state of matters respecting the land in question: they had no doubt those two ancient men could clear up the matter to our satisfaction, at a future opportunity, and would retire for the present.

In the afternoon, Obeal, son of Cornplanter, came with a message from the Indians, inviting us to council. We found a large body of them collected, Colonel Pickering, General Chapin, and three interpreters being in the centre, and the surrounding assemblage presenting a very striking aspect; the chiefs appeared solid and thoughtful. Captain John, and another of the Oneidas, spoke, addressing themselves to their brothers, the Senecas, Tuscaroras, and Delawares, who lived westward, holding in their hands, as they spoke, one after the other, several strings of wampum and belts; which they handed to the Seneca chiefs, one by one, at certain periods of their address, till they delivered all they had. As it was only an address to their brethren, the Indians of other nations, agreeably to their ancient custom, when they meet at a council fire, it

---

*Some members of the Society of Friends had purchased and settled upon lands about Hopewell, and there was reason to believe that the Indian title had not been extinguished by a fair and honorable purchase of the natives, by those occupants who had sold to Friends. The Society, consonant with its known principles, was desirous, that notwithstanding the Indians had left or been driven to remote parts, yet that if the original proprietors could be found, however feeble and insignificant they might now be, they should be fully compensated, in order that its members might hold those possessions on such a firm and justly acquired fee, as true Christian principles would dictate.

was not publicly interpreted; but we understood it was in the way of condolence, on account of the loss of many chiefs of the Six Nations by death, since they last met at a council fire. They expressed their desire to wipe the tears from their brethren's eyes, to brighten their countenances, and to unstop their throats, that they might speak clearly in the present council fire. The Fish Carrier, Clear Sky, and Red Jacket, returned a brotherly salutation, handing the eastern Indians belts and strings of wampum, to unite each to the other, and thus to open the council as with the heart of one man. They then informed Colonel Pickering, that the Six Nations were now embodied in council. He made them a complimentary and congratulatory address, informing them that he should hold a council of condolence to-morrow at four o'clock in the afternoon, to wipe away the tears from the eyes of the Delawares, who had lost a young brother, murdered by a white man at Venango, last summer; he would then take the hatchet out of the head of the deceased, and bury it in the earth, preparatory to the treaty. Several kettles of rum and glasses were brought, and the conference closed.

19th, First-day. Held a meeting for worship; a considerable number attended, who lived generally from two to ten miles distant. Many of them came on foot, there being but few horses in this country, and fewer wheel-carriages of any kind. One family came a considerable distance upon a sled drawn by four stout oxen. The people were solid, and through Divine favor it proved a good meeting, many were very tender and parted with us lovingly. It does our hearts good to see the gratitude some of the poor frontier people manifest, and the pains they take to be at a religious meeting. O Philadelphians, how abundant ought your gratitude to be for the enjoyment of your multiplied blessings.

Tenth month, 20th. Attended a very large Indian council, at which the commissioner condoled with the Delawares for the loss of one of their people, and by his speech and gestures performed the ceremony of burying him after the Indian custom, and covering the grave with leaves, so that when they passed by they should not see it any more. He took the hatchet out of his head, and *in words* tore up a large pine tree and buried the hatchet in the hole, then covered it thick with stones and planted the pine tree on the top of it again, so that it should never more be taken up. He wiped the blood from their beds and the tears from their eyes, and opened the path of peace, which the Indians were requested to keep open at one end and the United States at the other, as long as the sun shone. Many other things of the like nature he said to them, after the figurative style of the natives, that all might be cleared out of the way before the business of the treaty commenced. In the course of his speaking on different subjects, he gave them as many strings of wampum as were thought to be worth near one hundred dollars.

The Farmer's Brother then spoke with great energy to his Indian brethren, and they not being ready to answer Colonel Pickering's speech, the council fire was covered and the rum brought in as usual.

Third-day, 21st. Jemima Wilkinson being come to this place last evening, sent a message by two of her flock to James Emlen and myself, desiring our company; but as it snowed very fast and was a stormy time, we did not immediately obey the summons. After an early dinner, David Bacon being with us, we went and found her at Thomas Morris's, by invitation of Colonel Pickering to dine with him; D. Waggoner, and Enoch and Rachel Malin were also there. The Colonel paid great attention to Jemima, and seemed to be glad of having an opportunity to gratify his curiosity, as he had never seen her before. She was placed at the head of the table, and the conversation being on a variety of subjects, she bore a considerable part therein. A message was received informing that the Indians were collected. We went to council, whitlier Jemima and her disciples followed us, and were placed in the centre. Fish Carrier spoke in answer to the commissioner's address yesterday, till he had passed through his hands one by one, all the strings that were given them, and made a full reply: then with assurances of the determination of the Six Nations to keep hold of the chain of friendship with the fifteen fires, he delivered fifteen strings of chequered wampum as a seal to it. Colonel Pickering introduced himself as sole commissioner on the part of the United States, whom the Six Nations had requested might be appointed on the present occasion; gave them assurances of his desire to promote the happiness and peace of their nations, and told them that they might depend upon one thing at least, which was, that he never would deceive them. He also introduced us, their old friends the Quakers, as having come forward at their (the Indians') request, and with the approbation of the President. We then read the address from Friends, Jasper Parrish interpreting, which they received with frequent expressions of *entaw* or approbation; and afterwards Clear Sky said, they were glad to see us among them, and thanked us for our speech. It is however expected that they will give us a more full answer before the treaty is over. Immediately after we had read our speech, Jemima and all her company kneeled down and she uttered something in the form of prayer, after which she desired to speak, and liberty not being refused, she used many texts of Scripture, without much similarity or connection. The Indians having prepared belts as records of the death of several of their noted chiefs, intended to preserve the memory of their usefulness to the nation; a short speech was made on each of them to their brethren, and they were then delivered to the care of an ancient chief, whereupon the council fire was covered.

23d. Captain John, an Indian chief, visited us, and had much to say about the many deceptions which had been practised upon them by the white people; observing that however good and honest white men might be in other matters, they were all deceivers when they wanted to buy Indian lands; and that the advantages of learning which they possessed, made them capable of doing much good and much evil.

Colonel Pickering requesting our attendance at a council, we went about eleven o'clock. Nearly forty chiefs being assembled, Captain John, in a humorous manner, informed the commissioner of a council they were called to attend; but when the chiefs had collected, they were invited up stairs to take a dram before they began. Perceiving that Berry was to be the commissioner, they concluded it was no good council fire, so he came off and drew the rest of the Indians with him; it appearing that it was a design to get the chiefs to convey to him some Indian lands, after he should have filled them with liquor. The colonel highly approved of the Indians' conduct, and said he would have Berry removed off those lands. An account was brought to the council of the death of an ancient Oneida, upon which Captain John made a speech to their brothers of the other nations. They agreed that as the Great Spirit had brought them together to promote the work of peace, it could not be unacceptable to Him if they went on with the council, though it was contrary to their common custom. Being about to proceed to business, a request was made from three Indian women, to be admitted to the council, and deliver their sentiments, which being granted, they were introduced by Red Jacket. He addressed himself to the sachems and warriors, desiring their indulgence of the women, and also to the commissioner, enforcing their request by observing, that the other day one of our women had liberty to speak in council. He was then desired to act as orator for the women, and deliver to the council what they had to say. The substance of this was, that they felt a deep interest in the affairs of their nation, and having heard the opinions of their sachems, they fully concurred in them, that the white people had been the cause of all the Indians' distresses; that they had pressed and squeezed them together, until it gave them great pain at their hearts, and that the whites ought to give them back the lands they had taken from them. That one of the white women had yesterday told the Indians to repent; and they now called on the white people to repent, for they had as much need as the Indians, and that they should wrong the Indians no more.

The colonel thanked them for the speech, and replied, that it was far from him to think meanly of women: he should always be willing to hear them when they had anything of importance to say, but as they had mentioned as a precedent, the woman who spoke the other day, he must assure them, that it was not with his approbation; she had forced herself into council contrary to his advice; but as she was a woman, he was tender of her.

The commissioner gave us some information of the speech of the Indians yesterday, when we were not present. They said, when the white people first came on this island, they saw that they were men, and must have something to subsist upon, they therefore pitied them, and gave them some land, and when they complained that the land became too small for them, they gave them more, from time to time, for they pitied them. At length a great council fire was kindled at Albany, where a silver chain was made, which was kept bright for many years, till the United States and the great king over the water differed; then their brothers in Canada talked with them, and they let the chain fall out of their hands, yet it was not their fault, it was the white people's. They then repeated how things went at the end of the war, the substance of the treaty at Fort Stanwix, and several grievances which they had suffered. The commissioner spoke, perhaps two hours, respecting the ancient boundaries of the Six Nations' land, and inquired what was the extent of it. They told him, all the land from a point on Lake Erie to Muskingum was theirs, and that the council at the Miami, last summer, acknowledged it. This takes in a great part of what the Western Indians are fighting for. The commissioner told them, he did not approve of the conduct of the commissioners at Fort Stanwix—that they had just then become conquerors, and the Indians must make some allowances, if they spoke harshly and proudly to them. This council held five hours, and much was said on both sides.

This morning, the 25th, snow was seven or eight inches deep, and having been out in it yesterday, I was unwell. Abundance of deer are killed by the Indians, perhaps not less than one hundred to-day, within a few miles of this place, some in sight; one man killed three in a short time. A man named Johnson, having arrived two days ago from Fort Erie, with a message from Captain Brandt, a Mohawk chief, to the Six Nations, assembled some chiefs yesterday and delivered it to them. Being in the character of a British interpreter, he appeared at the council with the Indians to-day, and seemed very intimate with them. Cornplanter rose to vindicate his coming, being privy to the great uneasiness it had given Colonel Pickering: he expressed his surprise, that ever since the conclusion of the peace with the British nation, such an antipathy had existed, that the United States and the British could not bear to sit side by side in treaties held with the Indians. He said, Johnson had the care of the Senecas at Buffalo-creek, and had brought a message to the Six Nations assembled at this council fire, from Brandt, whom he left with Governor Simcoe at Fort Erie; they having just returned together from Detroit: that when he went some time ago to see the Western Indians, he sat in council with the Delawares, Shawnese [sic], Wyandots and Miamies, and the Western Indians expressed great joy at seeing the Six Nations represented by him among them; they told him he recollected that the business of the treaty last year did not go on, but the fault was not theirs, it was that of other people, and the Indians were led astray, for which they were sorry. The misfortunes that had fallen upon them were very heavy, and our brothers the British, who were sitting by, gave us no relief. We allow you who are listening to us, to be the greatest, we will therefore hear what you say. We desire a council fire may be kindled next spring at Sandusky, for all nations of Indians. Captain Brandt sends his compliments to the chiefs at Canandaigua, and says, you remember what we agreed on last year, and the line we then marked out: If this line is complied with, peace will take place; and he desires us to mention this at Canandaigua; after the council at Canada is over, it is my earnest desire you will immediately come to Buffalo-creek, and bring General Chapin with you—I will wait here till you return.

Colonel Pickering rose and said, he was sorry that anything should happen to interrupt this council fire: but it is now interrupted by the coming of Johnson, whom he considered as a British spy, and that his being here was an insult to him, to their friends the Quakers, and to the fifteen fires. That the intrusion of this man into our councils, betrayed great impudence, and was a fresh proof of British insolence. It was perhaps as well that there was no council yesterday, for he could not say how far the first emotions of his mind at seeing this fellow here, might have carried him; he hoped he was now a little cool, and would endeavor to moderate his expressions as much as he was capable of. He begged their patience, for he must be obliged to say a great deal to inform them of many of the reasons of his indignation at this step of the British government, and why it was totally improper to go on with the business while a British spy was present. He then went into a very lengthy detail of the ill-treatment of that government to the United States, for several years past, and concluded with saying, that either this man must immediately be sent back to those who sent him, or he, Pickering, would cover up the council fire; for his instructions from General Washington were, to suffer no British agents at the present treaty.

The Indians appeared in amazement at the warmth with which the commissioner delivered himself, and said, when he sat down, the council fire grows warm, the sparks of it fly about very thick. As to Johnson, he appeared like one that was condemned to die, and now rose and left us. The Indians requesting we would withdraw, counselled among themselves about half an hour, and sent for us again. Cornplanter rose and said, the reason why the council fire has not been uncovered to-day is, because of a British man being present. It was caused by us, we requested him to come here, it is true, but the fault is in the white people. I am very much surprised and deceived by what you told us at Fort Stanwix, when you laid before us a paper which contained the terms of peace agreed on between you and the English nation; and told us it was agreed on in the presence of the Great Spirit, and under his influence. We now discover what the commissioners then told us was a lie, when they said they had made the chain of friendship bright; but I now find there has been an antipathy to each other ever since. Now our sachems and warriors say, What shall we do? we will shove Johnson off: Yet this is not agreeable to my mind, for if I had kindled the council fire, I would suffer a very bad man to sit in it that he might be made better: but if the peace you made had been a good peace, all animosities would have been done away, and you could then have sat side by side in council. I have one request to make, which is, that you would furnish him with provisions to carry him home. The council having sat about five hours, adjourned till to-morrow. We dined by candle light, with the commissioner and about fifteen chiefs, among whom were Cornplanter, Red Jacket, Little Beard, Big Sky, Farmer's Brother, Fish Carrier, Little Billy, &c. Many repartees of the Indians, which Jones interpreted, manifested a high turn for wit and humor. Red Jacket has the most conspicuous talent that way; he is a man of a pleasing countenance, and one of the greatest orators amongst the Six Nations.

26th. First-day, several of our friends from parts adjacent came in, expecting a meeting for worship, but the commissioner having called the council together, no meeting was held. The council being assembled, the first business was the presentation of a letter which the Indians having got prepared since yesterday; they thought proper for the commissioner to see it, as they intended to send it by Johnson to Captain Brandt. The contents of it were not altogether agreeable to the commissioner. They expressed their sorrow that Johnson could not be permitted to stay, the reasons for which, he would doubtless inform them when he got home. It assured Brandt, they were determined to insist on the line agreed to last year, and expressed the sense they now had, that they were a poor, despised, though independent people, and were brought into suffering by the two white nations striving who should be greatest. The Indians appeared pretty high to-day, and little was done but clearing up some misunderstanding respecting the cause why the treaty was not held at Buffalo-creek, agreeably to the Indians' request—the disposition of the Senecas appeared rather more uncompromising than heretofore.

27th. Expecting a council, we went to the commissioner who was in private conference with some chiefs; but he informed us he is now preparing the way for a full and general council to-morrow, when he will cut the business short by decidedly opening the proposals of accommodation: this is agreeable news to us, who have been already much wearied with continual delays. Colonel Butler of Niagara, had despatched a runner, a Tuscarora, who brought intelligence of a late engagement between the Western Indians connected with some British soldiers, and General Wayne, fought near the forks of the Glaize, in which many on both sides were killed; and being weary, the combatants withdrew from the field of battle. The Indians appear cautious of letting out the particulars, probably from the fear that they may operate to their disadvantage at this critical juncture of the treaty; and the accounts being very various, nothing can be clearly ascertained. Sagareesa, chief of the Tuscoraras, and several others of his nation, spent most of the afternoon with us; a half-Indian who lives with them, interpreted, and the conference was to satisfaction. We endeavored to obtain a correct account of the numbers remaining in the Six Nations, and find as follows, viz: the Senecas number about nineteen hundred; the Tuscaroras, three hundred; the Oneidas, six hundred; the Cayugas, four hundred; the Onondagoes, five hundred; the Mohawks, eight hundred. A considerable part of the Cayugas and Onondagoes, have moved off their reservation and reside mostly with the Senecas and Tuscaroras, but some of them have gone over the lake to the Mohawks, within the British territories. By the best computation we can make, the number of acres that each nation still holds, is as follows, viz: The Senecas, about four millions of acres; the Oneidas, two hundred and fifty-six thousand; the Cayugas, sixty-four thousand; the Onondagoes, seventy thousand. The Tuscaroras have no land of their own, but are settled near the Senecas on their lands. The Stockbridge and Brotherton Indians, two small remnants, have some land which was granted to them by the Oneidas and confirmed by government, viz: Stockbridge, twenty-three thousand and forty acres; Brotherton, thirty-eight thousand and forty acres. The Brothertons are an assemblage of about one hundred and fifty Indians, of various tribes from New England, settled near Brotherton on the Mohawk river. The

Mohawks are at the Grand river and the bay of Quinta, on the North sides of Lake Erie and Lake Ontario, in the British government.

This evening Friends being quietly together, our minds were seriously turned to consider the present state of these Six Nations; and a lively prospect presented, that a mode could be adopted by which Friends and other humane people might be made useful to them in a greater degree than has ever yet been effected; at least for the cause of humanity and justice, and for the sake of this poor, declining people, we are induced to hope so. The prospect and feelings of our minds were such as will not be forgotten, if we are favored to return home. The happy effects of steady perseverance in the cause of the Africans, is an encouraging reflection, and may serve as an animating example in this. Our business here, though trying and tedious, is sometimes accompanied with an ample reward.

28th. Red Jacket visited us with his wife and five children, whom he had brought to see us; they were exceedingly well clad in their manner, and the best behaved and prettiest Indian children I have ever met with: Jones came to interpret. Red Jacket informed us of the views which the Indians had in inviting us to the treaty; which Jones confirmed, being present at the council at Buffalo-creek; viz. Believing that the Quakers were an honest people and friends to them, they wished them to be present that they might see the Indians were not deceived or imposed upon.

Yesterday many of the chiefs and warriors were very uneasy at Cornplanter's frequent private interviews with the commissioner, and Little Billy spoke roughly to him, told him he should consider who he was, that he was only a war chief, and it did not become him to be so forward as he appeared to be; it was the business of the sachems, more than his, to conduct the treaty. He told them he had exerted himself for several years, and taken a great deal of pains for the good of the nation, but if they had no further occasion for him, he would return home; and he really intended it; but Colonel Pickering and General Chapin interested themselves to detain him. The dissatisfaction of the Senecas rose so high, that it was doubtful whether a council would be obtained to-day, but about three o'clock they met; Cornplanter not attending. The commissioner spoke, and told them of the several conferences that had been held with a number of the chiefs since the last public council, and what the substance of their business was. He also told them he was sorry that they were made uneasy at the conduct of their war chief, but they ought not to blame him, for he, the commissioner, had invited Cornplanter to his quarters, and therefore if there was any impropriety, to blame him, for it was his fault. This pacifying them, he then said the business of the treaty had been retarded so long, that he was now determined to open to them, fully and candidly, the terms upon which the chain of friendship would be brightened, and the extent of what he intended to do towards it. He produced his commission, with full power to propose and adjust the accommodation of all differences between them and the United States; which he handed me to read.

After many observations upon former treaties, and the grant made by their old father, the king, to William Penn, he opened the terms which were as follows: but in the first place, perhaps, as this is an important matter, it will be most proper to take notice, that he acquainted the Indians now collected, both chiefs and warriors, being more than at any council we have yet had, that the chiefs had laid before him only two rusty places in the chain, one of which he had already brightened, the other was thought by their chief warrior to be very deep, though the sachems thought it not of so great moment; that in order to clean this rusty spot, their chief warrior had proposed a new line between them and the United States, to begin where the Alleghany crosses the north line of Pennsylvania, thence to French creek below the forks of —— creek; thence to the forks of Muskingum; thence down the Muskingum to the Ohio. This, he apprehended, would remove every cloud of difficulty. He observed to them, that the sachems had acknowledged it was now four years since he had been brightening the chain of friendship between them and the United States, and that it had been even as in the days of Sir William Johnson, that the rusty part now alluded to had never before been complained of to him, except by their elder brother, the Mohawk. Colonel Pickering thought it was rather within the claim of the Western Indians; and as they had, from time to time, acquiesced in the treaty of Fort Stanwix, they might reasonably suppose that their conduct in relation to the affair at Presque Isle must have given surprise to the President, who, feeling a fatherly care for their nations, had required of the persons to desist, who were about to form a settlement at that place; and had appointed him to inquire into, and endeavor to adjust, the difference subsisting between them: since which he had examined all former treaties, and reminded them, that at the treaty of Fort Stanwix, they had ceded all the lands within the bounds of Pennsylvania—that many of them were acquainted with the charter granted by the king of Great Britain to William Penn; that at the last treaty held before the war, at Fort Stanwix, about twenty-six years ago, they had received ten thousand dollars from Pennsylvania, and had agreed that they would sell no lands within the said boundaries, but to the proprietors of that (then) province. That treaty at Fort Stanwix had been confirmed at Muskingum in 1786, which was also acknowledged by the chiefs at Tioga; at which last place complaint was made that Phelps had cheated them, yet not a word of the former treaties. He then had reference to the triangle on Lake Erie, which Pennsylvania has purchased of Congress, and showed them on the map that it was ceded by them to the United States at the treaty of Fort Stanwix; and for which the State of Pennsylvania paid them two thousand dollars at the treaty of Muskingum, in confirmation of the title. Butler and Gibson, the commissioners at the last mentioned treaty, expected the east line of the triangle would have extended to Buffalo-creek; but that not being the case, he offered to cede back to them all the land between the triangle and a line running due south, from near the mouth of the said creek to the Pennsylvania line, which comprehends three or four times the quantity of land included in the triangle; and that the new line might run thus: to begin at Johnson's landing-place, about four miles distant from Niagara; thence along the inlet, including a strip of land four miles wide, till it comes within four miles of Buffalo-creek; thence to said creek at one mile distant from the mouth of it; thence along Lake Erie to the aforesaid triangle; bounded on the west by the said triangle, and on the south by the Pennsylvania line. The commissioner observed that the four mile path on the side of the inlet, between Lake Erie and Lake Ontario, was ceded to our predecessors, the British, in the days of Sir William Johnson; yet, that the Indians shall have the right of hunting on these lands, as well as on all those ceded at the treaty of Fort Stanwix; and on all other lands ceded by them since the peace; and their settlements thereon shall remain undisturbed; and also, that in addition to the annuity of fifteen hundred dollars which had heretofore been paid to them, the President had empowered him to add the sum of three thousand dollars more, amounting in all to four thousand five hundred dollars, to be paid to them annually, and to their posterity for ever; for the providing of clothing, encouragement of artificers, school-masters, &c., to settle among them. He had also goods at this place to the amount of ten thousand dollars to distribute among them, if the treaty should issue to mutual satisfaction. In consequence of the liberal offers now made, he hoped the Indians would cheerfully comply, and join him in digging a deep pit to bury all former differences, and take hold of the chain of friendship so fast, that nothing should ever be able to force it out of their hands. The Indians, after considering a few minutes what had been said, concluded to take it into further consideration, and return an answer.

29th. Sagareesa, or the Sword-Carrier, visited us; he appears to be a thoughtful man, and mentioned a desire he had, that some of our young men might come among them as teachers; we supposed he meant as schoolmasters and artisans. Perhaps this intimation may be so made use of in a future day, that great good may accrue to the poor Indians, if some religious young men of our Society, could, from a sense of duty, be induced to spend some time among them, either as schoolmasters or mechanics. At eleven o'clock, Colonel Pickering called and gave us an invitation to dinner; Captain Hendricks, an Indian, and several strangers, dined with us; after which Robert Nealy came in, who had been taken prisoner about forty years ago, being then about nine years old, and had continued with the Indians ever since, without any desire of returning or making much inquiry after his parents. Being entirely reconciled to the Indian life, he had taken several wives among them, none of whom were dead; but whenever they grew dissatisfied with each other, they parted and took others more agreeable, which, he said, was the general custom; and when the Indians lost a near connection, they were inconsolable till some of their friends made up a belt of wampum, and gave it to the family of the deceased, in remembrance of their deceased relation; after which, they betrayed no sorrow—a scalp from an enemy answered the same purpose, if taken with that design. Many of the Indian chiefs being drunk, no council was held to-day.

Fifth-day, 30th. A fine warm day, the Indians almost all turned out of their cabins; some of the young warriors having good horses, were running races all day with the white people; others engaged in different sports; dancing, &c., which is almost a daily exercise. They performed one which they call the brag-dance; when whoever deposits a bottle of rum, has the liberty to make a brag of the feats he has performed in war, the number of scalps he has taken, &c. A sensible man being present, after he had deposited his bottle, and the others had boasted of many marvellous exploits, made his brag, which was, that he had been a man of peace all his days, in the profession of a physician; that he had been very industrious, and restored many who had been ready to die. He said, all that the others had bragged of, was nothing to this, for any child might kill a man, but it required the judgment and wisdom of a great man to save another's life. They all acknowledged the doctor's was the best of all. The sachems and chiefs were engaged in council, by themselves, and sat till near night, and inform that they will meet us in council to-morrow. The interpreter says, parties rise high against Cornplanter, that he is in a difficult situation with his nation, and they are not able to conceive what he has done with eight hundred dollars received in Philadelphia, from the Pennsylvania government, and what induced the government to give him fifteen hundred acres of land for a farm; these things have created jealousies unfavorable to him.

There is a remarkable spring near this place, called the brimstone spring, which is so strong, as to have deposited in its course a large quantity of sulphur. Also, the salt springs of Onondago, which are said to be inexhaustible, and all this country is supplied with salt made from the waters.

31st. Red Jacket, Clear Sky, Sagareesa, and a chief of the Cayugas, waited on us at our lodgings, being a deputation from the Indian council that has been deliberating several days upon the proposals of the commissioner, bringing with them the interpreter. Several Indians and some white people being in the room with us, they were desired to depart, as the business they came about would not admit of their presence. Apprehending that we should be interrupted in the house, we retired to a distance, and sat down upon some logs, when Red Jacket spoke nearly as follows:

Brothers,—You see here four of us of the Six Nations, who are assembled at this place, in the will of the Great Spirit, to transact the business of the treaty. You have been waiting here a long time, and often visited by our chiefs, and as yet no marks of respect have been shown you.

Brothers,—We are deputed by the council of chiefs assembled, to come and see you. We understand that you told Sagareesa, that you should not have come, but at our request, and that you stood ready to afford us any assistance in your power.

Brothers,—We hope you will make your minds easy. We who are now here are but children; the ancients being deceased. We know that your fathers and ours transacted business together, and that you look up to the Great Spirit for his direction and assistance, and take no part in war. We expect you were all born on this island, and consider you as brethren. Your ancestors came over the great water, and ours were born here; this ought to be no impediment to our considering each other as brethren.

Brothers,—You all know the proposals that have been made by Cunnitsutty (Colonel Pickering, the commissioner), as well as the offers made by us to him. We are all now in the presence of the Great Spirit, and we place more confidence in you, than in any other people. As you expressed your desire for peace, we now desire your help and assistance—we hope you will not deceive us; for if you should do so, we shall no more place any confidence in mankind.

Brothers,—We wish, if you know the will of Congress, or the extent of the commissioner's powers, that you will candidly inform us.

Brothers,—We desire that what we are now about communicating, may be kept secret. We are willing to give up the four-mile path, from Johnson's landing-place to Cayuga-creek, agreeably to our compact with Sir William Johnson, long ago. The other part proposed by Colonel Pickering to be relinquished by us; that is, from Cayuga to Buffalo-creek, we wish to reserve on account of the fisheries; that our women and children may have the use of it for that purpose. We desire to know if you can inform us, why the triangle on Lake Erie cannot be given up.

Brothers,—Cornplanter and Captain Brandt, who were only war chiefs, were the persons who attended the treaty at Fort Stanwix, and they were to have sent forward the proposals for our more general consideration. At that time Old Smoke was alive, who was a man of great understanding; but they were threatened into a compliance, in consequence of which Captain Brandt went off to Canada, desiring Cornplanter to do the best he could.

They delivered us seven strings of wampum, and we desired them to call on us about three o'clock for an answer. We felt it to be a weighty and delicate matter to answer their request in our situation. They returned about the time fixed, but finding us not entirely prepared to give them an answer, told us not to hurry ourselves, and they would come to-morrow morning; for they are never in haste.

Eleventh month, 1st. Our house was full of Indians and others all the morning. About ten o'clock, the interpreter and the four chiefs came for our answer; we had endeavored to digest their request as well as we were capable of, desirous of dealing honestly with the poor Indians and of keeping a conscience void of offence. My friends laid it upon me to deliver the answer, which I did, holding the seven strings of wampum in my hand; and the reply being interpreted to them, I returned the strings at the end of our speech according to the Indian custom. Red Jacket went over the three points to which we had spoken, to know whether he had perfectly understood us, that he might deliver our sentiments to the great council. He thanked us for our advice, and said, though we might account it of small value, they did not consider it so, but thought it would afford them considerable strength.

After dinner, John Parrish and myself rode to view the Farmer's Brother's encampment, which contained about five hundred Indians. They are located by the side of a brook, in the woods; having built about seventy or eighty huts, by far the most commodious and ingeniously made of any that I have seen; the principal materials are bark and boughs of trees, so nicely put together as to keep the family dry and warm. The women as well as the men, appeared to be mostly employed. In this camp, there are a large number of pretty children, who, in all the activity and buoyancy of health, were diverting themselves according to their fancy. The vast number of deer they have killed, since coming here, which they cut up and hang round their huts, inside and out, to dry, together with the rations of beef which they draw daily, give the appearance of plenty to supply the few wants to which they are subjected. The ease and cheerfulness of every countenance, and the delightfulness of the afternoon, which these inhabitants of the woods seemed to enjoy with a relish far superior to those who are pent up in crowded and populous cities, all combined to make this the most pleasant visit I have paid to Indians; and induced me to believe, that before they became acquainted with white people and were infected with their vices, they must have been as happy a people as any in the world. In returning to our quarters we passed by the Indian council, where Red Jacket was displaying his oratory to his brother chiefs, on the subject of Colonel Pickering's proposals.

Eleventh month, 2d. Held a meeting for worship in the schoolhouse; a number of Friends residing in this part of the country, came in; and a considerable body of Indians were in and about the house; several of whom, as well as the white people of other societies, behaved well, and it was thought to be a good meeting. We went immediately after meeting to the council which had just assembled, and was very numerously attended both by Indians and whites. The business was introduced by Clear Sky, an Onondaga chief, in the following manner: He expressed a hope that there would be no hard thoughts entertained, on account of their having been several days deliberating on an answer; the subject was of importance, and he wished his brethren to be preserved in unanimity. Then Red Jacket being principal speaker, said,

> Brothers,—We request that all the nations present will attend to what we are about to deliver. We are now convened on one of the days of the Great Spirit; Then addressing Colonel Pickering:—
> Brother,—You now represent the President of the United States, and when you spoke to us, we considered it as the voice of the fifteen fires. You desired that we would take the matter under our deliberate consideration and consult each other well, that where the chain was rusty, it might be brightened. We took

General Washington by the hand, and desired this council-fire, that all the lines in dispute might be settled.

Brothers,—We told you before of the two rusty places on the chain, which were also pointed out by the sachems. Instead of complying with our request, respecting the places where we told you the chain was rusty, you offered to relinquish the land on Lake Erie, eastward of the triangular piece sold by Congress to Pennsylvania, and to retain the four-mile path between Cayuga and Buffalo-creek, by which you expect to brighten the chain.

Brothers,—We thought you had a sharp file to take off the rust, but we believe it must have been dull, or else you let it slip out of your hands. With respect to the four-mile path, we are in want of it on account of the fisheries; although we are but children, we are sharp-sighted, and we see that you want that strip of land for a road, that when you have vessels on the lakes, you may have harbors, &c. But we wish, that in respect to that land, the treaty at Fort Stanwix may be broken. You white people have increased very fast on this island, which was given to us Indians by the Great Spirit; we are now become a small people, and you are cutting off our lands, piece after piece—you are a very hard-hearted people, seeking your own advantages.

Brothers,—We are tender-hearted, and desirous of peace— you told us what you would give us for our land, to brighten your end of the chain. If you will relinquish the piece of land we have mentioned, our friendship will be strong. You say you are not proud; neither are we. Congress expects we are now settling the business with regularity; we wish that both parties may have something to say in settling a peace. At the time we requested a conference, we also requested that our friends, the Quakers, should come forward, as they are promoters of peace, and we wanted them to be witnesses to what took place; we wish to do nothing in private. We have told you of the rusty part, which the file passed over without brightening it, and we wish you to take up the file again, and rub it very hard; you told us, if it would not do without, you would apply oil.

Brothers,—We the sachems, warriors and others, all depend on you; whatever is done, we regard as final and permanent; we wish you to take it under consideration, and give us an answer.

Colonel Pickering replied, If I understand you right, your minds are easy excepting with respect to the strip of land between the two lakes. He then recapitulated what Red Jacket had expressed, which is the usual custom of the Indians in their answers; reminding them why they decreased, and the white people increased, and gave them advice in what manner they might increase also; observing that he did it as their friend, for he wished to see them rise and become a great people. Here Red Jacket called out earnestly, in his language, 'keep straight.' The commissioner proceeded.

Brothers,—You say you are anxious for peace; so are the people of the of the United States, anxious for peace with all the Indians on the whole island. We do not speak it with our lips only, it is the language of our hearts. You say, if we relinquish the four mile path from Cayuga to Buffalo-creek, a lasting peace will take place. The other day I gave you strong reasons why we could not give it up. I told you, if I could not rub out the rusty spots, I would cover them over, and I told you how I would cover this; alluding to the money offered as an equivalent. You seem to be sensible that the United States stand in need of a passage from lake to lake, by land. I therefore conclude, you would have no objection, if the land remains yours, to our cutting a road, and if we do so, it will be very inconvenient, unless we can have taverns to accommodate travellers, as the distance is great. You know they have a road and accommodations on the opposite side of the river, and as there can be no communication between the lakes, unless we have that privilege, the United States will have the same necessity for a road on this side.

Brothers,—If you should travel it yourselves, you would like to have a house to get a walking-staff; you justly observe, the United States will want harbor for their vessels on the lakes, but they can have no benefit from a harbor, unless they have the privilege of building houses and stores. If this is all the difficulty between us, I trust we shall not be long in coming to a conclusion.

Brothers,—When I came from Philadelphia, it was not expected I would relinquish a hand's breadth of land; but finding your villages on that part which I have offered to cede back, I freely give it up. I am growing impatient to conclude the business, and would be glad to know, whether you will give me an answer, or take some time longer to consider of it. As the Indians did not appear ready to give a final answer, he told them, he observed it to be a tender point with them, and proposed their taking it into consideration until to-morrow, and that he wished to confer with some of the chiefs at his lodgings, previous to their coming to council, which he thought would expedite the business.

It is a custom with the Indians, after the decease of one of their brethren, to return to the donor any present which he had received in his life-time as a mark of respect. In conformity with this usage, Red Jacket now returned to the commissioner a silver gorget, belonging to one of their chiefs, who died last year, which had been presented to him by the United States. Farmer's Brother made a speech of condolence on the occasion, and presented some strings of black wampum to the family of the deceased. Clear Sky, then in a short speech, covered up the council fire.

3d of the month. Big Beard, Sonochle, Canundach, Canatounty, and a John Whitestripe, all Oneidas, called at our lodgings. Big Beard mentioned, that some Friends whom they had seen at New York, requested them to make inquiry who were the original owners of the land about

Hopewell, and that if it could be ascertained, it was probable a present would be made them by the Friends who reside in that neighborhood. He said, they had accordingly made the inquiry, and although, it was beyond a doubt, that the original proprietors were incorporated with the Six Nations, yet they were so mixed and intermarried among the different tribes, that it would be difficult to point them out; they therefore apprehended, it would be most equitable, to distribute it among the Six Nations at large. No council was held to-day; a number of the chiefs being much intoxicated. We were teased by them for liquor and were, at last, obliged to flee from their persecutions.

4th. Sagareesa and Captain William Printup, a chief and warrior of the Tuscaroras, with an interpreter, visited us, to converse about the Hopewell lands, appearing to have no doubt that the Tuscaroras were the original proprietors. Colonel Pickering came to our lodgings, to read the proposed articles which were to conclude the treaty, the signing of which, as witnesses, if we were called upon to do it, had, for several days, been a subject of serious consideration with us. We told him, on hearing what was proposed, that we apprehended for reasons given, we could not be free to sign the treaty; which did not appear to be agreeable to him; but we have not now to begin to learn to suffer at Indian treaties. At two o'clock, an Indian messenger from the council, came to inform us they were assembled and waiting for us, the Indians not being disposed to proceed in our absence: a great number were assembled, and Red Jacket addressed the commissioner:

> Brothers,—We, the sachems of the Six Nations, will now tell you our minds. The business of the treaty is, to brighten the chain of friendship between us and the fifteen fires. We told you the other day, it was but a very small piece which was the occasion of the remaining rust in the chain of friendship.
>
> Brothers,—Now we are conversing together, in order to make the chain bright. When we told you what would give us satisfaction, you proposed reserving the piece of land, between Cayuga and Buffalo-creek, for building houses, &c., but we apprehend, you would not only build houses, but towns. You told us, these houses would be for the accommodation of travellers in winter, as they cannot go by water in that season, and that travellers would want a staff to help them along the road. We have taken these matters into serious consideration.
>
> Brothers,—We conclude that we do not understand this as the white people do; if we consent to your proposals, we know it will injure us. If these houses should be built, they will tend to scatter us and make us fall in the streets, meaning, by drinking to excess, instead of benefiting us: you want land to raise provisions, hay, &c; but as soon as the white people settle there, they would think the land theirs, for this is the way of the white people. You mentioned, that when you got possession of the garrisons, you would want landing-places, stores, fields to plant on,

&c; but we wish to be the sole owners of this land ourselves; and when you settle with the British, the Great Spirit has made a road for you, you can pass and repass by water; what you want to reserve is entirely in your own favor.

Brothers,—You told us, when you left Philadelphia, it was not expected by the President you would release a foot of land. We thank him for having left you at liberty to give up what you please.—You have waited with patience at this council fire, kindled by General Washington; it is but a very small thing that keeps the chain from being brightened; if you will consent to give up this small piece and have no houses on it, the chain will be made bright. As to harbors, the waters are between you and the British; you must talk to them, you are of the same color. I see there are many of your people now here, watching with their mouths open to take up this land: if you are a friend to us, then disappoint them, our patience is spent; comply with our request; dismiss us, and we will go home.

The commissioner then replied:

Brothers,—I wish your attention to a few words.—I thought you knew the necessity the United States had for a road from Fort Schlosser to Buffalo-creek. You appear sensible of it now, by referring to the road by water, made by the Great Spirit; you may see we can have no benefit of that without a passage by land. You have forgotten what I said the other day, respecting the treaty of Sir William Johnson, by which he obtained a right to pass and repass through your country. I then observed, that what was granted to the King was transferred to the United States by our treaty of peace with the British; now since so small a piece is between us, to convince you that I am not difficult, if you grant us but liberty to pass and repass, I will give up the rest. You know there is a path already from Buffalo-creek to Niagara; I only ask liberty to make a better path, to clear the stumps and logs out of the way. I am sure, that about so small a matter you can make no difficulty; I will sit down and wait your answer.

After a short space, Colonel Pickering observed, he had forgot to inform them that the road should be opened under the direction of the superintendent of the Six Nations, Canadesago; who would take care to have it done so as to be as little injurious as possible to the Indians.

The sachems having consulted together about half an hour, Red Jacket replied:

General Washington, now listen; we are going to brighten the chain of friendship between the Six Nations and the Americans. We thank you for complying with our request, in giving up the particular spot in dispute. You mentioned that you wanted a road through our country; remember your old agreement, that you were to pass along the lake by water; we have made up our minds respecting your request to open a road.

Colonel Pickering writing what was said, Red Jacket would not proceed till he looked him in the face.

Brothers,—It costs the white people a great deal to make roads, we wish not to put you to that great expense; we don't want you to spend your money for that purpose. We have a right understanding of your request, and have agreed to grant you a road from Fort Schlosser to Buffalo-creek, but not from Buffalo-creek down this way at all. We have given you an answer; if, on considering it, you have any reply to make, we will hear you.

Commissioner.—I confess, brothers, I expected you would have agreed to my proposal; but as this is not the case, I will give it up, only reserving the road from Fort Schlosser to Buffalo. There has been a mutual condescension, which is the best way of settling business. There are yet several matters to be attended to before signing the articles of the treaty; which I can best communicate to some of your chiefs, as it would not be so convenient to discuss them among large numbers. One matter is, how the goods and annuity had best be appropriated; and as there are some bad people both amongst you and us, it would be well to fix some modes of settling disputes, when they arise between individuals of your nations and ours. As soon as we have digested a plan, we will introduce it into the public council. I therefore invite two sachems and two warriors of the Senecas, and a sachem and a warrior of each of the other nations, to take an early breakfast with me to-morrow morning. I now cover the council fire.

5th of Eleventh month. No council to-day—Colonel Pickering and some chiefs busy in preparing the articles of treaty.

6th. An interpreter, with four other Indians, came to have further conversation about the Hopewell land. It does not appear probable, that the Conestogoes were the original owners. We requested them to convene some sensible chiefs of each nation, and we would meet them at General Chapin's, with a map of the United States, and endeavor to settle the matter, if possible. General Chapin is of opinion, that the Tuscaroras are the original owners of the Virginia land. No council in public, Colonel Pickering being engaged all day, in conference on the articles of treaty; new objections and dissatisfaction were started by several principal chiefs, who are unwilling to relinquish Presque Isle. They were surprised to find that Cornplanter, Little Billy, and others, had received two thousand dollars worth of goods from Pennsylvania at Muskingum, and two thousand dollars at Philadelphia. Their minds being much disturbed, they broke up the conference; this was a sad disappointment to us, who expected that all would be amicably settled, and we should set off to-morrow. General Chapin says, he hopes all will come right again, but the Indians must have time to cool. It is to no purpose to say you are tired of waiting, they will only tell you very calmly, Brother, you have your way of doing business, and we have ours; we desire you would sit easy on your seats. Patience then becomes our only remedy.

7th. No business to-day; many of the chiefs being drunk. Colonel Pickering spent the afternoon with us. The idea he entertains respecting the lands ceded at Fort Stanwix, is, that as the Indians did the United States a great deal of injury by taking part with the British in the late war, it was strictly just that they should make compensation by giving up the lands which they relinquished at that time. He instanced the case of an individual who had committed a trespass on another; the law determines that the trespasser shall suffer either in person or property, and this law is just. Such is the reasoning of conquerors.

8th. The Indians were sober to-day. General Chapin and the commissioner have determined to give them no more liquor, until the treaty is over. The chiefs and warriors were engaged til three o'clock with the commissioner, and agreed on all the articles of treaty to be engrossed on parchment, and signed tomorrow. At four o'clock, we met Cornplanter, Red Jacket, Scanadoe, Nicholas, a Tuscarora, Twenty Canoes, two ancient Conestogoes, Captain Printup, Sagareesa, Myers Paterson, a half white man who lives with the Tuscaroras, and several other chiefs at General Chapin's, to determine about the Hopewell land; examined maps and conversed with them on the subject, which resulted in the opinion, that the Conestogoes should quit claim to it; it appearing to those present, that the original right was in the Tuscaroras; one of whom, an ancient man, put his finger on the place in the map, saying, he had papers at home that would, as he thought, confirm their claim to it. We desired him to send them to General Chapin to examine, and if he thought they contained anything worth notice, he might forward them to us in Philadelphia.

First-day, the 9th. Several Friends in this part of the country came to the meeting; one of them thirteen miles. A number of other white people attended, and a large number of Indians. It was a solid meeting; several, both of whites and Indians, were tender, and wept; and after it was over, one man in a particular manner, confessed to the truth, and prayed that the Lord might bless it to all who were present. On my part, it was an affectionate farewell to the people hereaway. We returned to our lodgings, and before we had finished our dinner, a messenger came to inform us that the council was gathered, and waiting, which we immediately attended. Two large parchments, with the articles of the treaty engrossed, being ready for signing, we were in hopes the business would now close; but to our surprise and disappointment, we soon discovered some dissatisfaction among the Indians, by their putting their heads down together and whispering. After waiting impatiently for about an hour, not knowing what it meant, Cornplanter rose and spoke, as follows:

Brothers,—I request your attention, whilst I inform you of my own mind as an individual. I consider the conduct of the United States, since the war, to have been very bad. I conceive they do not do justice. I will mention what took place at New York at one particular time. After the treaty of Fort Stanwix, I went to New York under an apprehension, that the commissioners had not done right; and I laid before Congress our grievances on account of the loss of our lands at that treaty; but the thirteen fires approved to what the commissioners had done, and in confirmation of it, they held up the paper, with a piece of silver hanging to it; (the treaty with the British.) Now, Colonel Pickering, you have told us at this treaty, that what was given up by the British, was only the land around the forts. I am very much dissatisfied that this was not communicated to us before. There has already been too much blood spilt; if this had been known at the close of the war, it would have prevented any blood being shed. I have, therefore, told our warriors not to sign this treaty. The fifteen fires have deceived us; we are under the sachems, and will listen to what they do. Though we will not sign it, yet we shall abide by what they do, as long as they do right. The United States and the Six Nations are now making a firm peace, and we wish the fifteen fires may never deceive them, as they have done us warriors; if they once deceive the sachems, it will be bad.

He then took his seat, and after a short pause, said, "I will put a patch upon what I have spoken: I hope you will have no uneasiness hearing the voice of the warriors; you know it is very hard to be once deceived, so you must not make your minds uneasy." Eel, the herald, then made a warm speech to the Indians, exhorting them to abide by the decision of the sachems, which was received with loud shouts of applause. "Entaw! Entaw! Entaw!"

Colonel Pickering then addressed them as follows:

Brothers of the Six Nations and your associates,—I confess I am greatly surprised at the speech of your head warrior, after all the pains I have taken to make the articles of the treaty easy. I endeavored to please both sachems and warriors, they were both present when the articles were agreed on, and there was not a word of objection.

Brothers,—The design of this treaty is, to bury all differences; you know I candidly and explicitly disapproved of the conduct of the commissioners at Fort Stanwix, but as this treaty was to establish a firm friendship between the Six Nations and the United States, I did not wish to bring former transactions into view, which was also the desire of your chief warrior; now he brings up the old matters to make a division in your councils.

Brothers,—I wish for calmness and deliberation, as the subject is of importance to us, and of the utmost importance to you. He expresses his dissatisfaction that our treaty with the British was not explained before; but this was done last year to the Western Indians, when many of the Six Nations were present; I think many of the chiefs must remember it. I will explain it again to prevent mistakes. A certain line was drawn between the British and us; what the British had obtained of the Indians on our side of that line before the peace, was transferred by that treaty to the United States: it was agreed that the British should not interfere with the land on this side of that line, nor were we to interfere with the land on their side of the line.

Brothers,—I am very sorry that these objections are made now when we are just about to sign the treaty. The chief warrior has called it the treaty of the sachems, and said, that they only were to sign it; but the warriors, as well as the sachems, were present when it was agreed on, and made no objection to it. He says, they will abide by what the sachems do, as long as they do right. Does he mean they will abide by them no longer than the warriors think them right? If this be the case, we may as well let things remain as they are. He says also, the United States and the sachems are now making a firm peace, but I cannot consider it so, unless the sachems and warriors unite; for unless this is the case, it will cause divisions among yourselves; consider whether this will not be attended with dangerous consequences. He speaks of the United States deceiving the sachems; as I represent the United States, I have told you I will not deceive you; I can add nothing on that head to what I have told you already.

Brothers,—I cannot consent to close the business in this manner, after so much care and pains have been taken to make all things easy; but wish you to consider of it until to-morrow, and give me an answer. If the warriors expect to live in peace with the United States, as well as the sachems; if they desire to brighten the chain of friendship; if they wish to act for the advantage of themselves and their children, I am sure they will sign this treaty.

Cornplanter then addressed the warriors in a short speech, desiring they might be firm and steady to what they had agreed on.

10th. The warriors of the Six Nations met in council in the forenoon, to consult respecting signing the articles, and came to a judgment. In the afternoon they met again, expecting the commissioner and the sachems; but several of the principal sachems being intoxicated, did not come, so nothing was done. A number of the chiefs and warriors of the Tuscaroras came to pay us a visit respecting the Hopewell land. Captain Printup spoke for them as follows, viz:

Brothers,—We believe it was from motives of benevolence and good-will to us, that you were induced to make inquiry after the original owners of some land in Virginia.

Brothers,—You have now found them, and as you are a people that look up to the Great Spirit for direction, we hope you will now make us some compensation: we are in hopes the business may be accomplished at this time.

Brothers,—As the Friends on the land have long received the benefit of its produce, and live at so great a distance, it would be much more convenient to receive what they please to give, at one time, than to have a small sum paid yearly. We have been given to understand, that whenever the former owners of the land could be discovered, Friends stood ready to make them some compensation; as we apprehend this has been sufficiently ascertained, we are thankful to the Great Spirit, that there is now a probability of receiving something for the inheritance of our ancestors.

By the above speech, we found they had still some mistaken ideas, which we endeavored to remove, by again stating to them the true reason of the inquiry, and informing them we should represent to our brethren at home, what now appeared to us to be the state of the case, as soon as we conveniently could. This satisfied them, and they requested to sign their names to General Chapin's testimony, which most of them did in their usual manner.*

11th. Had much conversation with several of the Indian chiefs. In the afternoon, at two o'clock, we were sent for to council, where a great number were assembled. The Eel, an Onondaga chief, spoke to the Indians in a pathetic manner; which we understood to be an exhortation to unanimity among the chiefs and warriors in closing the business. Colonel Pickering then held up the two parchments containing the articles of the treaty, and asked if we should proceed, which they assenting to, he told them he would give one of the parchments to one of their friends to examine, while he read the other. I accordingly examined one, and informed them they were word for word alike. They then agreed to sign, and pointed out the two head warriors, who, though they were young men, were by some custom in their nation, the persons who were to stand foremost in ratifying contracts; they signed, and then the chiefs and warriors, some of the most eminent in each nation, being in all upwards of fifty.

---

*Some time after, a number of these Indians came to Philadelphia, for the purpose of examining more fully into the validity of their claims to be the original proprietors of these lands. Friends were very desirous of making a full compensation to the natives for any lands on which they had settled; and accordingly great pains were taken to adjust this business. But, after a close investigation of all the circumstances, and an examination of ancient maps and documents, by both Friends and Indians jointly, it did not appear that the Tuscaroras had ever been the possessors of the soil in question. Yet as they had entertained strong expectations of receiving a donation rather than disappoint them, Friends raised a considerable sum of money, and gave it as a present to them, with which they were highly gratified.

After the articles were signed, we desired Farmer's Brother and Cornplanter, to collect as many chiefs of the different nations as they thought proper, to go down to our lodgings; the interpreter was also requested to come with them: accordingly, about forty came. We smoked and conversed with them freely, on several subjects relating to their welfare, gave them further information of our principles, and expressed our good wishes for their prosperity. We then had our presents brought and spread upon two tables. They did not choose to divide them themselves, but left it to the interpreter; which being done, they were much pleased and satisfied with the division, and the articles were very agreeable to them. They soon after retired, informing us of their desire to see us to-morrow morning, as they had something further to communicate.

12th. About thirty or forty of the sachems and chief warriors met at our lodgings, and delivered the following speech, by Farmer's Brother, the chief sachem.

Brothers, the Quakers from Philadelphia! I wish you would attend to what we who are now present are about to say. We speak as one.

Brothers,—Yesterday, after receiving your invitation to come and partake of your presents, we agreed to meet here this morning to speak a few words, which we will now do.

Brothers,—We are very glad you have lengthened out your patience to see the end of the business which is now brought to a close. We thank the Great Spirit that he has preserved you in health, from the time you left your seats [homes], until you arrived here, and has continued to preserve you to this time. We put you under the protection of the same Good Spirit on your return, and shall be very happy to hear that you get safe home; and hope you may find your friends and families well on your return: it would be very acceptable to be informed of this, by letter to the chiefs now present.

Brothers,—We give hearty thanks to the descendants of Onas, that you so willingly rose from your seats to attend this council fire according to our request; here are the articles of treaty for you to look over, in order to impress them on your minds, that you may tell them to your brothers who are sitting on their seats at home.

Brothers,—You have attended this treaty a long time; the articles which we have now signed, we hope you fully understand. Now, as we have shown them to you, we would wish to know your opinion, whether we have made a good peace or not; as we cannot read, we are liable to be deceived; you have no doubt considered them; we want to know your minds, whether there is any flaw or catch in them, which may hereafter occasion uneasiness.

Brothers,—If you think that peace is now established on a good foundation, we wish you would come forward and sign the articles: as you are a people who are desirous of promoting peace, and these writings are for that purpose, we hope you will have no objection, but all come forward and put your names to them, and this would be a great satisfaction to us.

Immediately after this speech, the treaty being concluded, and the council having broken up, our friends took their leave and set out for home. The following memorandum is the first which occurs respecting the journey, viz:

13th. Rose at three o'clock in the morning, after a very poor night's rest in a cold open hut, where it snowed in upon us as we laid. The weather was very cold and the roads exceedingly bad; we had an uncomfortable ride of four hours, during which John Parrish had his face bruised by a fall; and such was the difficulty in part of the road, that it appeared as though we travelled at the risk of our lives. We at length arrived at a public house at the head of Canandaigua lake, thirteen miles, where we got breakfast and refitted. We then rode on seven miles, put up for the night, there being no stage ahead for twenty-two miles.

14th. Rose early and pursued our journey through bushes, swamps, and deep mud-holes; the road so bad that, with hard pushing, we could make but three miles an hour. In about three and a half hours, we found the remains of a fire where some travellers had fed yesterday, which was a pleasant sight; and having some oats with us, we fed our horses and breakfasted upon hoe-cake, dried meat, and cheese. We felt like poor, forlorn pilgrims, and mounted our horses again, the path being as bad as it could be; and the snow falling on us continually in passing among the bushes, it made the travelling truly hard. As it continued snowing very fast, and there being but one house to stop at between Bath and the Painted Post, we accepted the kind invitation of Captain Williamson to lodge with him at the former place. He is a very polite man, had been many years in the British service, and entertained us elegantly; a great contrast to our last night's fare.

15th. By daylight we left Bath, it still continuing to snow very fast. A most trying time it was to us, but in about two hours we reached a house where they were able to give us some breakfast, which was refreshing. We arrived at the Painted Post about one o'clock, got some corn for our horses, and eat our bread and cheese; after which we rode eleven miles crossing the Tioga several times, and arrived at the widow Lindley's who kindly invited us to stay at her house, where we were entertained very hospitably.

16th. After breakfast went for our horses, but the family were so friendly they would not receive any pay for their keeping. We crossed the Tioga twice more, and found the road so exceedingly fatiguing and the day unpleasant, that we rode only about two and a half miles an hour, and arrived at an ordinary about three o'clock in the afternoon. There being no house for about twenty-four miles ahead, we were under the necessity of lodging in a poor hovel, where there were already a man, his wife, and seven children. We laid our blankets on a bark floor, and endeavored to get some rest, but the cold pinched us to such a degree, that we had but little repose. We were all affected with an addition to our colds; this is hard travelling and living, and it is a mercy that we are preserved as well as we are.

17th. Rose between two and three o'clock, intending to make forty-two miles, as there is but one miserable house in the intermediate distance, which we desired not to lodge at, but disappointments and vexations are to be ours, and no doubt they are good for us. The depth of the snow, which was continually balling under our horses' feet, and the excessive badness of the path, it being little else but a continued succession of mud-holes, roots, and stones, rendered our hopes of getting through quite abortive; and from necessity we had to stop at the Blockhouse. Our horses had to stand out all night without hay, which gave us the most concern; as for ourselves, we procured a tolerable supper, and taking our lodging upon the floor, got some sleep. There being no chimney to the house, occasioned them to have but little roof, that the smoke might have sufficient vent to pass off, which gave us a pleasing view of the brilliancy of the stars, it being the first clear night since we left Canandaigua.

18th. Rising very early, we rode over the Alleghany mountain, which was covered with snow about ten inches deep. There were abundance of tracks of deer, bear, wild cats, white rabbits, &c. Near the top, a great bear raised up from the side of a log and frightened our horses. We fed our horses, and after eating some biscuit and dried beef at the foot of the mountain, proceeded on our journey, getting to the widow Harris's to lodge that night.

A few days after this, they were permitted to reach home in safety and good health. In closing the report of their proceedings, they remark in substance—that during a sojourn of seven weeks with the Indians, they had frequent opportunities of observing with sorrow the melancholy and demoralizing effects resulting from the supply of ardent spirits furnished them by the whites—that the difficulties and hardships to which those poor people, once a free and independent nation, are now subjected, appeared to them loudly to claim the sympathies of Friends and others, who have grown opulent in a land which was their former inheritance, and that they believed a mode might be devised of promoting their comfort, and rendering them more essential benefits than any which had yet been adopted. They likewise remark that the engagement was one involving trials of a peculiar and painful nature, yet they had reason to hope that the objects they had in view were in good degree answered, and that they were thankful in being permitted to return with the reward of peace.

As the articles of the treaty confirmed the right of the United States to large tracts of land which had been obtained by conquest, without making the Indians what Friends deemed an adequate and just compensation for it, they could not consent to the requests so frequently made to sign the treaty.

NOTES

1. Other editions of the Savery journal have imprint: London: G. Gilpin, 1844; Philadelphia: For sale at Friends' Book Store, 1861.

REFERENCES

Fenton, William N. *The Great Law and the Longhouse: A Political History of the Iroquois Confederacy.* Norman: University of Oklahoma Press, 1998.

Fenton, William N., ed. "The Journal of James Emlen Kept on a Trip to Canandaigua, New York, September 15 to October 30, 1794 to Attend the Treaty Between the United States and the Six Nations." *Ethnohistory,* 12, 4 (fall 1965): 279–342.

Savery, William. *A Journal of the Life, Travels, and Religious Labors of William Savery, a Minister of the Gospel of Christ, of the Society of Friends, Late of Philadelphia.* Compiled from his original memoranda by Jonathan Evans. Stereotype ed. Philadelphia: For sale at Friends' Book-store, [1837]: 88–155.

Center, George Heron, Past President of the Seneca Nation of Indians, and three members of the Philadelphia Yearly Meeting of the Society of Friends. Photo courtesy of George Heron.

1795: Text of the Canandaigua Treaty

At the treaty signing on November 11, 1794, in Canandaigua, New York, there were two handwritten copies of the treaty. After both copies were signed by representatives from the two nations, one copy was given to the Six Nations; the other copy was retained by the United States. A transcription of the United States' copy was issued as a U.S. congressional document on January 2, 1795, and is reprinted below. This transcription lacks the names of the Six Nations sachems and warriors and interpreters who signed the treaty. Another transcribed copy of the treaty was transmitted to the governor of Pennsylvania on January 27, 1795. This later transcription includes the names of the parties who signed the treaty and is also reprinted here.

UNITED STATES. CONGRESS. AMERICAN STATE PAPERS: DOCUMENTS, LEGISLATIVE AND EXECUTIVE, OF THE CONGRESS OF THE UNITED STATES . . .

Selected and Edited under the Authority of Congress. Volume 4. (Class II. Indian Affairs. Volume 1). 3d Congress, 2d Session, No. 58. Washington: Gales and Seaton, 1832: 544–45.

3d Congress.]   [2d SESSION

No. 58:

THE SIX NATIONS, AND ONEIDA, TUSCARORA, AND STOCKBRIDGE TRIBES.

COMMUNICATED TO THE SENATE, JANUARY 2, 1795.

Gentlemen of the Senate:

A spirit of discontent, from several causes, arose, in the early part of the present year, among the Six Nations of Indians, and, particularly, on the ground of a projected settlement by Pennsylvania, at Presqu' Isle, upon lake Erie. The papers upon this point have already been laid before Congress. It was deemed proper, on my part, to endeavor to tranquilize the Indians by pacific measures; accordingly, a time and place was appointed., at which a free conference should be had upon all the causes of discontent, and an agent was appointed, with the instructions, of which No. 1, herewith transmitted, is a copy.

A numerous assembly of Indians was held at Canandaigua, in the State of New York, the proceedings whereof accompany this message, marked No. 2.

The two treaties, the one with the Six Nations, and the other with the Oneida, Tuscarora, and Stockbridge Indians, dwelling in the country of the Oneidas, which have resulted from the mission of the agent, are herewith laid before the Senate, for their consideration and advice.

The original engagement of the United States to the Oneidas, is also sent herewith.

GEO. WASHINGTON.

UNITED STATES, 2d January, 1795.

A Treaty between the United States of America and the tribes of Indians called the Six Nations.

The President of the United States having determined to hold a conference with the Six Nations of Indians, for the purpose of removing from their minds all causes of complaint, and establishing a firm and permanent friendship with them; and Timothy Pickering being appointed sole agent for that purpose; and the agent having met and conferred with the sachems, chiefs, and warriors, of the Six Nations, in a general council: Now, in order to accomplish the good design of this conference, the parties have agreed on the following articles, which, when ratified by the President, with the advice and consent of the Senate of the United States, shall be binding on them and the Six Nations:

ARTICLE 1. Peace and friendship are hereby firmly established, and shall be perpetual, between the United States and the Six Nations.

ART. 2. The United States acknowledge the lands reserved to the Oneida, Onondaga, and Cayuga nations, in their respective treaties with the State of New York, and called their reservations, to be their property; and the United States will never claim the same, nor disturb them, or either of the Six Nations, nor their Indian friends, residing thereon, and united with them, in the free use and enjoyment thereof; but the said reservations shall remain theirs, until they choose to sell the same to the people of the United States, who have the right to purchase.

ART. 3. The land of the Seneca nation is bounded as follows: beginning on Lake Ontario, at the northwest corner of the land they sold to Oliver Phelps; the line runs westerly along the lake, as far as Oyongwongyeh creek, at Johnston's Landing Place, about four miles eastward, from the fort of Niagara; then, southerly, up that creek to its main fork; then, straight to the main fork of Stedman's creek, which empties into the river Niagara, above fort Schlosser; and then onward, from that fork, continuing the same straight course, to that river; (this line, from the mouth of Oyongwongyeh creek, to the river Niagara, above fort Schlosser, being the eastern boundary of a strip of land, extending from the same line to Niagara river, which the Seneca nation ceded to the King of Great Britain, at a treaty held about thirty years ago, with Sir William Johnston;) then the line runs along the Niagara river to Lake Erie; then along Lake Erie, to the northeast corner of a triangular piece of land, which the United States conveyed to the State of Pennsylvania, as by the President's patent, dated the third day of March, 1792; then due south to the northern boundary of that State; then due east to the southwest corner of the land sold by the Seneca nation to Oliver Phelps; and then north and northerly, along Phelp's line, to the place of beginning, on Lake Ontario. Now, the United States acknowledge all the land within the aforementioned boundaries, to be the property of the Seneca nation; and the United States will never claim the same, nor disturb the Seneca nation, nor any of the Six Nations, or of their Indian friends residing thereon, and united with them, in the free use and enjoyment thereof; but it shall remain theirs, until they choose to sell the same to the people of the United States, who have the right to purchase.

ART. 4. The United States having thus described and acknowledged what lands belong to the Oneidas, Onondagas, Cayugas, and Senecas, and engaged never to claim the same, nor to disturb them, or any of the Six Nations, or their Indian friends residing thereon, and united with them, in the free use and enjoyment thereof; now, the Six Nations, and each of them, hereby engage that they will never claim any other lands within the boundaries of the United States, nor ever disturb the people of the United States in the free use and enjoyment thereof.

ART. 5. The Seneca nation, all others of the Six Nations concurring, cede to the United States the right of making a wagon road from fort Schlosser to Lake Erie, as far south as Buffalo creek; and the people of the United States shall have the free and undisturbed use of this road, for the purposes of travelling and transportation. And the Six Nations, and each of them, will forever allow to the people of the United States, a free passage through their lands, and the free use of the harbors and rivers adjoining, and within their respective tracts of land, for the passing and securing of vessels and boats, and liberty to land their cargoes, where necessary, for their safety.

ART. 6. In consideration of the peace and friendship hereby established, and of the engagements entered into by the Six Nations; and because the United States desire, with humanity and kindness, to contribute to their comfortable support; and to render the peace and friendship hereby established strong and perpetual, the United States now deliver to the Six Nations, and the Indians of the other nations residing among, and united with them, a quantity of goods, of the value of ten thousand dollars. And for the same considerations, and with a view to promote the future welfare of the Six Nations, and of their Indian friends aforesaid, the United States will add the sum of three thousand dollars to the one thousand five hundred dollars heretofore allowed them by an article ratified by the President, on the twenty third day of April, 1792, making in the whole four thousand five hundred dollars; which shall be expended yearly, forever, in purchasing clothing, domestic animals, implements of husbandry, and other utensils, suited to their circumstances, and in compensating useful artificers, who shall reside with or near them, and be employed for their benefit. The immediate application of the whole annual allowance now stipulated, to be made by the superintendent, appointed by the President, for the affairs of the Six Nations, and their Indian friends aforesaid.

ART. 7. Lest the firm peace and friendship now established should be interrupted by the misconduct of individuals, the United States and Six Nations agree, that, for injuries done by individuals, on either side, no private revenge or retaliation shall take place; but, instead thereof, complaint shall be made by the party injured, to the other: by the Six Nations, or any of them, to the President of the United States, or the superintendent by him appointed; and by the superintendent, or other person appointed by the President, to the principal chiefs of the Six Nations, or of the nation to which the offender belongs; and such prudent measures shall then be pursued, as shall be necessary to preserve our peace and friendship unbroken, until the Legislature (or great council) of the United States shall make other equitable provision for the purpose.

NOTE. It is clearly understood by the parties to this treaty, that the annuity, stipulated in the sixth article, is to be applied to the benefit of such of the Six

Nations, and of their Indian friends united with them, as aforesaid, as do or shall reside within the boundaries of the United States: for the United States do not interfere with nations, tribes or families of Indians, elsewhere resident.

In witness whereof, the said Timothy Pickering, and the sachems and war chiefs of said Six Nations, have hereunto set their hands and seals.
Done at Canandaigua, in the State of New York, the eleventh day of November, in the year one thousand seven hundred and ninety-four.
                                                TIMOTHY PICKERING.
[Signed by fifty-nine sachems and war chiefs of the Six Nations.]

PICKERING, TIMOTHY. LETTER TO THE GOVERNOR OF PENNSYLVANIA. 27 JAN. 1795.

Ms. (letter only) Record Group 26, Executive Correspondence, Pennsylvania State Archives, Harrisburg. Letter and treaty published in Linn and Egle, eds., *Pennsylvania Archives*. Second Series, Volume 6. Harrisburg: State Printer, 1874–1890. 799–804.

TIMOTHY PICKERING TO THE GOVERNOR OF
PENNSYLVANIA.
                        ———
                                    DEPARTMENT OF WAR,
                                        January, *27th, 1795.*

SIR: I have the honor to transmit to you a copy of the treaty concluded with the Six Nations of Indians at Kanandaigua, on the eleventh day of last November, by which you will see, that the temporary obstacles to the establishment formerly contemplated by the State of Pennsylvania at Presqu' Isle are removed.
    I am, with great respect,
                    Sir,
                        Your most obed^t Servt,
                        TIMOTHY PICKERING,
                            Sec^y of War.

The Governor of Pennsylvania.

                        ———

PROCLAMATION OF THE PRESIDENT CONCERNING
THE INDIAN TREATY.
                        ———

GEORGE WASHINGTON, *President of the United States of*
                                        America,
To all to whom these presents shall come Greeting:
    WHEREAS. A treaty of Peace and Friendship between the United States of America and the Tribes of Indians, called the Six Nations, was made and con-

cluded on the eleventh day of November last, by Timothy Pickering, the Agent of the United States, for that purpose appointed, on the one part, and the Chiefs and Warriors of the Six Nations on the other part, which Treaty is in the form and words following:

A Treaty between the United States of America and the Tribes of Indians, called the Six Nations.

The President of the United States, having determined to hold a conference with the Six Nations of Indians, for the purpose of removing from their minds all causes of complaint, and establishing a firm and permanent Friendship with them, and Timothy Pickering being appointed Sole agent for that purpose; and the agent, having met and conferred with the Sachems, chiefs, and Warriors of the Six Nations, in a general Council, now, in order to accomplish the good design of this Conference, the parties have agreed on the following articles, which, when ratified by the President, with the advice and consent of the Senate of the United States, shall be binding on them and the Six nations.

ARTICLE I. Peace and Friendship are hereby firmly established, and shall be perpetual, between the United States and the Six nations.

ARTICLE II. The United States acknowledge the Lands reserved to the Oneida, Onondaga, and Cayuga Nations, in their respective treaties with the State of New York, and called their reservations, to be their property; and the United States will never claim the Same, nor disturb them or either of the Six Nations, nor their Indian Friends residing thereon and United with them, in the free use and enjoyment thereof; but the said reservations shall remain theirs, until they choose to sell the same to the People of the United States, who have the right to purchase.

ARTICLE III. The land of the Seneka nation is bounded as follows: Beginning on Lake Ontario, at the north-west corner of the land they sold to Oliver Phelps, the line runs westerly along the Lake, as far as O-yong-wong-yeh Creek, at Johnson's Landing place, about four miles eastward from the Fort of Niagara; then, Southerly up that Creek to its main fork; then straight to the main fork of Stedman's Creek, which empties into the river Niagara above Fort Schlosser, and then onward from that fork, continuing the same straight course to that river; (this line, from the mouth of O-yong-wong-yeh Creek to the river Niagara above Fort Schlosser, being the eastern boundary of a strip of land extending from the same line to Niagara River, which the Seneka nation ceded to the King of Great Britain, at a treaty held about thirty years ago, with Sir William Johnson;) then the line runs along the River Niagara to Lake Erie; then along Lake Erie to the North East corner of a triangular piece of Land, which the United States conveyed to the State of Pennsylvania, as by the President's Patent, dated the third day of March, 1792; then due South to the northern boundary of that State; then due east to the South West corner of the Land Sold by the Seneka nation to Oliver Phelps; and then North and Northerly, along Phelps's line to the place of beginning on Lake ontario. Now the United States acknowledge all the Land within the aforementioned boundaries to be the property of the Seneka nation; and the United States will never claim the same, nor disturb the Seneka Nation, nor any of the Six Nations or of their Indian Friends residing thereon and united with them, in the free use and enjoyment thereof; but it shall remain theirs until they choose to sell the same to the people of the United States who have the right to purchase.

ARTICLE IV. The United States, having thus described and acknowledged what Lands belong to the Oneidas, Onondagas, Cayugas, and Senekas, and engaged never to claim the same, nor to disturb them or any of the Six Nations or their Indian Friends residing thereon and united with them, in the free use and enjoyment thereof: Now the Six Nations, and each of them, hereby engage that they will never claim any other lands within the boundaries of the United States, nor ever disturb the People of the United States in the free use & enjoyment thereof.

ARTICLE V. The Seneka Nation, all others of the Six Nations concurring, cede to the United States the right of making a Wagon road from Fort Schlosser to Lake Erie, as far south as Buffalo Creek; and the people of the United States shall have the free and undisturbed use of this road for the purposes of travelling and transportation. And the Six Nations, and each of them, will for ever allow to the people of the United States a free passage through their lands, and the free use of the harbours and rivers adjoining and within their respective tracts of Land, for the passing and securing of vessels and boats, and liberty to land their cargoes where necessary for their safety.

ARTICLE VI. In consideration of the peace & Friendship hereby established, and of the engagements entered into by the Six nations; and because the United States desired, with humanity and kindness, to contribute to their comfortable support; and to render the peace and friendship hereby established strong and perpetual, the United States now deliver to the Six nations, and the Indians of the other nations residing among and united with them, a quantity of goods of the value of ten thousand dollars. And for the same considerations, and with a view to promote the future welfare of the six nations and of their Indian friends aforesaid, The United States will add the sum of three thousand dollars to the one thousand five hundred dollars heretofore allowed them by an article ratified by the President on the twenty-third day of April, 1792, making, in the whole, Four thousand five hundred Dollars, which shall be expended yearly for ever, in purchasing cloathing [sic], domestic animals, implements of husbandry, and other utensils suited to their circumstances, and in compensating useful artificers who shall reside with or near them, and be employed for their benefit. The immediate application of the whole annual allowance now stipulated, to be made by the Superintendent appointed by the President for the affairs of the Six nations, and their Indian friends aforesaid.

ARTICLE VII. Lest the firm peace and friendship now established should be interrupted by the misconduct of individuals, the United States and Six Nations agree, That for injuries done by individuals, on either side, no private revenge or retaliation shall take place; but instead thereof, complaint shall be made by the party injured to the other; by the Six Nations, or any of them, to the President of the United States, or the Superintendent by him appointed; and by the Superintendent, or other person appointed by the President, to the Principal chiefs of the Six Nations, or of the Nation to which the offender belongs; and such prudent measures shall then be pursued as shall be necessary to preserve our peace and Friendship unbroken, until the Legislature (or great Council) of the United States shall make other equitable provision for the purpose.

Note.—It is clearly understood by the Parties to this treaty, that the annuity stipulated in the Sixth article is to be applied to the benefit of such of the Six Nations and of their Indian Friends united with them as aforesaid, as do or shall reside within the boundaries of the United States; For the United States do not interfere with Nations, Tribes or Families of Indians elsewhere resident.

In Witness whereof the said Timothy Pickering and the Sachems and War-chiefs of the said Six Nations have hereto set their hands and Seals. Done at Kon-on-daigua, in the State of New-York, the Eleventh day of November, in the year one thousand seven hundred and ninety-four.

TIMOTHY PICKERING. [L. S.]

O-NO-YE-AH-NEE. † [L. S.]
KON-NE-AT-OR-LEE-OOH, or handsome lake. † [L. S.]
TE-KENH-YOU-HAU, alias Capt. Key. † [L. S.]
O-NES-HAU-EE. † [L. S.]
HENDRICK AUPAUMUT. [L. S.]
DAVID NEESOONHUK. † [L. S.]
KANATSOYH, alias Nicholas Kusick. [L. S.]
SOH-HON-TE-O-QUENT. † [L. S.]
OO-DUHT-SA-IT. † [L. S.]
KO-NOOH-QUNG. † [L. S.]
TOS-SONG-GAU-LO-LUS. † [L. S.]
JOHN SKEN-EN-DO-A. † [L. S.]
O-NE-AT-OR-LEE-OOH. † [L. S.]
KUS-SAU-WA-TAU. † [L. S.]
E-YOO-TEN-YOO-TAU-OOK. † [L. S.]
KOHN-YE-AU-GONG, alias Jake Stroud. † [L. S.]
SHA-GUI-E-SA. † [L. S.]
TEER-OOS, Alias Capt. Prantup. † [L. S.]
SOOS-HA-OO-WAU. † [L. S.]
HENRY YOUNG BRANT. † [L. S.]
SONK-YOO-WAU-NA, or Big Sky. † [L. S.]
O-NA-AH-HAH. † [L. S.]
HOT-OSH-A-HENK. † [L. S.]
KAU-KON-DA-NAI-YA. † [L. S.]
NON-DI-YAU-KA. † [L. S.]
KOS-SISH-TO-WAU. † [L. S.]

OO-JAU-GEHT-A, or Fish carrier. † [L. S.]
TO-HE-ONG-GO. † [L. S.]
OOT-A-GUAS-SO. † [L. S.]
JOO-NON-DAU-WA-ONH. † [L. S.]
KI-YAU-HA-ONH. † [L. S.]
OO-TAU-JE-AU-GENH, or broken axe. † [L. S.]
TAU-HO-ON-DOS, or open the way. † [L. S.]
TWAU-KE-WASH-A. † [L. S.]
SE-QUI-DONG-QUEE, alias Little Beard. † [L. S.]
KOD-JE-OTE, or half Town. † [L.S .]
KEN-JAU-AU-GUS, or Stinking Fish. † [L. S.]
SOO-NOH-QUAN-KAU. † [L. S.]
TWEN-NI-YA-NA. † [L. S.]
JISH-KAA-GA, or Green Grasshopper, alias Little Billy. † [L. S.]
TUG-GEH-SHOT-TA. † [L. S.]
T E H-ONG-YA-GAU-NA. † [L. S.]
T E H-ONG-YOO-WASH. † [L. S.]
KON-NE-YOO-WE-SOT. † [L. S.]
TI-OOH-QUOT-TA-KAU-NA, or woods on fire. † [L. S.]
TA-OUN-DAU-DEESH. † [L. S.]
HO-NA-YA-WUS, alias Farmer's brother. † [L. S.]
SOG-GOO-YA-WAUT-HAU, alias red Jacket. † [L. S.]
KON-YOO-TI-A-YOO. † [L. S.]
SAUH-TA-KA-ONG-YUS, or Two Skies of a length. † [L. S.]
OUN-NA-SHATTA-KAU. † [L. S.]
KA-UNG-YA-NEH-QUEE. † [L.S .]
SOO-A-YOO-WAU. † [L. S.]
KAU-JE-A-GA-ONH, or Heap of Dogs. † [L. S.]
SOO-NOOH-SHOO-WAU. † [L. S.]
T-HA-OO-WAU-NI-AS. † [L. S.]
SOO-NONG-JOO-WAU. † [L. S.]
KIANT-WHAU-KA, alias Cornplanter. † [L. S.]
KAU-NIH-SHONG-GOO. † [L. S.]
Witnesses—

Israel Chapin,	William Shepherd, Jun[r],
James Smedley,	John Wickham,
Augustus Porter,	James K. Garnsey,
W[m] Ewing,	Israel Chapin, Jun[r.]
	{Horatio Jones,
Intrepreters [sic],	{Joseph Smith,
	{Jasper Parish.
	Henry Abeele.

Now, know ye, that I, having seen and considered the said treaty, do, by and with the advice and consent of the Senate of the United States, accept, ratify, and confirm the same, and every article and clause thereof. In Testimony whereof, I have caused the seal of the United States to be hereunto affixed, and signed the same with my hand.

Given in the City of Philadelphia, the twenty-first day of Jan-
Seal of   uary, in the year of our Lord one thousand seven hun-
the United   dred and ninety-five, and in the ninteenth year of the
States.   Sovereignty and Independence of the United States.

G^e WASHINGTON.

By the President—

EDM. RANDOLPH.

True copy.

GE^O TAYLOR, J^r, *C. Clk Dep. Of State.*

George Washington, oil painting by Robert Edge Pine, *ca.* 1785.
Courtesy of Independence National Historical Park Library,
Philadelphia, Pennsylvania.

1795: Ratification of the Treaty by George Washington

On January 21, 1795, George Washington ratified the Canandaigua Treaty, upon the advice and consent of the United States Senate. On March 31, 1795, Timothy Pickering sent a copy of the ratification to the Six Nations.

Today the United States manuscript copy of the Canandaigua Treaty to which is appended the ratification by George Washington is housed in the National Archives in Washington, D.C. The Six Nations copy of the treaty is on display at the Ontario County Historical Society in Canandaigua, New York.

The February 23, 1920, minutes of the Ontario County Historical Society record the purchase of the Six Nations copy of the treaty as follows:

> Mr. Milliken gave an account of the auction of the library of Mr. Henry F. De Puy of New York, where he[,] with Mr. Clark Williams and Mr. Glenroy Vail, made several purchases for the Historical Museum.
>
> These purchases were made possible by the kindness of Mrs. L. F. Thompson—the most generous friend of the Society.
>
> Of these purchases the most important was the Indians' copy of the famous Pickering Treaty signed here in 1794. It seems a marvelous thing that after a hundred and twenty-five years—mostly cared for by wandering Indian tribes—it should find its final home within such a short distance of the spot where it was originally prepared and signed. *(Ontario County Historical Soc. 1914–28, 177–78)*

Appended to the minutes of the 19th Annual Meeting of the Ontario County Historical Society held on November 16, 1920, is the following note:

> Mr. Milliken reported a visit from a Mr. Kellogg of Elmira who said he had a copy of the our "Treaty" which he maid [sic] 17 years ago.
>
> The Treaty was then in the hands of the Indians.
>
> The Indians have since told Mr. Kellogg that the treaty was taken from them by a lawyer to use in connection with some trial and was never returned. The lawyer (said to be   ) holding it in payment of his fee. *(Ontario County Historical Soc. 1914–28, 188)*

WASHINGTON, GEORGE. RATIFICATION OF TREATY OF PEACE WITH INDIANS. 22 JAN. 1795.

Ms. Aboriginal Peoples in the Archives. Private Papers. 181. F 47. Simcoe Family Papers. Archives of Ontario, Toronto. In Cruikshank, E. A., ed. *The Correspondence of Lieut. Governor John Graves Simcoe, with Allied Documents Relating to his Administration of the Government of Upper Canada.* Volume 3. Toronto: Ontario Historical Society, 1925, 263–64.

RATIFICATION OF TREATY OF PEACE WITH INDIANS.

22nd January, 1795.

GEORGE WASHINGTON, President of the United States of America, to all to whom these presents shall come Greeting.

WHEREAS a Treaty of Peace, and Friendship between the United States of America, and the Tribes of Indians called the Six Nations, was made and concluded on the Eleventh day of November last, by Timothy Pickering the Agent of the United States for that purpose appointed, on the one Part, and the Chiefs, and Warriors of the Six Nations, on the other part, which Treaty is in the form and Words following.

(Here follows the Original treaty of which the like original is in the hands of the Chiefs of the Six Nations.)

Now Know Ye, that I having seen, and considered the said Treaty, do by, and with the advice and consent of the Senate of the United States Accept Ratify, and Confirm the same, and every Article and clause thereof.—In Testimony whereof I have caused the Seal of the United States to be hereunto affixed and signed the same with my hand.

	Given in the City of Philadelphia the twenty first day of January, in
Seal	the Year of our Lord One thousand seven hundred, and ninety five,
of	and in the Nineteenth year of the Sovereignty, and Independence of
the	the United States.
United	
States.	GEO. WASHINGTON.

By the President
    EDM. RANDOLPH.
Department of State of the   to wit.
United States of America.

I hereby certify that the above is a true Copy of original ratification,
    Seal   deposited in the Office of the Department of State.
    of the   Given under my hand, and seal of
office the twenty second day of
    Secre-   January, One thousand seven
hundred ninety five.
    tary   EDM. RANDOLPH,
    of   *Secretary of State.*
    State's
    Office.
Newark 31st March.
A true copy of the
Original Ratification
    JOHN BUTLER,
        Agt.

Endorsed;—Ratification of a Treaty of Peace and friendship concluded at KON on Daigue the 11th day of November 1794, between the Six Nations and the United States, signed by the President at Philadelphia, 22nd day of January, 1795.

PICKERING, TIMOTHY. LETTER TO THE SIX NATIONS. 31 MAR. 1795.

Ms. Aboriginal Peoples in the Archives. Private Papers. 181. F 47. Simcoe Family Papers. Archives of Ontario, Toronto. In Cruikshank, E. A., ed. *The Correspondence of Lieut. Governor John Graves Simcoe, with Allied Documents Relating to his Administration of the Government of Upper Canada.* Volume 3. Toronto: Ontario Historical Society, 1925, 339–40.

FROM TIMOTHY PICKERING TO THE SIX NATIONS.

31st. March, 1795.

To the Sachems Chiefs and Warriors of the Six Nations.

Brothers;—

It is with much pleasure I inform you that the Treaty of Peace, and Friendship, which in behalf of the United States, I concluded with you at Kon-on-daiguae on the eleventh day of last November, has been Ratified by the President, by and with the advice and consent of the Senate of the United States. Now that treaty is made strong. No act on the part of the United States can make it stronger.

Herewith I send you written Parchment the evidence of that Ratification, this you will keep with the Original treaty now in your possession.

Brothers;—

The United States will every year cause to be appropriated for the benefit of the Six Nations, and their Indian friends, dwelling among, and United with them, the sum stipulated by the treaty to be Annually expended for their use.

You may also rely on the complete performance of every Article of the treaty on the part of the United States, and we rely with confidence on the faithful execution on your part of a treaty so entirely calculated to promote the best interests of yourselves, and your posterity, the liberal and generous principles on which this treaty has been formed, are an evidence of the just and humane sentiments of the United States towards all the Indian Nations on our Borders, and should induce those also, who have long been hostile, to come forward with confidence that with them also the United States will negociate and establish treaties of Peace and Friendship on the Principles of Justice, and humanity, we persuade ourselves, that your friendship to us, and love to the people of your own Colour, will prompt you to embrace every occasion to accomplish a work so acceptable to the Great Spirit, and so interesting to all the Indian Nations.

I remain,

Your friend and Brother,

TIMOTHY PICKERING.

War Office,

PHILADELPHIA   NEWARK, 31st March, 1795.

22d, January, 1795.   A true Copy from the

Original letter,

JOHN BUTLER,

Agt.

ENDORSED;—Colonel Pickering's letter to the Six Nations informing them of the Ratification of the treaty concluded at Kon-on-daiguae, dated Philadelphia, 22d January, 1795.

REFERENCE

Ontario County Historical Society. Records of the Historical Society. 1914–28. Ms. Ontario County Historical Society, Canandaigua, New York.

THE LAST GENERAL COUNCIL OF THE UNITED STATES
WITH THE IROQUOIS CONFEDERACY WAS HELD
IN CANANDAIGUA, AND THE RESULTANT TREATY
WAS SIGNED NOVEMBER 11, 1794, BY
U.S. AGENT, TIMOTHY PICKERING

SACHEMS AND WARRIORS
FARMER'S BROTHER, CORNPLANTER, RED JACKET,
LITTLE BEARD, FISH CARRIER, LITTLE BILLY,
HEAP OF DOGS, HANDSOME LAKE, HALF TOWN,
AND FIFTY OTHERS:

WITNESSES
ISRAEL CHAPIN, JAMES SMEDLY, AUGUSTUS PORTER,
WILLIAM EWING AND OTHERS:

INTERPRETERS
HORATIO JONES, JOSEPH SMITH, JASPER PARRISH.

1902

Plaque on Treaty Rock, in front of Ontario County Courthouse, Canandaigua, New York. Photo © Helen M. Ellis.

Permissions

Permission to reproduce previously published material has been obtained from the following; their cooperation is gratefully acknowledged:

Nelson K. Benton III, for material from the Salem *Evening News*, Salem, MA
Peggy Carroll, for material from the *Daily Messenger*, Canandaigua, NY
George Heron, Past President of the Seneca Nation of Indians, and Sam Lemon, Clerk of the Indian Committee, Philadelphia Yearly Meeting of the Society of Friends, for material from *The Kinzua Dam Controversy*
Mary McNeil, University Press of Virginia, for material from *The Papers of George Washington*
Joyce Mitchell and G. Peter Jemison, for material from *Akwesasne Notes*
National Council for the Social Studies, for material from *Social Education*
James A. Purdy, Chief, Natural and Cultural Resources Branch, U.S. Army Corps of Engineers, Pittsburgh District, for material from *The Headwaters District: A History of the Pittsburgh District, U.S. Army Corps of Engineers*

Permission to reproduce unpublished oral history and manuscript material has been obtained from the following; their cooperation is gratefully acknowledged:

Meredith E. Cabe, Associate Counsel to the President, for material from William Jefferson Clinton letters
J. Sheldon Fisher, for material from personal interview
Geraldine Green, for material from Address at the 1989 Canandaigua Treaty Social
Margaret Heilbrun, Library Director, New-York Historical Society, for material from *O'Reilly Papers*
Martha LaFrance, for material from Address by Ron LaFrance at the 1989 Canandaigua Treaty Social
Jane LeClair, for material from Letter to editor
Vernon Jimerson, for material from Letter to editor
Lorraine Marchildon, Clerk, Ontario County (NY) Board of Supervisors, for material from *Proceedings of the Board of Supervisors of Ontario County, New York, 1899/1905*
Duane James Ray, President, Seneca Nation of Indians, for material from Basil Williams, Letter to John F. Kennedy
Ed Varno, Director, Ontario County (NY) Historical Society, for material from Ontario County Historical Society. *Records of the Historical Society, 1914/1928*

The following material is considered by the granting institutions to be in the public domain; no permission is required to publish from these sources:

The American State Papers. Class II. Indian Affairs. Vol. 1.

Savery, William. *A Journal of the Life, Travels, and Religious Labors of William Savery, A Minister of the Gospel of Christ, of the Society of Friends, Late of Philadelphia.*

Kennedy, John F., Letter to Basil Williams. 9 Aug. 1961.

The Pennsylvania State Archives, Harrisburg.

Leon Shenandoah, Tadodaho, Haudenosaunee Six Nations Confederacy, Canandaigua, NY. Treaty Commemoration public addresses, November 11, 1989, and November 11, 1994.

Simcoe Family Papers. Archives of Ontario, Toronto. In Cruikshank, E. A., ed. *The Correspondence of Lieut. Governor John Graves Simcoe, with Allied Documents Relating to his Administration of the Government of Upper Canada.*

200th Anniversary of the Canandaigua Treaty public ceremonial addresses, November 11, 1994, Canandaigua, NY.

Index

About the Contributors

Chief Irving Powless Jr., has been the leader of the Beaver Clan of the Onondaga Nation for the past 35 years. He has also been successful in raising consciousness regarding treaty obligations, non-taxable status, and land claims. He has helped to obtain an addition to the Onandaga Nation School, obtain a new health center, and return sacred objects and wampum belts. His work has appeared in various books and publications, including the *University of Buffalo Law Review* and *New York Folklore*, as well as several videotapes.

Paul Williams is a lawyer and historian whose work for the Haudenosaunee includes environmental protection and the recovery of sacred objects and land. He lives at the Six Nations Grand River Territory with his wife and two daughters.

John C. Mohawk, Ph.D., a member of the Seneca Nation, is an Associate Professor of History in the American Studies Department at the State University of New York at Buffalo. He is author of *Utopian Legacies: A History of Conquest and Oppression in the Western World*, and he edited *Exiled in the Land of the Free* and *A Basic Call to Consciousness*. He is one of the founders of the journal *Akwesasne Notes*.

Chief Oren Lyons (Joagquisho), Faithkeeper of the Turtle Clan, Onondaga Nation, is Associate professor of American Studies at the State University of New York at Buffalo. He has contributed to periodicals and books including *Exiled in the Land of the Free* and *Voice of Indigenous People* (Clear Light).

Daniel K. Richter, Ph.D., is Professor of History at the University of Pennsylvania, where he directs the McNeil Center for Early American Studies. His books include *The Ordeal of the Longhouse: The Peoples of the Iroquois League in the Era of European Colonization* and the forthcoming *Facing East from Indian Country: Rediscovering Colonial North America*.

Robert W. Venables, Ph.D., teaches in the American Indian Program and Department of Rural Sociology, Cornell University. He has written or coauthored several books, including *American Indian Environments*.

Doug George-Kanentiio, a member of the Mohawk Nation, is an award-winning columnist who has served as advisor, producer, and script-writer for national television documentaries on Iroquois subjects. He edited *Akwesasne Notes* from 1986 to 1992 and writes regular columns for the *Syracuse Herald American* and *News from Indian Country*. He is the author of *Iroquois Culture & Commentary*, and, with his wife, singer Joanne Shenandoah, is co-author of *Skywoman: Legends of the Iroquois*.

Laurence M. Hauptman, is Professor of History, State University of New York, New Paltz. He has authored twelve books on American Indians, including *The Iroquois Struggle for Survival*. He has served as an historical consultant to the Mashantucket Pequot, Oneida, and Seneca Indian Nations.

Joy A. Bilharz, Ph.D., is Associate Professor in the Department of Sociology and Anthropology, State University of New York College at Fredonia, Fredonia, NY.

Ron LaFrance, Ph.D. (1945–1996), a Subchief of the Mohawk Nation and a member of the Wolf Clan, founded the Akwesasne Freedom School, was the Director of the Native American Magnet School for the Buffalo Public School System, and was Director of the Akwesasne Mohawk Board of Education. He received his Masters and Ph.D. degrees at Cornell University, where he was also the Director of the American Indian Program.